The Human Potential

As men's interests become more diversified, and the splintered and fragmented mind becomes harder to avoid, reason has more and more to do. It must select some interests as central, discard or modify others, and ruthlessly subordinate minor interests to major.

BRAND BLANSHARD

We are weak today in ideal matters because intelligence is divorced from aspiration.

JOHN DEWEY

WILLIAM T. COUCH

The Human Potential

AN ESSAY ON ITS

CULTIVATION

Duke University Press

Durham, N.C.

1974

© 1974, Duke University Press

L.C.C. card no. 72–97940

I.S.B.N. 0–8223–0300–0

PRINTED IN THE UNITED STATES OF
AMERICA BY KINGSPORT PRESS, INC.

TO

ELIZABETH

FREUD IS RIGHT ABOUT REPRESSION BEING EVIL. What does not follow is the preposterous suggestion, sometimes confused with it, that it is good to indulge impulse regardless of circumstances. It does not even follow that we should allow the young to learn for themselves which indulgences are profitable and which are not. The race has acquired an immense capital of experience as to what kinds of behaviour irritate, what kinds of risks are over-dangerous, what are the most useful rules about sleeping and eating and exercising, even what studies it is profitable or otherwise to pursue; and if we decline to discourage firmly a good many youthful impulses, we are exhibiting not so much liberalism as a gratuitous denial of aid. Age owes more to youth than a bare sustenance; it owes it also such of its wisdom as is transmissible. . . . If experience can establish nothing, one wonders what education is for.

BRAND BLANSHARD

. . . IT IS NOT TRULY REALISTIC or scientific to take short views, to sacrifice the future to immediate pressure, to ignore facts and forces that are disagreeable and to magnify the enduring quality of whatever falls in with immediate desire.

JOHN DEWEY

Preface

I have had the privilege of making my living in work of extreme interest to me—twenty years as assistant director and director of the University of North Carolina Press, five years as director and general editor of the University of Chicago Press, ten as encyclopedia editor in chief in New York. I became aware during my early undergraduate days at the University of North Carolina that I did not know enough to choose my course of studies; and I soon discovered that nobody else knew, that knowledge of this kind, if it had ever existed as more than addiction to what habit had prescribed, had disappeared. My experience in scholarly publishing led me early to the conviction which I made public in an article in *Publishers Weekly* that the great need of our time was to educate our educators. I did not know at the time that Karl Marx had many years earlier asserted the existence of this need, but while I was not a Marxian, I would not have abandoned my conviction merely because Marx had expressed it. Not only have I never been able to abandon this conviction, my later experience at the University of Chicago and in encyclopedia editing in New York provided me with more and more evidence in support of it.

I do not intend to suggest that I am under the illusion that I am the only one besides Karl Marx who has seen the need to educate the educators. All scientific and scholarly research and experiment, writing and publishing, and a vast amount of oral academic argumentation could be regarded as effort by educators to educate each other. It would have been easy for me, occupying a position as I did in the middle of this effort and most of the time thoroughly enjoying my part in it, to fail to see the real effects of the effort and the painful truth that it was not only, in the main, failing in the way it most needed to succeed but was establishing the publish or perish principle that now dominates the scientific and scholarly world. After saying this, I have to say immediately that this principle is not wholly bad. There are many ways in which it is good, and I suggest these ways and the need for them in this book. But there is also dire need for much more, especially for knowledge of the fact that the intellectual world of today is dominated by an implicit orthodoxy of a nihilistic character. This orthodoxy, I believe, would be repudiated if the intellectual world were aware of its rule and of its destructive character.

The thesis of this book can be stated in many different ways. Several of these ways are stated at different places in the book. This is, perhaps, the best place to say that the title "The Human Potential" has been chosen because one way of stating the thesis of the book is that the intellectual life of man has now reached a level beyond which further advance is not only not possible but retrogression and severe stultification are in prospect unless the things that are necessary to raise the present level are done. This book is devoted to showing the present level and what is necessary to get beyond this level.

About ten years ago I laid before Eliseo Vivas certain ideas now embodied in *The Human Potential*. I had known Vivas and had published for him while he was in the department of philosophy of the University of Chicago and I was directing the Press of that institution. I knew I could rely on him to tell me gently but clearly if he thought I was talking nonsense. The tone of his discussion of my ideas, while clearly warning me that I was entering deep water, made me feel that I should go ahead and try to write the book that, except for certain basic notions, I then had only vaguely in mind. Mrs. Sheila Cudahy Pellegrini, friend of many years, showed in many conversations interest that made me feel that perhaps I had something to say worth saying. She saw the relevance of the quotation I give from Harold Pinter's play *The Homecoming* to certain views I had expressed, referred to this passage, and suggested that I read the play, which I did. She read and commented on several earlier versions of chapters, convinced me I had not done what I needed to do, and I abandoned these versions.

Fred Wieck, late director of the University of Pennsylvania Press, my chief editor for several years while I was in charge of the University of Chicago Press, read what at the time I considered a final version and gave me comments that again convinced me I had not done my job. So I abandoned that version and started over again. E. M. Adams, professor of philosophy in the University of North Carolina, read a couple of chapters and wrote so pleasantly that I couldn't help wondering whether he wasn't just being kind. I knew I needed kindness and I was grateful;

but these chapters too, I abandoned. Mrs. Emily Maclachlan of the department of social science of the University of Florida, Mrs. H. G. Baity, anthropologist, Mrs. Ruth Morris, good citizen, each read several chapters. Mr. Ivan Bierly, another good citizen, is largely responsible for my undertaking the task of writing this book, has read several versions, and has given me constant encouragement. J. O. Bailey, professor of English in the University of North Carolina, and Augustus Burns, professor of social science in the University of Florida, read and commented on the version that, except for some additions and minor changes is the one being published. My good friend of many years, Mr. Russell Kirk, my sister, Mrs. R. S. Haltiwanger, and my granddaughter, Miss Terry Nutter, read the prefinal manuscript and gave me stimulating comments. Mrs. Marion Wilson, who worked with me for several years as encyclopedia indexer and editor, made for me a study of the indexes of Americana, Britannica, and Collier's that supported the view expressed in this book that encyclopedia indexing is in a primitive stage.

Daniel Singal, a Columbia graduate student now writing on the intellectual life of the South in the second quarter of this century, read and criticized two versions of the manuscript, one of them a near-final version. He gave me criticisms which helped me to produce the form that is being published and that has continued to seem to me worth publishing as all other versions, after I have been helped to look at them coldly, have not.

I am under most pleasant obligations to the Duke University Press and especially to the director, Mr. Ashbel Brice, and the readers he selected and whose opinions made possible the publication of the work by the Duke Press. Mr. John Dowling has put my notes into good form, read and edited my copy with understanding care, and corrected errors that I would have found embarrassing if they had been allowed to get into print. I have found Mr. Dowling's slightest suggestions worth acting upon. Among the hardest tasks in university publishing, tasks that are least understood and given least recognition by outsiders are those of advertising, publicity, selling, and the management of finances. I know from years of hard experience how heavy my obligations are to the members of the Duke Press staff whose duties lie with these functions.

I could not have taken the time to write this book or incur the expenses that have been involved except for generous financial support from a source that prefers to remain anonymous. I am deeply grateful to this source for continued encouragement as well as financial support.

Of course, while I have taken the comments of all my readers seriously and take pleasure in thanking them in public for their help, I am wholly responsible for what I say in this book.

WILLIAM T. COUCH

Chapel Hill, North Carolina
January 29, 1973

Contents

The Human Potential

CHAPTER I

The Opportunity to Know

I don't even know what I am dying for
JEAN ANOUILH, *Antigone*

There are many ways of stating the purpose of this book. One is to show that the often proclaimed right of the public in the United States to know, so far as matters of basic importance are concerned, has been given, with rare exceptions, attention far short of that which is needed. Most of us today have no alternative except to rely on newspapers, television, radio, magazines, and books to provide us with the information we need in order to understand the changes that are occurring in our world and the world around us. We would have no chance whatever to understand if we did not have the information that these services provide. But while these services are necessary, they are far from sufficient. They do not provide the necessary background for understanding, and their current-periodical nature is such that any background they provide for the understanding of the changes that occur is soon as unavailable for common use as the printed matter that would swamp us if we did not get it out of our homes, or the particles or waves in space that bring us this information and then disappear forever.

Even in the intellectual world, the world that exists mainly for the purpose of providing the background that is necessary to the understanding of current events, the means necessary for the cultivation of this understanding do not exist. One of the purposes of this book is to show that there is only one possible means of doing as much as can be done, given the present state of human knowledge, to correct this condition.

But first we have to show that this condition which we have said exists, actually does exist; and this is not easy to do. Not that evidence of its existence cannot be piled mountain high, but that most of us are convinced that we already have the background necessary to understand current events and no evidence, no argument can arouse us from our dogmatic slumber. It is highly probable that some of us have this background, at least to some extent. But one thing is certain here: even those of us who have it, if any of us do, do not know how to convince others that we have it and they do not.

The ultimate purpose of this book is to promote the provision of means for cultivating better understanding of the changes that are occurring in ourselves and in the world around us. Since all education, beyond the elementary training in the use of the tools of learning exists for this purpose, and since vast sums of money and vast energies are currently devoted to this purpose, the question may reasonably be asked: Can it be possible that any great need essential to any genuine education has not been provided? It is necessary to show that this is the case—that there is dire need for means that do not now exist. If we fail in showing this, we fail to provide the ground that is necessary for our argument.

The most difficult problem in the writing of this book has been that of how to show the actual existence of this ground. Those who are already convinced of its existence do not need to be shown and to them the piling up of evidence of its existence will be not only unnecessary but redundant, a waste of the writer's energy and the reader's time. The case is so clear to those who are already convinced that only a skeleton argument is needed for them. But suppose the audience that one needs most to convince, the leadership in the contemporary intellectual world, is convinced that it already knows all that it needs to know: how is it to be waked from its dogmatic slumber—if this can be done at all—except by the piling up of evidence? This book is loaded, perhaps too heavily, with evidence of the need for the means that it proposes. The convinced reader can safely skip this evidence and pass on to the last two chapters. It is hoped that the unconvinced reader will study this evidence.

In the year 1756 Edmund Burke, a young man only twenty-seven years old, published anonymously a short work of around 20,000 words entitled *A Vindication of Natural Society*. The work is a powerful attack on government, perhaps the most powerful attack that has ever been made, possibly the strongest that can be made—incomparably stronger than has ever come from any anarchist. It shows, with such clarity that hardly anyone can fail to understand, that wars, as distinguished from individual and small-group violence, cannot exist in the absence of governments, and that since wars are incomparably the greatest scourges of mankind, the most certain way to get rid of them is to get rid of governments. One might wonder why Burke's *Vindication* has not been used effectively by advocates of anarchy and non-violent resistance. The reason could be that if one thinks with sufficient care about facts that Burke does not mention as well as those on which he bases his argument, one cannot escape a conclusion that is not new, that is still as inescapable as when it was first formed, but that nevertheless is shocking when one considers how far so much of the intellectual world of our time is from taking it into account in matters on which it is of decisive import.

Burke's *Vindication of Natural Society* was intended as a satire on the attack that Lord Bolingbroke (1678–1751), a prominent statesman and political philosopher of England, had made on the establishment of his time; but Burke's argument was so convincing, as far as it went, and the quality of the understanding that there was to deal with it was so low in many quarters—as it is today—that the satire was not seen. Furthermore, the style was such a perfect imitation of Bolingbroke's, or so it was thought, that the *Vindication* was widely attributed to Bolingbroke and accordingly was taken straight and seriously. Bolingbroke's main argument was really for the old establishment, which tended to look on political parties as disloyal, as conspiracies. Why have parties if the truth is available to men of ability? Bolingbroke's answer was that parties are not only not necessary, they are a hindrance to good government. His view on this subject has been the dominant one throughout most of the past in most societies; and the totalitarianisms of today, as well as of yesterday, are sufficient evidence of the great power in this view. Bolingbroke was therefore against the party system that had its beginnings in the period of the Glorious Revolution.

Burke's *Vindication* appeared to be in line with this main argument of Bolingbroke's. But the appearance was deceptive, and the deception went unnoticed by the leading intellectual lights of the time. The ability to read and remember and take into account problems closely connected with those in the text before one, and wide implications in the text extending far beyond it, was as rare then as now.

A careful reading today of Edmund Burke's *Vindication of Natural Society* brings up many questions as important as they were when, more than two hundred years ago, Burke wrote the work. The subject of the *Vindication* is suggested by the subtitle: "A View of the Evils Arising to Mankind from Every Species of Artificial Society." The extremely brief text is devoted to what Burke presents as a review of the wars of the world from the earliest times; to the different types of governments—despotic, monarchical, aristocratic, democratic; to legal systems; to the administration of law; to the structure of society; and to conclusions derived from consideration of the actual workings of all these. "War," says Burke,

War is the matter which fills all history. . . . The first accounts we have of mankind are but so many accounts of their butcheries. All empires have been cemented in blood; and in those early periods when the race of mankind began first to form themselves into parties and combinations, the first effect of the combination, and indeed the end for which it seems purposely formed and best calculated, is their mutual destruction [p. 12].[1]

Burke reviews the vast butchery, the suffering and death brought on all parties by wars—wars in which he says none of the participants could have had the least rational concern. All of the wars were provoked by ambition, pride, cruelty, madness. All the wars

ended as all such have ever done, and ever will do, in a real weakness of all parties; a momentary shadow and dream of power in some one; and the subjection of all to the yoke of a stranger, who knows how to profit of their divisions [p. 16].

"I charge," says Burke, "the whole of these effects on political society" (p. 20). Just get rid of states, of governments, of establishments of political society, Burke argues, and war will become impossible: "In a state of nature, it had been impossible to find a number of men, sufficient for such slaughters, agreed in the same bloody purpose" (p. 21). And, Burke goes on:

This artificial division of mankind into separate societies is a perpetual source in itself of hatred and dissension [p. 22]. . . . In vain you tell me that artificial government is good, but that I fall out with the abuse. The thing! The thing itself is the abuse [p. 37].

Burke repeats an ancient view:

The most obvious division of society is into rich and poor; and it is no less obvious, that the number of the former bear a great disproportion to those of the latter. The whole business of the poor is to administer to the idleness, folly, and luxury of the rich; and that of the rich, in return, is to find the best methods of confirming the slavery and increasing the burdens of the poor [p. 47].

1. References are to Volume I of *The Works of the Right Honourable Edmund Burke*, The World's Classics, 5 vols. (London: Oxford Univ. Press, [1906] 1925).

The remedy: get rid of artificial society:

In a state of nature it is an inevitable law that a man's acquisitions are in proportion to his labours. In a state of artificial society it is a law as constant and as invariable, that those who labour most, enjoy the fewest things; and that those who labour not at all, have the greatest number of enjoyments [p. 47].

Why this ridiculous constitution of things?

. . . the blindness of one part of mankind co-operating with the frenzy and villainy of the other, has been the real builder of this respectable fabric of political society; and as the blindness of mankind has caused their slavery, in return their state of slavery is made a pretense for continuing them in a state of blindness . . . [p. 48].

How could a man of the high intelligence of Burke say with satirical intent what many of our time say, and what is received by many in our intellectual world, as newly mined and freshly minted truth?

Much of the active intellectual life of the time of Burke was, like much of that of our time, antagonistic to the "establishment," convinced that man is by nature good, that his institutions have made him evil—that all that was needed for the flowering of the good in man was to get rid of the old institutions. So thoroughly steeped were many of the leaders of Burke's time in this notion—as, I repeat, are many in our time—that any argument to this effect was widely, even if not universally, accepted without serious question. Usually, it was simply assumed without discussion. And the emphasis was on the notion that man is by nature good. Hardly anyone held that the old institutions could not be improved or that some should not be abolished. It was possible to hold such views as that the old could be improved, as Burke did, and still not believe that man is by nature good.

Bolingbroke, as Burke represents him, did not base his work on any notion of the natural goodness of man, but, as I have suggested above, this was not noticed at the time, just as today the center of a subject, and the more important implications of this center, are often allowed to go unnoticed. Burke's argument appeared to be thorough, to those whose prejudices required that they believe it, and to hit squarely the target they assumed that it aimed at. There is no explicit statement in the *Vindication* that man is by nature good but his institutions have made him evil. Burke simply leaves the way open for the reader to make this assumption, knowing that he is most likely to make it, but hoping that in view of the facts that Burke states and, more important, those that he omits, the reader will realize its absurdity and begin to question it. This hope, if indeed he did have this hope—and it is hard to see that he could have hoped for anything else—was not realized. The question how it could be, if man is by nature good and reasonable—and both were assumed—that man throughout recorded time had set up and maintained institutions that were evil is not considered in the *Vindication*, simply because the asking of this and closely related questions and considering them carefully would destroy the basic argument of the work and its satirical character.

Wars always appear reasonable to those who initiate and engage in them; and to leave out discussion of this appearance, to treat it as having no weight when it is obviously decisive, is simply to falsify the discussion of wars. They are always fought on account of some interest that appears to be as important as life itself. It may, of course, be said that the appearances are false, utterly deceptive. The necessary response to this is that those who have had the power to make decisions that have led to wars obviously have not thought, when they made their decisions, that the bases on which they made them were mere appearances rather than realities.

There is no mistake that can be made so revelatory of ignorance of one's self and of others and of the world around one than the assumption so widespread today, in the intellectual world as well as among people generally, that it is always easy to distinguish realities from appearances. This assumption is clearly one of the major causes of wars. Burke obviously knew this and put before his readers everything necessary to get them to work this out for themselves—if they had the necessary reasoning powers. He knew very well that he could not create these powers, but if they existed he might stimulate them into action. He failed, and again, why he failed is fairly obvious.

Burke's ultimate intention was, of course, to show the shallowness of Bolingbroke's writings. In order to do this, he had to show that war and other evils are consequences of at least two aspects of the nature of man; and, further, that governments and other institutions actually express these aspects of man's nature; and this would suggest the fairly obvious truth, tabooed then as now, that the reduction and control of the human habit of resorting to violence, perhaps the transformation and elimination of this aspect of man's nature, is in actual practice, as opposed to utopian thought, an incredibly difficult task.

I assume that any reasonable person today will agree that war is one of the great evils, probably the greatest of the evils from which mankind suffers; but I have to add immediately and in the same sentence that the blanket condemnation of war as if all participants were equally guilty, as is so often implied in arguments for non-violence or non-violent resistance, is one of the major causes of war. The problem of aggressors, how to determine who they are and what to do about them, is sufficiently difficult without this complication. Non-violence and non-violent resistance have had their advocates for more than two thousand years, Jesus among them; but one cannot use Jesus honestly on this subject without taking into account that while he advocated turning the other cheek, he also refused to accept temporal power; and that if he was the son of God and one with God and really for peace, his rule could have brought only peace; and, in rejecting rule, he rejected peace; he clearly advocated obedience to existing governments, which were instruments of war as well as of peace; he said "Do not think that I have come to bring peace on earth: I have not come to bring peace, but a sword"; and he himself used physical means to drive money changers out of a temple.

The events in human history that can be used, that have been used, to illustrate this problem are innumerable. The literature in which these events have been used in discussion of one kind or another is vast, so vast that one could spend a lifetime studying it and, if one were not endowed with extraordinary mental powers, the only result could be that one would become utterly lost in it. Nothing could be clearer and more certainly true than the theory at the basis of the advocacy of non-violence and non-violent resistance that if everyone would stop using physical violence on other persons, and if no future generation anywhere on earth or any that might come to earth from outer space used physical violence in the settling of disputes among persons, then there would be no more wars, no more individual or group violence— and, I might add, no more persons who advocate non-violence and then, when they are displeased or angry or threatened with violence, themselves resort to violence.

If wishes were Cadillacs and palaces and whatever else one wanted, many more of us could live in luxury, and poverty might no longer be a problem. I say "might" because just what would happen when the wish to dominate met the equally strong wish not to be dominated, or the wish to be richer than anybody else in the world met somebody else's wish to be richer, I believe we cannot easily imagine if we have been able really to rule out violence. It might seem that if all we have to do to get what we want is to wish, then all our problems would be solved. The idea is so naive it is not worth discussing. Nothing can be done for or with people whose mental equipment works at this level. The best thing to do with such people, if it is at all possible, is leave them alone. And the human being who most ardently wants almost any particular condition does not have to be observed closely to discover that he, at some other time, also most ardently does not want it and is determined, so far as his power goes, not to have it. The human being who begins to understand the human condition in this respect may come to wonder whether man is not engaged in a task somewhat like that of Sisyphus in that somehow what he does is always being undone, but unlike the case of Sisyphus, man himself rather than an inscrutable fate too often does the undoing. All of man's efforts on earth to improve his condition, to improve his relations with his fellows, unsettle his condition and make problems for himself and others. A superficial view would say stop the effort to improve, but this would be to stop the effort to achieve more rather than less peace and justice.

I do not intend by these remarks any disparagement of the fantasies that have been built on imagining man to be capable somehow, sometime, somewhere, of finding fulfillment of his heart's desires. On the contrary, the portrayal of a heaven that would never become tiresome, monotonous, utterly boring, that would always be inviting, alluring, exciting, genuinely satisfying, and (since while we are human we have to think in terms of time) that would continue to provide these qualities throughout eternity—to imagine and portray such a heaven would be a real achievement. One does not have to be completely reconciled to creation as it is to be content with the days in spring when the fresh soft new leaves are coming out and flowers are in bloom, with the days of rain and storm and the hot sun that makes plants grow in summer, with the coolness and frost and colors of autumn, and even with the rain and snow and ice and slosh of winter. Both the change and the repetition, the differences and the constancies, may be found good; and, except for nature's terrifyingly destructive moods, it may not be possible to imagine much better. But nature's terrifyingly destructive moods can make one wonder whether nature may not be indifferent to man, perhaps even hostile; and if man is a mere product of nature, whether he does not deceive himself when he finds life good. If man is a product of nature, and there is nothing more, it would seem impossible that man should ever transcend nature, that qualities he did not have as an animal should float into existence, apparently from nothing, and become a part of his nature. But even here grounds for hope can be found, more than hope—some that has actually happened that is good. If man was once nothing, then dust of the earth, then mere animal, now a thinking animal—no matter how imperfect his thinking up to now—here is ground for hope; and if modern science is not completely deceptive in one of its most important teachings, at least part of this ground is solid. The rest is perhaps like the earth in the old lady's testimony in court, reported in one of his essays by William James. The old lady was being questioned about the solar system, had indignantly denied that the earth moved, and had asserted that it rested securely, not on mere air, or even sand, but on rocks. "And what do the rocks rest on?" she was asked. And she answered triumphantly: "It's rocks all the way down."

As I have said above, the satire in Burke's *Vindication of Natural Society* was completely missed at the time of its publication in 1756. Even men "of such sound judgment as Lord Chesterfield and Bishop Warburton," so F. W. Raffety tells us in his preface to the five-volume Oxford World's Classics edition of Burke, failed to recognize the satire.[2] Nine years later, in 1765, when Burke wanted to enter Parliament, and it had become known that he was the author, the satirical nature of the work was still not recognized, and his authorship was used in the effort to block his way to Parliament. One can easily imagine the alarms and excursions and the jokes about looking under beds to find Burkes; and the deep concern of those who knew, as Burke did, the horrors that otherwise good people could inflict on each other when seized by some utopian or diabolical extremism—a spectacle that one could weep over, as well as laugh over for relief, if one had any genuine understanding and human sympathies.

Burke found it necessary, in order to correct the suspicions that the discovery of his authorship of the *Vindication* had aroused, to bring out a new edition with a preface in which he explained his purpose. "Before the philosophical works of Lord Bolingbroke had appeared," says Burke, "great things were expected." When they were published, he goes on,

Those who searched in them for new discoveries in the mysteries of nature; those who expected something which might explain or direct the operations of the mind; those who hoped to see morality illustrated and enforced; those who looked for new helps to society and government; those who desired to see the characters and passions of mankind delineated; in short, all who consider such things as philosophy, and require some of

2. *Works of Burke*, I, xxix.

them at least in every philosophical work, all these were certainly disappointed; they found the landmarks of science precisely in their former places: and they thought they received but a poor recompense for this disappointment, in seeing every mode of religion attacked in a lively manner, and the foundation of every virtue and of all government sapped with much art and ingenuity. What advantage do we derive from such writings? What delight can a man find in employing a capacity which might be usefully exerted for the noblest purposes, in a sort of sullen labour, in which, if the author could succeed, he is obliged to own that nothing could be more fatal to mankind than his success [p. 3]?

Lord Bolingbroke's writings, says Burke, lead into "the fairy-land of philosophy." The word "philosophy" was used at that time as a synonym for what we today call "science," and also to refer to the effort to think seriously about almost anything; and thus, in the statement just quoted, Burke summarizes his low estimate of the quality of Bolingbroke's thought.

The low estimate that Burke gave to the quality of Bolingbroke's thought is strictly applicable to much of the most widely disseminated and dangerously influential thought of our time. The purpose of this book is to examine this problem and propose a means not only for dealing with it, but for going far beyond and trying seriously to see whether anything can be done to help human beings to develop their capacity for thought and to prepare themselves for the action necessary to improve the quality of their lives.

Many of us in the latter half of the twentieth century, more than two hundred years after Burke wrote his satirical *Vindication*, are still imaginatively on our way to "the fairyland of philosophy." We are most certainly living in a time of revolutions, and it is the great good fortune of those of us living in the United States, a good fortune of which we give little evidence of being aware, that we can do all the revoluting we please, and thanks to fundamental structures and processes that we did not create and that by misunderstanding and misusing we can damage or destroy, we can do our revoluting with relatively little violence. Fortunately, no one minority, or coalition of minorities, with the exception of one group, has yet been able to dictate to the majority. The power which minorities have had during the 1960's and the early 1970's has almost certainly been derived in the main from sentiments shared with large numbers, perhaps a majority, against certain governmental policies.

Both of the world wars of this century inaugurated revolutions of great portent for the future. In both, the power of the United States, supported by the overwhelming majority of the people, was the decisive factor. After both, great changes in opinion and in commitments occurred in the United States, changes that brought forth efforts by the United States to stop the revolutions it had been most effective in helping on their way. The question inevitably arises whether it is possible to discover any principles in international affairs to which a country such as the United States can commit itself and reasonably expect to be able, for more than a very few years, to continue to be convinced of the wisdom of its commitment, to want to keep it, and actually to keep it.

If revolution can be conceived as the making of commitments, the marshaling of all available resources to act on the commitments and make them effective, and then the reversal of commitments and marshaling of resources to act in the opposite direction, the United States has been during this century the country of permanent revolution. The communist countries, with their commitment to change in one direction and their resolute adherence to the stages they planned in that direction, have been, so far as the keeping of commitments is concerned, scenes of amazing stability. The revolutions in Russia and China and their satellites have been conducted along lines largely thought out in advance by governments that have used fear and force and fraud to the uttermost. The impression these countries now convey to the outside world is that their people are working happily and cooperatively for the general welfare; and if there are a few voices, suppressed in their home countries and barely audible in the outside world, that describe the fear and force and fraud necessary to achieve the apparently happy condition—such as the voice of the Russian nuclear scientist Andrei Sakharov in his *Progress, Coexistence, and Intellectual Freedom*—these voices are unheeded or quickly forgotten. The impression given to the outside world is that of a stability approaching a happily channeled progressive condition in which change in the channel is not permitted because change from such a happily channeled condition could only be change for the worse. The widely peddled legend that there is a visible youth revolt, a revolution in the communist countries, is simply false.[3] But the facts are not easy to find. They are buried beneath the legend of revolution.

There is a vast amount of unrest and gestation and revolution in

3. For a typical case, see Margaret Mead, "Youth Revolt: The Future Is Now," *Saturday Review*, 10 Jan. 1970.

countries of the world outside of the communist orbits. This unrest and gestation is extreme and widespread in the United States, perhaps more so than anywhere else in the world. It might not be totally wrong to see in this extremism a basic demand for a master, for rule by a power that has stability of purpose, even if that rule could be achieved only by the uttermost use of fear and force and fraud. The great danger of the United States today is that the demand for stability is not a monopoly of any one party or interest, and that it is in many ways an entirely reasonable demand.

During the last several years the unrest in the United States has been to outward view more anarchic than anything else. Anarchy of certain kinds and in limited ways is one of the chief characteristics of free societies; but anarchy of the complete and idealistic type has never existed on earth, and the varieties that have existed on earth have been exceedingly unstable. The basic and incurable cause of the instability of anarchism is discussed in Chapter III, where the encyclopedic treatment of basic types of government is discussed.

It is necessary in the interests of understanding to know that the two words "anarchy" and "communism" have attractive as well as repellent meanings and that the attractive meanings really do have attractive power in them. To fail to understand this is to be completely disarmed, completely ineffective in the handling of the arguments of anarchists and communists. And not only this. It can be a way of being unintentionally in league with them, and of helping them to destroy the last best hope of man on earth.

The idea of people working together freely and happily for the common good, everyone contributing everything he can, and everything being made freely available to everyone, beginning with the basic necessities of life and going on to the effort to satisfy the wants that seem always to grow as basic necessities are met—this idea is certainly among the world's most attractive ideas. It has been at the basis of all utopias and is the basis of the communist revolutions of this century. A society that actually worked in accord with this idea would soon, if it did not immediately, so the theory says, begin producing surpluses— primitive profits—beyond basic necessities. And, so the theory goes, no one would be allowed to have these "profits" for his private use. All would go into the common pot for the use of everybody. The theory assumes that there would be no bickering, no quarreling that ended in fighting over the distribution of goods from the common pot, and that there would never be any shortages that raised the question who would eat and live and who would starve and die—or if there were such shortages, the questions they raised would be settled peacefully and magnanimously. The theory assumes there would be no great differences over decisions, that these would somehow always be right and always accepted as right, either under leadership or upon group decision that, perhaps after discussion, was spontaneously and unanimously accepted. It is fairly obvious that any groups that succeeded in actually practicing such a theory, if no natural calamity intervened, would quickly become wealthy, and the necessity for such elementary things as food would cease to rule man, and he, instead, would rule necessity. Work would then become to a great extent a playful art, and everything would be done as well as possible. Nobody could make and nobody would want to make profits on shoddy work. Art would not be a separate activity and, like so much of the intellectual activity of our time, an activity doomed to become esoteric, largely a matter of posturing by the artist, and so specialized that the artist could not himself understand what he was doing and could not talk intelligibly to others about it. Religion would not be something that one could put on and take off as one does one's clothes. There would be no conflict between individual and social good, no conflict between groups or individuals for power, no causes for conflicts, and therefore no artificial divisions in society, no divisions within the individual, no need for the development of therapies designed to cure destructive aberrations produced by society; for society would be so organized that it, of itself, without any use of fraud or fear or force would create only a happy harmony.

In such a society, whole professions that are made necessary by the ills that afflict what we are in the habit of calling "free society," such as teachers who cultivate the competitive skills that serve the ambition that leads to the struggle for power, lawyers, psychoanalysts, psychiatrists, military men, police, politicians, labor organizers—the list would be long—would not exist. Who could reasonably object to getting rid of the tremendous burdens on society both of the professions that create and cultivate conflicts within individuals and societies and of those that exist to cure the havoc wrought by the conflicts—and that generally fail to cure?

The ideal society of communism is identical with the ideal society of anarchism. Every individual within this society, so the ideal says, governs himself in the ways (that is, by the necessities, the laws of physical and human nature) that have to be obeyed in order to allow the natural harmony of the genuinely good society to exist. Such individuals do not need any government or law over them. They have genuinely good government and law within themselves. All repressive governmental and legal apparatus are not only not necessary, they are a burden—a burden that is part of the cause of the ills they are intended to prevent. When people understand such basic truths as these, so the ideal says, they will get rid of all such burdens. The same grounds that require acceptance of the communist ideal also require acceptance of the anarchist ideal. The chief of these grounds, universal sympathy, is glorified in the following statement by Maximilien Robespierre:

It exists, I tell you, it exists: the soul sensitive and pure; it exists: the passion tender, imperious, irresistible, the torment and delight of the magnanimous heart, the profound horror of tyranny, the compassionate zeal for the oppressed, the sacred love of country, the love most sublime and most holy of humanity—without which a great revolution is only a terrible crime that destroys another crime—it exists: the generous ambition to found on earth the first Republic of the world, the elevated self-interest of the man who finds a heavenly pleasure and the calm of a pure conscience in the ravishing spectacle of the public welfare. You feel this spirit at this moment burning in your soul. I feel it in mine.[4]

Robespierre is only one of many in human history who have testified to the existence of this spirit and extolled it. The great skeptic David Hume sees sympathy as of the greatest utility to man in his *Enquiry Concerning the Principles of Morals* and bases morals on sympathy rather than on reason; and even Adam Smith, in his *Wealth of Nations* and *The Theory of Moral Sentiments*—helped to father the doctrine that so deep and wide and universal and useful is the sympathy that human beings have for each other that freedom will bring wealth to the nation that practices it. In the very first paragraph of *The Theory of Moral Sentiments*, Smith says:

How selfish soever man may be supposed, there are evidently some principles in his nature, which interest him in the fortune of others, and render their happiness necessary to him, though he derives nothing from it except the pleasure of seeing it. Of this kind is pity or compassion. . . . this sentiment, like all the other original passions of human nature, is by no means

4. This is my translation of a statement attributed to Robespierre in *The Origins of Totalitarian Democracy* by J. L. Talmon (New York: Praeger, 1960), p. 68. This work of Talmon's is superb in its presentation of the disasters wrought by reasoning concerning natural law and principles of universal validity that stops when it runs into such paradoxes as that of men being "forced to be free."

confined to the virtuous and humane. . . . The greatest ruffian, the most hardened violator of the laws of society, is not altogether without it.[5]

The notion that Adam Smith's *Wealth of Nations* was written by a man devoid of human sympathies, one mainly concerned with the removal of governmental restrictions on trade and industry—the establishment of laissez-faire—so that the rising class of businessmen who were in his time displacing the old landholding class could gain wealth and power, regardless of what happened to the general public, is a notion that can be supported only by passages taken out of context (such as the "invisible hand" passage) and using them without taking other passages into account. The same human sympathy that is expressed in *The Theory of Moral Sentiments* is in the *Wealth of Nations*. Human sympathy as expressed by Smith is not of the extremely abstract, completely doctrinaire form that is expressed by Rousseau. This could be at least a partial explanation of the comparatively benign influence that Smith has had.

This sympathy in its extreme form led Jean Jacques Rousseau to his doctrine that "whoever refuses to obey the general will shall be compelled to do so by the whole body. This means nothing less than that he will be forced to be free." [6] And so the sympathy that led to the demand for freedom for all in the interests of the welfare of all, in its extreme form led directly to the denial of freedom. So it is that when societies in which the most extremely radical doctrines, as far left as it is perhaps possible to go, gain power, such societies soon become the most authoritarian, the most oppressively conservative of all societies. Such has been the course in the communist countries of the world; and their experience seems to reflect certain necessities apparently unknown to the majority in the intellectual world of our time, in the structure of the political universe.

David Hume and Adam Smith, both in important ways severe critics of parts of the establishment of their time, did not let their abstract intellectual commitments lead them into political folly. They did not allow their ardor for the general welfare, an ardor no less genuine than that of Rousseau and Robespierre, go so far as to destroy their uncommon sense.

Can any person who feels and wills and thinks in ways that are genuinely good be opposed to the ideal society? How can he not be

5. L. A. Selby-Bigge, ed., *British Moralists*, 2 vols. (Oxford, 1897), I, 257.
6. Rousseau, *The Social Contract*, Book I, Chap. 7, in *The Social Contract and Discourses*, Everyman's Library (New York: Dutton, [1913]. 1937).

ardently for it? The answer obviously is, he cannot. Rousseau was in part certainly right. If man is by nature good, there is a general will and this general will most certainly is for the ideal society.

Why then do we not have it? Could it be that there are, say, metaphysical and perhaps other monsters in the woodpile? Thomas Jefferson, in a letter of March 5, 1810, to Governor John Langdon of New Hampshire, makes some remarks that might be relevant here on the way countries that have had kings have spoiled them: "Now, take any race of animals, confine them in idleness and inaction, whether in a stye, a stable or a state-room, pamper them with high diet, gratify all their sexual appetites, immerse them in sensualities, nourish their passions, let everything bend before them, and banish whatever might lead them to think, and in a few generations they become all body and no mind." [7] The light that illuminates our time, that comes in its fulgence from our intellectual world generally says that this notion of Jefferson's applies only to the special breed of animal that is chosen for kingship, that it does not apply to the ordinary breed; and besides, Jefferson's notion is not supported by social science and has long been out of date. Society undoubtedly has the power to do some molding, but it should be evident, without long disquisitions, that molding can be done in ways that are wrong as well as right.

Are there, then, metaphysical monsters, and perhaps others, in the woodpile? And if so, can they be liquidated?

If man is by nature good but ruined by his institutions, it is evident a new man, or a new something else, is needed, If we watch, look, and listen with sufficient care, we find in this body of doctrine many such plain copies of the old theology as this, without acknowledgments.

Where shall we start working for conversion? With man's institutions, with his society, with the individual man, or with some combination of these?

Let us look at a typical present-day, up-to-date diagnosis and prescription for our condition by a leading social scientist. "Society," as it actually exists, Margaret Mead tells us implicitly in most of her writings, explicitly in Appendix II of her book *Male and Female* (and she is far from the only one telling us this), "Society is the patient. Those who have been in some way hurt or distorted give us invaluable insights into what is wrong with it. But to cure society, we need also individuals who

7. Adrienne Koch and William Peden, eds., *The Life and Selected Writings of Thomas Jefferson*, Modern Library (New York, 1944), p. 603.

can use their strength in altering those cultural processes which lead toward disease." And so we do, we certainly do need such individuals. But first it would seem that we need to know the signs by which we can tell whether a society is diseased and what the disease is. So far as I am aware, Dr. Mead has not published a statement in which she has classified what she considers to be social diseases and the signs by which each can be identified. I judge from the little I know of her writings that some might read the signs differently from the way she seems to read them and might hold that what she considers to be health is really disease. I do not claim to know just what Dr. Mead's prescriptions are, or perhaps I should say what her prescription is, for she seems to have had only one. This prescription began to approach the clear side of haziness, though still not near enough to be certain about it, in her *Coming of Age in Samoa,* first published in 1928. That book, published some forty-five years ago, can be taken as prescribing more sex, much more sex and without inhibitions, without worry, as the cure for at least one of the ills from which American society apparently was assumed to have been suffering. How long does a prescription have to be taken by society, or some part of society, before its efficacy can be known? So far as I have been able to discover, this prescription has been tried many times in the past and one looks in vain for any society in which any ill has been cured by it. The societies that Margaret Mead has described and seems to have intended as possible candidates for imitation in this respect may have inspired imitation. I do not know. There is no room for doubt, however, that the United States for some years now has been in the midst of a revolution that has brought far more freedom in sex than at any previous time in the history of the country, and probably more, on a more widespread basis, than at any previous time in the past of the Western world. The real problem here is that of knowing the signs by which a social disease and a cure of this disease may be recognized with a reasonable degree of certainty. In the absence of such knowledge, talk about disease and cure has too much in it that is reminiscent of the sales harangue, from his wagon, of the patent medicine vender of former times to the villagers and the countrymen gathered in the village on a Saturday afternoon.

Our medical men have little difficulty recognizing many of the various diseases of the body that can become serious in the world today, but knowing when a society is sick, and especially what to do about it, is something else. If, for instance, a society uses color as a basis for discriminating among its members, or, as in India, uses anciently established membership in different groups with different and firmly held and seriously incompatible customs and habits—is it a sick society? Take the case of color as a basis for discrimination. Is this condition cured by establishing quotas based on color for determining legitimate mixtures in educational institutions, employment, and other such matters? Or is it likely to be more firmly established by such a practice? The real problem so far as the color question is concerned seems clearly to be that of standards that have nothing whatever to do with color. We hear little from social science today on this crucial question.

It could be that social science has not yet reached such a stage that it is capable of dealing with social problems of the more difficult kinds without running into the danger of creating more problems than it solves. But, let me say immediately, it is not enough merely to throw rocks at social science. Modern industrial societies pose problems on which decisions have to be made, and decisions made without the aid of social science are far more likely to be worse rather than better decisions. The social scientist is like all the rest of us in that he has an interest vested in his discipline and in his work, and this vested interest requires that he at least make his work appear to be worth its cost to society; otherwise he is in deep trouble. And I believe we can give him credit for much more than this. The social scientist, like the rest of us, is not likely to be satisfied with being able merely to create the appearance of being worth his cost to society. He is no more willing than the rest of us are to play the part of the charlatan or to be a deadbeat or to fail to do really good work.

It is not enough merely to ask, as we have done previously, whether there have ever been any such individuals as those for whom Margaret Mead calls—and if there have been, how they could have been so inattentive, so unconcerned, so blind as to allow society to become the patient. This is the same question that our discussion above of Edmund Burke's *Vindication of Natural Society* forced on us.

It may be that there are no lessons to be learned from human history. Still, there are some facts of the past that seem clearly to have some significance in them. One cannot help being moved by the sentiment expressed by Robespierre in the quotation from him above. One cannot help sympathizing with the young Robespierre and the ardor with which he cultivated his sympathies. One thinks immediately of his ardent opposition as a young man to capital punishment. And one also immediately thinks of, and has to take into account, if one wishes really to learn, his belief in and use, by the time he was thirty-five years old, of the guillotine as the sovereign remedy for vice in the body politic—vice being, in the main, opposition that threatened Robespierre's dominance over the government of France.

There could be instruction in the pathetic last words of Camille Desmoulins, leading journalist of the Revolution, in the note that he handed to his dear Lucile from the tumbril in which he was riding—his last ride anywhere on earth—on his way to the guillotine: "I was born to write verses, to defend the unhappy. . . . I have dreamed of an Otaheite which all the world would have adored. I could not have believed that men were so fierce and unjust." [8] One can only wonder what Desmoulins would have said if he had known that only a few days later his dear Lucile, suspect on account of her ardent relation with him, would be sentenced to make the same journey.

Learning, really learning and having something to teach that is worth teaching, that is not "true" today and "false" tomorrow, knowing what one has learned in such manner that a person of any intelligence cannot see the shabbiness of the teaching, is not as easy as falling off a log.

One does not understand any proposition whether it has to do with the existence of God, or the existence of the particles that are dealt with in nuclear theory, or the existence of the goodness in a charitable action, or the existence of the relation in arithmetic that says 2 and 2 are always and of necessity 4, or the existence of this pencil that I now have in my hand and with which I am now writing—I say one does not understand any such proposition until one understands all that can be said against it. At the same time, while the best teaching always tries to cultivate understanding, it cannot always do so successfully. Some authority simply has to be accepted. Elementary teaching of children at home, at play, and at school is of necessity largely authoritarian, whether it is the authority of the parent who says to the child, "Don't eat that, it will make you sick," or of the teacher who is trying to teach how to read or write or count, or of the playmate who throws a rock that hits and hurts. There is authority in rocks that are thrown and that hit, and in reading and writing and arithmetic, and in things that one

8. I picked this quotation up from a biography of Desmoulins many years ago but failed to note the source. My memory says it was presented as possibly of legendary origin. But if legendary, it is one of those legends that can have as much truth in it as any supposedly well-authenticated fact, and more than most.

eats; and if one is to survive and go beyond survival, one has to learn how to command these authorities rather than have them command and perhaps eliminate him.

But beyond the levels of the child, authority today of the kind that rests merely on the fact that somebody has declared something to be so is not enough. The acids of modernity have dissolved the authorities of former times, and this may either throw many of us into a freedom we cannot handle or transfix and paralyze us. It does not render the making of decisions and acting one way or another, or not acting, any less necessary. We are surrounded today by necessities that we do not understand and cannot escape.

The assumption that there has been increase over the ages in man's reasoning powers, but not necessarily any that is perceptible in the last three or four thousand years, is made necessary by the theory of evolution. This theory seems sufficiently well authenticated to warrant its acceptance until better grounds than any yet discovered are found for refusing to accept it. I call attention to this because modern science and modern knowledge generally involve many assumptions that cannot be finally and completely proved. Indeed, the tendency in the bodies of doctrine that are dominant in the English-speaking world today, relativity theory and logical positivism, is to hold that there are no propositions that have been or can be finally and completely proved, that all so-called knowledge is based on assumptions that are beyond final and complete proof. But man cannot live in an indecisive state. Such a state is, in fact, impossible. To be indecisive is to be impotently decisive. Furthermore, there is extreme confusion, appalling folly here.

Empirical doctrine, which includes logical positivism, is not, and never has been, a single consistent body of doctrine. One does not have to read very closely or carefully in John Locke or George Berkeley or David Hume (or all, as one has to do to understand any) or such present-day exponents of empirical doctrine as A. J. Ayer or Gilbert Ryle to discover that they contradict themselves as well as each other. It is impossible to show in the space available here where each contradicts himself and the rest. But to anyone who knows the literature, there should be no need to show that the very expression "empiricism" is riddled with ambiguity. We shall take a quotation from the 1967 edition of the *Encyclopaedia Britannica*'s article "Empiricism" to show this: "In its extreme form the empiricist doctrine is (1) that we have no ideas other than those derived from sense experience; and (2) that statements, other than those of logic, can be shown to be true only from experience." First, note the assertion here that there are different forms of empiricism. This is certainly true. But the form here described is not an extreme form. It is simply an unintended representation of the incoherence (the self-contradiction) in the doctrine. We proceed to show this.

Now whatever else the law of contradiction in logic is, it is certainly an idea. Clause (1) in our quotation above says all ideas are derived from sense experience. It follows that this idea is derived from sense experience. But clause (2) says the law of contradiction in logic is *not* derived from (sense?) experience. So (1) in the quotation contradicts (2). We now go beyond this and show further incoherence. Some empiricists, John Stuart Mill for instance, have attempted to derive the law of contradiction in logic from "sense experience" or "experience," and some who have made this attempt apparently have ignored, as in the quotation from Britannica above, the extreme ambiguity in the expression "experience" as compared with that in "sense experience." In our view all these efforts have been riddled with incoherence, but it would take a book of some length to show how we were forced to this view and we cannot include this book here. And we do not need to do this, for this is not the point at issue. The point at issue is this: whether Britannica's article is sufficiently coherent and free from ambiguity to make sense on the topic with which it deals.

The quotation above from Britannica's article "Empiricism," with all its incoherence and ambiguity, is a correct, even if unintended, representation of the incoherence and ambiguity in empirical doctrine in all its varieties.

When one considers the widespread use today of the assumption, often made without clear statement and possibly unconsciously, that man is by nature good, and the zeal with which those who make this assumption collect what they imagine to be facts to prove, as empirical doctrine in some of its phases requires, a thesis designed to save this creature by nature good, but who, despite his good nature, has somehow fallen into ways that the would-be doctor of society says are not good, one cannot help wondering what is going on here. Could it be that this doctor of society, instead of being really a doctor, is the epitome of the current ills of society? Edmund Burke answers this question in a teasing and implicative way which is at the same time the clearest possible way in his *Vindication of Natural Society*.

One has to understand these matters for one's self. The head cannot be cut open and understanding poured in. Burke was fully aware of the limits that nature imposes on the teacher. Burke sets the final test of the ability to learn when he states the evocative facts and leaves to his reader the task of understanding.

The skeptic or even the moderately cautious person may of course insist that as long as the theory of evolution has not been established finally and completely as certain—as is the case with any inductively based theory—it cannot reasonably be used as a basis for assuming increase in the reasoning powers of that something which we call "man" —something of which no one has ever had any sense experience, something which, if we take such bodies of doctrine as logical positivism seriously, we have to regard as a metaphysical monster. George Berkeley, one of the founders of modern empirical doctrine, made this clear more than two centuries ago; and no answer compatible with empiricism as currently conceived has ever been given to his argument. This portion of Berkeley's argument has been accepted in empirical doctrine. But Berkeley's basic argument has not been accepted. The failure of Berkeley's basic argument to carry conviction can be explained simply as the problem of an apparently clear demonstration up against an invincible prejudice. Hume was certainly right when he noted the failure of Berkeley's argument to carry conviction. Hume very carefully did not say why.

Most of us make decisions every day that involve the acceptance of doctrines such as that we know what we are talking about when we use common nouns—words like "man," "government," "state," "university"—and we have no alternative. Most of us do not stand transfixed before the puzzles such words pose even if we are aware of the puzzles, and generally we are not aware. Our education generally has been so imperfect that we do not know the most elementary things about the language that we necessarily use.

Whether fortunate or not, human beings generally seem not to have that perfect balance of rational powers and temperament ascribed to Buridan's ass which when he stood between two equally accessible stacks of hay, according to one version of the story, held him perfectly balanced between the two, kept him from moving in either direction, and thus doomed him to starve to death. Is it likely that a human being in such a situation would follow the example that we are told was set by Buridan's ass? I think not. Would we not say in this case that not acting was a decision just as much as acting? I think we would. But can any such question be answered in a way that satisfies everybody? The history of human argument says no. Shall we then give up arguments, the effort to understand?

Of all the answers that have been given to this question, Socrates gives in his discussion with friends, just before complying with the sentence that required him to drink the hemlock that caused his death, as good a statement, I believe as can be made:

> "How melancholy," said Socrates, "if there be such a thing as truth or certainty or possibility of knowledge—that a man should have lighted upon some argument or other which at first seemed true and then turned out to be false, and instead of blaming himself and his own want of wit, because he is annoyed, should at last be too glad to transfer the blame from himself to arguments in general: and for ever afterwards should hate and revile them, and lose truth and the knowledge of realities." [9]

When I urge that the strongest possible pro and con arguments are necessary to the understanding of a subject, I do not mean to suggest that the example set by Buridan's ass in the story be followed.

The skeptic is, like the rest of us, often faced with questions on which he has to make decisions, and then, if he has any reasoning powers, he, again like the rest of us, uses them as best he can. The reader of David Hume who stays awake while reading cannot help noticing how the utterly skeptical Hume of *The Treatise of Human Nature* to whom there is nothing whatever of necessity in the action of a billiard ball that moves when another hits it, to whom this is mere customary conjunction, association, also wrote political essays in which he speaks of "causes and principles eternal and immutable" [10] and "eternal political truths, which no time nor accidents can vary," [11] and does not hesitate to say "effects will always correspond to causes." [12] These quotations from Hume suggest that he may have intended by them to question the merely conjunctive or associative logic for which he laid the basis in his *Treatise of Human Nature* and his *Enquiry Concerning Human Understanding*. Whether he had this intention or not does not matter to our purpose here. In our view they do not affect his argument that if there are any necessary connections among events or facts, these con-

9. *Phaedo* 90, in *The Dialogues of Plato,* trans. B. Jowett (New York: Random House, 1937), I, 475.

10. David Hume, *Essays Moral, Political, and Literary* (New York: Oxford Univ. Press, n.d.), p. 16.

11. Ibid., p. 19.

12. Ibid. p. 22.

nections cannot be discovered by sense experience—that sense experience cannot discover more than external conjunction, association, regularity among facts. They obviously bear on his assertion at the end of the *Enquiry* that, so far as can be known a priori, anything or nothing can produce or create anything. But Hume has no grounds for saying this since he has denied that anything can be known a priori.

Now if Hume is right in the view that no necessary connections exist among facts, the pursuit of knowledge can lead only to the discovery of facts, if this pursuit is properly conducted. Facts, in this view, turn out to be innumerable. Thus, in this view, the pursuit of knowledge necessarily leads only to the fragmenting of knowledge; and the process of fragmenting knowledge, as we shall see in Chapters II and III, is necessarily a self-defeating process so far as any really important knowledge is concerned. The means that we propose in Chapter XII for the cultivation of human knowledge in the public generally makes no sense whatever if the doctrine concerning fact that stems from Hume and dominates our time is universally valid. This doctrine, we may as well note here, is self-contradictory in that it denies that there are any statements that are universally valid. However, since this self-contradictory doctrine is dominant in our time, it is necessary that we take it into account. We have done this indirectly throughout this book, and directly in Chapters II and XI.

The doctrines of Hume as modified and adopted in the dominant orthodoxy of our time enthrones physical violence as the only means of making decisions within and among societies and nations. It enthrones an associative or conjunctive logic that justifies whatever customs and habits different people have practiced throughout the centuries—or, if the customs and habits change, it enthrones the changes as long as they last. The process has been clearly exemplified in Hitler's National Socialism by a people that, so far as the formalities are concerned, have probably been the most highly educated in the world. The Humian doctrine as modified asserts rightly the importance of agreement on right and wrong in human actions, but its criterion of right and wrong is mere agreement. And this kind of right and wrong can be that of thieves and cutthroats—a kind that David Hume himself would most certainly have rejected.

It would be grossly wrong to take what has just been said as a mere polemic against the writings of David Hume. Hume's writings have gained their influence over our time because of the truth they contain about the animal becoming human. Despite all the contradictions in

Hume, his writings, especially his great *Treatise*, which he rejected, laid the foundations for modern psychology and for understanding the associative logic of the animal. No other body of writings in existence offers the material necessary to understanding the associative logic of the animal and the problems that have to be solved if the human being is to discover a better logic and use it to lift himself above the condition of the mere animal. The first steps toward the discovery of a better logic were made some two thousand years ago. But discoveries of this kind have to be made by everyone for himself. And such discoveries normally cannot be made without the help of the great leaders in the development of human thought. This book is devoted to showing the dire need for this help in a form that is available to the public generally.

It is not impossible to believe, and perhaps make an invincible case—despite the blinding enlightenment of this age in human history—for the belief that there never would have been any human bickering and quarreling and wars, there never would have been any human misery-making customs and habits and institutions if somehow human beings had not made them. It should not be necessary to read Edmund Burke's *Vindication of Natural Society* to be provoked into thinking one's way to this necessary conclusion. To see the necessity of this conclusion is easier today than it was in the time of Burke. One can no longer, unless one is utterly lost in madness, shake his fist at the skies, put the blame on gods or God, and declare war on them or him. For the gods of ancient times long ago disappeared from the skies; and it is no longer possible seriously to think of heaven and God up there above the clouds. One is forced by the overwhelming evidence to agree with Albert Camus that God is today out of style, but one does not have to follow the style even though the habitation and mode of existence, once thought possible, no longer are so. There is nothing whatever visible in the skies to which the ancient appeal for justice can be made.

Some two thousand years ago the Greek playwright Sophocles let his heroine Antigone make her appeal against the positive law proclaimed by her uncle, who was King Creon of Thebes, brother-in-law and successor of Oedipus, to what she held to be the natural law of God. "Your proclamation," Antigone said,

> "was not God's proclamation. That final justice
> That rules the world below makes no such laws.
> Your edict, King, was strong,
> But all your strength is weakness itself against
> The immortal unrecorded laws of God.

They are not merely now: they were, and shall be,
Operative for ever, beyond man utterly." [13]

What was King Creon's proclamation? Eteocles and Polynices, brothers and sons of Oedipus, and joint heirs to his throne of Thebes, had died fighting each other in a battle for Thebes outside the city walls. Eteocles had ruled for a year and if he had followed the arrangement to which he had agreed, he would have given the rule for a year to Polynices, and the two would have alternated in rule thereafter. But Eteocles refused to give the rule to Polynices. Polynices then raised an army and lay siege to Thebes. The city succeeded in defending itself, but Eteocles and Polynices eliminated each other from the scene, and Creon, their uncle, became heir to the throne. King Creon decreed decent burial for Eteocles but Polynices was to lie unburied because he had attacked his native land; "no man is to touch him or say the least prayer for him; he shall lie on the plain. . . ; and the birds and scavenging dogs can do with him whatever they like." According to the belief of the time, the refusal of decent burial with the customary ritual doomed the soul of Polynices to wander eternally and never find rest or peace.

Antigone disobeys the law the King has made, and Creon, applying the law rigorously and equally, sentences her to death. Haemon, Creon's son, engaged to marry Antigone, tells Creon that everyone in Thebes thinks Antigone did right, that his sentence is hurting him with his subjects because it is terribly wrong. Haemon begs for the revocation of the sentence. Creon refuses. Antigone and Haemon die together, Creon's wife Eurydice kills herself, and Creon, too late, sees the error of vengeance against the dead and becomes a walking corpse.

The French playwright Jean Anouilh uses this story in his version of *Antigone*, with some vast differences, but with a recognizable identity with and difference from Antigone I in the commitment and actions of just one person, Antigone II, and in the main outcome forced by the commitment and actions of the one person, *just one person*, Antigone II. Sophocles' King Creon is utterly impartial and unrelenting in his application of the law he has made. He makes no effort to persuade Antigone I to give up her commitment and to help him conceal her action, or even to convince her that in making his proclamation he was doing what he considered, whether mistakenly or not, in the interests of

13. Sophocles, *Antigone*, trans. Dudley Fitts and Robert Fitzgerald, in *Greek Plays in Modern Translation*, ed. D. Fitts (New York: Dial Press, 1947), p. 473.

peace and justice in Thebes. He holds to his sentence of death for Antigone despite extreme efforts to dissuade him and despite over-whelming evidence that popular sentiment would support, at least for a time, withdrawal of his sentence and even applause rather than condemnation for Antigone I. King Creon I, we cannot today avoid imagining, may have been acquainted with and in fear of wide shifts in public opinion, may have wanted to avoid making himself a target by relaxing his law for a relative—though he says nothing to this effect. His holding to his judgment is attributed by Sophocles to excessive pride; but the reader today who has thought at all seriously about government cannot help feeling that to see this alone was a lapse on the part of Sophocles. Pride was certainly involved, but the possibility of great shifts in public opinion could hardly have been absent from Creon's mind. What would people say, how would they begin to act, when they had the time to think, if a proclamation that was law and certain to be enforced against any ordinary citizen suddenly became not law when violated by a niece of the King? Creon I does not discuss this and related questions with Antigone. He appears to be a block of granite, totally without feelings. But in the end, he is broken to pieces by the action of Antigone and the hopeless position into which this action has put him with his hateful proclamation. His fate is worse than death.

Anouilh's King Creon II—again the portrait we have authorizes us to imagine—had no desire for the kingship and would have preferred to live his life as a private citizen. Before he took over, Thebes was burdened with crime, ignorance, poverty, and armed internal strife. Life for everybody tended to be nasty, brutish, and short. Some men of worse than barbaric temperament had formed bands and were fighting each other, looting, burning, and seizing food stores in the effort to get control of Thebes for themselves. Creon II could have left Thebes. The temptation to leave was strong. To leave meant relative safety, ease, and comfort. To stay meant danger, struggle, extreme and continual discomfort, possible torture, probable early death. The spec-tacle of destruction, the threat—becoming daily more than threat—of starvation for those not killed in the internal violence, moved him to decision and action. He could not act effectively without forming his own band, arming it, and destroying the other bands. It is necessary to say here that if the olive-branch wavers of our time had been there, they, if we believe them, could have brought peace without resort to violence. But somehow the olive-branch wavers almost always manage to be absent at those crucial times and places when and where their professions call for them. Creon II used the necessary means and he succeeded in bringing peace.

Jean Anouilh's *Antigone* is one of the great portrayals of all time of the central problem of government. Creon II makes strenuous efforts to show Antigone II that she did not know what she was doing, that while her sentiment was beautiful, and her concern about genuinely rightful law wholly and profoundly admirable, still, if she had just known and paid any attention to the facts about her brothers, and the quality of the myths to which she was devoted, she would have known that her sentiment was misdirected, and that commitment to it could bring only defeat and destruction on all that she most loved. Antigone II is a portrait, drawn true to the life of a vast number of the young people of the still relatively free societies of our time. Antigone II clearly loves more than life itself an abstraction that has no earthly embodiment, and her sentiment and action not only give no help to earthly embodiment but help to make it impossible. It is only when Antigone II finally, too late, begins to understand this and is about to die that she utters words that millions in the wars of this century could have uttered: "I don't even know what I am dying for." It would be impossible to find and erect any better memorial, any more truthful testimony, to the ignorance, the great failure of our time, than these words.

Despite all of our talk about education and the growth of knowledge, the opportunity of the public generally to know as well as is possible about matters that determine not only the quality of life but whether one is to live or to die—and whether one's living or dying makes any sense whatever—simply does not exist.

The purpose of this book is to show the conditions that have given rise to the appalling ignorance of the great questions that is characteristic of our time—an ignorance that threatens to destroy the spirit of American life—the efforts that have been made to correct this ignorance and their failure, and to show that one and only one institution, an institution that does not now exist, is the only possible means of working toward the correction of this condition. Chapter II will deal with the fragmentation that has gone along with the extreme specialization of our time and that is tending to reduce the world of learning to a world of barbarians. General education is the name that we, in common with others, give to the remedy for this condition. But very little is known about what this remedy is, and very little serious effort has been made to find out. Chapters III and IV examine our leading encyclopedias to see whether they serve the purpose of general education. The original idea of the encyclopedia, suggested by the name, is that it would serve exactly this purpose. Our examination of our leading encyclopedias shows that none do this, and that this, their great purpose, is as if forgotten. Since the encyclopedia is the only means of general education that can be made available generally in homes, the questions we discuss in these two chapters cannot be ignored in any serious consideration of the problem of general education. Chapters V and VI constitute a case study. In them the two books by Marshall McLuhan that have brought him fame—books that have stimulated the writing of four books about McLuhan's doctrines with probably more to come—are examined in order to prepare a background for Chapter VII. In Chapter VII our encyclopedias are examined to see whether they help the typical reader—not to speak of the typical literary critic—to judge the soundness of McLuhan's work. Chapter VIII examines the most thoroughgoing criticism of higher education of our time, that of Robert Maynard Hutchins. Chapter IX examines the most serious effort yet made anywhere to establish general education—that made in the College of the University of Chicago under the regime of Chancellor Hutchins. Chapter X discusses briefly the best of the great-books projects as a means to a general education, and then passes on to discussion of the suggestion that the great books make for our time and that generally has been completely ignored. Chapter XI states and examines in a preliminary way principles by which the subject matter of a genuine general education can be determined. Chapter XII states and discusses the only possible means—a new type of encyclopedia, prepared on a basis worked out by a projected institute for general education—by which a general education can be made available to the whole public as well as to the barbarians now crowding the intellectual world and who, because of the tremendous power they have in their hands, are most sorely in need of this remedy. Whether they will take it is the great question. It cannot be forced on anybody. Almost anybody who chooses can make a train of death and destruction as did our burningly intense, our marvelously well-intentioned and ignorant Antigone II. And finally Chapter XIII explores the relations between learning and the cultivation of the human potential.

CHAPTER II

Education and Disintegration

'Tis all in pieces, all coherence gone
JOHN DONNE

Is education in the United States in such condition that it is largely a fragmenting and disintegrating rather than an integrating influence? And if so, how did it get this way?

It would be possible to write many volumes on this subject, and we can be sure many will be written. The outpouring, the creation of avalanches of words on large and extremely difficult and important subjects, as well as trivial ones, has become a habit of literate societies. This habit is not necessarily a helpful one. For the avalanche of words can bury the important subjects.

The most important influence in education in the United States today is the centrifugal force in higher education. The United States is simply repeating in this field the catastrophic mistake that Germany made in the late nineteenth century; and up to now in the twentieth, most of us are unaware of the fateful tendencies of this mistake.

Candidates for the highest degree may not make any real contribution to knowledge, but this is the ideal at which they are supposed to aim. In order to have a relatively easy opportunity to make what may be regarded as a contribution, the candidate has to go to the periphery of the field in which he has chosen to work if he is to find materials that have not been threshed over many, many times and about which he may find it very difficult, if at all possible, to say anything new that is worth saying. It is always possible at the periphery to find something to talk about and write about that has previously been given little attention; and, as this is done, the field in which he is working is expanded. Instead of thinking of this field as a circle, it is perhaps more illuminating, and more nearly true, to think of it as a sphere. The sphere of any subject is susceptible of indefinite expansion. Every subject involves innumerable facts and every subject is connected with others that also involve innumerable facts, with perhaps sharp divisions, such as that between what we think of as animate and inanimate matter, between collections of subjects. There is thus practically no limit to the work that can be done that may in some sense, trivial or other, be said to be a contribution to knowledge in any field, no matter what the size of the field was thought to be when work was started in it.

It usually takes around four years beyond an undergraduate degree for a person of normal competence to win the highest degree, that of doctor of philosophy. When the candidate finally wins his degree, he has a heavy investment of time and money in it. He can recover this investment most easily only if he can teach the subject in which he has specialized. This will be a peripheral subject, one far from the central subjects that everybody needs to know. And he very likely will not be able even to name some of the central subjects or discuss them intelligibly. He may be employed as a teacher if he is fortunate and has cultivated with sufficient zeal the orthodoxy to which his teachers subscribe. His interests, as I have said, require that he teach his speciality, and in the empire building in which universities are engaged under pressures which they cannot control, there are more forces that help him go in this direction than there are that hinder him. In ways somewhat like this, courses are added to curricula, and college and university catalogs grow. It is necessary only to examine a few catalogs to see why some students get the notion, not entirely wrong, that the faculty and administration have done a bad job of deciding what should be taught, and that they, the students, could hardly do worse.

Joseph Schumpeter, late professor of economics in Harvard University, somewhere remarks that it might be better, instead of continuing to use the currently established methods in higher education, to give every child at birth a set of stamps or patches, which when he grew up he could wear as one would wear a medal, to show that he had won the degree of doctor of philosophy. If this were done, it might then be possible to treat seriously the problem of education in a way worthy of the tremendous importance of the genuine process. I have some reservations as to this suggestion. The currently established processes do help in learning to read and write insofar as the entirely outward and superficial aspects of this learning are concerned. In some cases, they help to cultivate a highly persuasive rhetoric, such as that which Ruth Benedict exhibits in her *Patterns of Culture*, which I discuss later in this chapter. All this is in the right direction provided, and provided only, that the knowledge and skill central to all genuine education are also cultivated and are used to keep the centrifugal tendency in higher education as now constituted from becoming a fragmenting and disintegrating tendency. Awareness of this problem is rare, but some exists. Professor Gerald F. Else in Greek and Latin at the University of Michigan exhibits this awareness with the highest degree of clarity in an article "The Old and the New Humanities" in the Summer 1969 issue of the periodical *Daedalus* devoted to "The Future of the Humanities." Robert Maynard Hutchins exhibits this same keen awareness in several books, and as Chancellor of the University of Chicago worked perhaps as hard as is possible to establish in the College of the University an educational process that would have genuinely integrating effects. I discuss Hutchins' effort at the University of Chicago in Chapter IX, and his educational philosophy, which somehow had little effect on the College, in Chapter VIII. Hutchins' effort failed, not, I believe, because his ideas were unsound. I believe they were in their broad outlines sound. I believe the cause of the failure, as I show in my discussion, is that he could not find teachers who understood his ideas and were able to use them in teaching.

The question what is worth teaching is not nearly so difficult in introductory courses to the physical and biological sciences and mathematics as in the humanities and social sciences. In the natural sciences generally and in mathematics the reasons for doing certain basic teaching and learning are comparatively clear and compelling. If there is any rationale for the teaching and learning that are required in the humanities and the social sciences, this rationale is rarely expressed in more than an utterly superficial manner. The only rationale, if we may call it that, is you do this and you do that, or you may even choose as you please, and after certain processes are completed, you get your credits and finally your undergraduate or graduate degree, and the only real reason given is: Thus saith the authority.

When our candidate gets his degree of doctor of philosophy and gets a job and begins teaching, he may never have read more than a very little of the writings of any of the great philosophers or scientists or historians. It long ago went out of style to read any of the great theologians if one is not preparing to be a theologian. The typical candidate who receives a Ph.D. degree will have read widely in his field and in works currently considered important that bear on his field. For instance, no candidate for a Ph.D. in anthropology who had not read Ruth Benedict's *Patterns of Culture* and was not able to give an account of the Pueblos of New Mexico, the Dobuans of the

D'Entrecasteaux Islands, and the Kwakiutl Indians of Vancouver Island would be likely to have any chance; and most important, the candidate would be expected to know the argument for cultural relativity that Miss Benedict makes in *Patterns of Culture*. The candidate would be expected to know other works, such as those of Edward Westermarck and Melville Herskovits that make this same argument. He would not be expected to know of any current and powerful arguments by anthropologists against cultural relativity, for, until recently, there were very few; or rather, I should say, few that were recognized as worth serious attention by anthropologists. If the candidate adopted as his main purpose the making of such an argument, he could, until very recently, ruin his chances to get his degree, no matter what his degree of competence, if at an early stage he let his purpose be known. No candidate aware of the orthodoxy, the doctrines that dominated the field until very recently—and even recently have been only somewhat loosened—would adopt such a purpose if he put first his chances of getting ahead in anthropology. It should be said immediately that anthropology is not unique in this respect. I discuss below one of the very recent events that bear on this problem in anthropology. The extreme bias that has prevailed in the field has been so strong, however, that there can be no certainty that it will be abandoned or even modified.

The candidate would be expected to know all the most important works that bear on his subject. This means his chances of getting his degree depend on his having a memory well-stored with information that his examiners expect him to have. A candidate for a degree in any field may have, however, an enormous store of information that bears on his field, acquired from the reading of many books and articles— hard work over a long time—and still be an ignoramus so far as other fields of knowledge are concerned. One can, for instance, easily find persons with Ph.D.'s teaching courses in, say, history, who cannot talk intelligibly about the meaning of the words "naive realism" or give an account of the theories of causation of Aristotle and David Hume and distinguish clearly between them. Many will not have the slightest idea what is meant by the expression "the objectivity of value." One can find persons in almost any field who cannot state the principles that for centuries have been used to discredit old ideas and establish new ones. One can find even in physics persons who have little awareness of the revolutionary effect that the particle theory as inherited from the Greek atomists and modified by Galileo and Newton and others has had on theories of knowledge. One can easily find in any field, except that of specialists in theories of knowledge, persons who cannot state the more important theories of knowledge of the present.

This lack of knowledge of subjects of great importance to all fields of knowledge is not the fault of any particular group or institution today. It is the inevitable sequel to the division of knowledge into different fields. This division has been necessary and it is necessary that it be continued; but in the division, awareness has been lost of the importance of the knowledge of principles that are necessary to all knowledge whatever in any and every field. The opportunity to acquire this kind of knowledge and gain skill with it exists today only for the rare student who discovers that his formal education does not provide it and who then works as he can to get this knowledge and skill independently and entirely by his own efforts. The student who does this will certainly get out of line with others in his field and will only make trouble for himself if he lets others discover how far out of line he is. The problem of orthodoxy is a perennial problem in all fields of knowledge. No field can do without its orthodoxy. The real problem is how to do with and to it. The person who is not willing to take the chance of making himself a sacrifice for something that he believes is worth more than himself will always tamely choose the prevailing orthodoxy as long as it appears to be strong.

Let us turn now to another aspect of the problem of the division, the specialization and the fragmenting of knowledge.

Suppose a person discovers that his formal education has not given him the background that he needs in order to understand himself and his world as well as his mental abilities will allow him. It ought, perhaps, to be said first that the making of this discovery is not very likely. It is only when one has a really good general education that one begins to lose the intellectual assurance, the ability innocently to make ludicrous errors, the ability to tell people generally what's what when one is one's self in a state of blessed unawareness. The paradox of knowledge is difficult enough at best. If when we start learning, we are ignorant, we cannot know that we are learning. It would be necessary already to know what it is to learn in order for us to know this. Our learning is most likely in many ways to be a mere plastering over, a hiding from us of our ignorance, a mere acceptance of an authority that is drilled into us and that we take for knowledge. It may be to some extent a drawing out of what was already present in us, but in some mysterious way, even while present, unknown to us. But this process requires teachers of genius. The formal education that most of us get leaves us almost totally unaware of our ignorance, and not only this—it also cultivates the assurance that hides our ignorance from ourselves and others. The teachers in the system are themselves produced by the system and they tend to perpetuate it in the form in which they receive it, good, bad, or indifferent as this may be. They are unable generally to do other than establish it more firmly, even when they are trying most seriously to be original and improve on it. Fortunately, however, there are teachers here and there who have taken thought, gone into the wilderness, lived on locusts, scourged their egos and put them down, and learned some of the great truths of life. There are not enough of these to transform and govern the system. The specialists, the mere specialists are in an overwhelming majority. They know enough to say what their clientele at the moment wants to hear. And while they do not always defeat every tendency toward the provision of some genuine general education in the formal processes, if they allow anything of this kind, they allow it only by chance.

This is one, and only one, of the extreme difficulties that the person faces who, regardless of how many years of formal education he has had or what eminence he has reached as a specialist, becomes aware of his ignorance. What can such a person do?

The most difficult problem for him is that even if he has been using printed materials since his childhood, he cannot find his way around today in the flood of printed materials or among the offerings of one kind or another that are constantly being made to illuminate his darkness. If he does not know the right questions to ask and where he can find the most cogent and best informed discussion of his questions, he is unlikely to be able to solve his problem. Even within specialties, the difficulties here have become far too great even for the genius to solve them—given only the currently existing means. Consider the testimony of the distinguished physicist Max Born on the state of this problem in the field of physics:

Physics has expanded in such a way that nobody is able to survey the whole. The following data give some idea of it: The Encyclopedia of Physics (being published by Springer) is planned to have 54 volumes, each of them between 300 and 1,000 pages. Nobody knows more than a small fraction of this enormous amount of material. Yet it goes on increasing from day to day, and many a volume may be outdated on publication. Still more terrifying is the accomplished fact, that the Transactions of the International Congress on the Peaceful Uses of Nuclear Energy, held in Geneva, 1958, are now published in 27 volumes, many of 500, some of 800 pages. Each volume addresses specialists of a narrow section of this special branch: nuclear physics.[1]

This is really only a small part of what could be said about the mass of printed materials in the field of physics. It is not necessary to take into account the classics and periodicals that deal with physics in order to show that the person who wishes to make his mark in physics has to be an extreme specialist. Fortunately, some persons in the field are likely to know about or can find out about existing books that review the whole field as well, perhaps, as this can be done. But the non-specialist in physics—and all of us outside of our specialties are non-specialists—will find it extremely difficult, if at all possible, to locate books that are helpful to him and that are worth his time.

Max Born goes on to say:

This boundless increase of material is common to all the sciences. It is caused not only by the continuous expansion of research inside the older group of civilized nations, but participation of newly developing nations all over the world.

Thus the very meaning of the concept "knowledge" has undergone fundamental change. It does not refer any more to a single person but to the community of all men. While the total of what has been found and deposited in print grows in an unlimited manner that part of it which an individual can possibly know and handle becomes relatively smaller and smaller. Thus the gigantic increase of knowledge of the human race as a whole may mean that individuals become more stupid and superficial. There are unfortunately many indications that this is happening.[2]

It would be possible to pile up mountain high evidence on all other fields of knowledge of the same kind that Max Born gives on physics.

As to scientific journals, here is the testimony of Derek J. de Solla Price from his book *Science Since Babylon:*

The earliest surviving journal is the *Philosophical Transactions* of the Royal Society of London, first published in 1665. It was followed rapidly by some three or four similar journals published by other national academies in Europe. Thereafter, as the need increased, so did the number of journals, reaching a total of about one hundred by the beginning of the nineteenth century, one thousand by the middle, and some ten thousand by

1. Max Born, *Physics and Politics* (New York: Basic Books, 1962), p. 5.
2. Ibid., p. 5.

1900. According to the *World List of Scientific Periodicals*, a tome larger than any family Bible, we are now well on the way to the next milestone of a hundred thousand such journals.[3]

I will not take the space to estimate here how much printed material a person can examine hastily, how much he can read rapidly, how much he can read closely, how much he can read and re-read and study with extreme care in a certain period of time. One may be able to read a book such as Alfred North Whitehead's *Science and the Modern World* in a few hours, but unless one already has wide acquaintance with the subject, one will not get much unless he reads and re-reads closely. My copy of *Process and Reality* bears dates showing I have read certain portions as many as a half-dozen times. I would have to read more, and very closely and carefully, really to understand the book. No one really reads a book such as Kant's *Critique of Pure Reason* the first time he goes through it even if he tries to read closely, sentence by sentence. Such works require many readings, and even then one cannot be sure that a passage that is still puzzling is so because of a failure of one's own or of the author.

Problems such as these make estimates of how much reading a person can do in a limited period almost useless. Furthermore, the amount of material in print is so far out of proportion to the ability of any one person to read and understand it that estimates on this question are practically meaningless. No person who tries to get a general education today is likely to get very far unless he has a lifetime before him and just happens early to find the things that lead him to reading the right materials. He cannot get the help that he needs from any materials now in print or from any existing institutions.

Educational television has not reached a level such that it is worth discussion so far as general education is concerned. Educational television cannot possibly be any better, except by accident, than the specialists who plan the programs. Generally, what they provide, beyond some well-organized specialized courses that are in no way integrated with other knowledge, and beyond some extraordinarily well-chosen and well-performed plays, is just a little bit of this and a little bit of that. Moreover, one cannot do with television what one can do with a book—pick it up when one wants, examine this part and that closely and repeatedly, compare this part with that and hold the parts before one as long as one needs to do so, and so on. There are

3. New Haven, Conn.: Yale Univ. Press, 1961, p. 95.

things television can do better than print, some it can do that print cannot do at all. There is nothing today, no micro card system, no computer-storage electronic push-button retrieval system, nothing that serves the purpose of general education so well as the printed book, or that imaginably can do so. One of the insuperable difficulties in the way of understanding why this is so is that one has to have some of the elements of a general education in order to understand discussion of the questions involved. We shall give more attention to these questions in subsequent chapters.

Let us now look at some of the specific consequences of the fragmentation that we have been discussing.

Ruth Benedict's *Patterns of Culture* and a recent event in anthropology illustrate perfectly the problem created by the division and vast proliferation of what it pleases us today to call knowledge, but which is rapidly becoming a most destructive ignorance. In the last sentence of the last paragraph of the last chapter of *Patterns of Culture*, Miss Benedict summarizes her argument for cultural relativity. She says here, in effect, that there are no reliable bases for saying that one culture is better than another, that when we understand this, we arrive "at a more realistic social faith, accepting as grounds of hope and as new bases for tolerance the coexisting and equally valid patterns of life which mankind has created for itself from the raw materials of existence."[4] A copy of the first printing of *Patterns of Culture* was given to me by the distinguished southern sociologist Howard W. Odum in 1934, the year when the book was first published. I read the book, was delighted with Miss Benedict's rhetoric. She had more than rhetoric. She had obviously worked hard and carefully to get command of those facts of her subject that appeared to her most important. But her conclusions, while completely in accord with the prevailing orthodoxy in anthropology, were totally at odds with her facts. The orthodoxy was so powerful in her mind that she sacrificed her facts to it and was apparently totally unaware that this was what she was doing. This condition in her book drove me to lamentations that I expressed orally on many occasions and in writing when I had the opportunity.[5]

4. Ruth Benedict, *Patterns of Culture*, Mentor Books (New York: New American Library, 1953), p. 257. My references are all to this edition.
5. See W. T. Couch, "Objectivity in Social Science," in *Scientism and Values*, ed. Helmut Schoeck and James W. Wiggins (Princeton, N.J.: Van Nostrand, 1960).

Miss Benedict, if we judge by the language she used to describe them, regarded the quiet, calm, genuinely cooperative and peaceful life of the Pueblos as admirable. She equally obviously regarded the suspicions and hatreds, the institutionalized antagonisms of the Dobuans, and the competitive and conspicuous and destructive consumption, the potlatches that dominated Kwakiutl culture, as anything but admirable. Her descriptions of all three cultures were in language that unambiguously evaluated the cultures, as language has to do if the effort is made to be truthful. In these descriptions she clearly denied the orthodoxy, the theory she asserted in her conclusion—the theory of cultural relativity that all cultures are of equal value.

In the next to the last paragraph of *Patterns of Culture*, Miss Benedict speaks of culturally supported forms of ego gratification by "arrogant and unbridled egoists as family men, as officer of the law and in business." In the preceding paragraph she characterizes the Puritan divines as psychopaths who put to death confused and tormented women as witches and, as the voice of God, "put the fear of hell into the heart of even the youngest child" and condemned sinners to lives of anguish and remorse with threats of final and eternal damnation. The arrogant family men, officers of the law, and businessmen of her generation, she says, are like the Puritan divines. Their "courses of action are often more asocial than those of the inmates of penitentiaries."

I cannot interpret these words of Miss Benedict's in these two paragraphs next to the last in *Patterns of Culture* as saying anything other than that any culture that supports the characters she specifies deserves only to be destroyed. From her own language, it is clear she considers Pueblo culture idyllic in comparison. And in expressing this judgment, even though it is spread out in a lot of words, she contradicts her judgment, also expressed at the end of *Patterns of Culture*, that all cultures are of equal value, or, to say the same thing in another way, no one culture is better than any other. This, as I have said, is the doctrine of cultural relativity; and it has been for a long time, and probably still is, despite some heresies, the orthodoxy in anthropology on this subject.

One may doubt the truth of the two paragraphs next to the last in Miss Benedict's *Patterns of Culture*, but this is not the point we are discussing. The point is that Miss Benedict was as rigidly bound by her orthodoxy, despite the facts that she herself clearly states, as were the Puritan divines by their orthodoxy.

It is impossible to overemphasize the importance of the fact that, according to the Editor of *Psychology Today*,

Soon after World War II, Ruth Benedict's elegant little classic, *Patterns of Culture,* became one of the few standard works of social science, required but surprisingly pleasant reading for millions of students. . . . Ruth Benedict showed us how a people organize themselves around a set of values so that all institutions tend to play up or put down particular traits of character. Each "system," as we now say, has a distinctive configuration. Mores such as polygamy or private property can lead to bitter competition in one culture, but encourage gentle unpossessive ways in another. It depends upon the configuration of that culture.

  And that's where she left us, as if her life had been broken in the middle of a sentence. She had refused in *Patterns of Culture* to argue for one style of life over another. . . . Among the professionals of anthropology, anything but neutral categories might have been attacked as "unscientific"— the sin of sins. . . . She was, however, never a neutral person. You can feel passion in the rhythmns of her prose.

The statement quoted above from *Psychology Today* is from an editorial "About Ruth Benedict and Her Lost Manuscript." The statement is excellent, true, important—with one exception which, also important, is simply not true. We will identify this statement below. The lost manuscript has been published in the April 1970 issue of the *American Anthropologist.* A part of it is published in the June 1970 issue of *Psychology Today* from which the quotation above has been taken.

  The "lost" manuscript is Miss Benedict's last testament on the conclusion to which she came when she wrote her *Patterns of Culture* and which I have stated above. In this last testament of Miss Benedict's she completely repudiates the theory of cultural relativity which she asserts in the last paragraph of *Patterns of Culture.* There is no evidence in this last paragraph that she was "in the middle of a sentence" as the editor of *Psychology Today* suggests. The evidence is conclusive that when she wrote her *Patterns of Culture* she was in the middle of an orthodoxy that had such complete control of her that she was totally unaware of this control and therefore totally unable to do anything to get better control. Better control would have been to derive her conclusion from her facts.

  How many of the "millions" of students who were exposed to Miss Benedict's *Pattern of Culture* discovered for themselves the self-contradictory nature of the book? How many of the teachers who prescribed it as "required" reading discovered this fact? How many who made this discovery ever made their discovery public in print and known to their students? How long will it take for the correction that Miss Benedict made in her last testament to catch up with and correct the spurious conclusion for cultural relativity in *Patterns of Culture?*

These are not trivial questions. The mantle of science cannot safely be spread over activities supposed to be of a serious intellectual nature that in drawing conclusions ignore the facts on which the conclusions are supposed to be based. The problem involved here is not new but ancient. The myth that Aristotle was a mere theorizer, that he made no effort to base his theories on fact, is widely believed today and repeated over and over despite the evidence in Aristotle's writings and in the writings of students of Aristotle to the contrary. This myth received its first powerful expressions in the sixteenth and seventeenth centuries. It is not at all clear that the facts will ever catch up with the myth. The myth of *Aristotle, Galileo, and the Tower of Pisa,* as exposed in the book under this name by Lane Cooper, is an object lesson in the making of myths and their tendency to become immortal. I tell about this myth in Chapter XI. Among the scholars and scientists and philosophers who have repeated it are John Dewey, Alfred North Whitehead, C. I. Lewis, W. D. Ross, C. A. Coulson, Carl Becker, Louis Trenchard More, and Albert Einstein.

One of the theories of this book is that the more important theories of man and the universe constitute the major part of the subject matter that is necessary to a general education. And we really should know by this time in human history that theology has no monopoly of the problems of dogma and doctrine and orthodoxy. The problems these terms pose are present in all science and are inescapable. The word "dogma" designates a doctrine or theory that is still expressed but that has ceased to be meaningful. Every field has its dogmas. The words "doctrine" and "theory" are indistinguishable in their meanings. The word "orthodoxy" designates a body of doctrine or theory in any field, and every field has its dominant orthodoxy. Scientific work would be impossible without a dominant orthodoxy. Yet, at the same time, some of the most important work in science may involve attack on the dominant orthodoxy. If science is to be taken seriously, it is absurd to expect no serious effort to be made to repel such attacks. For attacks and efforts to repel them to occur is simply a sign that science is still alive. The real problem here is that of distinguishing between attacks that lead to improvement and those that lead to confusion and destruction of standards.

All intellectual work is done under more or less control by certain theories or myths which may be consciously or unconsciously held.

The highest grade and by far the most difficult and important intellectual work is that which shows the misleading character of accepted theories and the more fruitful, possibly more truthful, character of new theories—or of old ones that have been abandoned. The heliocentric theory had been advocated in ancient times by the Pythagoreans and Aristarchus, but the geocentric theory of Aristotle and Ptolemy is the one that was held generally until about the time of Copernicus. It is hardly possible today to imagine the extreme difficulties that had to be overcome in thinking through and establishing the Copernican theory. Even though Copernicus clearly pointed toward a heliocentric theory, he did not prove the theory as is widely thought, in terms that were acceptable up to the advent of relativity theory. None of our leading encyclopedias tells in its article on Copernicus what had to be done to prove the heliocentric theory in pre-relativity terms, and what Copernicus did and did not do in the provision of this proof. None collects this information and presents it in any one place. I shall not take the space to present this information here; and I have to confess, in spite of much time taken in searching, I cannot tell the reader of any one place where he can find it. I content myself with remarking that on some questions of world-shaping importance, our encyclopedias as sources of information are grossly inadequate. And all other sources are scattered and practically impossible for the layman to use. I return to evidence of the extreme difficulties that leaders in the development of Western thought have had in overcoming the dogmas in their fields.

Copernicus did not succeed in freeing himself from the Aristotelian notion that the movements of the heavenly bodies are in circles. The very idea that the motions were not circular, so Copernicus said, "made the mind shudder." He, too, had to have epicycles to explain apparent motions, just as Ptolemy did. Kepler was the first astronomer to work out, on the basis of actual observations, the theory now accepted, that the orbits of the heavenly bodies are not circles but ellipses. This theory had been suggested previously by Nicholas of Cusa in his *De Docta Ignorantia*, and possibly by others, but never worked out on the basis of observed fact. Kepler appears to have been totally unaware of any earlier suggestions and resisted the idea until his calculations finally forced him to accept it. Galileo was not convinced by Kepler's demonstrations and to the end of his life held the theory that the orbits were circles. The extreme difficulties in the discovery of the inadequacy of the old dogmas, and the demonstration of the more nearly adequate character of the new theories, are illustrated probably as well as is possible in the work of Copernicus, Kepler, Galileo, and Newton; but to this day these difficulties are not as clearly understood as they need to be. For the scientist cannot work without theory, and the history of science tells us that theory has always contained what in the course of work that is fruitful is finally seen to be dogma, and that the progress of science is the overcoming of dogma. Herein lies whatever truth there is in the Hegelian doctrine of contradiction; and there is certainly some truth there. The sifting of the true from the false here is one of the great, and so far as I have been able to discover, unattempted tasks of our time. I shall criticize our encyclopedias in much of the discussion throughout this book, but I wish to say here that encyclopedia editors cannot solve problems that the members of the intellectual world are not even attempting to solve. But they can and should call attention to them.

The contrast between the care with which leading physical scientists generally have proceeded in disestablishing old and establishing new theories, on the one hand, and the looseness of the procedures and demonstrably faulty reasoning that characterize much of modern sociology and anthropology, on the other, is startling. I have shown above the faulty reasoning in Miss Benedict's *Patterns of Culture*. I shall now tell of a great error made by Galileo—one that is not widely known, possibly because of devotion to the idea, or perhaps I should say the myth, that the great leaders in physical science did not make any great errors, or possibly because by shifts in definitions and by judging the work of one time by the standards of another it is so easy to show error to be not error. I have given in the case of Miss Benedict's *Patterns of Culture* an example of the irresponsible procedure of social scientists in establishing their dogma of cultural relativity. I do not know of any case in which a physical scientist has proceeded in a way as socially irresponsible as the way of some social scientists. There was nothing socially irresponsible in Galileo's error—unless, and this is a big unless, zeal for the propagation of truth and overweening confidence that one has it is in itself socially irresponsible. I suggest there is a problem of the greatest difficulty and importance here—a problem of which the ancients were far more aware than we are—the problem of pride in knowing, a pride that can become demonic, and I hope the following discussion will throw some light on it.

It is still widely held that the action by the Inquisition against Galileo was a great error, and in a sense, the sense that it had tremendous, probably decisive, effect in the way of strengthening the forces already working for the destruction of the spiritual and intellectual unity of the Western world, it certainly was. It strengthened these forces by opposing them with means that not only were inadequate to its purpose but made a horrible caricature of its purpose in the case of Giordano Bruno and others and went far in this direction in the case of Galileo. Yet its purpose, its intention was the maintenance of the spiritual and intellectual unity of the Western world. And so it may really be that Hell is to some extent paved with the very best of intentions. But bad as the judgment of those in power in the case of Galileo was in this respect, their judgment was not in all respects wrong. The wisdom and tolerance of the leadership of the time in one respect is clearly demonstrable. The theological leadership of the time held the theory that the Copernican theory was hypothetical in nature. The theory that all scientific propositions are hypothetical in nature is dominant in physical science today. The Church in the time of Galileo was thus far ahead of its time so far as the hypothetical nature of the Copernican theory is concerned. Was it behind so far as censorship is concerned? I now turn to this question in order to show the quality of the wisdom of our time on it. But first some words on Galileo.

The book that Galileo wrote that got him into trouble with the Inquisition, his *Two Great World Systems*, used a theory of tides based on the newly developed theory of inertial motion—largely the work of Galileo, and now universally accepted as one of Galileo's great achievements; but Galileo's use of his theory of inertial motion to try to prove his theory of tides, which in turn he used to try to prove the Copernican theory—none of this has been accepted since Isaac Newton published his *Principia*. Galileo's real trouble, as I have suggested, was that he was not willing to present the theories on which he based his argument as hypothetical, as the Church advised him to do. He insisted on presenting them as true, and he did so at the end of his book with a sneer at those who had advised him to present them as hypothetical.

Newton's theory of tides, based on gravity, is the generally accepted theory today, but it is accepted only as an hypothesis. Newton himself wobbled—as has been told many times—from the theory of action by contact to action at a distance; and the question which of these two theories is the better one for the purposes of science is today an unsettled question. If contact wins (and Einstein seems for it), Newton's theory of the tides will have to be abandoned.

I have said above that the effort that the Inquisition made to stop

Galileo from publishing his *Two Great World Systems* in the way in which he wanted to publish it, that is as an argument for what he thought to be true rather than what he regarded as only hypothetical, while a catastrophic blunder in its main bearing, contained a judgment that is upheld by present-day scientific theory. Now our question is, do we really believe and practice today the theory that the judgment of scientists does not justify censorship?

The problem involved here is a perennial one that comes up every now and then in every important field of knowledge; and the notion, the theory that the solution of it is easy, that all that has to be done is just get rid of censors, of inquisitions, is utterly puerile and false. Its falsity is easy to show, but nevertheless the theory, the dogma, is so firmly held that getting rid of it would make a lot of minds do more than engage in a Copernican shudder. There is much evidence to show that censorship, driven out the door, comes in the window. Each of us has in his own mind a collection of unexamined commitments, or notions that we have no commitments, some held unconsciously, that serve a censorial, thought-stopping process. Sigmund Freud did not create the superego and plant it in our minds along with a subconscious receptacle for ideas we are unable to tolerate consciously as well as a lot of we know not what else, and his theory of them is not an exhaustive one. I will now come to the point of this discussion and tell of an instance in our time that illustrates perfectly the problem of censorship and especially its perennial nature. There is no discussion in existence that is easily available to the general public and that illuminates the more difficult aspects of this problem.

In the year 1950 a leading American book publisher, the Macmillan Company, issued *Worlds in Collision* by Immanuel Velikovsky. I did not buy the book, did not read it, and though I have a copy, have not read it to this day. This, however, is totally irrelevant to the problem with which we are here concerned, except for one important consideration. This is that when a case such as this one is told about, the question usually is asked: Was the book worth publishing? And if you say you haven't read it, the conclusion usually is: You have no basis for a judgment as to whether it should have been published. This question and this conclusion, instead of working against censorship, work for it. I do not have to read a book to know that some people may think it was worth publishing; some that it was not worth publishing; some that it is so misleading, so bad, that it should not be issued by a reputable publisher; and some that its publication should not be allowed by anybody, reputable or not. The question whether the last group should be allowed to make its opinion effective easily turns into the question of censorship by a public agency, one perhaps established by a government. But it is fatuous to assume that there can be no effective censorship in the absence of public agencies established to perform this function.

I repeat, I am not concerned here with the question whether *Worlds in Collision* was an unskillful or a skillful but fraudulent example of scholarship and science, or was a work of great originality that offended the high priests of science because it attacked with great persuasiveness and some truth the prevailing orthodoxy. If I concerned myself with this question, I would be trying to establish myself as an authority; and if I then tried to do what some physical scientists ganged up and actually did, I would be trying to establish myself as an authority with the rightful power of censorship. I am concerned here only with the question whether modern scholars and scientists believe any more than the scholars and scientists who guided the Inquisition in its affair with Galileo the proposition that the true cannot be crushed by the false, that men do not have to rush to defend what they think is true if they wish for it to survive, that the true can safely be left, without human intervention, to defend itself.

It has been the almost universal habit among intellectuals in the United States during the last thirty years to condemn the intellectuals of Germany who sat idly by during the period while Hitler was spreading his racistic and other poisons and preparing for World War II. On what grounds can this condemnation be justified other than that truth does not rise of itself and defend itself—that men have to rise and defend it?

I witnessed the storm that started at the time of the publication of *Worlds in Collision*. This storm came as a concerted effort on the part of leading American astronomers and physicists, members of such faculties as those of Harvard University and the University of Chicago among them, to frighten the publisher, the Macmillan Company, into dropping the book from its list and firing the editor who secured the manuscript from Velikovsky for Macmillan. The effort succeeded.[6]

It might be said that the astronomers and physicists have learned

6. See "The Politics of Science and Dr. Velikovsky," *American Behavioral Scientist*, 7, no. 1 (Sept. 1963), for an excellent account of this affair. The article by Ralph Juergens, "Minds in Chaos: A Recital of the Velikovsky Story," bears specially on the problem of censorship.

better, that this will not happen again. This is again to deal with a problem of the greatest difficulty in a way that is puerile. No one would employ an accountant who refused to accept the authority of the multiplication table. No candidate for the degree of doctor of philosophy in, say, history, would get very far if he refused to accept the orthodoxy that says there is in some way that makes sense a past that can be studied and about which statements can be made that are probably true—even though that past, as distinguished from mere signs of its existence, cannot be seen, touched, tasted, smelled, or heard and, if empirical dogma is true, cannot be an object of study. Every field of knowledge, every human activity has its orthodoxies. These orthodoxies cannot be violated except at more or less risk, depending on the kind of society in which one lives. Every great advance in knowledge involves a violation of an orthodoxy. But, it has to be remembered, a violation is not necessarily an advance.

It is, I believe, clear from all the evidence we have that if Galileo had not claimed to prove *the truth* of the Copernican theory, if he had been willing to treat it as an hypothesis, as Osiander did in his preface to the *De Revolutionibus*—a preface that for a time was thought to have been written by Copernicus—Galileo would not have been called before the Inquisition. But this tolerance does not solve the problem. The willingness of the high priests of the orthodoxy of Galileo's time to allow dissenting theories to be presented if they were presented as hypotheses could be interpreted either as a weakening of belief in the orthodoxy or as a belief that the orthodoxy was so strong it could stand the tensions that might be produced by the publication of hypotheses that were incompatible with it. There is much evidence that both convictions were widely prevalent in the intellectual leadership of the time. Both were effective in the action taken against Galileo—an action that while deeply humiliating still eventuated only in what amounted to house arrest. I repeat, there is plenty of evidence that if Galileo had been willing to treat the Copernican theory as an hypothesis, that is, as an astronomer in accord with relativity theory would treat it today, rather than as absolutely true, it would not have been possible for individuals to organize any effective action against him.

It happens that since the development of non-Euclidean geometries and relativity theory, the notion has gained widespread acceptance that there are no principles that are known to be true, that all principles are imaginary constructs, fictitious, mythical in character—except, one has to say, this principle; and when one makes this exception, one has to scurry around to justify it, if one understands what one has done. There is very, very little of this understanding among us, and virtually no agencies that are effectively cultivating it. Euclidean geometry was based on what were accepted for around two thousand years as self-evident axioms or truths. There is room for doubt whether Euclid regarded his axioms as self-evident truths, but there is no room for doubt that others at later times did, up until the development of non-Euclidean geometries. The non-Euclidean geometries are widely held to have destroyed the idea of self-evident truths, but this view has not gained universal acceptance. In relativity theory, truth is most often held to have lost status—though Einstein himself can be quoted against as well as for this view. And the same is true of Einstein on the question of self-evident truths. The message that requires the relaxation of claims to truth in physical science that is generally thought to be in relativity theory had not reached the astronomers and physicists who ganged together against Macmillan and Macmillan's editor and the author of *Worlds in Collision*. This message had, however, without benefit of the conclusion derived from non-Euclidean geometry, reached the papal power in the time of Galileo. And, again I repeat, it is crystal clear from the records of the time that as long as Galileo did not claim to have proved the absolute truth of the Copernican theory, the papal power would not have molested him. I now add there is plenty of evidence that says it not only would not have molested him, but would have supported him and showered him with honors. But the Church did not solve the problem of hypothetical vs. true premises. This is a perennial problem. And whether human beings can really know or not, they have to make decisions as if they know. Our educational institutions of today, including our encyclopedias, are not helping to find better rather than worse solutions of this problem.

The doctrine developed from the non-Euclidean geometries that there are no self-evident truths in physical science was extended by Gunnar Myrdal in his work *An American Dilemma* to social science and makes a shamble of the truths held to be self-evident in the American Declaration of Independence. This doctrine is not yet reflected in any of the articles in any of our encyclopedias that have to do with any of the great problems of human rights. A powerful argument that this doctrine is false is possible. The reader who does not already know where such an argument can be found will not be able easily to locate it.

In her powerfully persuasive *Patterns of Culture*—persuasive, as I have shown, if and only if one is unable to read closely and think while one is reading—Ruth Benedict tells a story the point of which is crucially important, but she misses it, as, I believe, most of her readers have done. She tells how Ramon, a chief of the Digger Indians, once interrupted his descriptions "of grinding mesquite and preparing acorn soup," and said to her:

In the beginning, God gave to every people a cup, a cup of clay, and from this clay they drank their life. They all dipped in the water, but their cups were different. Our cup is broken now. It has passed away [p. 19].

Miss Benedict tells us that she did not know

whether the figure of the cup occurred in some traditional ritual of his people that I never found, or whether it was his own imagery. It is hard to imagine that he had heard it from the whites he had known at Banning; they were not given to discussing the ethos of different peoples. At any rate, in the mind of this humble Indian the figure of speech was clear and full of meaning [p. 19].

One may be profoundly grateful to Miss Benedict for treasuring and recording this beautifully simple figure, but one may still disagree completely with her interpretation of it.[7] I have discussed above the last sentence of *Patterns of Culture* in which Miss Benedict summarizes the thesis of her book when she speaks of all cultures as having "equally valid patterns of life." Miss Benedict's conclusion, as I have shown, clearly contradicts the substance of her book, just as Ramon's story clearly contradicts Miss Benedict's conclusion. For the cup of Ramon's people, if we accept Ramon's testimony, was not able to stand the strain of contact with other cultures, or of time, or of something else, any or all of which some other cultures were able to stand, but perhaps not forever. It should be clear by this time in human history that cups can be broken without war, without any physical conquest, without the organized violence of one culture against another. The cup of a culture may fall to pieces simply because it has lost the power to hold itself

7. I do not intend in my criticism of Miss Benedict's *Patterns of Culture* to suggest that this work of hers is of no value. On the contrary, I consider it of great value; but if this value has ever been suggested by any anthropologist, I have been unable to find this suggestion. Miss Benedict's notion of patterns of culture is a perennial notion anticipated more than two thousand years ago by Plato's notion of the form of the good. Her *Patterns of Culture* is a superb working out of Plato's notion despite the fact that she clearly did not know that this is what she was doing. Ramon's account of the cup of the Digger Indians is a beautiful instance of the embodiment in a myth of a truth of profound importance in the life of a people. Ramon's cup is, of course, a symbol representing the pattern of the culture—the form of the good—of the Digger Indians.

together; its life, for internal reasons, may just have gone out of it. Mere cultural contact may be enough to break cups. The industrialization of China that is going on today is not being forced on China by any of the powers in the world that led in industrialization—except as example may be a force. One may hope that the industrialization of China will not break the cup of that great people. The Chinese family has been in the past one of the world's great institutions. It performed, and appears to have performed amazingly well, many such functions as social security and old age, unemployment, and health insurance—as the society of the southern United States did, but probably not as well, prior to the American Civil War. Governments in the Western world perform these functions today, but it is not clear that they are doing better than the family did in these older cultures. That the Chinese family will survive modernization and the emancipation that tends to go with modernization appears hardly possible at this time. However, the Chinese are a marvelously tenacious people—equal in this respect to the Jews, who, despite all tribulations and changes in the world, have had a continuing and benign influence, beginning in ancient times and continuing until today, that has been powerful in determining the best in the cultures of the Western world. The Jews appear to have kept their cup unbroken and perhaps greatly to have strengthened it. One can only hope the same for the Chinese in the ordeal through which they are passing.

The tolerance that Miss Benedict pleads for in *Patterns of Culture* is, I believe, necessary up to a point; but there are points beyond which tolerance is an evil thing, and it is of the utmost importance to find these points. No people, primitive or civilized, has ever practiced tolerance unlimited. One cannot know whether one's cup is as good as or better than other cups unless one has valid standards by which to judge; and while apparently hopeless dilemmas arise when one thinks he knows that his standards are valid, and tendencies toward arrogance and overweening pride appear, still one has to try to get standards that are valid and to use them in his judgments, and, in fact, everybody does this; but none have as yet been able to convince all or even most others that their own are the best and should be universally adopted. It is easy for one to deceive himself about the strength of his cup, but still one has to have and willy-nilly does have a cup, unless one is all in pieces, all coherence gone—meaning personality disordered—as many in highly industrialized, highly sophisticated societies are today. Ethnocentrism is no longer adequate. And even less adequate is the notion which many at the top of the social hierarchy have today that since they are at the top, they belong there. We have to look hard at any claim of any group or culture to be the best. Such claims, generally, we may say, are not soundly based. But neither is know-nothingism, follow-any-immediately-attractive-thingism. We cannot escape the burden; standards that are universally valid are absolutely necessary if any judgments that are valid are to be made. Consider the statement from Miss Benedict's *Patterns of Culture* which we have previously quoted in which she tells her audience that there are arrogant and unbridled family men, officers of the law, men in business, whose courses of action "like the behaviour of Puritan divines . . . are often more asocial than those of the inmates of penitentiaries." Now I believe we can be sure Miss Benedict did not just sort of think that perhaps maybe what she said on this subject is possibly a quarter of the way or halfway or some unknown portion of the way toward the truth. The firmness of her statement says: I, Ruth Benedict, say this is it. Now I do not bring this up again in order to repeat the charge that she contradicted her orthodoxy when she expressed this judgment. I bring it up for two reasons: first, the empirical dogma that dominates most ethical theory today regards such judgments as nonsense. Miss Benedict obviously worked on empirical principles and was apparently unaware of this problem. Second, it is possible to reject empirical dogma on this point, but if one does so and holds that such judgments as those expressed by Miss Benedict may be tested and either validated or rejected, one has to have an ethical theory that shows how this is possible. No such theory that is compatible with empirical doctrine is generally accepted by social scientists today. I go into this because I believe such judgments as those referred to above and that Miss Benedict made are among the most important judgments that human beings can make, but, I repeat, standards that are universally valid are necessary if such judgments are to be more than mere prejudice, mere personal opinion, or perhaps the opinion of a group or a tribe, or even the majority in a nation. Opinion may of course be true, but on matters of such great importance as those on which Miss Benedict expressed herself so freely and, so far as I can see, just as harshly as any Puritan divine, there is dire need not merely to opine, but really to know. In saying this I do not intend to suggest the possibility of human omniscience, no matter how great the need for the achievement of this state. I wish to suggest simply that some charity in judgments would seem to be as much needed by social scientists as by Puritan divines. We cannot correct the Puritan divines, but we can suggest the need for charity in judgments today—but not to the point of refusing to make any judgments at all.

I intend to suggest in this discussion only the crucial human interest in achieving that which is humanly possible. Joseph Schumpeter comes near stating the principle I am seeking when he says in his *Capitalism, Socialism and Democracy*, "To realize the relative validity of one's convictions and yet stand for them unflinchingly is what distinguishes a civilized man from a barbarian." [8] I accept this with the very important substitution of the words "humanly limited" for the word "relative." I do not expect judges and juries and police and legal systems to be a great deal better than they are until the people generally for whom they exist are a great deal better. I do not expect the Prosperos of the world to be omniscient or perfect. They are limited to what it is possible for human beings to know and to be. To know what they know, to pattern one's life after them, is to know and be the best one can. The task of finding out how to recognize them is not an easy one. But the difference between them and the Calibans and Callicleans of the world—even if these are social creations—is so great that if one is unable to recognize this difference and if one is not attracted by the better, there may be very little that one can do for one's self, or that others, no matter how hard they try, may do for one.

In the specialization of our time, as I have shown in the preceding cases of Ruth Benedict's *Patterns of Culture*, Galileo's *Two World Systems*, and Velikovsky's *Worlds in Collision*, we have lost knowledge of and skill with the principle that has always and everywhere been necessary to the cultivation of theories or myths that are more rather than less true. I rely throughout this book, as well as I can, on the universal validity of the law of contradiction in logic. I cite it here as a principle that is basic in the cultivation of human knowledge, and I have been using it to illustrate its gross violation in quarters especially charged with responsibility for the cultivation of skill in its use. I have no doubt that I violate it. Practically everybody does if he ever engages in lengthy discussion of any subject of any importance; but those who know the importance of this law do not violate it knowingly. To do so is a stain on one's intellectual honor, and there are still people around, rare but still extant, who take honor seriously. I shall not attempt to prove that this law is really a law or that it is universally valid. And I

8. Schumpeter, *Capitalism, Socialism and Democracy*, 2d ed. (New York: Harper, 1947), p. 243.

cannot take the space to try to distinguish it from what Hegel mistakenly, I believe, called contradiction when he perhaps should have said contrariety or opposition, and in doing so gave his sanction to the essential element in the body of doctrine that has been transforming the world during this century and thus giving a worldwide demonstration of the power that a doctrine that has some truth in it but that is basically false can generate. One cannot find any illuminating discussion of the truth and falsity of this doctrine in any of our leading encyclopedias. The typical reader who becomes aware of the importance of this question is today utterly helpless in the face of it.

The best discussion of the law of contradiction of which I know—by far the best—is in Book Gamma of Aristotle's *Metaphysics*. It is easy to understand, but very difficult, if at all possible, to practice in extended discussion. I grant, as Aristotle did and as everyone since his time has done who has shown any understanding of the problem, that proof cannot be given of the basis of all proof. I invite the reader to examine the history of human thought and find one instance, if he can, of the advancement of knowledge without the rigorous use of this principle. The only discussion of the Hegelian doctrine in relation to the Aristotelian is scattered, incidental, brief, too slight to have any wide influence. An example is Morris Cohen's essay "Hegel's Rationalism" in his book *Studies in Philosophy and Science*. It is an excellent statement and should have stimulated more extensive work on the same subject; but apparently it is unknown even to specialists in the field of logic. The article on Hegel in the *Encyclopaedia Britannica* (1967) completely ignores this crucially important subject as well as the errors Hegel made in his philosophy of nature. Britannica's bibliography should list one or two works that contain illuminating discussion of these problems in Hegel, and particularly of Hegel's doctrine of contradiction in relation to Aristotle's, because of the paramount practical as well as theoretical importance of this subject. So far as Britannica and our other leading encyclopedias are concerned, this subject is not of sufficient importance even to be mentioned.

If Ruth Benedict had been fully aware of the decisive importance of the law of contradiction and skilled in its use, she would not have blundered into self-contradiction as I have shown she did. The editors of *Psychology Today* report that John J. Honigman, professor of anthropology at the University of North Carolina at Chapel Hill, who, along with Professor Abraham Maslow, was responsible for the preservation of Miss Benedict's lost manuscript after her death in 1948, "noticed in some discomfort, a vague similarity between synergy [the name Miss Benedict gives to the cooperative doctrine in her lost manuscript] and Adam Smith's argument that private greed serves the public good." The notion that Adam Smith ever held this doctrine in any pure and unadulterated form is a consequence of not having read with care all of Adam Smith's *Wealth of Nations*. It is a consequence of exclusive attention to the "invisible hand" passage, and of the making of myths about Adam Smith on the basis of this passage. Most of us do not have the time to read even the relatively few great seminal works such as Smith's *Wealth of Nations*. If we read anything of such writers as Smith, we read excerpts, or comments by writers who have read only excerpts. It is a very difficult, an extremely exacting task to write a fair summary of a work such as *The Wealth of Nations* in a few thousand words. Summaries that can be trusted of the work of men of great importance, such as Kepler, Galileo, Newton, Smith, Marx, Darwin, Freud, are extremely rare. The 1967 edition of the *Encyclopaedia Britannica* has an article on Adam Smith that is almost a model of excellence. The 1967 edition of *Collier's Encyclopedia* has an article on Galileo that, with one or two exceptions, so far as I can see, leaves practically no room for improvement. The article on Adam Smith in the 1967 edition of *Collier's Encyclopedia* is hardly worth reading. The reason for this may not lie with the author of the article, since he was not allowed enough space to give Smith anywhere nearly adequate treatment.

It is on encyclopedias that most of us, when working outside our specialties, have to rely for discussion of the subjects that constitute a general education. Most of us do not live in university communities, do not have easy access to large libraries, do not have time to search in libraries even if they are easily accessible to us—and those of us who have these advantages are as likely to be ignorant on the great questions and as impotent in our efforts to find out about them as the John Does in Podunk. Encyclopedias are the only practical resource for most of us. Millions of us have them in our homes, and around a million until very recently have been going into homes every year—and none of them come anywhere near doing the job that a properly made encyclopedia could do. There simply is nowhere else for most of us to go for discussion of the great questions such as these that bear on the present. Our encyclopedias are being edited by the dead hand of the past and in apparent total unawareness of this fact.

If Professor Honigman had read the article on Adam Smith in the *Encyclopaedia Britannica* (1967) and if he had considered what he was reading at all seriously, he would have recognized Miss Benedict's synergy as old doctrine under an unfamiliar name.

In addition to contradicting herself, as we have shown above Miss Benedict doing, she tells us, also on the last page of her *Patterns of Culture*, that "it is only the inevitable cultural lag that makes us insist that the old must be discovered in the new, that there is no solution but to find the old certainty and stability in the new plasticity." I suggest that despite this utterance, Miss Benedict's words do not have magical powers. If Miss Benedict were expressing some such doctrine as that quantity at some stage in its increase brings change in quality, I assume she would not deny at least some permanence in the actual working of this doctrine. I do not know in any omniscient way that there is any permanence of any kind, any continuity whatever in the world, and I would not attempt to prove any because I know very well this is not possible except on grounds that in turn cannot be proved. Again I suggest, and I only suggest, that the notion implicit in the quotation immediately above from Miss Benedict that suggests that the world may be born wholly new in every successive moment is also not susceptible of any proof; and if it were, Miss Benedict's synergy, however admirable in the moment of its appearance, would be doomed to non-existence in the next moment. And unless there are persisting magical powers, such as Miss Benedict's powerfully evocative words, it cannot be known that Miss Benedict's synergy will ever again appear on earth.

Finally, on the question of the comparative excellence of cultures, Miss Benedict must have known when she wrote her *Patterns of Culture* about such customs as those of the Aztecs of Mexico. And surely such knowledge is not kept secret from anthropologists generally. It was, one might say, not necessary to wait for the example of Hitler's National Socialism to be shocked into questioning the dogma of cultural relativity. But the public generally had no chance to know the appalling character of this doctrine. The best of the summaries of human knowledge available to the general public, the *Encyclopaedia Britannica*, has no entries in its 1967 index of the words "cultural relativity" or "ethical relativity." Until very recently, one would have had to search long and hard to find an anthropologist willing to write on cultural or ethical relativity and use such evidence as that which can be found in ancient writings—say the histories of Herodotus and Thucydides—or such as that which can be found in current editions of Britannica but which, if one does not already know the subject, one will find practically impossible to locate.

The article "Aztec" in Britannica provides an excellent example of the kind of information that is indispensable to the understanding of the doctrines of cultural and ethical relativity; but before examining this sample, if our purpose in this chapter is to be understood, it is necessary to keep clearly in mind that the public is not likely to recognize the decisive importance of such samples as this one if the specialists, the scholars, the supposed authorities do not recognize this decisive importance. It is impossible to overemphasize the importance of this problem. We have chosen Ruth Benedict's *Patterns of Culture* and have discussed it at length because it illustrates a blindness on this subject that pervades the intellectual world of our time. Miss Benedict's work is far better than most current intellectual work and, despite the failures on which we have harped because they are so widespread, is worth far more attention than we have given it. Cultures are most certainly patterned as her title says; and the study of cultural patterns and how they may be changed for better or worse is a subject of the very greatest importance. General education of a kind that is worth having is not possible by any means whatever unless there is some understanding in the intellectual world of problems of this kind. Fortunately, there is some such understanding; otherwise this book would be an utterly hopeless effort.

Let us now consider certain information in Britannica's article "Aztec." The Aztec god Huitzilopochtli

had to be well-nourished, vigorous and healthy. His sustenance was human blood. . . . the Aztecs were people of the sun, chosen by Huitzilopochtli to provide him with nourishment. War was, therefore, their favorite occupation and religious obligation. In war they captured their enemies and sacrificed them to the sun, opening their chests and tearing out their hearts barehanded. As the Aztec power grew, the number of human sacrifices increased. Prisoners from all parts of the country were put to death in Tenochtitlan [the site of present-day Mexico City] so that the universe and man might survive. The Aztecs' cult of the sun was not to go unrewarded; Huitzilopochtli therefore promised them no less than domination of the world.[9]

Could any people within reach of the Aztecs reasonably tolerate them if it was within their power to do anything else? One may urge the

9. *Encyclopaedia Britannica* (1967 ed.), article "Aztec."

appeal to reason—but the use of reason to eliminate the horrible worship of the Aztecs, even if reason alone could be successful, would have meant the breaking of the Aztec cup, that is, the destruction of Aztec culture; and the destruction of the culture of a people is the destruction of the people as a distinct people. It is a forcing of them, whether by rational persuasion or otherwise, to become something other than what they have been. Now it would be a mistake of the most serious kind to imagine that the quality of the thought given in our time to such cults as that of the Aztecs is unique.

The quality of the thought on matters of the greatest importance that dominates our time may be further illustrated by two quotations from Bertrand Russell—not a social scientist, but a philosopher thoroughly in accord with the spirit of modern social science. Russell first says, "There is something Hitlerite in objecting to people on account of birth," [10] and one can hardly disagree. Yet if the Aztecs really could not themselves somehow free themselves from their horrible worship, if outside interference was necessary and proved ineffective insofar as it did not resort to physical force, one faced a hard decision. One could reasonably hold, as Miss Benedict held with reference to the Puritan divines, that Aztec society, in so far as it held to its murderous worship, deserved only to be destroyed. Or could one? I ask the question because I deny that it is possible reasonably and in the name of humanity to avoid saying yes or no to this question. I hold the view that Aztec worship was evil just as Hitler's attitude toward race was evil; but I am unable to escape the conviction that I face an almost hopeless dilemma when I say this. For the judgment that the Aztecs could not free themselves from their worship plus the judgments that their worship was evil and deserved destruction adds up inescapably to the judgment that they as a distinct people deserved destruction—and I find this judgment as arrogant as it is inescapable. I turn back then on my hard judgments, as I wish Miss Benedict had done, reexamine them, and persuade myself that the notion of equality must in time, if not immediately, have application here; and that while one cannot tolerate the worship of such gods as Huitzilopochtli, one has to find ways of expressing intolerance that do not condemn whole people, or classes of people, as distinct groups to destruction, though it may be necessary to eliminate certain types of distinctness. One can accept and try to practice, even

10. "Reply to Criticisms," in *The Philosophy of Bertrand Russell,* ed. P. A. Schilpp (New York: Tudor, [1944] 1945), p. 731.

if it is old, apparently immortal, hackneyed, and at times a mask for evil, the principle of trying to correct the error, the sin, and save the person. I do not know of any mode of procedure, invented by modern social science, that compares even remotely in its genuinely humane quality with this ancient one, even if I grant, as I have to do, that it is not a solution of the problem of what might be called the right of peoples to maintain their cultural differences. It is one of the great tragedies of history that this humane doctrine of correcting the error but saving the person, even if it is not a final solution of the problem with which it deals was ever closely associated with physical torture and physical force—but then I have never lived close to any people with practices such as those of the Aztecs, and I believe it best not to form harsh judgments of people who had to do this or its virtual equivalent, people who have had to find ways to deal with problems such as those posed by people like the Aztecs.

I find no awareness of problems of this kind in Bertrand Russell's writings on ethical and social subjects. I find no principles such as that of correcting the error and saving the person that have any chance to solve them. And I find the same true as far as I am acquainted with the writings of social scientists. One cannot identify error if one does not have standards that are wider and more genuine than mere opinion, even if the opinion is that of social scientists.

Within eight pages of the quotation above from Russell is the following sentence also by Russell: "Consider one simple fact: that the wheel was unknown in America until white men introduced it. No doubt the wheel was the product of an evolution which took a considerable time, but each step required brains, and among the Indians the necessary brains did not happen to occur." It is necessary today to point out that Russell himself says here the "something Hitlerite" that he condemns in the previous quotation from him.

It would be grossly wrong to assume that all modern thought is riddled with dangerously self-contradictory nonsense of this kind. There would be no hope for modern man if this were the case. But so much that is of appallingly low quality comes from sources from which better can reasonably be expected that one can only wonder whether there really is any hope. For instance, look at this from a book on *Bertrand Russell's Philosophy of Morals* by a professor of philosophy in a well-known American institution: "The democrat believes flatly and finally that all human beings are to count as one and be regarded as morally equal; the Nazi believes that some men are inferior to others and, hence, the inferior races are to be treated as a means and not as an end." [11] So, in any society which happens to be so unfortunate as to have a majority of Nazis—who presumably, like the Aztecs, despite the horrors for which they stand, are still human beings—"the democrat believes flatly and finally" that nothing should be done to thwart the democratic political process by which power would be turned over to the Nazis. One cannot possibly have read John Stuart Mill's great essay *On Liberty* with any understanding and then write a sentence such as that quoted immediately above. I do not mean to say that Mill solves the problem embedded in this quotation. I find utterly repugnant his statement that "Despotism is a legitimate mode of government in dealing with barbarians" unless the spirit in which he makes this statement is taken into account—and that spirit would not lightly consider any people to be barbarian nor would it accept as rightful just any kind of despot. The real problem in all its extreme difficulties is to be seen only in the struggles between the Antigones and Creons of this world.

Was there ever any Antigone among the Aztecs who protested and sacrificed her life in protest against the worship of the god Huitzilopochtli?

If this question evokes the reproach that the human sacrifices of the Aztecs to their god Huitzilopochtli are as nothing compared with the sacrifices of the Western world in the two world wars of this century to their god, the nation-state, I say the reproach is well-deserved. But I ask, and I insist on asking, what is this nation-state, this mortal god that is worshiped by modern man but modern man himself? One does not have to read Thomas Hobbes' *Leviathan* to know this; but the *Leviathan* helps. I suggest there may be far more old than new in modern man, especially those varieties of modern man that are illuminated by what is imagined to be strictly modern light.

We have seen in the first part of this chapter the processes in education that have led to the fragmentation of what is called human knowledge, and we have seen that the fact of fragmentation reveals the self-deception and utter falsity in the claim made by the words "human knowledge." We have seen in the second part of this chapter the consequences of this fragmentation as they have affected the ability to think

11. Lillian W. Aiken, *Bertrand Russell's Philosophy of Morals* (New York: Humanities Press, 1963), p. 142. This quotation is one of the many ways of stating what seems to me the great dilemma of democracy. If recognized as a dilemma, the quotation has tremendous illuminating powers.

about the fragments in the various fields of so-called human knowledge. In the course of this discussion we have been led by necessity to the conclusion that the great problem of modern man is his worship of himself without knowing that in him—the image of God—which points toward that which is worthy of worship and that in him—the diabolical self-centeredness—which points only toward his self-centered self, the self that is one thing today and another tomorrow, that rejects and destroys today what it did yesterday, the self that is utterly unable to achieve unity with itself. In the course of time, as has been suggested in Chapter I, the animal in process of becoming human has been becoming conscious of the volatile self and has begun the quest of the real self. It is in the nature of man to want to be real, to want to escape being nothing—less than mere shadow—even though life has been so hard for some peoples, and so apparently hopeless, that escape into nothingness has been for them the most desired goal. There are depths in the animal becoming human of which he is still little more than vaguely if at all aware. The stories of the two Antigones, the one by the ancient Greek Sophocles, the other by the modern French playwright Jean Anouilh, which we summarized at the end of Chapter I, are rich in their meaning and illustrate the painful struggles, the necessary sacrifices, in the growth of awareness. One of the purposes of this book is to suggest the learning of infinite importance to human beings that may be done by the contemplation of such stories. Greek literature has no monopoly of such stories, but it and the Bible, the book of books, provide the great paradigms. One knows, for instance, the essence of the story of Petalesharoo, son of Knife Chief of the Loup band of the American Pawnee Indians, if one really knows the story of Antigone. In such stories one finds the potential in man that perhaps could be realized almost universally and that is most worthy of attention and cultivation. One is forced to wonder from much of what one reads whether many modern social scientists are fully aware of this.

We have reviewed in this chapter, first, the fragmentation of higher education; and, second, we have examined a few of the consequences of this fragmentation in addition to those examined in our first chapter. We have shown in many of the cases we have examined the loss of knowledge of and skill with an intellectual tool that in over two thousand years of experience in the Western world has proved necessary to the cultivation of human knowledge and the improvement of the quality of human life on earth. We have recognized the necessity of specialization, but we have shown in our sample cases that specialization which leads to fragmentation and then does not give adequate attention to integration is self-destructive. We have pointed out the only possible means of integration as far as this is possible—a new type of encyclopedia. Our next two chapters will show by the only means that is practicable—a sampling procedure—that our best encyclopedias not only fail at the task of integration but provide no evidence of awareness that though this in complete form is not possible in the present state of human knowledge, the better understanding of the problem of integration is one of the great purposes that encyclopedias can serve and that they must serve if they are to serve general education.

CHAPTER III

Facts and Fragments

The world divides into facts. Any one can either be the case or not be the case, and everything else remain the same.

LUDWIG WITTGENSTEIN

Is it true as is said in the quotation above that any one fact in the world "can be the case or not be the case, and everything else remain the same"? At any particular moment, your finger, let us say, is in a certain position. Is it possible that you can move your finger without moving all the particles in the air around it? There are doubtless millions of these. To move any one is to change the fact of its location and perhaps the shape of that of which it is a part. Suppose you get up in the morning in a house that is cold. The house has central heating and you turn the thermostat to the heat you want and the heat comes on. If you attempted to describe on paper every movement of yours, internal and external, and every change of fact involved in this process, every change in the particles in your body and in the particles surrounding your body, you would probably find that even if you were a mathematical physicist as well as expert on motions in and of and around the body, and unless you made certain assumptions you could not prove, you were attempting an endless task and would give it up.

It would be possible to give innumerable illustrations that would show that any change in any fact in the world is accompanied by changes in other facts, that these latter are perhaps endless in number, that "in fact" there is no such thing as a change in one of the facts of the world and all the other facts remaining the same.

How then can we explain the quotation above? Could it be only a reaction from the Hegelian dictum that "if the least grain of dust were destroyed, the whole universe must collapse"?

The author of the quotation above, Ludwig Wittgenstein, at the end of his *Tractatus Logico-Philosophicus*, from which this quotation is taken, labels his *Tractatus* as nonsense, but important nonsense. Hegel never does this with reference to the statement quoted from him in the paragraph immediately above, or with reference to the work in which he makes this statement, his longer *Logic*. From the point of view of common sense, Hegel's statement too undoubtedly is nonsense.

Why this nonsense, common sense might ask? Let common sense try to consider seriously the various ways in which the word "fact" is used. Let it use all the help it can get from the various sciences. Let it go beyond questions of mere usage into the question whether the world really divides into facts and what the relations are among these facts and it will, if it proceeds in a way that is not utterly superficial, run into puzzles that so far in human thought have proved beyond solution in a way that is demonstrably true or that has been so clear and convincing as to gain general acceptance. For instance, every fact in the physical universe is in modern thought assumed to be in a process of change. Where does the newness in the changed facts come from? Does the word "potential" explain, or is it at least partly a label for our ignorance? Where does that which is eliminated by the change go? Is it nonsense to ask these questions? If so, it is nonsense to try to understand the processes that in modern thought are assumed to occur in the universe.

The quotation above from Wittgenstein, despite the fact that the book is labeled nonsense by its author, has had tremendously important consequences in the intellectual world. The reason the work was labeled nonsense by its author almost certainly is simply that it is clearly an exercise in metaphysics. The audience for which the work was mainly intended was committed to logical positivism in which metaphysics is rejected as nonsense. The labeling of the work as nonsense by its author gave the work the best chance it could have of acceptance by logical positivists. They saw how they could use it and despite their general rejection of metaphysics did not hesitate to do so.

The nature of Wittgenstein's *Tractatus* and the use that has been made of it has not gone unobserved and uncriticized. Brand Blanshard, by far the leading exponent of objective idealism in the world in this century, has provided in his *Reason and Analysis*[1] and especially in Chapter IV, "Logical Atomism," a powerful criticism of Wittgenstein's notion of fact and works that have been based on this notion.

Blanshard links Wittgenstein's notion of fact to that of Hume and the

1. Brand Blanshard, *Reason and Analysis* (La Salle, Ill.: Open Court Publishing Co., 1962).

logical positivism that is largely derived from Hume. He holds that this notion provides the basis for Whitehead and Russell's *Principia Mathematica* which in turn is the basis for the symbolic logic of our time. He holds that *Principia Mathematica* and symbolic logic are erected on a basis that will not stand serious examination and that there are other invalidating objections, some of them made by the later Russell. And the doctrine of internal relations in Whitehead's *Process and Reality* suggests that when Whitehead wrote this work around fifteen years later, he had abandoned Hume's doctrine of external relations as he and Russell had worked it out in the *Principia*. It would be impossible to find two doctrines more clearly incompatible than these two.

We have said all that we can on the pros and cons of this subject without going too far afield, and without going beyond the limits of our competence. The presentation of the pros and cons on this subject is one of the jobs that our encyclopedias should do but that they do not do. Britannica does even worse by presenting one side in this argument not even as argument but as final authority. We shall have more to say on this subject in Chapter XII.

Why is the subject Fact important? One of the great questions that divides the world today is that of the nature of a large class of what are called "facts." Is it a fact that the potentials in the universe and in the animal becoming human are such that the process called "dialectical materialism" (which we shall discuss in Chapter IV) is working inevitably toward the establishment of Communism throughout the world? Is it possible for the people of the United States to form sane attitudes toward this and other closely related questions unless they have some real understanding of them? Is government of the people by the people for the people a process that has inevitably developed and that will inevitably continue, or is it one that insofar as it has been established at all has been established by understanding and great risk and sacrifice of life and that perhaps cannot be further developed without more of the same? Can it be that far better and far more widespread understanding are not necessary to maintenance and further development?

This book is devoted to showing the need for and the means necessary to far better and far more widespread understanding of the great questions on which the people of the United States are having to make decisions.

In this and our next chapter we shall discuss the treatment of particular subjects in our encyclopedias in order to throw further light on what our encyclopedias currently do and do not do. References are to the 1967 editions of the *Encyclopaedia Britannica* ("Britannica"), the *Encyclopedia Americana* ("Americana"), and *Collier's Encyclopedia* ("Collier's"). As we have shown in our preceding chapter, the members of the intellectual world today are almost of necessity specialists and are, like the members of the general public, lost in the wilderness that modern man has made of what should be knowledge and reasonable belief. A new effort toward as much synthesis as is possible, or perhaps I should say a stimulus toward synthesis, is needed. This new effort should be directed toward serving the purpose of general education— a purpose that is not being adequately served by any existing agency and, as we shall show, cannot be; and at the same time the new effort toward synthesis could serve, better than is now being done, the present purpose of the leading encyclopedias, a purpose that is none too clear but that might perhaps be correctly stated as serving as compendia of fact, perhaps also of theories.

The need for the work which is envisaged here and will be described as far as possible in this book is far greater, far more urgent than that which existed in the middle of the eighteenth century when the greatest of encyclopedia editors, Denis Diderot, with the aid of an equally brilliant and well-qualified colleague, Jean Le Rond d'Alembert, launched the epoch-making French Encyclopedia. The distinctive achievement of that work was to make available to the literate public the best thought of the age on the great issues of all time as these stood at the middle of the eighteenth century. The encyclopedias of our time do not do this. They are mainly helter-skelter collections of miscellaneous materials, much fact with some attention to theory, but with very little to the relations of fact to theory, and none to the question whether there is any evidence of any general hierarchical order of fact and theory. The collection and recording of facts in print is necessitating at present rates of increase the doubling of university libraries every twenty or thirty years. The notion that the facts that are recorded in print constitute human knowledge is, as we have shown in Chapter II, a dangerous illusion. Suppose that the facts in print can all be recorded—and there is little room for doubt that anything in words can be recorded—in electronic storage-and-retrieval systems. Who will know enough to get the relevant ones out when someone needs them? Who will know enough to distinguish the facts from the alleged facts in print? We have laid the basis in Chapter I and shall show in Chapter VII that the answer to these questions is incomparably more difficult than it is currently thought to be. The intellectual activities of Western man have reached a stage such that unless he finds far better ways of dealing with facts and alleged facts he accumulates, all further accumulation will only increase the size and the jungle-like character of this accumulation. The volume of "fact" has swollen far beyond the possibility of recording in any encyclopedia that would not be so large as to be useless to the general public. And the number of theories has also swollen.

Selection of theories to be treated and of facts that are most relevant to theories has become mandatory. Furthermore, modern man has been becoming aware that, throughout human history, some of the theories, the beliefs, man has held have had a large share in the making of fact. Attention to theory, far more serious than has ever before been given, has also become mandatory. None of our encyclopedias has been made with sufficient awareness of the multiplicity of theories, of their various relations to fact, of the urgent need for better understanding of these relations, and of the absolute necessity, if knowledge and reasonable belief are not to be smothered in the multiplicity of detail, that principles of selection that drop out the less important detail in both theory and fact be developed and used in the making of encyclopedias. The smothering effect of the vast proliferation of theories and facts is already visible in our leading encyclopedias. They are seriously deficient in their treatment of subjects of the greatest importance, they omit some entirely, and they give far too much attention to subjects of no importance and no educational value to the general public. Their treatment of controversial subjects frequently fails to reveal the real issues. And even if they contain the help that is wanted by somebody, the task of finding that help is often impossible.

It is not possible in this book to do more than provide samples of the great subjects that are not given adequate treatment in our encyclopedias, and also suggest what adequate treatment would be. I shall now discuss a few samples.

Government, Anarchism, Communism, and Democracy are among the numerous great subjects that are in some ways given excellent treatment, but not in the most important ways. And too frequently, the mass of verbiage obscures rather than brings out clearly the real questions. Let us begin our samples with Government.

"Anthropologists have shown conclusively," so Britannica tells us in its article "Government," "that all [so-called primitive peoples] possess governments, be they ever so rudimentary." This is a clear, positive, and emphatic assertion of crucial importance. There has never been any doubt, among qualified observers, that government of some kind, even if it is only that of the dissident individual engaging in violence and terrorizing a neighborhood, or of dissident and perhaps warring bands, has always existed among peoples beyond the primitive. The fact that government of some kind exists always and everywhere among all peoples has tremendous implications. Britannica does not discuss any of the more important of these implications or the questions to which the universality of government gives occasion. Neither does Collier's or Americana.

Among the most important of these implications is that unless human beings change in ways that seem clearly impossible, the ideal of anarchism as presented in the fully developed forms of both anarchism and communism, that is, the total absence of government, is not possible. We have only to consider what government always and everywhere and of necessity is in its central meaning to see this. Government is always either internally imposed control by each individual in a society on himself, or it is control imposed externally by society, or it is a combination of these two.

The statements we have just been making are what have traditionally been known as statements of natural law. A natural law statement is an assertion of a regularity, a process of any kind that has been observed always and everywhere in human affairs. This definition of ours does not rest the case for natural law on the discovery among different peoples always and everywhere of "a system of right and justice . . . common to all mankind and so independent of positive law" as Britannica's article "Natural Law" defines the term for the simple reason that it has been known for centuries that no such system exists. The term "natural law" has to do with the quest for such a system, with the bases on which this quest has been conducted, and with the question whether any elements that might be part of a system have been found to exist always and everywhere. The notion of natural law is thus, at this stage in history, not a static notion. Britannica's article "Natural Law" is helpful in that it provides some of the more important definitions that have been worked out in the past. Americana has an article that does the same. But neither goes beyond discussing the definitions it presents and showing that if they are accepted, natural law doctrine based on any of them has to be rejected. Colliers' does not have an article "Natural Law" or any discussion of the subject in other articles.

The lines along which for many centuries the effort was made to solve the problem of natural law are well illustrated by a passage from

Richard Hooker: "The general and perpetual voice of men is as the sentence of God himself. For that which all men have at all times learned, Nature herself must needs have taught; and God being the author of Nature, her voice is but his instrument. By her from Him we receive whatsoever in such sort we learn." [2] This approach seems not to have been fertile. For we know only too well that what some human beings consider good is to others evil. Any unanimity that can be derived from "the general and perpetual voice of men" seems so abstract as to be virtually meaningless. Milton's Satan illustrates one extreme of the problem when he deliberately chooses evil to be his good. But still the idea persists, and has persisted through the centuries, that there is a potential harmony, a harmonious set of universally valid principles, in the nature of human things and of reason that would bring harmony—peace and justice—into human relations if it were discovered and obeyed. The search for this set of principles and means for getting it obeyed has undoubtedly been a perennial human activity, one that we can be fairly sure will continue. There is no other activity that is humanly so important. It is, of course, possible that the principles are known in the sense of having been declared and recorded, but that too many human beings make the choice, perhaps unknowingly, that Milton's Satan made.

In this discussion which began with Britannica's article "Government," I have considered only the individual in society because such creatures as those of whom Rousseau has written, individuals living by themselves outside of society, are, with perhaps extremely rare exceptions, like unicorns and centaurs, purely imaginary creatures. There are no grounds whatever for believing that normal human beings have ever existed outside of society. Rousseau was fully aware of this despite his use of the myth of the individual outside of society. The evidence is overwhelming that the normal human being, or the animal becoming human, has always lived in society, small perhaps, but still society. Men are undoubtedly social animals, as Aristotle says, but I will add even though I cannot take the space here to follow up and discuss its importance: they are, and especially as they become what we call "civilized," also individuals.

I continue with the implications from Britannica's assertion concerning government quoted above. Now while government in the sense of externally applied controls seems clearly to have existed always and

2. Hooker, *Of the Laws of Ecclesiastical Polity*, Everyman's Library (New York: Dutton, [1907] 1925), I, 176.

everywhere to prevent deviations by penalizing them, the understanding that some deviations were helpful while others were harmful to society must have occurred early, for all legal codes, all customs and habits of which we know, reveal that the effort to make distinctions in this respect began early. But the further fact that this effort was not always successful, that failures occurred, is made evident by the execution of Socrates and Jesus. Both were, in terms of the ruling powers of their times, deviates.

The question whether people generally owe a debt that can never be paid to the persons who have deviated in ways that have proved helpful and have taken the risk of being penalized by externally imposed government seems the only factor worth considering until we consider another factor. In speaking of the deviate, we have by implication assumed that society consists mostly of persons who conform. The person who conforms is often in our time described in terms that make him look like a mere shadow of a shadow, a something that hardly exists. Here, for instance, is the French sociologist Gabriel Tarde's description of this person: "The typical social man is a hypnotical creature, a somnambulist acting under suggestions from others, though he does not know it, and is under the illusion that he is himself." [3] But the mass constituted by the typical social man may perhaps more truthfully and more importantly, despite deviations at times of such masses, be regarded as the balancing mechanism of human societies. The typical social man, the man who conforms, can be seen as a man who is integrated within himself and his society. When we understand that a man can be integrated within himself and at the same time with a gang of thieves and cutthroats, we begin to understand that there is a problem of kinds of integration.

Now if the individual never can completely escape reflecting to some extent the culture of the society in which he is born and grows up, if most individuals tend merely to reflect and except in minor ways never to deviate from the prescriptions of the culture in which they grow up, then what the anarchist regards as internally imposed government by the individual on himself is merely what his culture has first imposed on him, and there is no such thing as government in the individual that originates in him and that is imposed by him on himself, except in extremely rare cases. And it is in the nature of things that such cases

3. Tarde quoted in Bernard Bosanquet, *The Philosophical Theory of the State* (London: Macmillan, 1899; rpt. New York: St. Martin's Press, 1958), p. 42.

can only be rare. For it is not possible that culture should both shape all except the rare individual, and even the rare individual in most ways, and at the same time not shape them. And to say this and to recognize its truth is to see the truth of the first and most important rule, in the strictest sense of rule, of reason in what has been traditionally called "natural law."

Furthermore, if it is true, and it seems beyond question that it is true, that there have been in all societies everywhere, but perhaps not always, persons who have deviated from the established customs and habits, we have further questions of very great importance to consider. One of these arises from the fact that the first use of fire, the first planting of a seed, the first making and using of a wheel—all were acts of deviates. It seems clear beyond question that if societies for long periods of time have no deviates that do such things as these, they become static societies, perhaps even retrogressing or declining societies. When we mention acts of deviates that society in time deems helpful and incorporates in its customs, we must not fail also to mention the fact that some acts of deviates have been deemed harmful and punished. Among these have been acts that, first deemed harmful, later were deemed helpful, as well as such acts as murder and theft that have been widely, perhaps universally condemned, and on which opinion has tended to remain stable. It is necessary to say "perhaps universally condemned" because killing most certainly is not always murder; and it is not clear that any people has ever existed that has not shared the condemnation expressed by the English word "murder" for certain types of killing. The differences in types chosen for condemnation can be explained to some extent, but not always by differences in circumstances. The same spirit necessarily expresses itself to some extent differently under different circumstances. To reason and act otherwise is to descend to a literalism in spirit as obscurantist as a literalism in words. It is at this point that the failure to make necessary distinctions can lead to the adoption of an ethics of circumstance which is in reality the simple negation of ethics. The distinctions that are necessary are not easy to make in a way that is clear and convincing. We cannot take the space to make them here. One can search far and wide and fail to find them made clearly and convincingly. They are not made in any of our encyclopedias.

If the advocate of anarchy, in the effort to disprove what is said above regarding the possibility of anarchism, resorts to the argument that we have misrepresented anarchism when we say it has as its ideal internally imposed government—that, on the contrary, anarchism in its true form rejects all imposition of controls, that the true anarchist holds that when all imposition is removed, the individual can act spontaneously, and that when such action occurs, the result will be a natural harmony in the actions of all normal individuals—we have to say that anarchists have not agreed on the nature of their ideal. Some have held to the spontaneity doctrine, some to the pure self-government doctrine, and some to other doctrines, none of them defensible. The spontaneity doctrine was expressed by Karl Marx in one of his very rare excursions into utopian thinking when he said that "in communist society, where nobody has one exclusive sphere of activity but each can become accomplished in any branch he wishes, society regulates the general production and thus makes it possible for me to do one thing today and another tomorrow, to hunt in the morning, fish in the afternoon, rear cattle in the evening, criticize after dinner, just as I have a mind, without ever becoming hunter, fisherman, shepherd or critic." [4] If it is not immediately evident that the goods and services that people have to have in order not to starve could not be produced and distributed if such spontaneity were allowed to prevail, no piling up of words will help. Only bitter experience in such cases has any chance of instructing.

One may dislike extreme specialization as both Karl Marx and Adam Smith did, and as many other people do, but specialization is not going to evaporate because it is disliked or because it has brought grave handicaps with it. The fact is that it has brought far greater advantages, and the recognition of this fact gave rise to the cultivation of specialization as far back in time as we have any knowledge of human history. It may be that the returns to society from specialization are diminishing, but except for the problem about which this book is written, there are no visible signs to this effect. It may be that automation—an extreme specialization—will increase to the point that human beings will have the time to cultivate more than one specialty, or perhaps will choose to extend their specialties and to some extent generalize them by gaining command of those involved with the one with which they start, just as we are now discussing specialization because of its bearings on the possibility of anarchism of any of the ideal types, and of specialization and anarchism and natural law because of their relations to government. If we could see all these subjects as they really are, we would see them

4. Robert C. Tucker, *Philosophy and Myth in Karl Marx* (London: Cambridge Univ. Press, 1961), p. 197.

simultaneously in a motion-filled network that contains pitfalls, illusions as well as realities, and much that we have not discussed—and that, if we did discuss here, would take us away from the center of the subjects and the interrelations of the centers with which we are concerned here.

A good answer to the spontaneity statement by Karl Marx quoted above is given in the Epilogue to Milton Mayer's book *On Liberty: Man v. the State*. This answer was given by a student, Susan Rosenblum, a graduate of Washington University with a special interest in the communitarian movement. She gave it in a group engaged in discussion of the subject man vs. the state, and it is so exactly to the point that I quote it here:

I've had some experience living in a non-violent community in Pennsylvania. It included a group of high school and college students who were strongly politically oriented toward social change. There also was a group of young people who were very much interested in art and sensitivity experience, who saw the real revolution as an individual and experiential process. There was a great deal of conflict the summer I lived in the community. The art group people kept going off during the work hour and playing the guitar instead of helping out with the community chores. At the same time the political people were out demonstrating and leafleting in town when they were supposed to be at the farm. The community didn't work because some were not willing to do as Marc suggests—weigh the advantages of what you give up to balance what you receive. The idea of doing your own thing is not the purpose of living in community. It's a mistake to think that community is something that just spontaneously comes about; it has to be created through the experience of sharing. It requires effort and cooperation.[5]

This excellent statement could be used as a basis for an argument against the quotation from Britannica that governments of some form have always existed, but it can also be interpreted in a way that is entirely compatible with this quotation. It is reasonable to assume that there never was a moment in human history when human beings started making efforts toward cooperation. It is reasonable to assume that they have always to some extent made such efforts. Differences of opinion could lead to differences in the direction of efforts, and these in turn could lead to destructive conflict. And while the destructive conflict lasts, it rules—it, in its destructive way, is the government. Differences of opinion do not necessarily lead to destructive conflict. They can

5. Milton Mayer, *On Liberty: Man v. the State* (Santa Barbara, Calif.: Center for the Study of Democratic Institutions, 1969), p. 161.

lead to competition, as in play in games, and such competition can be a most fruitful form of cooperation. Our encyclopedias have many articles that engage in much speculation, and, we shall see, this is one of the necessities to the advancement of knowledge. But all of our encyclopedias are almost completely devoid of such speculation as this that is most needed in our time and that has the best chance to be socially fruitful.

The history of man on earth could be written in terms of the implications of the statement concerning government quoted from Britannica at the beginning of this discussion. Britannica cannot reasonably be expected to do this, but it can reasonably be expected to discuss this statement enough to show its wide implications. Britannica, as I have said, completely ignores this whole problem. There is a reference at the end of Britannica's article "Government" that says: "See also references under 'Government' in the index volume." On looking under "Government" in the index volume, one does not find any such subject as natural law. None of the articles, or passages in articles, referred to under "Government" in the index volume, with one exception, even mentions, much less discusses, any of the implications we have discussed above. The one exception is an article "Political Philosophy." Let us see what this article does to help us understand the basic problems of government. The first paragraph in the article is as follows:

The traditional problems of political philosophy have been the nature and the justification of political obligation and authority. There are here two essentially different sets of questions. First, there are the questions how men came together under governments and what were the motives which originally influenced them to do this and which still prevail to keep them obedient to government orders. These are questions of fact and they are properly studied by social historians, sociologists, and psychologists; but before sociology and psychology were established as independent sciences, many political philosophers included speculations on these historical and psychological topics in their works. The second question is that of the ethical justification of obedience to government; or, if we look at it from the point of view of the rulers, that of the moral basis of their authority. This question is the proper concern of political philosophy. In this article some representative answers to it are considered.

As to "how men came together under governments," the answer which Britannica gives in its article "Government," and which we have quoted, is that they never did, that they have always and everywhere lived under governments of some kind. The notion of solitary individuals living by themselves, as it is met in political theory, is sheer myth. There is no evidence, we repeat, to support the view that, beyond extremely rare cases, human beings, or animals becoming human, ever lived solitary lives. All of the factual evidence we have that is worth consideration in political and social thought is that individuals have always lived in groups, at times very small groups, always under governments. This is not to say that the myth of the solitary individual, when it is recognized as myth, has not been instructive in the effort to form true political theory. Government can be discussed intelligibly in the case of just one person whether the person is solitary or in society. Governments have always been more or less extensive and when widely extended have at times broken up into smaller governments, perhaps at war among themselves. The individual almost always already belongs to a group, and a group, whether large or small, is always under a government of some kind. While groups have changed, have grown or diminished in size, or have joined or separated from others, and individuals have left one group to join another, most individuals have always, even in extremely rare cases or while shifting from one group to another, lived under externally imposed controls in addition to those imposed by physical nature, that is, under government.

This criticism is not intended to suggest that since the notion of solitary individuals coming together to form a government is a sheer myth—and presented as myth by some writers on the subject of government, for instance, Rousseau—therefore this notion should not be taken into account. On the contrary, the notion is of perennial importance in political philosophy, there are reasons for it, and these reasons should be stated; to omit discussion of its more influential expressions, from that, say, of Glaucon in Book II of Plato's *Republic* to that of Rousseau in *The Social Contract*, is simply to leave out a large part of the subject. And the same is true of the opposing view—that governments of some kind have always existed among all peoples, and that they exist by nature.

The treatment of the subject government in our encyclopedias illustrates one of the problems that the author of an article for an encyclopedia cannot solve. This is the problem of the pros and cons of subjects, the organization, and the space allowed for articles.

The question of the existence of governments always and everywhere among all peoples is obviously a question of what has been traditionally called "natural law" as well as a question of political philosophy. The author of an article on political philosophy cannot know, unless he is told, whether he should include discussion of the contract and natural law theories of government. These could be covered as well in the articles "Government" or "Natural Law" or perhaps under some other caption. The choice of captions for articles is not a trivial matter as the "perhaps" in the last sentence might suggest. The traditional terms, usually the most widely used and best known, are probably the best. The best answers to questions of this kind cannot be given in the absence of an overall scheme, worked out with extreme care and in great detail when an encyclopedia is first made and before any but sample, model articles are written. The scheme should be such that in all cases it suggests, if it does not prescribe exactly, under what captions subjects, and parts of subjects, should be covered. A mere list of titles of articles is worthless. This problem will be taken up again in Chapter XII. Our purpose in discussing it now is only to suggest that there is a serious problem here.

It would be impossible to show in the space that can be taken here how badly the problem of the interrelations among subjects is being handled today in the only place where it is possible to show these interrelations in public, that is, in our encyclopedias. The simple faith that this showing of interrelations is done better in the numerous courses given currently in colleges and universities is not even understood to be a simple faith. It is a problem that is simply ignored. The invisible authority, the authority utterly beyond examination even by those in whose hands the authority is vested in this case, is worth contemplating. The dogmas of the church were public, open to public examination— but only after the early days when to suggest that public examination was needed was to endanger one's livelihood and one's freedom, to risk torture and death. It is time that the learned world begin paying serious attention to this problem as it relates to the nature and work of the institutions that exist for the cultivation and advancement of knowledge and that talk, when it suits them, about the right of the public to know.

Both the author and the editor of Britannica's article "Political Philosophy" were almost certainly aware of this problem of inadequate coverage of the subject. The problem of space is what defeated them. They might have solved this problem in this particular case, but this would have taken far more doing than we can do more than suggest here. Britannica, as I have already said, allows entirely too much space to articles that are written by specialists on subjects of interest only to specialists—and the specialists, since they have their own reference works and monographs, do not need the articles. Britannica cannot be redesigned to cut these articles out except at tremendous expense.

Britannica is already about as large as an encyclopedia can be and still be really needed by and really useful to the general public and within its purchasing power. Both considerations have to be taken into account. Mere expansion in size is no solution of the problem of making an encyclopedia that will be most useful to the general public. The notion of greater size as a solution is, on the contrary, an infantile notion, one to which the American public unfortunately is addicted but one that no educational institution can honestly encourage, one that cannot be held by anyone with any experience with the editing and the business side of the handling of encyclopedias and with any understanding of the problem of the kind of encyclopedia that is most needed by and would be most useful to the general public. To resort to increase in size is not only to evade and not only to increase the difficulty of the real problem, it is to surrender abjectly in the face of it. This problem is the choice of subjects, the determination of their arrangement, such questions involved in treatment as how the pros and cons of subjects should be handled, and the allocation of space in accord with the importance of subjects in comparison with each other, their need for more or less extensive treatment, and their relation to the overall purpose to be served.

With respect to the question of the existence of institutions that are now serving the purpose contemplated here, there are none; and with respect to the question whether any institution other than an encyclopedia designed and made for the purpose can meet the dire need that exists, no one has ever imagined and proposed such an institution that comes within the realm of practicality.

I have said much and will say more to the effect that our existing encyclopedias are to a great extent haphazard collections of miscellaneous materials, in articles that sometimes break subjects up into little pieces and scatter the pieces according to their place in the alphabet, in articles that sometimes combine pieces, and, in general, with the content of articles determined by a space allowance that excludes the discussion of important parts of subjects in the places where discussion is most appropriate, that ignores the relative importance of subjects to each other; and worse, collections that include many articles that serve no purpose that makes any sense and thus waste space that is sorely needed for the adequate treatment of other subjects. I would like to repeat, but of course I cannot, in connection with all such criticisms of our encyclopedias, that this condition in them is not the fault of the present or of any recent editors. They inherited the condition, and while they can, within the existing limits, do some things to correct it, they cannot do nearly as much as needs to be done, and the making of even moderate improvements is exceedingly difficult.

The encyclopedias that our editors inherit are not entirely unlike the culture that our society inherits. Our culture is changing and our editors try to keep our encyclopedias up to date by annual revisions that reflect the more important changes. But the basic mold, the basic pattern that was made for our encyclopedias at some time in the past, does not change from year to year; and the basic mold, the basic pattern that was made in the past, was made with reference to conditions that, in decisive ways, no longer exist. A new stage has arrived. A need that is imperative has come with it. And only a new encyclopedia made in a new mold, a new pattern, can meet this need.

At the same time it is held in this book, as the reader who stays with us will see, that there are principles, such as that of the mold or pattern used in the forming of things, that are universally valid, principles that have been true always and everywhere in the past and that cannot imaginably be other than valid in the future. Still, we have to grant that the human imagination cannot be trusted to set limits on the future and that things may happen that we cannot now imagine. So far as encyclopedias are concerned, we hold it is best to restrain the urge to be prophetic. It is held further that those principles that have been found to be universally valid in the past provide at least one of the important clues to the determination of the relative importance of subjects and such questions as the allocation of space to them. We do not mean by this that always the more important a subject, the more space should be given to it. Abraham Lincoln gave us our answer to this question in a story that we do not hesitate to butcher in the retelling. Somebody in a discussion with him said something that suggested that a certain man's legs were not the right length. Lincoln settled the matter, at least to our satisfaction, by saying a man's legs were the right length if they reached the ground. We hold that an article is the right length if it covers, or rather, if it uncovers, its subject, no more, no less. A great subject uncovered as briefly as possible is a great achievement, one for which all people who want to know ought to be grateful. And it is just possible that when Aristotle wrote the first sentence of his *Metaphysics*, "All men by nature desire to know," he was right, and still is right, even though this desire has been so badly abused in our time that it has to a great extent retreated into apparent non-existence.

A great deal has been said in our time about the right of the public to know. It was appreciated by the founders of this republic that the continued existence and health of a society of the type they were founding, one in which the people set up and maintained their own government, depended on the institutions that the people established and maintained for the purpose of serving their desire and their right to know. The major concern of this book is that this service, on which the life of this republic in large measure depends, is not being provided in our time.

Let us return now to Britannica's article "Political Philosophy" for some final remarks on the treatment of this subject in Britannica and in our other encyclopedias. Britannica's article is excellent as far as it goes. It is especially good in its discussion of the ethical justification, the basic why of governments. The lack of understanding of this subject is widespread today and exists in high as well as low quarters, in intellectual circles as well as outside. Britannica's article quotes Lenin on this basic question of the why of the state and of government:

We are not utopians, and do not in the least deny the possibility and inevitability of excesses on the part of *individual persons*, or the need to suppress *such* excesses. But, in the first place, no special machine, no special apparatus of suppression is needed for this; this will be done by the armed people itself, as simply and as readily as any crowd of civilized people, even in modern society, interferes to put a stop to a scuffle or to prevent a woman from being assaulted (V. I. Lenin, *The State and Revolution*, ch. 5, sec. 2, in *Lenin, Selected Works*, vol. ii, pt. i, pp. 293–294, Lawrence and Wishart, London, 1951).

Britannica's article follows this quotation with the comment:

But crowds do not part combatants and men do not violate women when there is a crowd standing by. Lenin's recipe is lynch law, and lynch law is notoriously incapable of dealing with most crimes or of dealing justly with those which it does assail. Here then is a clear case for government action. . . .
    If government were to wither away, the victory in every dispute would go to the stronger or to the possessor.

The truth of this comment—except for the possessor when he is not the stronger—has been illustrated so many times in human history that one wonders how anyone could be widely accepted as having an opinion on this subject worth any attention who betrays in his public utterances or actions total lack of awareness of this truth.

The *why* of governments, including such subordinate subjects as the *why* of jails and such significant facts as that pre-literate peoples generally do not have them and literate peoples do—is not an unimportant subject. One can search long and hard and fail to find, either in encyclopedias or in books, discussion of this subject which is as exactly to the point as that above from Britannica and for this reason is worth reading. The subject lynching can, of course, be dealt with in separate articles under the caption "Lynching."

All three of our encyclopedias have articles under the caption "Lynching," Britannica's by far the best. All three are perfectly clear on the point that under the type of government that exists in the absence of a regularly established police and legal procedures for the trial and punishment of alleged offenses, lynch law is likely to prevail. None discusses the very important question of the feelings, values, and attitudes of the public, of custom and habit in relation to mob violence and its expression in such ways as lynching. And so far as the reader who wants to know whether any qualified authority has held that there is an important relation between the type of government in a society and the problem of lynch law, the passages quoted above from Britannica's article on this subject might as well not exist. He is not likely to be able to find them. There is no index entry "Mob Violence" or "Lynch Law" that refers to these very important passages. And so far as the reader who is familiar with the subject of political philosophy is concerned, he will not expect to see the passage quoted above. Comment of the extraordinarily important kind that the author of the article makes on the exactly pertinent quotation from Lenin that he chose to give is exceedingly rare in our encyclopedias. The best of political philosophers could be helped by contemplating the passages quoted above, but he will be no more likely to find them than the least informed reader, since they are not indexed as they should be. A big book could be written on the failures of Britannica's index. It is by far the worst of the three. Collier's index is the best.

We have already engaged in much discussion of anarchism, and we have done so only because it is impossible seriously to discuss government without discussing anarchism. We now turn to the articles "Anarchism" in our encyclopedias. Britannica's article does not do what an article on anarchism ought to do. It does not even refer to the question whether government of some kind or other is always found wherever there are people. It is only two pages in length. Adequate treatment of such subjects as anarchism in the most highly condensed form that is possible would require at least three or four times the space Britannica devotes to the subject. Britannica devotes over five pages to the mathematical article "Analysis, Complex"—an article typical of many that Britannica has, written by a specialist, for specialists, and readable only by specialists, an article entirely out of place in an encyclopedia designed for the general public. Such articles give an impression of expertness, profundity, and ultimate authority and may be used by highly skilled salesmen to dazzle the prospective purchaser and get him to sign on the dotted line. There are many gimmicks of this kind that salesmen have become accustomed to demanding that editors provide, such as numbers of articles and numbers of index entries, knowing that the American public has been taught to believe that the bigger something is the better it is. The skilled salesman can, however, be convinced that, as the American public learns, and it is learning, it will see through the gimmicks; and that the salesman, if he does not want to bring hard times on himself, had better become seriously interested in the quality of the work he is selling, demand that he be given products of better quality to sell and, and then use his great skill to sell such products.

Britannica wastes much space on subjects of no conceivable interest or importance to the general public—far more than the other two leading encyclopedias, Collier's and Americana. Such space is taken away from space that ought to be devoted to subjects which are of great importance, on which the general public needs and can use help, and on which Britannica, along with Collier's and Americana too, often fails to provide the help that is needed.

Collier's article "Anarchism" occupies about three inches in one column and is worthless except as an effort to state the basic belief of anarchists. The effort could not possibly be successful in more than a superficial and seriously deceptive way in the extremely small space that is allowed. For instance, in the first sentence of the article it is said that anarchism is "primarily a nineteenth-century movement holding the belief that society should be controlled entirely by voluntarily organized groups and not by the political state." This statement is an accurate representation of widely held anarchist belief and it appears to make sense. But if there is any truth in the way American history is usually represented in its most general aspects, it is that the United States of America was first organized in the main "by voluntarily organized groups," though certainly not entirely so; but it is practically certain that nothing involving many people has ever been done that has not involved some coercion. Furthermore, men generally do not join groups unless they have ideal or practical interests that make them feel that they should join. We may question whether such action is "voluntary."

But our answer has to be—because when we understand the question and what it involves, no other answer is possible—that no tyranny, no matter how terrible, could stand unless some men chose voluntarily to support it, and unless others chose, also voluntarily, not to risk their lives by opposing it.

We will not repeat here David Hume's brief, careful, and decisive discussion of this subject in his essay "Of the First Principles of Government." If what Hume says on this subject is true (and if what we have just been saying on it is true), the groups that the anarchist believes should determine human affairs are in their voluntariness indistinguishable from the groups that support governments generally, as well as from the groups that originally formed the United States and that have supported or opposed changes of one kind or another throughout its history. And so far as the "political state" is concerned—a something that as purely political has never existed—if the "voluntarily organized groups" chose to establish the "political state" and were able to do so, anarchist theory is self-contradictory if it says they should not do so, and it says exactly this. Ability to understand this is an elementary test of intelligence. Many of us today who are yowling about government and justice are unable to pass this test, and it is no wonder that we at times make terrible trouble for ourselves as well as others.

It would be a mistake to regard what we have just said as a criticism of the author of Collier's article "Anarchism." Instead of criticizing him, we should commend him for making an accurately descriptive statement, only a part of which we have quoted, of the anarchist's belief. An accurate statement of a self-contradictory belief necessarily contains the contradiction, and this one does. It could reasonably be held that such a statement may be grossly misleading if its author does not point out the contradiction and explain its effect on the doctrine; but to do this would be to assume that the audience to which the encyclopedia is directed and which in the main will use it probably will not recognize the contradiction and understand that it demolishes the doctrine unless this is made clear to them. In the present state of American education and the American intellect, this assumption should be made and is necessary if gross misunderstanding, rather than its opposite, is not to be cultivated.

The really serious problem here is that mere literacy, mere ability to look at a written or printed sequence of words and recognize the words and pronounce them, or possibly to read a paragraph that poses no real problem and restate correctly the idea of the paragraph, is in American education today widely thought to be completely satisfactory evidence of ability to read. It would be worth more than the trouble it costs to put short passages such as the one quoted above before groups of recent college graduates and recent Ph.D.'s to see whether they would recognize the self-contradictions in the passages. It would seem important to know whether the schools, colleges, and universities of the country are helping people to learn really to read, or whether they are, for large numbers, creating a vast and mere semblance of this learning. It should not be necessary to urge the practical importance of this question.

Finally, on this subject we should say that even if the position that we took in our discussion of the articles in our encyclopedias on "Government" that anarchism is a doctrine which in its fully developed form cannot be practiced—a position we are making more specific by seizing this opportunity to show that the basic reason is that it is self-contradictory—even if this argument is valid and granted, it does not follow that widespread belief in anarchism cannot have effects. It certainly can, just as any gross error can. It can tear a country to pieces. As with all error that has to do with matters of widespread practice, it can have terribly destructive effects. At the same time it is clear, even from our brief discussion, that there are elements common to the theories of anarchism and free society, or what has come to be called democracy. One of these elements is belief that individuals and groups should be able to act voluntarily. The anarchist holds or appears to hold that ability to act voluntarily should be unlimited, that freedom can be and should be for individuals unlimited. But then he also denies that certain kinds of voluntary action, such as that of forming a state, should be taken, and he is blissfully unaware that he does this. And worse, he is unaware that whether he acts or not, he lives under conditions that constitute a state and that his real problem is to have a better rather than a worse one, that he does not have the choice of having none at all.

While the anarchist holds that coercion can and should be dispensed with, the believer in free society who understands the more serious problems of freedom and justice and the elementary cooperation that is necessary to any type of decent society will say it would be just fine if we could dispense with coercion, but we still have among us some animals in human form who are not willing either always to be available to help put out the fire that is destroying a neighbor's house or to pay their share of the taxes necessary to make specially qualified persons available to do this job. None of our encyclopedias is clear on this crucial issue.

Collier's article "Anarchism," in accord with the basic plan of the set, does not provide any bibliography with the article. If there is any bibliography for the article "Anarchism," it is in the bibliography in the index volume and can be located by looking under anarchism in the index. There is no reference in the index to a listing of books on anarchism in the bibliography. Both Britannica and Americana provide bibliographies. Britannica's bibliography is more for the specialist than for the general reader. Americana's bibliography is better in this respect.

There is, so far as I have been able to discover, no book in existence mainly devoted to such questions as how far anarchism in its peaceful aspect as a constant quest for a reasonable freedom, equality, and justice is present in the theories of democracy and communism, or whether it has ever had any existence in any society in any way that anywhere nearly approaches its ideal form, or whether it has usually been merely a stage on the way to some other type of society. There are books such as *The Ruling Class* by Gaetano Mosca and *Political Parties* by Robert Michels that are relatively easy to read and understand and that deny the possibility of dispensing with governments, whether formal or informal, with coercive powers over individual and groups. If the principle that a subject is not known as well as possible unless all the arguments in it, both pro and con, are known, then such books as those of Mosca and Michels should be listed in bibliographies on anarchism unless better books, better suited to the general public, can be found. No such books are now listed. And it might be that one of the most helpful uses of the space in encyclopedias would be to use some of it to characterize items listed in bibliographies. Long lists of books, with no characterization of each book, can prove so wasteful of the time of the general reader that he may tend to avoid trying to use them.

A good article on anarchism would include discussion of the strongly individualistic element in anarchistic thought and the presence of this element in the thought of such very influential American authors as Emerson, Thoreau, and Whitman as well as in such doctrines as that of laissez-faire economics. The American businessman is not the only one in American society who often, except when his direct interests have called for it, has not been an enthusiastic supporter of more and more externally imposed controls such as those of governments usually are. Whether consistency on this subject would be a hobgoblin of little minds is a question we need not discuss here. But it would be possible to show in an article on anarchism deep and lasting contradictions in thought and action in the Western world on this rather important subject. It could be helpful for Americans as well as others, for leaders as well as led, to understand that a reasonable integration of the self may be necessary to the reasonable integration of society, and that both require more serious concern than any that the intellectual leadership of the Western world has yet given to the question what is reasonable.

Britannica's article "Anarchism" suggests but does not say explicitly that anarchist doctrine in its full-fledged form is not likely to survive in practice when it tells us: "In revolutions and civil wars, communists and anarchists sometimes started as allies but usually ended as adversaries. The anarchist headquarters in Moscow, for example, were attacked by artillery in April 1918, on Trotski's orders, and all anarchist activity was suppressed."

The Civil War in Spain in the 1930's began with the communists and anarchists in a united front against the uprising led by Francisco Franco against the popularly and legally elected Republican government. In the section on the Civil War in its article "Spain," Britannica tells us: "The Republican cause suffered from internal differences much more fundamental than were to be found on the other side, and serious clashes occurred." Noam Chomsky, professor of linguistics in Massachusetts Institute of Technology, prominent opponent of the participation of the United States in the war in Vietnam, provides much evidence in the first chapter of his book *American Power and the New Mandarins* to support the view that the strife between communists and anarchists, rather than the forces of Generalissimo Franco, brought defeat to the Republican cause. Professor Chomsky says nothing, however, to suggest that anarchist doctrine is self-contradictory and that anarchists of all varieties give no signs in public of awareness of this fact. This is the basic problem in anarchist theory. If anarchists understood this, they would move on to some other theory. It cannot reasonably be expected, however, that the understanding that anarchists have of this problem should be a great deal better than that of the intellectual world generally.

Britannica's article "Anarchism," while it suggests that something basic is wrong with the theory of anarchism and that as long as anarchists try to practice their theory—which of course in honesty they should do—their efforts are bound to be self-defeating, does not even attempt to say precisely what is wrong. Collier's article exhibits the theory in its correct form, but does not examine it to see whether anything self-destructive is in it. Americana's article is even more bland and smooth in its evasion of the real issue in anarchism than Britannica.

Here, for instance, is Americana's statement of anarchist theory with reference to the problem of crime: "The repression of crime, where crime might arise, could safely be left to spontaneously created organizations, such as the vigilance committees in early California, where no state government existed." This is simple, elementary testimony to the fact that wherever there are people, there is some kind of government, and in the absence of better agencies of government, such agencies as vigilance committees will spring up. But as we saw above in our discussion of Britannica's article "Political Philosophy," vigilance committees can be agencies for the administration of lynch law. It is true, of course, that courts operating under the best rules that human beings have yet been able to devise may also at times become agencies for the administration of lynch law; but the existence of courts and of rules that are supposed to be impartially applied is at least testimony to the fact that there is on this point some public understanding of a great problem which can be given better rather than worse handling. In discussing this problem, the avoidance of reference to intense public feeling, of anger that can move groups and break into violence—of feelings of anger that people ought to have against criminal actions, of feelings that are absolutely necessary to the maintenance of a decent society but can be channeled in directions that destroy the decency—is one of the worst forms of evasion in the discussion of human relations. This problem is not peculiar to anarchist theory. It exists in all types of society.

When we hear that a person about to be murdered has cried for help, that dozens of persons could not possibly have failed to hear the cries, that dozens could have called police but none did so, that not one raised a finger to help in any way, we wonder what could have brought about this appalling torpor. Well, here it is in our encyclopedias, in a most respectable and apparently innocent form: an apparently complete lack of the feeling that draws and drives thought to the central issues of a subject, in this case a subject that is brought into existence by feeling and that is falsified if the feeling is excluded with which, in its living form, it is imbued. To fail to recognize that mob violence is always an expression of group feeling, that it is even more horrible for people to be without feelings that move them to good actions than it is for them to have the same feelings but by gross error be driven by them to viciously destructive actions is, in our view, a rather serious failure. For the viciously destructive always appears under the guise of the good. It is only the feelings of people which, directed one way, lead to the prevalence and continuance of lynch law or, in Americana's whitewash term, "vigilance committee" law; and it is only the feelings of people which, directed another way, lead to the effort to get a better and more just type of law. All directing of feelings is done by thinking, and only thinking and feeling together can determine which is the better type of directing. In speaking of Americana's whitewash term "vigilance committee," I have not meant to suggest that this term should not be used. On the contrary, it is highly appropriate that it be used, but it should be used along with the term "lynch law" and the near equivalence of the terms indicated. If this is done the whitewash that probably was not intended but is there nevertheless is removed, and one of the very difficult and obscure problems of law is made somewhat clearer.

When our encyclopedias fail to reflect awareness of the problems we have just been discussing, they merely reflect a condition that is all too common among us. We see in this discussion where this condition is made. It is made by the nature of things, particularly by that part of the nature of things which has to do with what human beings have made of government. This nature in its primal state is unshaped. One of the tasks of men is to shape it and to shape it for better rather than worse. This shaping is mainly the task of the intellectual leadership that a people is able to generate.

We have seen in this discussion some failures to do shaping as well as it might be done. The evasion that characterizes the articles on anarchism in Britannica and Americana is in their failure to show, first, that the basic theory is self-contradictory, and second, that their theory of government, or no government, would lead to the establishment of mob violence and lynch law. These are hard but necessary judgments. If such men as Voltaire and Diderot had been soft in their judgments on the great errors in theory and practice of their time, the wheel and the rack would still be among the approved means for the maintenance of civilized life on earth.

CHAPTER IV

Fragments and Understanding

> I understand nothing. . . . If I try to understand any thing,
> I shall be false to the fact and I have determined to stick
> to the fact.
>
> FYODOR DOSTOYEVSKY

In order to avoid extending the length of this book beyond all reasonable bounds, I shall from now on limit my discussion, with a few exceptions, to Britannica. I take up now Britannica's article "Communism."

The article opens with the statement that the term "communism is used to denote systems of social organization based upon common property, or an equal distribution of income and wealth." If we take this statement strictly, there has never been any actual practice of communism. If the words "in theory" were inserted before the word "based," the statement would be more nearly correct. After this statement, reference is made to the many small communities intended to be of utopian character that have been founded in the United States. One might expect that the chief interest in such communities would be to find out why some failed so quickly and others had relatively long and successful careers. No light is thrown on this question, and there is no reference to any article where any may be found. Britannica has much extremely interesting discussion of many communities, much of it in an article entitled "Utopia," but some of the most illuminating discussion is widely scattered and hard to find. Robert Owen's effort at New Harmony is, for instance, mentioned in the article "Communism." It is discussed in both the biography of Owen and in the article "Utopia." In both, the fact that Owen's effort failed within two years is mentioned and reasons for the failure are discussed. The reasons given are incompatible. This might be taken as a sign of failure in Britannica's editing, but this would be to treat as easy a very difficult matter. People generally accepted as of the highest competence often disagree on questions of this kind. Britannica did right in presenting the disagreements, but it failed badly in not referring the reader from the mention of New Harmony in the article "Communism" to them.

It would seem most highly appropriate in Britannica's opening paragraph on communism to give the reader the opinion of Karl Marx on the subject of utopian communities. This is not done. According to Marx, all such efforts "correspond with the first instinctive yearnings of the proletariat for a general reconstruction of society." The proponents of such action "reject all political, and especially all revolutionary action; they wish to attain their ends by peaceful means, and endeavor, by small experiments, necessarily doomed to failure, and by the force of example to pave the way for the new social Gospel."[1]

Britannica's article is only about four pages long, about a third or fourth the length needed to deal adequately with the subject. There are separate articles "Marxism" and "Dialectical Materialism," the first of about two and a half pages, the second about one page. The three articles are located in their alphabetic positions, and these positions occur in separate volumes of Britannica. If a subject can be understood only when its more closely related parts are seen together, Marxism and Dialectical Materialism should be sections of the article "Communism" and at least sixteen to twenty pages should be allowed for the whole subject. Collier's one article "Communism" covers the more important subjects that are spread out in Britannica's three articles and does in eleven and a quarter pages an incomparably better job. All three encyclopedias, Britannica, Collier's, and Americana, are seriously defective in that none deals anywhere with the horrors of the Civil War in Russia that lasted from about October 1917 until 1921 and the various liquidations and purges through the years thereafter, and the continued use of a rigorous censorship and threat of the extreme use of fear and force to secure compliance with governmental edicts right up to the present.

Britannica's article "Communism" of only about four pages tells us correctly that more than a third of the world's population is now living under communist governments, and that this growth—all in this century and most of it since World War II—has been to a large extent a consequence of the blindness of the democracies: "Against the strict unity and carefully planned strategy of the Communists the democracies

1. Karl Marx and Friedrich Engels, *Manifesto of the Communist Party,* in *Great Books of the Western World* (Chicago: Encyclopaedia Britannica, 1952), L, 433.

showed neither unity nor an understanding of the issues involved."

Britannica adds to the vast amount of evidence of lack of understanding by allowing the author of the article "Communism" only about four pages and by dividing the subject into parts so that only the most determined reader will have a chance—a chance Britannica does not provide—to get a view of the whole subject. The criticisms that we have to express of the article are all on account of the brevity and butchered presentation forced on the author.

The careful and informed reader will see in the article many clear instances of the effects of the strait-jacket put on the author by the inadequate space allowed him. None of the suggestions made above with reference to the first paragraph could have been carried out as well as possible without more space. I will now discuss this problem as it exists in the second paragraph. The author says in the first sentence that "Marx did not find the basis for the communist movement in religious or ethical assumptions but in the new social sciences." One could quarrel with one point in this sentence. The outcome of the historical process that Marx says is inevitable is the establishment of the communist heaven on earth in which "the free development of each is the condition of the free development of all" and the principle "from each according to his powers, to each according to his needs" will be improved on in the communist heaven. Marx did not regard this outcome as an assumption. It was, in his view, and is in the view of his followers, as certain as any predicted outcome could be in physical science. But so far, the chief use has been that of powerful propaganda. The author did not have the space to make these clarifications. The author is certainly right when he says Marx used principles that he found "in the new social sciences" as the basis for his doctrines. But he did not have the space to say what these doctrines were, and that Marx used them only in his own very special way—a way that these doctrines did not make necessary. One of the doctrines of the classical economics that Marx used, that of value, contained ambiguities. The other, that of the so-called iron law of wages, was simply wrong. Marx gave these doctrines his own special interpretations, and it was on such as these that he based his own doctrines. Somewhat the same is true of his relation to Hegel. The author certainly is right when he says Marx "claimed as a disciple of Hegel an infallible certainty for his analysis of the historical forces at work in society," but, again, in the space allowed he could not say in what respects Marx not only did not claim to be a disciple of Hegel, but clearly rejected him. Marx certainly used Hegel's dialectic as a method when it suited his purpose to use it, but he equally certainly rejected Hegel's idealism.

Since the doctrines of Marx, or what have been thought to be his doctrines, have been the inspiration of all the more powerful communist and socialist movements of this century, and since the advocates of these doctrines have been reshaping the world during this century, it is clearly of the greatest importance to understand the doctrines. And the first and by far the most important question to ask is, What is Marxism? Is it a body of doctrines on the basis of which predictions can be made that events verify, as in the physical sciences? Is it one body of doctrine that, except for minor deviations, is the same for Marx and his followers, as, say, Newtonian doctrines were for all physical scientists until the advent of relativity theory?

The writings of Marx are pervaded with the claim that his doctrines constitute a social science with predictive powers comparable to those of the physical sciences. This claim is made explicit by Marx himself in his preface to the first edition of *Capital*. Marx says there "the final purpose of my book is to reveal the economic law of motion of modern society." This claim is also made in the contrasts that he and Engels drew between what they called scientific socialism on the one hand and utopian socialism on the other and in the scorn they expressed for the latter. The followers of Marx have repeated the claims made by Marx and Engels and have, so far as their words go, committed themselves to these claims. But their words are at many points self-contradictory; and their actions belie their words.

It seems clear that the tremendous and continuing growth of communism in this century is attributable in the main to five factors: (i) an almost universal faith in science; (ii) the fact that there is a body of doctrine that has given communism its power and the belief that this body of doctrine constitutes a science; (iii) the development of a missionary spirit that is dedicated to this body of doctrine and to cultivating and spreading it—a spirit that is so well-trained in the essentials of the doctrine and the actions it calls for that continuing directions from any center are not needed; (iv) the use of terror, of fraud and force, whenever and wherever it is thought they can be used effectively; and finally, (v) an extremely widespread lack of understanding in high as well as low quarters in free society of the conditions that are necessary to the health of free society. Of these five factors, the first two, faith in science and the belief that communist doctrine constitutes a science are basic. Without them, the other factors, except the fifth, would not exist. We shall not discuss faith in science here because we regard this faith as justified insofar as it is limited to the sciences that have been shown to have truly predictive powers, and insofar as this faith sharply excludes the belief that these sciences can be relied on to determine the ends they should be made to serve. In the view held here, the interests of better rather than worse life for human beings on earth require that these sciences be made the servant rather than the master of man. We shall not discuss this issue here, but shall limit our discussion to the belief that communism is a body of doctrine that constitutes a science. We shall discuss the problems of free society, and certain problems that are common to all types of society, when we take up Britannica's article "Democracy."

Britannica's article "Communism" does not attempt any strict examination of the claim made by Marx to have developed or laid a basis for a social science. The doctrine called "historical materialism" by Engels, but never so labeled by Marx,[2] is given one of its expressions in the following quotation from Marx:

At a certain stage of their development, the material productive forces of society come in conflict with the existing relations of production, or—what is but a legal expression for the same thing—with the property relations within which they have been at work hitherto. From forms of development of the productive forces these relations turn into their fetters. Then begins an epoch of social revolution. With the change of the economic foundation the entire immense superstructure is more or less rapidly transformed. . . . *No social order ever perishes before all the productive forces for which there is room in it have developed; and new, higher relations of production never appear before the material conditions of their existence have matured in the womb of the old society itself.*[3]

I have italicized the demonstrably false portion of this statement. The communists themselves have given this demonstration, as we shall see in the discussion of their actions that follows. However, the part of this statement that is not italicized certainly points toward problems that leaders and followers in free society have long known to exist and for which they have been trying to find, and to a great extent have succeeded in finding through the years, better rather than worse solutions. The communist solution of a dictatorship would, as the communists would have to say if they used their own logic honestly on this problem,

2. Z. A. Jordan, *The Evolution of Dialectical Materialism* (New York: St. Martin's Press, 1967), p. 404, n. 67.
3. Sidney Hook, *Marx and the Marxists*, Anvil Books (Princeton, N.J.: Van Nostrand, 1955), p. 141.

negate the freedom of a genuinely free society and therefore would not be acceptable to such a society; nor would it be acceptable to communists if their aim was a reasonable freedom.

By far the most fair-minded and the best brief discussion in every way of the italicized portion of the statement from Marx quoted above and other questions in communism is that of Sidney Hook in his excellent little book *Marx and Marxists*. Hook says (p. 38) on the italicized portion of the quotation above: "Historically, there is no evidence whatsoever that in October, 1917, when the communists took power in Russia, capitalism had run its course." Hook could have added here, as he does elsewhere, that communists have never secured power except by the use of fear and fraud and force, and that, after securing power, one of their chief concerns, along with the extermination of possible sources of opposition, has been the development of industry: the industry that necessarily brings with it the division of labor that Marx so vigorously condemns in *Capital*. This kind of action is sufficient to refute the claim that such passages as that italicized in the quotation above describe an inevitable process in the inevitable passage from capitalism to communism. As Hook makes clear in the work of his from which I have just quoted, the process is not inevitable and the passage is not inevitable. On the crucial question of the predictive powers of Marxism in general, Hook remarks (p. 38) that "neither Marx nor Engels nor any leading protagonist of historical materialism predicted the rise of Fascism in any of its varieties."

The reader who already knows that communism as practiced in Russia and China has derived much of its attractive power from the claim that communism is a body of scientific doctrine will see that much that is said in Britannica's all-too-short article is evidence of the falsity of this claim. But if he does not have this knowledge, and Britannica does not provide it as clearly as is possible, he is almost certain not to see the meaning of this evidence. It is a serious mistake to assume that readers generally have this knowledge. And in any case, if they can reasonably be assumed to have this particular and decisive knowledge, it is not clear that this assumption cannot be made with equal safety about every particular portion of knowledge provided by Britannica in other articles as well as this one. The only possible conclusion from any such assumption is that encyclopedias such as Britannica are superfluous—not really needed by anybody.

Next in its importance to the idea that communism is basically a science probably is the idea derived originally from the writings of

Marx that the leaders in the development of communist theory and practice have been men of complete integrity, utterly dedicated to the destruction of all classes in society other than that of the working man, and even of his class, since the existence of any one class in communist theory depends on the existence of more than one. The description which Marx presents in great detail in *Capital* of the conditions under which poor people and their children worked in the period of which Marx writes—children even as young as five—creates a feeling of horror in the reader and a concomitant feeling that Marx was a man of deep and genuine compassion, of profound understanding, and absolutely devoted to the cause to which he had dedicated his life. That Marx was devoted to the communist cause is beyond doubt. That he would have used fraud and force and fear as far as he might think necessary to forward the cause is debatable. There are grounds in his writings for supporting both sides in such a debate.

The reader, deeply and rightly impressed by the utter devotion of Marx to his cause and not worried over the question whether fear and force and fraud as means may defeat the utopian end, is not likely to stop and ask why the poor people that Marx describes crowded into the towns and cities seeking employment in the new industries established in them—and the old such as mining—or perhaps crowded in because they had nowhere else to go, despite the horrors. Can it be that they felt compelled to do so by what seemed to them, and what may really have been, worse horrors? Marx discusses the enclosures that forced people to move in rural areas, but whether the enclosures explain all or most or any substantial part of the moving that led to the conditions he describes, he does not discuss, though he does suggest that they could and did lead to both rural and urban horrors. The reader is not likely to consider the meaning of the fact, on which Marx does not remark, that a large portion of the description of horrors is provided by reports of official investigations of the effects of industrialization authorized and paid for by the British Parliament that was dominated by the aristocrats and bourgeoisie that Marxian theory requires be exterminated. It is true, as has at times been charged, that the landholding aristocrats to some extent supported and used the reports in the effort to discredit the rising class of industrialists, the bourgeoisie. But the bourgeois themselves also to some extent attacked the ways in which industry was conducted. And in some cases they went much further. Robert Owen (1771–1858), a highly successful industrialist, was a most severe critic of what he considered abuses of industrialism and gave impetus to reforms that have had continuing greatly helpful effects. A large part of the money that supported Karl Marx came from his wealthy friend and collaborator Friedrich Engels (1820–95). The wealth of Engels was derived from the new industrialism. Both classes, aristocrats and industrialists, were divided internally on the question what policies should be followed with reference to the so-called "working classes." This mode of speech tended and still tends to hide the fact that the fruitful use of the mind is the most rare, the most difficult, the most wearing and tearing, the most hazardous—if anything greatly worth while is attempted—and, if successful, by far the most productive and satisfying of all kinds of work. It has been this kind of work that has invented and developed sources of physical energy other than the human body, has made it unnecessary for human beings to be beasts of burden, and has invented machines that at a more and more rapid pace are displacing physical labor. It has been only the fruitful use of the mind, along with physical labor, that has opened the way for the potential in some animals to begin becoming human. This kind of labor, or work, has not been the exclusive occupation of persons who have had their origins in any particular class.

One of the great problems of this kind of work is that a class of persons often thought to be its chief beneficiaries tend to live on it only as parasites. Many persons at the top in society make no contribution whatever except in spending and consuming and consequently creating demand for labor and management and production, but providing none themselves. The pattern for and the practice of this particular kind of parasitism were certainly first made and followed in the main in and near the top levels in society. In the lower levels the principle expressed in the folk-saying "root hog or die" was so generally true, and from primordial times, that parasitism of this particular kind, except for the mentally and physically deficient, was rare until physical labor was to a great extent displaced by machines propelled by energy derived from sources other than human beings.

The parasitism at the top levels in society and the surface relations of this parasitism to the production of the economic goods necessary to society had become so obvious by the eighteenth century that it was possible then to make seriously the argument that privates vices are public benefits, since these vices generally consume without producing and thus provide employment. The Dutch physician Bernard Mandeville (1670–1733) made this argument in his poem *The Fable of the Bees* published in 1714 and widely influential at the time.

The parasites on society of whom Mandeville wrote and who certainly existed then and still exist now, often considered privileged, can perhaps even more truly be considered deeply underprivileged if work of a fruitful nature is necessary to the best development of human personality. The question what kind of work needs most to be done in our time and whether the public generally can engage fruitfully in this kind is just another way of stating the subject to which this book is devoted. Before leaving the subject of parasitism, we should say that parasitism is not in itself evil unless man's relation to the world is evil. For man is certainly, contrary to Hegel, a parasite on the world. He did not create it or himself or the potential in him. Even in his most active and fruitful use of his mind he creates nothing in any primary and complete sense. Hegel has him engaging in creation unlimited. Other doctrines of our time do the same. These doctrines are strictly indefensible. Man uses products of the earth, discovers the art and science of cultivating it and the plants and animals that he selects and breeds for his use. He invents new forms and combinations of materials provided by earth, air, and water. He "creates" great works of art and literature, of science and industry and commerce. But he did not create the world and the potentials in it, or himself and the powers and potentials in himself that enable him to "create." All these were somehow from some source given to the animal becoming human, or its predecessors. The human being can use the word "create" without self-deception or the deception of others only if he and they know and remember that there are limits on human powers of creation, limits largely unknown, but still certainly limits. Hegel should have known this, as Plato certainly did, for in his doctrine, as in Plato's, anything or something without limits is nothing. And the human being, while he exists, whatever else he is, is certainly not nothing. Human beings sustain themselves only on that which they find or cultivate on the surface of the earth or extract from under its surface. Human parasitism therefore cannot be condemned without condemning man for existing. The real problem of parasitism is whether there are types that are evil and types that are good, and whether human beings can discover and cultivate the good.

The reader will not know, unless he is told, that there have been incomparably worse horrors under communism than under any phase of industrialism, and that communist policy does not permit the investigation and establishment of facts on subjects of this kind and the making of them known to its own public, and to anybody else anywhere who wants to know about them.

As to whether the new industrialism made the plight of the working man worse, as Marx says, consider the simple elementary problem of the craftsman with his own shop and perhaps one or two apprentices in addition to sons of his own in the time of which Marx was writing. If his sons or his other apprentices on having finished their apprenticeship wished to set up shop for themselves, they might have a serious if not impossible problem getting the tools necessary to do so. And the craftsman-owner and operator of a shop might have more sons than he could train as apprentices and provide with tools.

F. A. Hayek says that

for the greater part of history, for most men the possession of tools for their work was an essential condition for survival or at least for being able to rear a family. The number of those who could maintain themselves by working for others, although they themselves did not possess the necessary equipment, was limited to a small proportion of the population. The amount of arable land and of tools handed down from one generation to the next limited the total number who could survive. To be left without them meant in most instances death by starvation or at least the impossibility of procreation.[4]

Hayek gives many references, but he does not indicate which provide evidence on particular questions he discusses. He does not give any references to more extended discussion of the availability of tools and their relation to survival. He thus makes the assumption often made by scholars and scientists and perfectly illustrated in Britannica and our other encyclopedias that people generally, including scholars and scientists, either are not interested in knowing about subjects outside their specialties or have unlimited time to spend in the quest for knowledge.

Marx discusses in many passages in *Capital* the subject of tools. His discussion in *Capital* and elsewhere often implies that the working man before capitalism had tools of which capitalism deprived him. He presents no real evidence to support this implication. None of his discussion of tools throws any light on the questions raised in the passage quoted above. Marx refers to the discussion of pin making in which Adam Smith engages in the third paragraph of the first chapter of his *Wealth of Nations*—except that Marx speaks of needles whereas Smith's discussion is of pins; and Marx does not discuss the point Smith makes that a person who had never before made a pin, even if he had the necessary tools and materials, could not produce many or "perhaps not one pin in a

---

4. "History and Politics," in *Capitalism and the Historians,* ed. F. A. Hayek (Chicago: Univ. of Chicago Press, [1954] 1960), p. 15.

day." Poor people at the time of which Marx was writing almost certainly would not have the tools or materials necessary to make tools, nor would they normally have the necessary skills.

Britannica gives no attention to this problem and could hardly be expected to do so in the skimpy space allowed to its three articles on aspects of communism. Britannica has an article "Hand Tools" which one may discover by looking in the index under "Tool." There is no discussion of the question whether the person in need of tools before the rapid development of industrialism or at any stages of its development might find it extremely difficult or impossible to get them.

In view of the great emphasis Marx puts on his argument that the industrial system made the plight of the working man and his family worse rather than better, and of the possibility that this is not true, it would seem that someone should have collected the evidence on this question and rendered a verdict that is worth attention. There is plenty of documentation of the horrors of industrialism. But if there has been any documentation of the conditions that preceded industrialism, our encyclopedias ignore it.[5] So far as Britannica is concerned, and on this point Britannica's performance is the same as that of our other encyclopedias, a large part of the verdict of Marx stands—the part that says early capitalism brought horrors to the working man from which he previously had been free. Marx predicted that late capitalism was going to bring the working man even worse horrors. This prediction has so far proved false. There is no discussion of this prediction in any of Britannica's three articles. But Britannica's article "Communism" does make it fairly clear, despite the extremely limited space, that if the predicted communism is to be utopian rather than tyrannical, there will have to be further and miraculous transformations.

The charge of Marx and his followers that there is a class struggle and no genuine class cooperation is patently false. The proof of this is implicit in what leading communists themselves have said. On this question again, the testimony of Sidney Hook merits attention: "The

---

5. L. M. Hacker in his essay "The Anticapitalist Bias of American Historians" in *Capitalism and the Historians* tells us that P. Boissonade's *Life and Work in Medieval Europe* (New York: Knopf, 1927) strips "bare all the pretensions of those who were seeking to pretty up the medieval world." Hacker says, "The common charge of inhumanity against the nineteenth century—for that is the popular reading of laissez-faire, is it not?—would be an idle slander if it were not so gross." Hacker's article is devoted to the effort to show the falsity of the charge. As suggestion the article is helpful. As proof or even weighty evidence, it is wholly inadequate.

frequency and intensity with which Marxists have denounced 'class collaboration' is eloquent testimony of how pervasive such cooperation is even in areas where one might expect open clash of interests. It proves that 'the law of class struggle' is either not a law, since it has so many exceptions, or is of very limited validity." [6]

Britannica's only reference to classes has to do with the Marxian doctrine that the bourgeoisie must be completely eliminated; and Britannica says correctly and much too briefly that the communists have not only preached this doctrine, they have practiced it. There is a problem here, however, to which careful attention is needed. While the communists have certainly eliminated the bourgeoisie as a class devoted to free or relatively free enterprise and competition in the making of profits, they have developed a new and utterly ruthless class devoted to government; and the only means they have so far developed for determining who rises and falls in this class has been the ancient method of secret intrigue and, at times, murder within a relatively small group. The practitioners of this method do not hesitate to extend it to the whole of Soviet society when they deem this necessary in order to stay in power. The horrors of the industrial system that were revealed in investigations authorized by the British Parliament and other writings and that Marx reports in *Capital*, terrible as they undoubtedly were, have been greatly exceeded by the communists in the purges and liquidations that have occurred under their auspices. Sidney Hook suggests the immensity of the communist crime when he says that "the number of individuals destroyed or sentenced to living deaths in the concentration camps of the Communist countries of the world is greater than the whole Negro population of the United States." [7]

The purges and liquidations that have occurred at various times under communist rule in Russia and China and their satellites are among the most significant events that have ever occurred in human history. They are most certainly of sufficient importance to warrant detailed statement for each period of communism since October 1917, either in the article "Communism" or in the article on each country where communism is dominant. And if this highly relevant information is not in the article "Communism," there should be a cross reference saying where it is. This information is not in Britannica's article "Communism"

6. *Marx and the Marxists*, pp. 39 f.
7. Hook, *Political Power and Personal Freedom*, Collier Books (New York: Macmillan, 1962), p. 30.

and there is no cross reference saying where it is. Our other ency-clopedias are no better than Britannica in this respect.

Let us turn now to the promise made by Marx and Engels that the state would wither away when the classless society was established.

Marx held that the state is not natural, that it was a creation of the bourgeoisie, and that it would disappear with the disappearance of the bourgeoisie. It would not be reconstituted by the classless society be-cause the classless society not only has no need for the state, but the state is its greatest enemy. We shall see later how Engels dealt with this problem. The author of Britannica's article could not possibly deal with it in the skimpy space at his disposal without pushing other im-portant subjects out or compressing them to the point of unintelligibil-ity.

Before going further with the question of Marx's doctrine on the withering away of the state, let me say it is not my intention in this discussion to suggest that the problem of power within and among societies arose with communism. It has always been here. But while communism has not created this problem, it was developed to solve it; and it not only has not done so, it has so far made the problem in-comparably worse. The horrors of early industrialism as recounted by Marx, copying reports of official investigations authorized by the classes in society that Marx would exterminate, are as nothing in com-parison with the horrors imposed by the communists on the people of their own countries. At the same time, if we wish to understand, we must remember that communism in its utopian aspect, and this aspect clearly seems to have become to some extent real, is undoubtedly by far the most attractive of all bodies of social doctrine. It is not enough to know that the utopian aspect, whatever the original intention of its makers, is a mask for what has been most of the time up to the 1970's the most dangerous, the most murderous tyranny in human history. We can be sure that not all the leaders in the development of communist power had this intention. We can be sure the intentions of some were as good as the best of those who have led in free society. It is of the ut-most importance that we learn from communist mistakes, and that we think of what the communists have done, as far as we possibly can, as catastrophic mistakes for mankind rather than as cynically intended crimes against mankind; and that we try as hard as we can to establish and maintain the peaceful relations that are necessary to mutual learn-ing.

Marx clearly believed that the social process was bringing a time when men would not struggle for power and would not, as a consequence of this struggle and more or less success in it, create the social pyramid, the hierarchical order of more and less power that has characterized all human societies so far as these are known and that is analogous to the pecking order among chickens. We have no intention when we say this of resorting to the notion that what has been always will be. Our intention is not prophetic. We do not know and cannot know what time will bring. Our intention is not to praise hierarchy. Our intention is simply to say there is a problem here of the greatest importance to every human being on earth, that communism has not solved it but has instead made it far worse, that free society has not solved it but at least has found and tries to use the methods it has found in ways that make hierarchy work more for human good than for human misery. None of our encyclopedias even recognizes the universality of hierarchies in human societies and the great problem of making them serve human welfare, if it is impossible, as it may be, somehow to get rid of them.

In this notion of a classless society, a society that would not be a hierarchical ordering of power, Marx committed himself completely to utopia, despite his utter condemnation of utopianism. In the following passage from *The Communist Manifesto*, though the word "state" is not used, Marx clearly predicts the withering away of the state:

When in the course of development class distinctions have disappeared and all production has been concentrated in the hands of a vast association of the whole nation, the public power will lose its political character. Political power, properly so called, is merely the organized power of one class for oppressing another. If the proletariat during its contest with the bourgeoisie is compelled, by the force of circumstances, to organize itself as a class; if by means of a revolution it makes itself the ruling class, and, as such, sweeps away by force the old conditions of production, then it will, along with these conditions, have swept away the conditions for the existence of class antagonisms and of classes generally, and will thereby have abolished its own supremacy as a class.[8]

Again, when Marx forecasts the elimination of the bourgeoisie and says, in Sidney Hook's translation in Hook's excellent book *From Hegel to Marx*, that "the modern state power is merely a committee which manages the common business of the bourgeoisie," he says implicitly that this power will disappear with the disappearance of the bourgeoisie.

---

8. Marx and Engels, *Manifesto of the Communist Party*, in *Great Books*, L, 429.

Here is what Britannica says, and obviously correctly, on the withering away of the state:

Marxism and Leninism originally expected that with the triumph of the proletariat the state which Marx defined as an organ of class rule would "wither away" because class conflicts would come to an end. Communist rule in Russia, however, resulted in an ever increased power of the state apparatus. The Communist dictatorship created the first and most perfect example of the totalitarian state in which no sphere of individual life was allowed to remain outside its all-inclusive grip.

When the state under communism, during the period of Lenin's rule, did not wither away, critics of communism, anarchists, and others called attention to this fact. Lenin already had his explanation ready in his book *State and Revolution*. Lenin is among the world's great explainers. He has used language more than once that has appeared to be clear and that has aroused hopes that have trapped people in action that served Lenin's ends, Lenin intending all the time later to take action that would betray the hopes. He did not hesitate to use the desire of the vast numbers of poorer peasants of Russia for land to disrupt the state. He encouraged the peasants to kill the owners of small as well as large estates and to seize the land, and to think they would be allowed to keep it—knowing all along that his program required the abolition of all property in land and that to achieve this many peasants would have to be killed. No capitalist in human history has ever practiced fraud and fear and force on so many people, so utterly without scruples and so ruthlessly as Lenin did. He clearly prepared the way for Stalin.

Let us follow as briefly as we can Lenin's tergiversations on the question of the withering away of the state. In his *State and Revolution*, written just before the Revolution of October-November 1917, Lenin says: "According to Engels the bourgeois state does not 'wither away,' but is 'abolished' by the proletariat in the course of the revolution. What withers away after this revolution is the proletarian state or semistate." [9] Lenin quotes a long passage from Engels to show that Engels held the view that after abolishing the bourgeois state, the proletariat would reconstitute a state of their own that would gradually transform the society, and as this occurred, the proletarian state would wither away. The quotation from Engels can be interpreted as saying

9. Arthur P. Mendel, ed., *Essential Works of Marxism*, Bantam Books (New York: Grosset and Dunlap, 1961), p. 148.

what Lenin says it says. And who knows any better? Perhaps some day the proletarian state will really wither away.

However, Lenin also says in *The State and Revolution*, "The proletariat needs the state only temporarily. We do not at all disagree with the anarchists on the question of the abolition of the state as the aim." [10] As is said above, *The State and Revolution* was written just before the Communist Revolution of October-November 1917, that is, more than fifty years ago. How much longer will "temporary" be before the state finally withers away? Lenin says, "Clearly there can be no question of defining the exact moment of the *future* 'withering away'—the more so since it will be a lengthy process." [11] Maybe a thousand years? Maybe ten thousand? One has only to consider the illuminating character of these quotations from one of the classics of communism to see the need for widespread knowledge of them, and therefore the need for much more space than Britannica devotes to its article "Communism."

Let us now examine as briefly as we can Britannica's article "Marxism." First, the question has to be asked, Why a separate article? Are not Marxism and communism identical? If not, and the only reason for a separate article is that they are thought to be not identical, would it not be better to make Marxism a separate division of the article "Communism"? They certainly are identical in some respects, different in others. Some of the differences, however they are regarded by communists, amount to criticism, even rejection, of points in original Marxism. If there are two articles, where should these points be dealt with? If they are only in the article "Communism," the person who reads only the article "Marxism" will not be helped by them; and if they are only in the article "Marxism," the person who reads only the article "Communism" will not be informed of them. Clearly, anyone who wishes to be informed on the subject with which both deal has to read both articles. Why, then, were they not put together?

The article "Marxism" has sections on "Determinism," "Economic Interpretation of History," "Dialectics," "Class Struggle," "Labour Theory of Value," "Theory of Alienation," "Appraisal of Marxism," "Austro-Marxism," "Neo-Marxism." The last two sections, "Austro-Marxism," and "Neo-Marxism," obviously have to do with modifications of Marxism and could more appropriately be in the article "Com-

10. Ibid.
11. Ibid., p. 167.

munism." Not one of the other sections could not just as appropriately be in the article "Communism" as in the article "Marxism."

In the first sentence of the article "Marxism" it is said that "in his analysis of capitalism, Marx had been concerned almost exclusively with a highly competitive kind of capitalist system in which entrepreneurs were in the main opposed to state intervention." I quote this passage to illustrate the difficulty of discussing certain points in Marxism intelligibly. Marx clearly did not regard the state as something separate and distinct from capitalism. On the contrary, he clearly regarded the state as an instrument of the capitalist. Surely, it makes no sense to talk about "intervention," as is done in the quotation above from Britannica, by the bourgeoisie in what Marx has clearly and carefully defined as their own affairs. The fact that there was intervention, and the significance of this fact, is ignored in the section "Appraisal of Marxism."

In the section "Determinism," the author says:

Marxist determinism promises victory to the working class and thus is apt to strengthen the latter's self-confidence in the class struggle, but at the same time the question arises as to why workers should sacrifice in order to bring about developments that are inevitable in any event. . . . For Marxists, this fundamentally insoluble dilemma is particularly important because they regard themselves not only as scholars but also as active promoters of social change.

The answer to the question asked here—why workers should sacrifice in order to bring about developments that are inevitable in any event— was given by Georgi Plekhanov in his essay *The Role of the Intellectual in History*, first published in Russia in 1898. Plekhanov is correctly represented in Britannica's biography of him as "the founder and for many years the leading exponent of Russian Marxism." Here is Plekhanov's answer:

. . . history shows that even fatalism was not always a hindrance to energetic, practical action; on the contrary, in certain epochs it was a *psychologically necessary basis for such action*. In proof of this, we will point to the Puritans, who in energy excelled all the other parties in England in the seventeenth century; and to the followers of Mohammed, who in a short space of time subjugated an enormous part of the globe, stretching from India to Spain. Those who think that as soon as we are convinced of the inevitability of a certain series of events we lose all psychological possibility to help on, or counteract these events, are very much mistaken.

Here, everything depends upon whether my activities constitute an inevitable link in the chain of inevitable events. If they do, then I waver less and the more resolute are my actions. There is nothing surprising in this: when we say that a certain individual regards his activities as an inevitable link in the chain of inevitable events, we mean, among other things, that for this individual, lack of free will is tantamount to *incapability of inaction,* and that this lack of free will is reflected in his mind as the *impossibility of acting differently from the way he is acting.* This is precisely the psychological mood that can be expressed in the celebrated words of Luther: "*Here I stand, I can do no other,*" and thanks to which men display the most indomitable energy, perform the most astonishing feats.[12]

If the "fundamentally insoluble dilemma" of determinism is sufficiently important to be pointed out as the author of Britannica's article "Marxism" points it out, surely its psychological solution is sufficiently important to be reported somewhere. It is not reported in Britannica. Plekhanov's psychological solution does not state all the aspects of the psychological solution. For many persons, the desire to be on the side which they think has the greater power and apparently is going to win is the dominating desire.

The psychological solution of the problem of determinism is not reported in any of the three articles "Communism," "Marxism," or "Dialectical Materialism." It is not reported in the article on Plekhanov. It should be added that true and important as the psychological solution is, the dilemma that determinism posed in Marxist doctrine was a cause of much dissension among the persons who were competing for leadership in the transformation of Russian society in the period before the advent of communist rule. Plekhanov's solution quoted above did not eliminate or, so far as we know, reduce this dissension. The dissension was of tremendous importance, and the problem from which it arose is still a basic contradiction in communist doctrine. The dissension of pre-revolutionary times, but not Plekhanov's solution, is clearly and briefly indicated in the article "Plekhanov," discussed in some detail in the article "Lenin," and in lesser detail in the article "Russian Revolution."

The important point here is, however, lost in the mountain of verbiage. This point is that Marxism as it came from Marx, or from Marx and Engels, was riddled with what we can only call "contradictions," and in the rigorous traditional sense, not in the confused Hegelian sense. And communist doctrine to this day is still in this condition.

Let us turn now to Britannica's article "Dialetical Materalism" and

12. Plekhanov, *The Role of the Intellectual in History* (New York: International Publishers, 1940), pp. 11 f.

discuss it first in connection with Britannica's articles "Communism" and "Marxism." Since dialetical materialism has been held, and is still held by the leading communist theorists since Marx and Engels, to be the basic doctrine of Marxism and communism, it necessarily follows if this is true, and there is no room for doubt that it is, that Marxism and communism cannot be understood without first understanding dialectical materialism.

Britannica's article "Dialectical Materialism" is written by the British communist Maurice Cornforth. It is reasonable to assume that Britannica took care to see that the doctrine in Cornforth's presentation is that officially held. It is essential that this be the case, otherwise examination of the doctrine would be a waste of time or worse—an exercise in self-deception. We need to know as well as is possible what we are dealing with when we deal with communism. I shall assume that Britannica took the necessary care and that Cornforth's representation is authentic.

If it is true that a doctrine is not understood, and cannot be understood, unless everything of any importance that can be said against it as well as for it is understood, then Britannica did well in securing a statement of the official communist doctrine of dialectical materialism; but in presenting Cornforth's article, Britannica did only half of its job. There is nowhere in Britannica careful, concise, and specific criticism of dialectical materialism that appears under this specific name. There is criticism, but it is seriously inadequate, and it does not appear under the heading "dialectical materialism." The uninformed reader will not recognize the criticism as relevant to dialectical materialism. If he were able to do this, he would not need to go to Britannica for information on this subject.

The words "dialectical materialism" are not used in Britannica's article "Communism." There is at the end of the article a reference that says "see also references under 'Communism' in the Index volume." There is no reference to the article "Dialectical Materialism" under the entry "Communism" in the Index volume.

The words "dialectical materialism" are not used in Britannica's article "Marxism." The discussion in the article "Marxism" that relates to dialectical materialism serves only to show serious lapses in the author's treatment of his subject. For instance, the author says:

Marx tended to believe that all historical progress is achieved through an all-out conflict between an old and a new *principle* of *social organization*, and that consequently progress would be impeded if the tension between these two *principles* were "prematurely" reduced by limited reforms of the old system. This belief is based on *dialectic philosophy*, which Marx took over directly from the German philosopher Hegel and indirectly from ancient Greek philosophers [all italics mine].

This quotation is grossly misleading, and much is said in the article that is incompatible with it. I shall not discuss the incompatibilities, most of which point in the right direction, but only the errors in the quotation.

First, Hegel wrote in terms of the conflict of principles. Hegel's philosophy is correctly described as a "dialectic philosophy." But Marx clearly rejected Hegel's dialectic of principles, that is of reason, and the historical process as the realization of reason that of itself has moving power. Marx goes to physical nature for motion, for the power that moves the historical process.

The quotation above from Britannica's article "Marxism" would, as far as it goes, represent dialectical materialism correctly if the word "mode" or "modes" were substituted for "principle" or "principles" and the word "production" for the words "social organization." In Marxian doctrine, social organization is part of the superstructure of a society and is determined by the mode of production. The word "mode" is certainly ambiguous and in Marxian doctrine may be interpreted as economic or technological or characterized by the type of labor used—slave or serf, wage or free. It may be taken as a combination of any two or all of these; but if Marx ever thought just what he meant on this particular point, he never set this thought down clearly in writing. In any case, at this crucial point in Marxian doctrine, Marx certainly rejected Hegel's dialectic philosophy instead of taking it over, and he was perfectly clear about this.

While Marx clearly and explicitly rejects Hegel's idealism, he equally clearly adopts and uses Hegel's dialectic in his exposition of the historical process. Marx never used the expression "dialectical materialism" in any of his so far known writings. Neither did Engels. But this is, of course, no proof that their views, scattered through their writings, cannot be correctly interpreted as supporting what is now the official communist doctrine of dialectical materialism. The argument has recently been made by Z. A. Jordan in his very important book *The Evolution of Dialectical Materialism* that Engels was a metaphysician, that Marx was not a metaphysician but an empiricist, that Marx developed, beyond his youthful period when he identified materialism and naturalism, a world view that repudiated both materialism and the idealistic doctrine that the universe is all mind; that Marx was *not* a dialectical materialist in Engels' sense.

According to Jordan, the currently accepted orthodoxy of dialectical materialism goes far beyond anything for which support can be found in the writings of either Engels or Marx. And while Jordan does not say so, Marx, as an empiricist, would have to condemn the total failure of the heads of communist states to use the method of testing theory by fact and the making of the methods and the results of the tests publicly available. Such testing is not only not done, it is not permitted in the case of facts that might conflict with the theory of dialectical materialism. Communist practice excludes testing that is public and that can be repeated by parties that have no interests vested in the outcome of the tests.

Since Jordan's book was not published until 1968, it would be unreasonable to expect it to be taken into account in the 1967 edition of Britannica, the edition I am using. But it could be taken into account in later editions. Furthermore, Jordan's argument while in detail containing much that is new is, as he himself says, in line with much that has been said previously by Sidney Hook in a series of books.

In Britannica's article "Dialectical Materialism," one reads:

[1] Marx and Engel's conception of dialectics owes much to Hegel. [2] In opposition to the "metaphysical" mode of thought, which viewed things in abstraction, each by itself as though endowed with fixed properties, dialectics considered things in their movements and changes, inter-relations and interactions. [3] Everything is in continual process of becoming and ceasing to be, in which nothing is permanent but everything changes and is eventually superseded.

Statement [1] seems clearly true. But statement [2] is a typical example of the use of language in a way totally different from customary usage. There can be no objection to this if the usage is consistent. In the theory of dialectical materialism it is not consistent. It would be impossible, for instance, to make a statement of a more clearly metaphysical nature than [3]. Since the time of Aristotle, a metaphysical theory is a theory of a speculative nature that cannot, as it stands, be directly tested by fact.

I shall discuss statement [3] of the quotation above further below, but here I should like to dispose of the argument concerning abstraction in statement [2]. Let us assume for the moment that Britannica's article "Dialectical Materialism" is right when it says "all knowledge is derived from the senses." Now let us ask, how do sense impressions come to us? Do they come to us of everything all at once, or of only a part? The answer obviously is of only a part, and there is a statement in the article "Dialectical Materialism" that says so. A part is undeniably an abstraction from a whole. Now no matter how many parts, that is how many sense impressions a person gets, he cannot possibly get, even in a lifetime, sense impressions of everything. The sense impressions that he gets cannot possibly be more than abstractions from the whole. So dialectical materialism while labeling abstraction as metaphysical and rejecting it on this account, engages in abstraction and metaphysics.

Modern physical science would be impossible without abstraction of the kind that dialectical materialism condemns. Dialectical materialism is, I think, right in the notion that if what is abstracted is to be fully understood, it has to be considered in the context of a whole. But to do this is one of the ways of engaging in metaphysics.

Some of the particulars that constitute "everything" can be involved in propositions that can be tested by facts of sense experience; others cannot. No one has ever yet had any sense experience of the particles that in present-day atomic theory constitute the universe. Their existence, if they exist, is wholly an inferred existence. Proposition [3] above about "everything" is certainly beyond any testing by any facts derived from sense experience.

The tendency in most discussion of so-called metaphysical propositions since the great and obvious achievements of modern physical science has been to try to draw a sharp line between metaphysical and empirical propositions and to hold that metaphysical propositions cannot be tested by any factual evidence that is derived from sense experience, whereas empirical propositions can. But that a sharp line can be drawn and that statements on the metaphysical side of the line are nonsense, as is widely held today in the variety of empirical doctrine called logical positivism, is not beyond question. For instance, there has been during the last century, and especially in this century, a tremendous amount of scientific study of the atom. But in all this study only perhaps an infinitesimal fraction of the atoms of the universe have been studied. None have been objects of direct sense perception. The existence of atoms is a logically inferred existence. The physical scientist does not hesitate to assume that some of what he assumes he has discovered about some atoms is true of all the atoms of the universe. But he cannot prove this or disprove it by any of the standard methods of physical science. He is ready to alter this assumption if he discovers evidence that calls for alteration, but meantime he certainly makes this assumption and builds on it. Newton in his *Principia* makes the assumption that time and space are absolute, and Einstein in his relativity theory makes the assumption that time and space are relative. But neither of these assumptions is subject to any testing by sense experience; they are never tested except as parts of a system of testing in which they may not be the decisive factors. This fact would seem to be sufficient to point up the need for more care in the distinguishing of metaphysical from empirical statements, or perhaps for the admission that this cannot by any means whatever be completely done.

Britannica's article "Metaphysics" gives us very little help on this exceedingly difficult problem. There is no bibliography and no reference to E. A. Burtt's *Metaphysical Foundations of Modern Physical Science*, published almost fifty years ago, or to the questions that Burtt discusses, or to Einstein's work and opinions which clearly support Burtt's argument that assumptions that cannot be tested by any empirical procedures are deeply involved in modern physical science. Moreover, the question of the nature of the subject matter that Aristotle discusses in the work on which someone else, after his death, put the label "metaphysics," could have been briefly characterized in Britannica's article in a more illuminating way. This subject matter is clearly of the kind that cannot be directly subjected to empirical testing. This fact and other comparable facts have often been taken to mean that Aristotle discounted, if he did not ignore, the importance of facts established by sense experience. It would have helped to clear away centuries of fog on where Aristotle really stood on this question if this quotation from him had been remembered: "The facts [about the generation of bees] have not yet been sufficiently grasped; if ever they are, then credit must be given rather to observation than to theories, and to theories only if what they affirm agrees with the observed facts." [13]

It is not my purpose here to beat the drums for metaphysics. It is my purpose to suggest, since I cannot take the space to do more, that the case against metaphysics is not as strong as it is in the intellectual world today generally held to be. And, of course, the case for metaphysics is lost if everything that is presented under that name is accepted as metaphysics. To think of metaphysics in this way is exactly on a par with thinking of Lysenkoism as a part of biological science.

It would be a mistake to assume, as is so often done, that the discussion of theory that is not reflected in practice is of no value. No theory

13. W. D. Ross, *Aristotle*, Meridian Books (New York: World, 1959), p. 121.

or orthodoxy that attempts to be comprehensive, that includes human thoughts and feelings and will and actions and ultimate goals as well as natural processes, has ever been completely and correctly reflected in practice. All have been infected with error or failure to take some facts into account. The error, or failure in comprehensiveness of facts, is clearly perceptible to those students who have concerned themselves seriously with the relations of fact and theory. When one finds that no orthodoxy has yet been developed that takes into account and is completely compatible with all the known facts about man and the universe, one may either attempt to develop a new orthodoxy that satisfies the demand for comprehensiveness and compatibility, or one may concern himself with discovering and adopting that orthodoxy which seems to offer man the greatest and best hope. Dialectical materialism abandons the demand for compatibility. It substitutes conflict for compatibility, and apparently on the assumption that conflict will in time eliminate conflict—an assumption which makers of war have often made and which is in practice indistinguishable from the warmakers' assumption. Dialectical materialism claims to offer man the greatest and best hope. It claims further to be a science, but it does not stand any of the ordinary tests of a science and will not allow, insofar as it can prevent them, any of the ordinary tests of a science to be made on its claims.

Dialectical materialism while claiming to get rid of social or economic classes has brought into existence new classes in a hierarchical arrangement, as classes have always been, and in the top class a certain type of person, a type as old as human history, uninhibited by any notions of human rights or by any of the customs and habits that traditionally have tended, even though often imperfectly, to safeguard the human decencies. The type is described by Machiavelli in his account of Cesare Borgia and Remmiro de Orco in Chapter VII of *The Prince*. Cesare Borgia sent Remmiro, "a cruel and able man," with full authority to establish order into a region of "every kind of disorder," knowing that Orco would have to use the most extremely brutal means to succeed in his commission. Orco carried out his commission, but in doing so, naturally incurred the hatred of many of the surviving inhabitants of the region. Then since Orco was no longer useful to him, Cesare Borgia appointed a commission to investigate the means that Orco had used. The commission condemned Orco, and Cesare Borgia had him "cut in half and placed one morning in the public square at Cesena with a piece of wood and a blood-stained knife by his side." Thus Cesare Borgia showed to the satisfaction of the people that he was not responsible for the atrocities which Orco, under his direct orders and with his full understanding, had committed.

The great tragedy of communism today is that the beautiful-sounding theory supports most highly deceptive and most inhuman practices. The practices have been described to some extent, but nowhere nearly as fully as is needed, in numerous well-authenticated books such as *How Russia Is Ruled* by Merle Fainsod, late professor of government and director of the Russian Research Center in Harvard University, and in a very limited sampling way by such as *Progress, Co-existence, and Intellectual Freedom* by Andrei Sakharov, top-ranking Russian nuclear scientist, and in a Nobel-Prize-winning novel, *The First Circle*, by the Russian Aleksandr Solzhenitsyn. The theory of dialectical materialism has been competently discussed in a number of books such as *The Illusion of the Epoch* by H. B. Acton, professor of philosophy in the University of London, and *The Theory and Practice of Communism* by R. N. Carew Hunt, late fellow of St. Antony's College in Oxford University. Unfortunately, the title of Carew Hunt's book is seriously misleading, since he deals very little, except in generalities, with communist practices. The only exposition of dialectical materialism that is accompanied by tests of the doctrine in practice of which I am aware is in *Reason, Social Myths and Democracy* by Sidney Hook, the philosopher that New York University has been fortunate enough to have in its faculty for many years. Hook's treatment of testing by practice is, however, entirely too brief and amounts to little more than a sampling. Space in the book that could have been used on this subject is devoted to other topics remote from it.

Another quotation will illustrate again the confusion and misunderstanding in Britannica's article "Marxism": "Apparently Marx was not prepared to rule out peaceful progress unconditionally, and he may also have found it difficult to reconcile philosophy with the economic interpretation of history, since technological progress is the very model of 'straight-line' gradual evolution." It is true that Marx "was not prepared to rule out peaceful progress unconditionally"; but the evidence for this is derived only from patches that he made on what he and others seem clearly to consider his basic doctrine. Lenin paid no attention to these patches. Neither did Stalin or Khrushchev. The question naturally arises whether the patches Marx made are all the patches needed, and if all needed were made, whether anything would remain, and if anything, how much of the original doctrine. I do not mean by the word "patch" nothing but disparagement of Marxian doctrine. No theory of man and the universe, I repeat, has ever yet been stated that has not needed patches; and most have not stood up even when they have been freely patched. Marxian doctrine, whether largely a collection of patches or not, has demonstrated far more power than any other social doctrine in many centuries, probably more than any other since Christianity. It has been taken seriously and excellent studies of it have been made; but so far as the general public is concerned, and especially so far as the young people of the United States are concerned, these studies might almost as well be non-existent.

Let us return to the quotation on pp. 107–8 above, from Britannica's article "Marxism." The words "dialectic philosophy" are used in this quotation without distinguishing between the dialectic philosophy of Hegel and that of Marx, or even suggesting the existence of a crucially important distinction.

Finally, the quotation seems to equate the economic interpretation of history with the technological interpretation. This is again grossly to misunderstand and misrepresent Marxian doctrine. In Marxian doctrine, economic and technological forces are clearly different forces and at times are in harmony, at other times in conflict with each other. This conflict Marx, following Hegel, miscalls "contradiction" and thus continues the confusion that Hegel introduced by this practice; and it is by Marx, again following Hegel but on a basis certainly opposed to that of Hegel, perhaps empiricist (but this is not entirely clear), considered the moving force of history. It should be added here that if we correct Marx's language as we have just suggested, this is one of the many points at which there seems to be crucially important truth in Marxian doctrine, truth that poses a problem that so far has defied solution, either by communists or others, except by the sacrifice of freedom, and that can be justified only on the grounds that some freedoms have to be sacrificed in order to save others. A free society, as we shall see when we discuss Britannica's article "Democracy," is one that makes an empirical approach to this problem, one that constantly compares the various possible freedoms, one that concerns itself to discover and choose always the basic freedoms on which all others depend.

Let us now take sample statements from Britannica's article "Dialectical Materialism" alone, without reference to the article "Marxism," and examine them. The first paragraph of the article contains the statement, "The essential feature of dialectical materialism is the combination of philosophical materialism with dialectics." If metaphysics is defined as speculative reasoning of the type which proceeds on the basis of pure reasoning, that is, reasoning that cannot be checked by facts derived from sense perception, this statement is an example of metaphysics. The habit of proceeding without concern for checking by such facts is what I would call the metaphysical habit. Now philosophical materialism has never been validated by any facts derived from sense experience. And neither has any variety of dialectics, either that which may occur in an argument or that which the theory of dialectical materialism says occurs in natural and historical processes. The dialectical process that occurs in an argument can be seen only by the mind. It is not and cannot be in any way an object of sense experience. If there is a dialectical process in nature or history or both, it too can be seen only with the mind. To speak of, say, the growth of an oak from an acorn as a dialectical process is an analogical mode of speaking, and analogies are modes of mental seeing and cannot be tested by any facts derived from sense experience.

Let us take another example: "For Marx and Engels, materialism meant that the material world, perceptible to the senses, had objective reality independent of mind or spirit." Nobody denies the existence of particulars such as dogs, chairs, other persons, stars, etc., that can be objects of sense experience. "The material world" is, however, in materialistic doctrine, only a logical implicate of the particulars of which it consists. It is, in Hegelian terms, a universal that expresses or unfolds itself only in particulars. In the jargon of the Hegelian philosophers, it is a concrete rather than an abstract universal; and there is much that can reasonably be said for its reality. But it, in contrast with the particulars in which it expresses itself, is an object only of mental experience. No one has ever had any sense experience of "the material world." It is possible to have only mental experience with it, and the mental experience may be rational or irrational. As to independence of mind or spirit, if "the material world" exists only as a logical implicate of mind, it, as distinguished from the particulars from which it is logically derived, can exist only in minds, and is therefore *not* independent of mind. Furthermore, if sense experience is the only source of knowledge, and knowledge is something that can be realized only in a mind, it cannot be known even that the particulars exist when they are not perceived by a mind.

Dialectical materialism simply ignores large considerations of the greatest importance in human thought. I quote again from Britannica's article:

[1] The theory of knowledge of Marx and Engels started from the materialist premise that all knowledge is derived from the senses [2] But against the mechanist view which derives knowledge exclusively from given sense impressions, they stressed the dialectical development of human knowledge, socially acquired in the course of practical activity.

Sentence [1] says *all* knowledge is derived from sense experience; sentence [2] says that some knowledge is derived from "the dialectical development of human knowledge." So *not all* knowledge is derived from sense experience; some is derived from dialectics. Thus [1] contradicts [2]. Furthermore, it should be clear, without reading the vast amount of discussion that there has been of this question—and I repeat—that if all knowledge depends on sense perception, there can be no knowledge of objects that are not being perceived. On this point, again we have to say as we have above, dialectical materialism is self-contradictory. And there is no dialectic process by which this contradiction can be removed unless the dialecticians involved want to remove it and are willing and able to use the perfectly clear and many times illustrated rules of logic by which only it can be removed. One of the steps in removing it is to drop the metaphysical assumption that all knowledge is derived from sense experience.

Second, the doctrine that "all knowledge is derived exclusively from given sense impressions," is no more exclusively mechanist than it is materialist or idealist. And it is contradicted by the notion that there is a "dialectical development" in which some knowledge that is not in sense experience can arise in thinking about sense experience and thus float into existence from nothing. It should be noted here that the thinking that is now assumed—which has not previously been mentioned and is here merely assumed and perhaps very carefully not mentioned, or perhaps merely overlooked—is necessary if sense impressions are to be more than merely separate impressions, that is, if they are to become really worthy of the name "knowledge." To proceed: by "nothing" I mean what I find when I imagine I have $100 in my pocket and reach for it and find no $100 and no part of $100 but only emptiness where I imagined there was $100. Or when I think of my existence as an object of the sense experience of other people prior to the year 1900— more than a year before I was born. The idea is important and needs to be familiar, and, unfortunately, in some crucial respects it is.

Dialectical materialism is not the only doctrine that is infected with the notion that something can float into existence from nothing. All doctrines that do not assume a basic reality that contains all possibilities and that itself is never an object of ordinary sense experience but is the source of all such objects assume that something can float into existence from nothing. Aristotle's potentiality, which plays a large and apparently indispensable part in modern science, is merely another name for this source. The notion of such a source may be either metaphysical or religious, depending on how it is treated. But however it is treated, there is no alternative: either one subscribes to the doctrine that something can and does come from nothing, or one assumes a source and, in general, there are only two other possible sources. We shall discuss these below. There are no other possibilities.

The argument just made concerning the infection of dialectical materialism with the notion that something can come from nothing is a metaphysical argument. It is like the argument that ghosts do or do not exist. It cannot be tested by fact derived from sense experience.

Let us proceed with the examination of sample statements in Britannica's article "Dialectical Materialism":

[1] Motion, Marx and Engels insisted, was the mode of existence of matter. [2] Within the material world there was continual change and development, one form of motion arising from another. [3] For example, chemical processes gave rise to living processes and living organisms developed consciousness—life and consciousness being higher forms of the motion of matter, arising from and based on lower forms but having their own qualities and laws of development. [4] Materialism, therefore, must cease to be "mechanistic" and become "dialectical."

Statement [1] cannot be subjected to comprehensive and finally decisive empirical tests for the simple reason that one cannot test matter. One can test only samples of matter and then assume that all the infinitely numerous particulars that constitute what is called matter are like, or somewhat like, those tested. In saying this, I intend no denial that "motion is the mode of existence of matter." A denial as well as an assertion would be strictly metaphysical. I intend to deny that it makes any sense whatever to say that "motion is the mode of existence of matter," and then deny the assumption necessary to the truth of this proposition.

It happens that the weight of modern physical and biological science is overwhelmingly on the side that says every particular in the universe is in the process of change. I see no good reasons for doubting that this is true. But this is a metaphysical proposition, whether it is asserted by dialectical materialists or others. And some change, as we shall see, may be of a merely repetitive nature.

Statement [2] in the quotation above is of the same character as [1] with the addition of the notions of development and new forms. The notions of development and of new forms were "explained" before the time of Darwin by the doctrine of potentiality and afterward, by the doctrine of evolution—with potentiality still in the background because the word "potentiality" is a more general term. It merely names, as does the word evolution, and in no sense explains a basic problem. Its workings can be described and to some extent the descriptions can be tested in scientific work. But when we try to explain "potentiality" we are deep in the realm of metaphysics. The history of the discussion of this subject is sufficient proof that the human mind in its quest for knowledge and reasonable belief is unwilling to refrain from entering and trying to explore the metaphysical realm. It is as easy to get lost there as it is to get lost in the exploration of the unconscious mind of man. But both explorations are necessary to the proper cultivation of human knowledge.

We shall now indulge in what seem to us inescapable metaphysical propositions on the subject of potentiality. Potentiality has to have been always either in the particulars of the universe, or to exist in the form of motion in the particulars, or to have come into the particulars from some source beyond the universe; or it floats into existence from nothing. Let us assume for the moment, in consonance with most of modern thought and dialectical materialism, that there is no source beyond the universe. We have thus in this theory the alternatives (i) either the particulars invested with potentiality have existed always and in their transformations produce whatever exists; or (ii) the particulars or potentiality or both come from nothing. Alternative (i) has led to cyclic doctrines that assume the universe to be somewhat like a perpetual motion machine, or at least perpetual in existence and in motion, if not like a machine. Many problems arise in connection with this notion. None of them can be explained or even discussed intelligibly in terms of any knowledge that human beings have derived from sense experience. So this alternative is ruled out and, since we have no other alternative, we have to accept (ii). But we no sooner say this than we know that dialectical materialism with its doctrine that all knowledge is derived from sense experience also rejects (ii)—unless we assume that nothing doing something can be an object of sense experience.

The problem touched on here is so important that we go further with it. Even David Hume, with his denial of causation as necessary connection asserted conjunction or association in the sense of one thing preceding or following another. Now if we take the word "universe" as meaning what it says, and what dialectical materialism says it is—that is, one and only one system of things—and if we assume, as dialectical materialism requires that we assume, that there is nothing beyond the universe, then if we use ordinary language in the ordinary way, we have to say that the universe exists in conjunction with nothing. Furthermore, the universe, in this theory, in addition to having nothing as the cause of its existence, is conceived as self-existent, self-caused. And so it is that the metaphysician who denies metaphysics takes, without knowing what he is doing, a position that if followed up, leads directly to a conclusion that is identical with a conclusion reached by the great theologians: that the notion of something that is a cause of itself, in a strictly necessary sense of cause, is an intelligible notion. Next, we have to ask, what is the meaning of the word "nothing" in this context? Can it be the absence of a particular something, such as the $100, or of the person living at one time but not at another, and that we find nothing when we look for something and do not find it? Ordinary usage says this is one meaning of the word. But can we look for the universe and find it? And if not, and if therefore we cannot have sense experience of it, shall we conclude that it does not exist, that in our looking we have found nothing?

Words are helpless things, and we can easily use them in ways that befuddle ourselves as well as others. We, of course, cannot conclude that since the universe is not and cannot be an object of any human sense experience, therefore it does not exist, therefore it is nothing. If we did this, we would be using the word "nothing" as the great theologians have used the word "God." We would be, without knowing it, beyond metaphysics and deep in the realm of theology.

I return now to propositions in the last quotation above.

Statement [3] is simply an elaboration of [2].

Statement [4] is an assertion that ignores the possibility that if the dialectical process is a process that occurs in nature, as is asserted in [3], and if this process is inevitable, as is apparently assumed and certainly basic in Marxian doctrine, it cannot be distinguished from a mechanistic process. An inevitable process is a wholly deterministic process, and a process that is wholly determined is mechanistic even if it is called dialectical. This condition would not be affected in the slightest even if consciousness and will were attributed to nature. A deterministic idealistic process is in its mechanistic character indistinguishable from a deterministic materialistic process except in the language used to describe the process. The language does not have magical powers and does not change the process from a rigorously determined one merely because different words are used to describe it.

It is reasonable to expect a theory that claims to be comprehensive to be really so and to deal with all the major problems involved in it. When we consider closely what is said in the quotation above and in Britannica's article, the question arises, How can it be known that real rather than merely apparent change is occurring? Now in raising this question I am not denying change. If I were expressing my own opinion I would assert that change does occur, and I would hope to be able to give a satisfactory basis for believing that it occurs. I am simply asking whether it can be known to occur on the basis of anything said in Britannica's article. I find nothing in the article on this question that goes beyond naive assertion, nothing that even suggests there is a real problem here.

In Einstein's relativity theory the assumption is made that everything is in motion but that some things are at rest with reference to others, and in order to know what is in motion or even to talk intelligibly about motion, a point of rest has to be assumed and the motion of other points observed with reference to it. All motions within, say, the solar system, except those of things that enter and leave, are, with reference to other systems, only local motions. They are not motions of the solar system with reference to other systems. The local motions are totally deceptive if taken as evidence of changes in the position of the solar system in its relation to other systems.

Even if everything is changing, the change may be analogous to the motion that occurs only within the solar system, that is, the change may be only of a kind such that the object that is changing, or something that takes its place, returns to its former state, as in birth, growing up, becoming old, dying, and then again birth, and the cycle over and over again. This is, of course, not necessarily the only kind of change that occurs. It is highly probable that all things that are changing in ways that may be compared with the local motion in the solar system are also changing in other ways and in one or more directions. This is where, in the present epoch of human history, the real problems of change arise. Dialectical materialism, as presented in Britannica's article, makes no contribution whatever to the understanding of these problems, and not only this. It does not even suggest that they exist. It makes the assumption that all change is in one direction and is inevitable. Such a notion of change can be held as a faith, but it cannot possibly be known.

At the same time, dialectical materialism claims to be both a philosophy and a science.

In all of this discussion, I assume the reader will understand that it is very difficult, if it is at all possible, to make any statement to which apparently legitimate objections cannot be raised. This is the occasion for the beginning of the dialectical process; and if properly conducted, it is one of the most genuinely educational of all processes in which human minds can engage. I will illustrate with a statement of my own in a preceding chapter that could give occasion to the process. I deliberately made the statement in Chapter I that it is no longer possible to believe that God is up there above the clouds. I made this statement in the hope that the reader would recognize it as the mixture of sense and nonsense that it is and be stimulated by it into the use of his mind to distinguish the sense from the nonsense. To make such use of his mind would be to engage in the dialectical process. I would like to do this here for my own benefit, if not for that of others. But if I tried to do this on every subject of great importance, I would be trying to write an encyclopedia rather than a book that tries to show how at least one encyclopedia should be written, and the dire need for it. Our encyclopedias, if they are not to be a disgrace to the term, should contain a doctrine of God that makes as much sense as possible. None even attempts this. Far better sense can be made of a doctrine of God than has yet been made of dialectical materialism. And this is far from all that needs to be done in our encyclopedias.

It would take far more space than we have available here thoroughly to examine the theory of dialectical materialism merely as theory. A competent summary examination of the main points, intelligible to the non-specialist, would require at least a half-dozen pages of the size of Britannica's pages; and this brevity would be possible only in case such articles as "Empiricism," "Naturalism," "Realism," "Idealism," "Materialism," "Metaphysics," "Locke," "Berkeley," "Hume," "Kant," "Hegel," "Marx," "Engels," "Lenin," "Stalin," "Government," "State," "Anarchy," "Communism," "Democracy," "Ethics," "Political Philosophy," "Power, Political and Social," "Logic" dealt adequately with all the more important problems involved in them. None of our encyclopedias has an article on Power, Political and Social. Such an article would show that power is a perennial problem within nations as well as among nations. It is necessary to know this and much else about political and social power, if one is to understand any basic theory of society.

We have seen in this chapter some of the lapses in the articles "Communism," "Marxism," and "Dialectical Materialism." We shall conclude now our discussion of dialectical materialism by pointing out what we consider by far the most important failure by those who subscribe to the doctrine. This is the failure to test it by practice. To apply this test in a comprehensive way would require a large book. Free society, as well as communist society, has failed to produce a careful, reliable comprehensive book that applies the test that is most needed.

The kind of specific evidence on the quality of the social and political life in the Soviet Union that is most needed is, I believe, best illustrated by such first-hand testimony as the following from the top-ranking Soviet nuclear scientist Andrei Sakharov:

Fascism lasted twelve years in Germany. Stalinism lasted twice as long in the Soviet Union. There are many common features but also certain differences. Stalinism exhibited a much more subtle kind of hypocrisy and demagogy, with reliance not on an openly cannibalistic program like Hitler's but on a progressive, scientific, and popular socialist ideology. . . . At least 10 to 15 million people perished in the torture chambers of the N.K.V.D. [secret police] from torture and execution, in camps for exiled kulaks [rich peasants] and so-called semi-kulaks and members of their families and in camps "without the right of correspondence" (which were in fact the prototypes of the Fascist death camps where, for example, thousands of prisoners were machine-gunned because of "over-crowding" or as a result of "special orders").

Sakharov's testimony was first published in 1968 in the *New York Times*—a service for which every civilized person should be grateful. His testimony was shortly thereafter published as a book under the title *Progress, Coexistence, and Intellectual Freedom* [14] by W. W. Norton, with Introduction, Afterword, and Notes by Harrison E. Salisbury of the *Times*. While one has to be deeply grateful to the *Times* for publishing Sakharov's testimony, one cannot be grateful to it for supporting the policy that not only led to making World War II by far the bloodiest in human history, but also to the tremendous expansion and increase of communist power in the world. The policy the United States should have followed was a balance-of-power policy. Such a policy can be conducted cynically and be as viciously and appallingly destructive as any; but it and, in the present state of human affairs, only it can keep the war god from raging freely. No other policy can be made to work so effectively for a genuine peace and justice both within

14. The quotation is from p. 52.

and among nations. The United States has during most of its history tended toward a policy of treating all individuals as equal before the law, and the practice of equality is the practice of balancing, of allowing no power in one to operate that is not allowed in another, of allowing individuals wide freedom to organize voluntarily in groups for the pursuit of legitimate purposes; and the effort was made and is made to prevent any one group from dominating any other—that is, the effort was made and is made to maintain a balance of power among groups. If this effort has not been entirely successful, if it has posed many problems for which adequate solutions have not been found, if it has threatened by balancing at times to create situations in which nothing could be done to correct sore evils, still freedom of speech and press and assemblage guaranteed that proposals for correction that had any appeal to the public could be heard; and in free societies, such proposals could be acted upon. And herein lies the greatest danger and the greatest hope of free societies. For freedom of speech and press and assemblage can be used to destroy a reasonable freedom just as they can be used to cultivate it. In this respect they pose exactly the same problems that are posed by the use of power. Majorities can be wrong—but they can also be right. But they cannot be right, except by accident, if they are not informed. The American public is not informed on the basic meaning of a balance-of-power policy either in domestic or foreign affairs. Hans Morgenthau's superb book, *Politics Among Nations*, published in 1949, much too late to be taken into account in the shaping of World War II policies, is known to only a relatively very small portion of the American public and cannot be made and kept more widely known except by encyclopedias. The problem of political and social power within and among nations is not the only subject on which the American public is not informed and currently has no opportunity, no means of being informed.

Let us turn now to Britannica's treatment of the subject "Democracy." The article is a careful, straightforward exposition of the different types of society to which the term "democracy" is customarily applied. It is, with two exceptions, probably as good an article as can be written on the subject within the eight and one-quarter pages allotted.

One of the exceptions is a paragraph in the section Origins of Modern Democracy that begins with the sentence, "[1] According to Rousseau's Social Contract, no law is legitimate unless it is an expression of the general will, a consensus of the whole community." But

Rousseau says in *The Social Contract*, "[2] There is often a great deal of difference between the will of all and the general will; the latter considers only the common interest, while the former takes private into account, and is no more than a sum of particular wills: [3] but take away from these same wills the pluses and minuses that cancel one another, and the general will remains as the sum of the differences" (p. 25).[15] Since a consensus is merely the will of all or of a majority at a particular time, it may not be the general will. Thus statement [2] may in some cases contradict [1]. As to statement [3], apparently intended to tell when there is a contradiction, let us consider such practices as that of the Aztecs in making war to secure captives to sacrifice to their god Huitzilopochtli; or that of peoples who have engaged in headhunting in the belief that in removing a head the soul within is captured and added to the general stock of soul matter belonging to the community, contributing to the fertility of the human population, the cattle and the crops; or that of the white southerners whose will in the middle of the last century was to maintain slavery even though doing so meant war. When we consider such wills as these, we realize not only the absurdity of the quotation from Britannica above but also the absurdity of the method Rousseau proposes in [3] of discovery of the general will.

Rousseau clearly meant by the general will a will that would serve a genuine and not a spurious common good or general welfare. But he involves himself in a mass of contradictions on this subject. "The general will," he tells us (p. 94) "is found by counting votes." But nothing is clearer in the history of vote counting than that what is voted for one day is not voted for another. So Rousseau also tells us (p. 93) "the constant will of all the members of the State is the general will." But when we look for this constancy, we do not find it; and neither does Rousseau. He tells us "the people is never corrupted" (p. 25). But he also speaks of "the simple morals, the disinterestedness, the liking for agriculture and the scorn for commerce and for love of gain which characterized the early Romans," and then asks, "Where is the modern people among whom consuming greed, unrest, intrigue, continual removals, and perpetual changes of fortune, could let such a system as that [of the early Romans] last for twenty years without turning the State upside down?"—(p. 101). And he says that "when

15. References are to Jean Jacques Rousseau, *The Social Contract and Discourses*, Everyman's Library (New York: Dutton [1913] 1937), p. 25.

the social bond begins to be relaxed and the State to grow weak, when particular interests begin to make themselves felt and the smaller societies to exercise an influence over the larger"—which is to say that the people certainly can be corrupted—"the common interest changes and finds opponents: opinion is no longer unanimous; the general will ceases to be the will of all" (p. 91).

But, Rousseau goes on (p. 91), "Does it follow from this that the general will is exterminated or corrupted? Not at all: it is always constant, unalterable and pure."

Now, as we have said above, we obviously have a mass of contradictions here. But is this all that is important that can be said on these passages? Consider the discussion of this same subject in which St. Paul engages in Chapter 7 of the book of Romans in the Bible. "Wherefore the law is holy," says St. Paul, "and the commandment holy, and just, and good." But, St. Paul goes on, that which I know I ought to do, I do not do. And that which I know I ought not to do, that I do. The whole text of St. Paul's discussion is better than my paraphrase; and if the reader wishes to understand Rousseau and get a taste of the wisdom that is in the Bible, of discussion that goes to the point without any wasting of words, he cannot do better than study St. Paul.

I do not intend to suggest by reference to St. Paul that there is knowledge of good and of what would be the common good, if human beings could be persuaded to serve it, and of a general will that would serve the common good that would necessarily be in accord with the ultimate good. Even if some human beings have known this good, nothing could be clearer than that others have not or, if they have known it, have not had the will to serve it. I do intend not merely to suggest but definitely to say that there are problems of extreme difficulty and of extreme importance in Rousseau's notion of the general will for the common good, and that Britannica's article "Democracy" fails completely even to suggest this in its treatment of this subject that Rousseau correctly saw as basic to democracy.

The other exception to Britannica's article that I have to discuss is the statement: "Down to the time of the American and French revolutions, there was only one major theorist who maintained a strictly democratic position, Jean Jacques Rousseau." Now my exception is not to the accuracy of this statement. I think it is true. My exception is to the use of it or rather, the failure to make illuminating use of it, in Britannica's article. The ordinary notion of democracy is that of people making their own constitution and their own laws and obeying them because they are their own. Rousseau clearly expresses this notion. But he also clearly goes beyond it. His constitution maker, his lawgiver, is not a mere human being or mere collection of human beings. The only way we can avoid seeing in Rousseau at this point an utterly barren contradiction is by seeing human beings in their constitution- and law-making capacities as illuminated by truths they themselves did not make.

I repeat, Rousseau clearly meant by the general will a will that would serve a genuine and not a spurious common good or general welfare. "All that destroys social unity," he tells us (p. 117), "is worthless; all institutions that set man in contradiction to himself are worthless." "The opinions of a people," he tells us (p. 111) "are derived from its constitution," but the constitution is not made by the people. "In order to discover the rules of society best suited to nations, a superior intelligence beholding all the passions of men without experiencing any of them would be needed. . . . It would take gods to give men laws" (p. 35). And while Rousseau does not say so, it would take beings better than any ordinary gods human beings have imagined, and only one god has been imagined by human beings who, without experiencing any of the passions as human beings experience them, is passionately concerned for human good. The constitution is something "graven . . . on the hearts of the citizens" in the course of obeying the constitution prescribed by their god. "This forms the real constitution," this "keeps a people in the ways in which it was meant to go, and insensibly replaces authority by the force of habit. I am speaking," says Rousseau, "of morality, of custom, above all of public opinion; a power unknown to political thinkers, on which none the less success in everything else depends. With this the great legislator concerns himself in secret" (p. 48).

We must not allow ourselves to be distracted by flaws in Rousseau such as the statement just quoted that political thinkers have not concerned themselves with public opinion. The really important consideration is that in these passages Rousseau is deep in metaphysics and theology, and that if we think in these terms, profoundly good sense can be made of his doctrine of democracy. Britannica's article "Democracy" could in its treatment of Rousseau's contribution at least suggest this possibility. It does not do so.

Let us now look at the problem of omissions from Britannica's article. The different types of democracy—direct, representative, and totalitarian—are first briefly characterized; then follow sections on Ancient Greece, Origins of Modern Democracy, The United States, The

French Revolution, Great Britain, Other European Countries, Totalitarian Democracy, and finally The Twentieth Century. There are no sections devoted to Equality, Freedom or Liberty, Justice, and Order. There is no discussion of freedom of speech, press, and assemblage, none of the fact that all societies from the most primitive tend to be hierarchical in shape—which could be taken as suggesting that, insofar as they are ordered, they are ordered by something in and beyond them—none of the basic importance in all societies of custom and habit, none of the fact, and especially of the significance of the fact, that all societies, even the Aztec with their blood-drinking god Huitzilopochtli and many other societies with equally horrible gods, have had their objects of worship. It is just possible that the quality of a society depends on the quality of its object of worship. This possibility would seem worth some attention.

Britannica does not provide in other articles adequate discussion of these topics. They are basic to the understanding of democracy. There is no article in Britannica on Equality. There is a short and wholly inadequate article on Liberty. There is no article on Justice. There are none on the other topics of basic importance that I have mentioned above. There are at the end of the article "Democracy" two cross references: "See Natural Rights; see also references under 'Democracy' in the Index volume." The article "Natural Rights" is about three-quarters of a page in length. The briefest possible anywhere nearly adequate discussion of the problems in the subject would require at least a half-dozen pages. There are no cross references. The bibliography lists *Natural Right and History* by Leo Strauss. In this volume Strauss shows that historicism and positivism, a form of empiricism, and particularly the form of positivism known as logical positivism, are wholly incompatible with natural right. Historicism and logical positivism are the dominant doctrines among intellectuals in the United States, and not a few give strong evidences from time to time of what it is that is dominating them. The case of Ruth Benedict with which we dealt in Chapter II tends to be typical.

There is nothing about either historicism or logical positivism in Britannica's article "Natural Rights." The word Historicism is not entered in Britannica's index. There is an article "Positivism" and an article "Logical Positivism," but neither has under its index entry a reference to the other, and their relations are nowhere discussed in the detail that is necessary to understand them. There is a reference under the index entry Positivism to Auguste Comte, as there should be, but none

under either Positivism or Logical Positivism to David Hume—by far
the most important source of positivism, and particularly of the variety
of positivistic influence, that of logical positivism, that is dominant
today.

Why are historicism and logical positivism important? Historicism
because it says that human beings in their thinking cannot transcend
the influences of their times—something that all the great thinkers from
the earliest times have done; and positivism because in its diabolically
religious and metaphysical way it is both antireligious and antimetaphysi-
cal. Logical positivism not only denies that there can be knowledge of
God—and knowledge of God certainly includes knowledge of good
—it holds that statements concerning both God and good are meaningless. It goes further and denies that there can be any knowledge whatever other than that of facts and such relations of ideas as are involved
in mathematics; and it holds that these relations are true only because
they are based on definitions that are made by human beings. The basic
doctrine of logical positivism was stated by David Hume at the end
of his *Enquiry Concerning Human Understanding:* "If we take into
our hand any volume; of divinity or school metaphysics, for instance;
let us ask, Does it contain any abstract reasoning concerning quantity
or number? No. Does it contain any experimental reasoning concerning
matter of fact and existence? No. Commit it then to the flames: for it
can contain nothing but sophistry and illusion."

Britannica's articles on David Hume and Auguste Comte both correctly ascribe the origins of the positivistic influence of our time to
David Hume. But neither quotes in any of its several articles that have
to do with positivism the passage from Hume quoted above which is
the classic statement of the doctrine and has to be understood in the
sense Hume intended, if the doctrine is to be understood.

As has been suggested above, the intellectual world of our time is in
the main addicted to positivism without being aware of this fact and
without understanding the doctrine or having any clear knowledge of
its existence. The best statement to this effect is in the opening pages of
Natural Right and History by Leo Strauss, formerly Robert M. Hutchins Distinguished Professor of Political Philosophy in the University of
Chicago. *Natural Right and History*, as I have suggested above, is
devoted to showing the origins of historicism and positivism, their
effects on political theory, and why they have to be overcome and
abandoned if there is to be any valid doctrine of natural right. The best
concise statement on this subject is also by Strauss. It is the concluding

essay, "An Epilogue," in *Essays on the Scientific Study of Politics*, edited by Herbert J. Storing. This volume is a devastating criticism of the school of thought that is dominant in political science today.

If one checks the references under Democracy in Britannica's index, one finds that there are no references to discussion of equality, freedom or liberty, justice, good, order, worship—all deeply involved in democracy. There is an article "Civil Liberties," in Britannica. This article should be listed under Democracy in the index. It is not listed. There is an article "Natural Law" in Britannica. It also is not listed under Democracy in the index. One wonders how the editors of Britannica expect uninformed readers to find discussion of closely related subjects. The article "Natural Law" suffers from its brevity and its blindness to problems that involve natural law doctrine, such as those of historicism and positivism, which have become crucial during the last hundred years, have been taking seriously destructive social and political forms in recent decades, and can destroy American democracy in the absence of better and far more widespread understanding of them. The article "Civil Liberties" is good in its discussion of the liberties and rights of the individual, but it is written as if individuals and groups could have rights and liberties without also having duties and obligations—as if there were in existence a great deposit or bank of rights and liberties on which every individual and group can draw and into which no one and no group ever has to put anything. This is the kind of wild metaphysics—just one example of many—that the antimetaphysicians of our time are spawning. Our encyclopedias, others as well as Britannica, are today in the main governed by this wild metaphysics.

One would have to be a genius far transcending any that is very likely to appear in our time to be able to say anything not of a cheaply demagogic, not of a viciously misleading propagandistic character, usually also self-serving, on the subject of natural right unless he had the benefit of the understanding that can be got from study of the great thinkers of the past on this subject. But while we know that such transcendence occurs, we know this usually only because there are those who know the great tradition and are thus able to recognize the transcendence when it occurs. This knowledge is being lost, is rapidly disappearing, and nothing effective is being done to cultivate it on the scale on which it is most urgently needed. This, again, is just another way of stating the purpose of this book and the dire need for the institutions that we shall propose in Chapter XII.

I leave the subject democracy with regret because there is so much in the subject with which I have not dealt—such as the great dilemma of democracy which is stated briefly in Chapter II. This dilemma can be anticipated and prevented in only one way, and that is by a genuine general education that is practically non-existent today. There is much that is known, in the sense that it has been worked out with extreme care by superior minds in the past, and this working out is on record for use today. But this known is known to only a relatively very few and is practically unavailable to the vast public, including the leadership in the intellectual world that is most in need of it. I cannot, however, write a book on the subject of democracy and at the same time write the same book on the subject to which this book is devoted—the dire need for means for a general education for all members of the public.

CHAPTER V

Don Quixote Rides Again

And here's a prophet that I brought with me
SHAKESPEARE, *King John*

Suppose you are reading Marshall McLuhan's books *Understanding Media* and *The Gutenberg Galaxy* and you begin wondering about the truth of some of his statements and wish to check them. Suppose you turn to your set of Britannica and begin trying to find answers to particular questions that seem to you most important. How much help will you get? The next three chapters are intended to throw light on this question. Chapters V and VI examine the books and indicate subjects about which questions might be asked. Chapter VII selects the more important questions and examines Britannica to see what help, if any, it gives on them. I have selected these two books of McLuhan's for this test because *Understanding Media* has been one of the most discussed works of the last ten years. I include *The Gutenberg Galaxy* because *Understanding Media* is a continuation of it and to some extent based on it.

Understanding Media has been compared to Oswald Spengler's *Decline of the West* and Arnold Toynbee's *Study of History* and a few other of the best-known writings of this century. I have chosen it for discussion not merely because of the prominence it has had on the intellectual scene but also because it illustrates so well the need that so many intellectuals have today for general education; and second, because McLuhan holds, as I do, that modern conditions have made general education a matter of the greatest importance. I hope to show that *Understanding Media* and *The Gutenberg Galaxy* are in large measure unintended exhibits of the need for general education. And this book of mine will also be such an exhibit, except as it escapes being one by great good fortune. For no one, except by the gift of good fortune, can transcend the conditions that make general education practically impossible today.

The first chapter of *Understanding Media* is entitled "The Medium Is the Message," and McLuhan tells us in the Introduction to the McGraw-Hill paperback edition (1965), the edition I am using, that this title "can, perhaps, be clarified by pointing out that any technology gradually creates a totally new human environment." In both *Understanding Media* and *The Gutenberg Galaxy*, McLuhan gives much attention to the effects of media or technologies, all of which he considers extensions of man comparable to the tools that man has invented.

According to McLuhan, if I read him correctly, of all technologies, modes of communication have been most important. They have shaped human cultures. His theory is thus, as he says, in competition with other theories such as that of Karl Marx. According to McLuhan there have been five stages in the development of Western culture. (1) Preliterate culture was oral, and the audile sense (or the audile-tactile senses) dominated. (2) Preliterate culture was succeeded by pictorial or sign writing; this stage was also oral, and the audile sense (or audile-tactile senses) continued to be dominant. (3) Pictorial or sign writing was succeeded by the invention of the alphabet; while writing by hand continued, the writing by hand was now alphabetic rather than pictorial or sign. This inaugurated alphabetic-manuscript culture. The phonetic alphabet, McLuhan tells us, abstracts meaning from sound and translates sound into a visual code, and "the phonetic alphabet . . . lands men at once in varying degrees of dualistic schizophrenia." Its chief effect is to separate thought from action (GG 22).[1] "By the meaningless sign linked to the meaningless sound, we have built the shape and meaning of western man" (GG 50). But even so, the visual element did not become dominant as long as writing was done by hand. Alphabetic-manuscript culture, even though it had this meaningless visual element, remained oral and audile-tactile. (4) Alphabetic-manuscript culture was succeeded by typographic culture, inaugurated by Gutenberg with moveable type and the printing press. In this culture the visual sense became dominant. The effect of this dominance was to "homogenize" human beings in the Western world, to alter sense ratios, and to establish the process of "stripping" or "denudation" by which men translated themselves from a world of roles into a world of jobs. (5) Typographic culture has been in the process of being displaced by electronic culture since the invention of telegraphy. Auto-

1. References are to *The Gutenberg Galaxy* (Toronto: Univ. of Toronto Press, 1962; U.S.A. paperback ed., 1965), "GG," and *Understanding Media*, paperback (New York: McGraw-Hill, 1965), "UM."

mation, the computer, and television are the chief factors in electronic culture. In electronic culture the audile-tactile senses regain their ascendancy and a new and wonderful era comes into existence when "we have only to name and program a process or a product in order for it to be accomplished."

Is it not rather like the case of Al Capp's Schmoos? One had only to look at a Schmoo and think longingly of pork chops or caviar, and the Schmoo ecstatically transformed itself into the object of desire. Automation brings us into the world of the Schmoo [UM 352].

All that we had previously achieved mechanically by great exertion and coordination can now be done electrically without effort [UM 357].

The need for intellectual and moral as well as physical muscular exertion, according to McLuhan, does not exist any longer: "The computer, in short, promises by technology a Pentecostal condition of universal understanding and unity" (UM 80).

I have said above, "according to McLuhan, if I read him correctly," because summarizing any part of McLuhan's doctrine in one's own words is a hazardous task. For instance, he hedges his bets on such prophecies of his as those above by suggesting that the visual culture will not peacefully resign and let itself be replaced by the coming electronic audile-tactile culture. There will be bloody conflict, and while previous conflicts have been comparable to nuclear fission, this one will be comparable to nuclear fusion—far more destructive (UM 50): all because the devotees of the visual culture are too stupid to understand that electronic culture is going to be victorious anyway. The devotees of the visual culture are like the anticommunists of the period before World War II, says McLuhan:

Being anti-Red made it impossible for them to read the message of Hitler. But their failure was as nothing compared to our present one. The American stake in literacy as a technology or uniformity applied to every level of education, government, industry, and social life is totally threatened by electric technology. The threat of Stalin or Hitler was external. The electric technology is within the gates, and we are numb, deaf, blind, and mute about its encounter with the Gutenberg technology, on and through which the American way of life was formed. It is, however, no time to suggest strategies when the threat has not even been acknowledged to exist. I am in the position of Louis Pasteur telling doctors that their greatest enemy was quite invisible, and quite unrecognized by them. Our conventional response to all media, namely it is how they are used that counts, is the numb stance of the technological idiot. For the "content" of a medium is like the juicy piece of meat carried by the burglar to distract the watch-dog of the mind [UM 17–18].[2]

I suggest that the reader consider this quotation from McLuhan care-fully, and then reread the three immediately preceding quotations from him. In this last quotation, the one immediately above, according to McLuhan, the main influence in the shaping of American life is totally threatened by electric technology, and McLuhan is trying to tell us that electric technology is "our greatest enemy"; and we are, he says, "numb, deaf, blind, and mute" in the face of his efforts. In the three immediately preceding quotations, McLuhan tells us electric technology is bringing us a veritable utopia, and not only to us but to the whole world, and, glory be, a "Pentecostal condition of universal understand-ing and unity."

It is, I believe, clear that this part of the message that McLuhan is bringing us is badly mixed up. It has not been possible for us to dis-cover who did the mixing, the medium who gave the message to McLuhan, or McLuhan himself. Such mixing as that we have just ex-hibited is typical of both *The Gutenberg Galaxy* and *Understanding Media*. Why then do we bother? A serious examination of McLuhan is called for because of the widespread attention given him, and par-ticularly because of the high critical appraisal, with a few exceptions, that his work has been given.

As a consequence of the publication of *Understanding Media*, McLuhan received an appointment in 1966 that was subject to annual renewal to the Albert Schweitzer Chair in Humanities at Fordham University in New York City. The appointment was to pay $100,000 a year for McLuhan's salary and staff and expenses. The $100,000 was to come from the Treasury of the State of New York, that is, from taxes. There are several such appointments in New York state financed by the state and administered by universities in the state. The appoint-ment was completely in accord with the chorus of enthusiastic critical approval that was given to McLuhan's work, and it was a shocking thing to learn later that funds were not available and could not be found to finance the appointment. So McLuhan did not leave Toronto for New York. Now despite the criticisms I express in this chapter and the following two, I have to say this was New York's great loss and Toronto's corresponding gain. For whatever one may think of

2. Note the first sentence in this quotation. One cannot say that being anti-Hitler—as any decent person had to be—can also have its blinding effects with-out making himself a target for attack by intellectuals.

McLuhan's work, it has certainly been extremely stimulating to many people, including myself. Entirely too much professorial writing not only says little or nothing at all that is greatly worth saying, but says it in a way that wakes none of us from our dogmatic slumber. Any university that makes McLuhan's talk available to its students is, we can be sure, making a treasure beyond monetary estimate available to them.

McLuhan is at the time of this writing (January, 1973) still at the University of Toronto, where he has been a teacher of English literature since 1946 and director of the Centre for Culture and Technology —a small affair until after the publication of *Understanding Media*— since 1963. In 1962 McLuhan received the Canadian Governor General's award for *The Gutenberg Galaxy*. The award is made to the author of the book by a Canadian judged to be the best published during the year. If the acquisition of degrees in formal learning qualifies a person for the prophetic office, McLuhan is well qualified. He has two B.A. degrees and two M.A. degrees, one of each from the University of Manitoba in Canada, and one of each from Cambridge University in England, and one Ph.D. from Cambridge. His Cambridge doctoral dissertation was on *The Place of Thomas Nashe in the Learning of His Time*. At Cambridge, McLuhan was under the influence of F. R. Leavis, best known perhaps for his attack upon Sir Charles Snow in his Rede Lecture at Cambridge, *Two Cultures? The Significance of C. P. Snow*. Anthony Burgess, in his article "The Modicum Is the Messuage," in the highly readable and unusually illuminating collection *McLuhan: Pro and Con*, speaks of "the terrible magic of F. R. Leavis" and speculates on the effect on McLuhan of the doctrine of Leavis that "in an acceptable work of literature, it is not possible to separate content from form. You can't talk about the meaning of a poem: to explain it in terms of a prose paraphrase is not merely heretical but destructive of a highly wrought artifact."[3] It was from this doctrine of Leavis, Burgess suggests, that the light after some years dawned on McLuhan that "in a work of art the form is the content, 'the medium is the message.'" "McLuhan's gimmick," says Burgess, "has been to push an esthetic doctrine to the limit. Nobody denies that a piece of music represents the condition to which all works of art must tend—a condition of unparaphrasability, total identification of form and content." This theory, if adhered to, would, I believe, make all art into cliché; but to discuss this question here would take us too far away from our subject.

3. R. Rosenthal, ed., *McLuhan: Pro and Con* (Baltimore: Penguin, 1969), p. 230.

In 1936 McLuhan published an article, "G. K. Chesterton: A Practical Mystic," in the January issue of the *Dalhousie Review*. This article and other writings of McLuhan's establish an important identity in the doctrines that McLuhan held at that time and those of the Southern Agrarians, also known as the Fugitives, then located mainly at Vanderbilt University in Nashville, Tennessee. McLuhan speaks at the end of the Introduction to the paperback edition of *Understanding Media* (1965) of maintaining "an even course toward permanent goals, even amidst the most disrupting innovations. We have already discussed the futility of changing our goals as often as we change our technologies." If in my discussion of McLuhan, our strangely modified Don Quixote as to goals, this voice crying in the wilderness and telling us of the salvation to come from television, automation, and the computer, I betray fears that McLuhan, like Don Quixote, is suffering from the effects of the books he has read, I will have accomplished part of the purpose I wish to serve. For modern man is lost in the wilderness of print that he has made.

The argument that McLuhan makes in both *The Gutenberg Galaxy* and *Understanding Media* rests on notions that he presents of the role of sense perceptions in human existence. I should say immediately that McLuhan would, and does repeatedly, deny that he is making any "argument." He claims to be making "probes." But then every piece of writing by every author from the invention of the alphabet to the present can be considered a "probe." McLuhan carefully avoids saying so, but what he is really doing is imparting to his readers revelations that his fertile mind has helped him to secure.

McLuhan often speaks of the tactile sense as involving maximal interplay of all the senses without reference to any particular culture; but he also speaks of it, or of the audile-tactile senses, as dominant or basic until Gutenberg came along with movable type and the printing press and created the possibility of wide degrees of literacy among people generally. McLuhan presents no evidence of a scientific nature to support his notion of the crucial importance of the tactile or audile-tactile senses in the evolution of man, and the reader is left to wonder, Could primitive man have survived without eyesight? Certainly, primitive man's sense of hearing was necessary to communication, if communication depended on noises that became speech. But what of motions, of gestures? They cannot be heard. They can only be seen. If the origin of speech was naturalistic, it is highly probable that gestures, along with vocal organs, eardrums, eyesight, and minds, played a necessary part. The only clues that McLuhan provides on the question what theory he holds of the origin of speech are so absurd that we find it difficult to believe they point toward his theory. For instance, he quotes the following passage from Plato's *Cratylus*.

Socrates: But if these things are only to be known through names, how can we suppose that the givers of names had knowledge, or were legislators before there were names at all, and therefore before they could have known them?

Cratylus: I believe, Socrates, the true account of the matter to be, that a power more than human gave things their first names, and that the names which were thus given are necessarily their true names.

"This view of Cratylus," McLuhan tells us,

was the basis of most language study until the Renaissance. It is rooted in the old oral "magic" of the "momentary deity" kind such as is favoured today for various reasons. That it is most alien to merely literary and visual culture is easily found in the remarks of incredulity which Jowett supplies as his contribution to the dialogue [GG 27–28].

If we accept the views of those scholars who have given most careful attention to the subject McLuhan is discussing here, we have to reject his statement that "this view of Cratylus was the basis of most language study until the Renaissance." It may have been the primitive tribal view that McLuhan says has been demonstrated in many modern studies, but it certainly has not been the basis of most language study in the Western world from the time of Socrates until the Renaissance. McLuhan cites Ernst Cassirer to support his view. I shall later quote Cassirer to show how utterly misleading McLuhan's procedure is on this question. Cassirer agrees with McLuhan up to a point, but beyond this point disagrees about as completely as is possible.

The views of Socrates, Plato, and Aristotle on the nature of language were totally different from the view of Cratylus, and their views in more or less modified forms, along with nominalistic views, have shared the stage from their time to the present. McLuhan does not quote the view of Socrates which Socrates expresses toward the end of the *Cratylus* that "the knowledge of things is not to be derived from names." Both Plato and Aristotle certainly agreed with Socrates on this point. So far as I know, the primitive idea was, as McLuhan holds, that of Cratylus—it was rooted in the notion that names are not in their origins noises assigned to things by chance, custom, or convention or by an imagined relation between the sound of the name and the object to which it pointed, but are derived by revelation that comes from a god and that, as Cratylus says in the passage quoted above, "the names which were thus given are necessarily their true names." I am not sure what McLuhan means when he says this idea "is favored today for various reasons." He cites no references other than Cassirer. There are, as I have said, good reasons for thinking this was the idea of many primitive peoples, and there certainly are some scholars, Ernst Cassirer, for instance, who recognize this. But to recognize that primitive peoples had a certain notion of the origin of names is not to accept this notion as correctly representing the actual origin of names. For the primitive notion could be wrong. Can McLuhan possibly mean that serious students of this subject today are adopting the doctrine that "the names originally given to things are necessarily their true names"? If this is what McLuhan means, the only possible response is laughter.

McLuhan's lucubrations on this subject remind us of the question that a certain scientist of some prominence asked and that caused widespread hilarity when the name Uranus was given to the newly discovered planet now known by this name: "What guarantee have we that the planet regarded by astronomers as Uranus is really Uranus?" [4]

The most serious and careful and prolonged discussion of the nature of names (words) is probably that which occurred between realists and nominalists from the twelfth through the fourteenth century. None of the leaders in this discussion held the doctrine of Cratylus. All held that words as spoken are noises and as written refer to the noises as spoken. All held that words are not in any respect the things to which they refer. The difference between them was wholly on the nature of universals (common names or nouns), the realists holding that universals exist both in minds and in things, extreme nominalists holding that they have no existence either in minds or in things except as conveniences for purposes of classification, moderate nominalists tending toward conceptualism, the notion that universals exist in minds but only in minds. There were refinements in these two opposed views, but we do not need to take these into account here. The point is that all serious students of language, from the time of Plato and Aristotle to the present, would have laughed at the notion that Cratylus' doctrine of names is the

4. C. K. Ogden and I. A. Richards, *The Meaning of Meaning* New York: Harcourt, Brace, 1956), p. 109, n. 1.

true doctrine.[5] How widely it has been held to be the primitive doctrine, as I have said, is a totally different question. We shall return to this subject later when we discuss certain statements of McLuhan's concerning myth.

I turn now to examination of the summary statement I made above of McLuhan's doctrines. I begin with his thesis that the modes of communication determine cultures and ask, What determines modes of communication? Let us grant, to begin with, that a god might determine them. But if we grant this, the question arises whether there are any things that a god or gods did not determine—and many other such questions such as whether they continue determining things. We do not have to follow this line of thought very long before we realize that it is utterly incompatible with scientific thought. Scientific thought, in its widest meaning, is the effort to understand as far as possible things and events in terms of natural processes. So we have to ask, Is human speech such that its origin could conceivably have been in a natural process? If our answer is yes, then we have to ask, Is it conceivable that animals on the way to becoming human beings could have developed human speech by any natural process without involving senses comparable to what we today call the "human senses" and without involving that which we call "mind"?

The human senses, along with minds, are the means and the only means by which, in naturalistic and empirical doctrine, knowledge of any kind whatever is possible to human beings. There cannot be, according to this doctrine, anything in human minds that was not first in the senses. If we hold to this doctrine, there can be no beginnings whatever of any of the knowledge that is necessary to any mode of communication that does not depend on the senses and the mind. And the question arises, How did human beings get the minds that have been generally held to distinguish them from animals? Could minds have developed by any natural process? One can assume that the answer is yes, and one can make long arguments to support this view. But it is beyond proof. If Cratylus had held that mind was a gift of a god to man just as, say, the human senses and, indeed, all existence can be considered a gift, and if he had developed his notion of the origin of speech

5. I cannot document this statement, but I can refer the reader to an excellent discussion of the medieval controversy over universals. See Meyrick H. Carré, *Realists and Nominalists* (New York: Oxford Univ. Press, 1946). The doctrine of Cratylus was too absurd to be discussed by serious students except as it represented a primitive belief.

in a way compatible with this assumption, he would have escaped the absurdity into which he fell, and into which McLuhan seems to have fallen with him.

Rousseau stated the paradox that is involved here when he said, "If men need speech to learn to think, they must have stood in much greater need of the art of thinking, to be able to invent that of speaking."[6] The question whether McLuhan is right in arguing that modes of communication determine cultures does not depend on the solution of this paradox. For it is clear that without mind and the senses, there would be no chance for communication beyond that of animals to start. And once communication started, though a case may be made for the view that often nothing but noise or confusion or a combination of the two is communicated, if anything cogent is communicated, mind and the senses continue to be necessary.

The fallibility of mind and the senses is illustrated by error and superstition. The potential—a most seriously question-begging idea, but we have to assume it or assume supernatural intervention at every moment —that the animal becoming man has in him, with the aid of the means that nature provides him of unknown measures of development, seems clearly illustrated in the process of evolution—a process that as it has to do with the senses and the mind can perhaps be summarized in the words "growth of consciousness." We shall later give our reasons for believing that McLuhan's view of the computer as an extension of human consciousness is grossly misleading. McLuhan's thesis certainly includes the growth of human consciousness. We see no grounds for disagreeing with this thesis. We could not disagree without rejecting the doctrine of evolution, which, however, we do well to remember, is supported by assumptions that cannot be proved to be true. We do not know that at some stage in evolution mind was not a gift of a god to man. The assumption that it was not requires the assumption that it was all along potentially present in the animal becoming man, or that it just developed from nothing. We simply do not know about the origin of mind any more than we know about the origin of speech.

But however this may be, if what we have said about mind and the senses being necessary to communication in the human sense, then, contrary to McLuhan these have determined the modes of communication rather than the other way around. Furthermore, if the doctrine of

6. "A Discourse on the Origin of Inequality," in *The Social Contract* . . . , p. 190.

revelation that we have discussed above is McLuhan's—and he clearly appears to subscribe to it, though he equally clearly avoids explicitly saying so—since a revelation can be made only to a mind, or to a mind through the senses, if there was any revelation of the "true meanings" of words, this revelation determined the first use of the word by human beings. And if this revelation was real, that is, was not merely imagined, it occurred outside the naturalistic process and proves that if this process is to exist, it has to be involved with a supernatural process. Thus McLuhan has, if I have judged and represented him correctly, two independent factors—one, modes of communication, the other, revelation determining cultures; but if revelation provided the word, and if the spoken word is a mode of communication, the two factors are not independent. They are, on the contrary, moments in a process, a cyclic or non-cyclic linear process, and we have to add, if true, the most important of all linear processes. This particular linear process receives no attention so far as its transforming effects on man are concerned, while the linear process of literacy cultivated in typographical culture is given credit by McLuhan for working great transformations in man.

It is worth noting here that while we have dwelt on the question how this linear process was started, it happens that even if the answer that the process was started by a god or gods can be wrong, this possibility does not affect the fact that if evolutionary theory is true, there was such a process, with or without the help of a god; and there is little room for doubt that such a process would have transforming effects probably greater than any that the animal becoming man has ever undergone. Now we have no doubt that literacy in typographic culture has had transforming effects on man; but we hold with Lewis Mumford that man has undergone many transformations; and all of the most important ones of which we know or can reasonably guess anything have contributed to the growth of consciousness of themselves and their surroundings in human beings. The phrase "growth of consciousness" may be, however, grossly misleading; for while consciousness may suggest the icon, that is, one object which at the same time may represent an infinity of objects and their qualities and relations past, present, and to come—a notion of which McLuhan makes a great deal—this representation by the icon, to which McLuhan appeals, is itself mere suggestion. It is extremely doubtful whether the human consciousness can be aware of more than a very few subjects and details of subjects at once. To be aware of everything at once, and McLuhan suggests that electronic technology extends man's nervous system everywhere in the world and enables man to be instantaneously aware of everything at once, is to imagine that man has acquired one of the attributes that theologians in the Western world have generally considered as belonging only to omniscience. McLuhan correctly says that in such awareness there are no points of view and no need for argument. He repeatedly disclaims having any point of view of his own and of making any arguments. In this respect he assimilates himself to omniscience and expresses a doctrine that Marx, Feuerbach, Bernard Shaw, and a host of others have flattered man and themselves with—and that many intellectuals flatter themselves with today.

Socrates, without benefit of Christian theology, understood that the desire for knowledge and its apparent, perhaps even its real, acquisition within limits leads to this doctrine if the limits are ignored. Socrates rejected this doctrine, as an expression of human pride, a swelling of the ego which, if not checked by the recognition of human fallibility, destroys what it should protect.

Speech has never been explained naturalistically, though many efforts have been made. Revelation seems to have been necessary—but not the type which derives from Cratylus and which McLuhan seems clearly to support. In fact, any appeal to revelation can easily be shown to rest on assumptions that cannot be proved. It is at such points as this that the human mind reaches one of its limits; and at this point myth, even though it is essentially an abdication of reason, becomes far more reasonable than any other human exertion of reason. It is at such points as this that if there is to be any representation at all of what may have happened in the most remote past, and if false claims to knowledge are not to be cultivated, myth becomes necessary, the only possible means other than speculation, which tends to become endless and buries under mountains of words the mystery it tries to uncover.

"Myth," McLuhan tells us, "is the instant vision of a complex process that ordinarily extends over a long period. Myth is contraction or implosion of any process, and the instant speed of electricity confers the mythic dimension on ordinary industrial and social action today. We live mythically but continue to think fragmentarily and on single planes" (UM 25). If the story of the origin of the world and of man told in Genesis is a myth, McLuhan's definition misses the mark, not, perhaps, as far as is possible, but by a long distance. Brief as it is, and carefully as it avoids elaboration and efforts to explain that could not possibly succeed, the story in Genesis is told in parts which succeed one another. In fact, there are two stories, and this is true of both. The complex process in both, while for good reasons not elaborated, is certainly not in Genesis an "instant vision." Myth is, as McLuhan says, a "contraction or implosion," but not of *any* process. Myth, on the contrary, has to do with processes, or aspects of processes, that are utterly beyond the reach of scientific observation and experiment; and electricity and ordinary industrial and social action today are certainly not utterly beyond scientific observation and experiment. Insofar as existence is a mystery and all efforts to explain how it first came to be—or that it has always been—soon reach an impasse, there certainly is a mythical element in our lives and I will risk the opinion that there always will be. But this element or dimension of mystery was not conferred by the "instant speed of electricity." It was already there and has always been there. And if when McLuhan says we "continue to think fragmentarily and on single planes" he means to say we continue to engage in analysis and try to understand things and processes in terms of their components, he certainly is right; and despite his predictions to the contrary, as long as we want to know as much as we possibly can about ourselves and our world, it is highly probable that we shall continue with this procedure. McLuhan suggests that this is the whole of our procedure. When he suggests this, he is simply ignoring easily available evidence, evidence that indeed is so public and pervasive that it is difficult to understand how anyone can be unaware of it. There may be problems of great public importance of which no one is aware and about which no thinking is being done. But there certainly are many of great public importance about which organized groups of people, as well as individuals, in the Western world are trying to think in the largest possible and most general terms, often under the best-qualified leadership that is available. Take, for instance, the large general problem, of worldwide scope, of the growth of the human population during the last two hundred years or so. Whenever anyone today who is sufficiently well-informed and sufficiently intelligent to realize its importance faces the fact that the growth and application of scientific knowledge has led to the growth of human population at rates that make some form of control in the future inevitable—either by starvation or by war or by some other abhorrent means, or by some worldwide procedure that may be impossible to enforce except by abhorrent means—he cannot escape asking large questions and trying as hard as he can to include all the small and intermediate ones that have any bearing on his large questions. To imagine, as McLuhan does, that this effort has not been made all along is simply to ignore easily available evidence. To imagine, as McLuhan does, that the advent of automation, television, and the computer will bring, after the violent fusion that he prophesies, a guarantee of procedures that will be adequate to solutions of problems such as those of world population or world peace or world justice is simply to engage in fantasy.

Much of both *The Gutenberg Galaxy* and *Understanding Media* is devoted to the thesis that "specialist technologies detribalize. The non-specialist electric technology retribalizes" (UM 24). This *is* news. Why does McLuhan say this? He cannot possibly be unaware that "electric technology" or electronics is among the most highly specialized of all disciplines that are cultivated today, and there is no evidence whatever that it will have tribalizing effects.

And, according to McLuhan, in the tribal mode of life of today and of the future that electric technology has brought, communication is mythical in that it is mosaic in form, iconic; it present wholes, not parts; is not discursive—does not analyze, does not break subjects or things into parts, does not consider one thing after another—but is instead characterized by immediate knowledge of everything, all-at-once aware-ness in which points of view disappear since everything is seen all at once from every point of view. These latter are, of course, as I have said above, characters of omniscience. The mythical mode as it is com-ing to be in modern retribalized society is, in McLuhan's view—we have to use the word "view" even though McLuhan rejects its applica-tion to himself—like cubism in art, which

substitutes all facets of an object simultaneously for the "point of view" or facet of perspective illusion. Instead of the specialized illusion of the third dimension on canvas, cubism sets up an interplay of planes and contra-diction or dramatic conflict of patterns, lights, textures that "drives home the message" by involvement. . . .

In other words, cubism, by giving the inside and outside, the top, bottom, back, and front and the rest, in two dimensions, drops the illusion of per-spective in favor of *instant sensory awareness of the whole* [my italics]. Cubism, by seizing on instant total awareness, suddenly announced that *the medium is the message* [McLuhan's italics; UM 13].

McLuhan tells us, and such students of myth as Ernst Cassirer have said very much the same, except for the passage that I have italicized:

The myth, like the aphorism and maxim, is characteristic of oral culture. For, *until literacy deprives language of his* [sic—its?] *multi-dimensional resonance* [my italics] every word is a poetic world unto itself, a "momen-tary deity" or revelation, as it seemed to non-literate men [GG 25].

McLuhan goes on to say:

Ernst Cassirer's *Language and Myth* presents this aspect of non-literate awareness, surveying the wide range of current study of language origins and development . . .

and this is certainly true. But while McLuhan tells us that myths represent wholes and that the theoretical mode of representation is *only* analytic, *only* takes things apart, and considers parts one after another in linear fashion part by part, that is discursively, Cassirer says the direct opposite:

The aim of theoretical thinking . . . is primarily to deliver the contents of sensory or intuitive experience from the isolation in which they originally occur. It causes these contents to transcend their narrow limits, combines them with others, compares them, and concatenates them in a definite order, in an all-inclusive context. It proceeds "discursively," in that it treats the immediate context only as a point of departure, from which it can run the whole gamut of impressions in various directions, until these impressions are fitted together into one unified conception, one closed system. In this system there are no more isolated points; all its members are reciprocally related, refer to one another, illumine and explain each other. Thus every separate event is ensnared, as it were, by invisible threads of thought, that bind it to the whole. The theoretical significance which it receives lies in the fact that it is stamped with the character of this totality.

Mythical thinking, when viewed in its most elementary forms, bears no such stamp; in fact, the character of intellectual unity is directly hostile to its spirit. For in this mode, thought does not dispose freely over the data of intuition, in order to relate and compare them to each other, but is captivated and enthralled by the intuition which suddenly confronts it. . . . For a person whose apprehension is under the spell of this mythico-religious attitude, it is as though the whole world were simply annihilated; the immediate content, whatever it be, that commands his religious interest so completely fills his consciousness that nothing else can exist beside and apart from it. The ego is spending all its energy on this single object, lives in it, loses itself in it.[7]

Among the authors that McLuhan relies on most heavily is Bishop George Berkeley. Berkeley, as every student of the history of Western thought ought to know, had an important part in determining the course of Western thought, and present problems in this thought cannot be understood without understanding his part. For instance, consider Einstein's doctrine of modern science conveniently summarized for us by him:

7. Ernst Cassirer, *Language and Myth*, trans, Suzanne K. Langer (New York: Dover, rpt. n.d.), pp. 32–33.

The belief in an external world independent of the perceiving subject is the basis of all natural science. Since, however, sense perception only gives information of this external world or of "physical reality" indirectly, we can only grasp the latter by speculative means. It follows from this that our notions of physical reality can never be final. We must always be ready to change these notions—in order to do justice to perceived facts in the most perfect way logically. Actually a glance at the development of physics shows that it has undergone far-reaching changes in the course of time.[8]

This statement of Einstein's is utterly meaningless to us unless we know why it is that he says "sense perception only gives us information of this external world *indirectly*" (my italics). To understand Einstein's "indirectly," we have to understand certain speculations of Galileo and Newton and the efforts made by John Locke, Bishop Berkeley, and David Hume—and especially Berkeley—to make sense of these speculations. To understand this line of thought is basic to understanding McLuhan, and I shall give some time to it, and especially to certain points that have not been given the attention they deserve.

The atomic theory of the early Greeks Democritus and Leucippus was embodied in a philosophical system by Epicurus and was beautifully summarized, with what appears to have been extreme care and accuracy, in a poem, *The Nature of Things*, by the Latin poet Lucretius. *The Nature of Things* is generally accepted today by students of early Greek thought as the best available representation of early Greek atomism. Early Greek atomic theory is clearly the source of the atomic ideas as expressed very briefly by Copernicus in his epoch-making *Revolutions of the Heavenly Spheres*, and Galileo was using it when he wrote a sheerly speculative and amazingly prophetic passage in *The Assayer*. The passage that I shall quote does not mention atoms or the names of the persons who formed the theory or recorded it for the future. Early Greek atomic theory holds that color is not in atoms, but somehow becomes present when atoms join to form objects. Color in early Greek atomic theory is thus in objects in what, since the time of Bishop Berkeley, has come to be called, by students of sense perception, the "external world." Color in the theory expressed by Galileo, still sheer speculation in his case as it was with the early Greeks, is not in objects in the external world. The theory that Bishop Berkeley expresses

8. Albert Einstein, "Maxwell's Influence on the Evolution of the Idea of Physical Reality," in *Ideas and Opinions* (New York: Crown, [1954] 1963), p. 266.

is not, except in details, his invention. The speculation by Galileo is so interesting and important that I quote it in full:

It now remains for me to [express], as I promised, some thoughts of mine about the proposition "motion is the cause of heat," and to show in what sense this may be true. But first I must consider what it is that we call heat, as I suspect that people in general have a concept of this which is very remote from the truth. For they believe that heat is a real phenomenon, or property, or quality, which actually resides in the material by which we feel ourselves warmed. Now I say that whenever I conceive any material or corporeal substance, I immediately feel the need to think of it as bounded, and as having this or that shape, as being large or small in relation to other things, and in some specific place at any given time; as being in motion or at rest; as touching or not touching some other body; and as being one in number, or few, or many. From these conditions I cannot separate such a substance by any stretch of my imagination. But that it must be white or red, bitter or sweet, noisy or silent, and of sweet or foul odor, my mind does not feel compelled to bring in as necessary accompaniments. Without the senses as our guides, reason or imagination unaided would probably never arrive at qualities like these. Hence I think that tastes, odors, colors, and so on are no more than names so far as the object in which we place them is concerned, and that they reside only in the consciousness. Hence if the living creature were removed, all these qualities would be wiped away and annihilated. But since we have imposed upon them special names, distinct from those of the other and real qualities mentioned previously, we wish to believe that they really exist as actually different from those.[9]

In the very next paragraph, Galileo speaks of "the primary phenomena of motion and touch." McLuhan could have used this passage to support his thesis as to the prime role of touch—if he had known of it and had not bothered to read on and take into account the following passage:

And as these four senses [those of touch, sound, taste and odor] are related to the four elements [shapes, number, motion, body], so I believe that vision, *the sense eminent above all others* [my italics] in the proportion of the finite to the infinite, the temporal to the instantaneous, the quantitative to the indivisible, the illuminated to the obscure—that vision, I say, is related to light itself.[10]

If McLuhan had used Galileo's *Assayer*—and the first passage above supports his thesis about touch far better than many he quotes—and if

9. Stillman Drake, trans., *Discoveries and Opinions of Galileo*, Anchor Books (Garden City, N.Y.: Doubleday, 1957), pp. 274 f.
10. Ibid., p. 277.

he used Galileo as he uses Berkeley, he would, as I have shown in the case of Cassirer and shall show further, quote the first passage above and ignore the second. It would take two volumes longer than McLuhan's *Gutenberg Galaxy* and *Understanding Media* to check on all of McLuhan's selective uses of quotations, his contradictions, and his plain errors of fact. Obviously, I cannot do all this in three chapters. But I can and will check a few cases.

Isaac Newton is important along with Galileo as an example of the kind of thinking and speculating to be found in early modern scientific writing on the theory that the material universe consists of particles in motion, and that while these cause the sense perceptions of human beings, they are utterly unlike what is perceived.

In Book I, Part II of Newton's *Opticks*, there is the following passage:

The homogeneal Light and Rays which appear red, or rather make Objects appear so, I call Rubrifick or Red-making; those which make Objects appear yellow, green, blue, and violet, I call Yellow-making, Green-making, Blue-making, Violet-making, and so of the rest. And if at any time I speak of Light and Rays as coloured or endued with Colours, I would be understood to speak not philosophically and properly, but grossly, and accordingly to such conceptions as vulgar People in seeing all these Experiments would be apt to frame. For the Rays to speak properly are not coloured. In them there is nothing else than a certain Power and Disposition to stir up a Sensation of this or that colour. For as the Sound in a Bell or musical String, or other Sounding Body, is nothing but a trembling Motion, and in the Air nothing but that Motion under the form of Sound; so Colours in the Object are nothing but a Disposition to reflect this or that sort of Rays more copiously than the rest; in the Rays they are nothing but their Dispositions to propagate this or that Motion into the Sensorium, and in the Sensorium they are Sensations of those Motions under the Forms of Colours.[11]

This passage is important in the early history of scientific thought about sense perception, since it is based partly on actual experiments and partly on speculation. Newton demonstrated by actual experiments that light consists of colors, and he used prisms to break light down into colors and to reverse the process and show that the same colors can by the use of another prism be made to join the colors together again as light. But he did not show that the "rays to speak properly are not coloured," and that "in them there is nothing else than a certain Power and Disposition to stir up a Sensation of this or that Colour." This is

11. Newton, *Opticks* (New York: Dover, rpt. 1952), pp. 124–25.

speculation based on analogy. Newton assumes that the case of color is the same as that of sound.

There is no room whatever to doubt, as Newton suggests in this passage, that if a tree falls in a forest and if there is no human being with an eardrum to receive the impact of the particles of air put in motion by the fall, there cannot be any sound produced in consciousness by means of impact on an eardrum. But there is room to doubt Newton's assumption that the case of color is like that of sound—that the color that human beings see in objects is not in the objects but is instead an effect produced in the mind by the impact of particles that are not colored on the eyes. The cases of sound and sight are certainly different in that the particles involved are different, in the case of sound, particles of air; in the case of sight, certainly not merely particles of air. There may be further and profound differences; and no experiment yet tried has proved beyond reasonable doubt that color is not in the external object. The present state of informed opinion on this subject is well illustrated in the two following statements, the first from A. J. Ayer, formerly Wykeham Professor of Logic in Oxford University, later at the University of London, and leading exponent of logical positivism, a variety of modern empiricism, author of *Language, Truth and Logic* and *The Problem of Knowledge*, other books and numerous essays: "Physics does *not* [my italics] prove that we do not perceive physical objects as they really are." [12] Ayer does not give the reader any reference to any scientific work in which experiments are described that validate this statement of his. We are forced to wonder whether there have been any such experiments and to wonder further, if there have not been any, how a strict empiricist such as Ayer could come to the conclusion that we have just quoted from him.

The second statement is from Bertrand Russell, most influential perhaps for his writings on the philosophy of mathematics and his joint authorship with Alfred North Whitehead of *Principia Mathematica*, in which the effort was made to show the unity of logic and mathematics, but best known probably for his numerous popular writings and adamant positions on public questions. Russell's statement brings out perhaps even more clearly than that of Ayer the fact that modern physical science has not yet settled beyond reasonable doubt some crucial questions such as that of the role of vision in sense perception. "Common sense," according to Russell, says:

12. A. J. Ayer, *The Problem of Knowledge* (Baltimore: Penguin, 1956), p. 93.

"I see a brown table." It will agree to both the statements: "I see a table" and "I see something brown." Since, according to physics, tables have no colour, we must either (a) deny physics, or (b) deny that I see a table, or (c) deny that I see something brown. It is a painful choice; I have chosen (b), but (a) or (c) would lead to at least equal paradoxes.[13]

At the end of his *Opticks*, Newton asks a number of questions and gives speculative answers to them, answers suggested by his experiments with light, but still speculative, as Newton himself clearly recognized. Question 30, the last one at the end of the *Opticks*, contains Newton's speculation on the atomic theory:

. . . it seems probable to me, that God in the Beginning form'd matter in solid, massy, hard, impenetrable, moveable Particles, of such Sizes and Figures, and with such other Properties, and in such Proportion to Space, as most conduced to the end for which he form'd them; and that these primary Particles being Solids, are incomparably harder than any porous Bodies compounded of them; even so very hard, as never to wear or break in pieces; no ordinary Power being able to divide what God himself made one in the first Creation. While the Particles continue entire, they may compose Bodies of one and the same Nature and Texture in all Ages: But should they break away, or break in pieces, the Nature of Things depending on them, would be changed.[14]

The train of thought that led John Locke to classify and name qualities as primary, secondary, and of a third sort to which he did not give a name did not originate with him. He was simply following Galileo and Newton, and they were following, with some changes, the early Greek atomists. The two kinds, primary and secondary, and their locations, the primary outside the mind and the secondary inside, posed a problem in Galileo and Newton that Locke despite some confusion repeats. It is not necessary that we consider what Locke said on this subject, since he, in the respects with which we are concerned here, simply examined and gave his sanction, with clear warnings about the fallibility of human authorities and the vast and perhaps insuperable extent of human ignorance, to the theories expressed in the quotations above from Galileo and Newton.

The position that Berkeley took on the question of primary and secondary qualities and their location called for a theory of perception that Berkeley expressed. McLuhan claims that Berkeley's theory sup-

13. Russell, "Reply to Criticisms," in P. A. Schilpp, ed., *The Philosophy of Bertrand Russell* (New York: Tudor, [1944] 1951), p. 705.

14. *Opticks*, p. 400.

ports his. We shall show that Berkeley's theory not only does not support McLuhan's, but contradicts it.

Let us first consider the following quotation from Berkeley:

For my own part, I see evidently that it is not in my power to frame an idea of a body extended and moved, but I must withal give it some colour or other sensible quality which is *acknowledged* [Berkeley's italics] to exist only in the mind. In short, extension, figure, and motion, abstracted from all other qualities, are inconceivable. Where therefore the other sensible qualities are, there must be these also, to wit, in the mind and nowhere else.[15]

The questions that a thorough consideration of this passage would raise, even today, more than two hundred years after it was written, are utterly foreign to the popular mind. The popular mind is the mind of all of us. It is the mind of naive realism, which says that objects are outside of minds and that we see and experience them, not in all cases, but probably in most, very much as they are.

One may imagine one refutes Berkeley as Samuel Johnson did by kicking a rock. But the rock and one's body and the kicking, in Berkeley's argument, all are in the mind. The whole world, the whole universe, in Berkeley's argument, is in God's mind, and there is nothing outside God's mind. In order to understand Berkeley, we first have to get rid of the tyranny that words and their usual definitions exercise over us. For instance, the word "idea" has to be redefined as referring to tangibles as well as intangibles. The word "mind" can no longer be used as referring to something in what is called a skull in one's head that contains a brain in which, somehow, there is a mind—a notion about as absurd as can be imagined; if we accept it, we do so only because it has been indirectly drilled into us. There are problems in Berkeley's notion of mind, but we cannot go into them here, since they have no bearing on McLuhan's use of Berkeley.

Berkeley is of the greatest importance to the understanding of McLuhan's misuse of the authors that he quotes. McLuhan's whole argument in both *The Gutenberg Galaxy* and *Understanding Media* rests on notions that he attributes to Berkeley—notions of sense perceptions—which Berkeley did not have. And not only this. Berkeley's notions, in the main, are the direct opposite of those that McLuhan attributes to him.

15. George Berkeley, *Principles of Human Knowledge*, in *A New Theory of Vision and Other Select Philosophical Writings*, Everyman's Library (New York: Dutton, [1910] 1926), p. 118.

The importance of the theories that we have outlined above extends far beyond the aid they give in understanding McLuhan. They illustrate the fact that there are permanent problems in human history. The theories we have outlined have been held in various forms from the time of the early Greek atomists to and including the time of Einstein. There is not the remotest prospect that any experiments or other procedures will solve all the problems posed in these theories at any time soon. For instance, even the existence of the particles assumed in the theory is subject to doubt. No particle, I say again because to get this firmly in mind is necessary to understanding the problem we are now discussing—no particle has ever been an object of sense experience. Their existence is only an inferred existence—a fact that suggests that logic may have a far more powerful role in the acquisition of knowledge than empirical doctrine generally allows to it.

It is worth noting here that ever since Locke's time, he has been considered the founder of British empiricism and very little attention has been given to the fact that there are elements in this empiricism that are not empirical. In Locke's empiricism, for instance, our knowledge, if we have any, of the so-called external world is based on the assumption that there is such a world, and the attempt is made to buttress this assumption by inferences based on a logic to which the founder of the empiricism that we have today was unwilling to grant any positive role in the acquisition of knowledge.[16]

Berkeley's doctrine of mind is so foreign to our usual modes of thinking that before passing on I should like to quote the passage which perhaps has received, and justly, more attention than any other, and which, if approached without prejudice, is probably most helpful in the understanding of Berkeley's doctrine and why he developed it:

Some truths there are so near and obvious to the mind, that a man need only open his eyes to see them. Such I take this important one to be, to wit, that all the choir of heaven and furniture of the earth, in a word all those bodies which compose the mighty frame of the world, have not any subsistence without a mind, that their *being* (*esse*) is to be perceived or known; that consequently so long as they are not actually perceived by me, or do not exist in my mind or that of any other *created spirit*, they must either have no existence at all, *or else subsist in the mind of some eternal spirit. . . .*[17]

16. John Locke, *An Essay Concerning Human Understanding* (Oxford, Clarendon Press, 1894), II, 277 ff., Book IV, Chap. 7, Sec. 11.
17. Berkeley, pp. 115 f.

Berkeley's interest went far beyond that of an academic discussion of the grounds of human knowledge. He was most concerned with making a conclusive argument against skepticism, atheism, and immorality and for the existence of a world that could not exist unless sustained by an all-encompassing and all-powerful mind that gave laws to man which were necessary to his welfare but which he was free to violate. Berkeley intended a doctrine of objective idealism—a doctrine that says there are necessities in nature and reason that have to be observed in the interests of human welfare. His doctrine has been mutilated by an invincible prejudice into various species of subjectivism, and particularly into doctrines that say that thinking something is good, without reference to its connections, makes it so. This problem has been of perennial interest in the tradition of the Western world. We shall find it dealt with by McLuhan in a way that is typical of the way in which the intellectual world of today deals with ethical problems.

I proceed now to show McLuhan's misuse of Berkeley. I quote from *The Gutenberg Galaxy:*

. . . by 1709 Bishop Berkeley in his *New Theory of Vision* was denouncing the absurdity of Newtonian visual space as a mere abstract illusion severed from the sense of touch [GG 17]. Berkeley's *New Theory of Vision* (1709) is now favoured by psychologists of our sense lives. But Berkeley was concerned to refute Descartes and Newton, who had wholly abstracted the visual sense from the interaction of the other senses [GG 53]. . . . in 1709 Bishop Berkeley had published *A New Theory of Vision,* which revealed the lop-sided assumptions of Newtonian optics. Blake, at least, had understood the Berkeleyan critique and had restored tactility to its prime role as agent of unified perception. Today artists and scientists alike concur in praising Berkeley [GG 271].

All that we have to do is go to Berkeley to see the gross misrepresentation in these passages. Berkeley himself committed the "absurdity" with which McLuhan charges Newton and Descartes of setting up "visual space as a mere abstract illusion from the sense of touch." Berkeley himself abstracted "the visual sense from the interaction of the other senses." Berkeley clearly denies "unified perception." And finally, as we shall see, not all scientists today concur in praising Berkeley, and McLuhan does not name any who do and refer the reader to where they do so.

Let Berkeley speak. I quote from *A New Theory of Vision:*

. . . the ideas intromitted by each sense are widely different, and distinct from each other; but having been observed constantly to go together, they are spoken of as one and the same thing [XLVI].

. . . that there is no necessary connexion between visible and tangible ideas suggested by them, we need go no further than the next looking glass to be convinced [XLV].

. . . a man no more sees or feels the same thing, than he hears and feels the same thing [XLVII].

. . . if we take a close and accurate view of things, it must be acknowledged that we never see and feel one and the same subject. That which is seen is one thing, and that which is felt is another; if the visible figure and extension be not the same with the tangible figure and extension, we are not to infer that one and the same thing has divers extensions. The true consequence is, that the objects of sight and touch are two distinct things [XLIX].

The extension, figures, and motions perceived by sight are specifically distinct from the ideas of touch, called by the same names, nor is there any such thing as one idea or kind of idea common to both senses [CXXVII].

I cannot imagine any clearer statements on this subject than these from Berkeley himself.

McLuhan speaks many times in both *The Gutenberg Galaxy* and *Understanding Media* of tactility as interplay among the senses. I will give a few instances:

Hildebrand had shown how tactility was a kind of synaesthesia or interplay among the senses [GG 41]. I would suggest that "touch" is not so much a separate sense as the very interplay of the senses [GG 65]. Gombrich records the stages of nineteenth-century discussion and analysis of "sense data" leading to the Helmholtz case for "unconscious inference" or mental action even in the most basic sense experience. "Tactility" or interplay among all the senses was felt to be the very mode of this "inference" [GG 81]. An oral manuscript culture had no fear of tactility, the very crux of the interplay of the senses [GG 106]. . . . tactility is the interplay of the senses [UM 314]. . . . TV is, above all, an extension of the sense of touch, which involves maximal interplay of all the senses (UM 333). The tactual mode of perceiving is sudden but not specialist. It is total, synesthetic, involving all the senses [UM 334].

Berkeley's answer to the question posed by these quotations is completely unambiguous. I add another statement of his to those above: "*The two distinct provinces of sight and touch* [my italics] should be considered apart, and as if their objects had no intercourse, no manner of relation to one another, in point of distance or position" (CXV).

I have nowhere nearly exhausted the opposition between McLuhan's views and those of Berkeley. For instance, McLuhan tells us in his usual oracular manner that "number is the dimension of tactility" (GG 81). Berkeley tells us in his *New Theory* that number "is entirely the creation of the mind" (CIX). But it would be a waste of time to pile up more instances.

Touch certainly establishes in Berkeley's system degrees of hardness or softness, of heat or cold, of roughness or smoothness, and so on, and, as it is presented in the *New Theory*, might be taken to establish a physicalistic or materialistic order. But to do this would be to falsify Berkeley. It would be to ignore his intention in the *New Theory*, as well as in his *Principles*, to establish a non-materialistic doctrine. Furthermore, Berkeley himself admits in his *Principles of Human Knowledge* that he made at least one serious error in his *New Theory*. His admission concerns the sense of touch and is as follows:

XLIV. The ideas of sight and touch make two species, entirely distinct and heterogeneous. *The former are marks and prognostics of the latter* [Berkeley's italics]. That the proper objects of sight and touch neither exist without the mind, nor are the images of external things, was shown even in the [*New Theory of Vision*]. Though throughout the same, the contrary be supposed true of tangible objects; not that to suppose *that vulgar error* [my italics] was necessary for establishing the notions therein laid down, but because it was beside my purpose to examine and refute it in a discourse concerning vision. So that in strict truth the ideas of sight, when we apprehend by them distance and things placed at a distance, do not suggest or mark out to us things actually existing at a distance, but only admonish us what ideas of touch will be imprinted in our minds at such and such distance of time and in consequence of such or such actions. It is, I say, evident from what has been said in the foregoing parts of this treatise, and in Sect. XCLVII, and elsewhere of the essay concerning vision, that visible ideas are the language whereby the governing Spirit, on whom we depend, informs us what tangible ideas he is about to imprint upon us, in case we excite this or that motion in our bodies.

This correction, however, still leaves crucial questions about Berkeley's theory unanswered. Although the contradiction concerning touch —having its objects both in the mind and not in the mind in the same way at the same time—is removed by this correction, sight and touch are still left totally separate in different spaces "in the mind." It is not clear just how far Berkeley goes in his later writings in making further corrections. For instance, in his *Visual Language, Vindicated and Explained*, he repeats (Sect. 15) his argument "that there is no such thing as a common object, as an idea, or kind of idea perceived by both sight and touch." But whatever Berkeley we appeal to, the early, middle, or late, we find only one idea of sense perception that is compatible with McLuhan's. This idea is that visual perception is two-dimensional.

However, if any psychologist has produced experimental evidence for the validity of this idea, Britannica fails to report it.

It is possible, by picking and choosing what serves one's purpose and excluding what does not, to "prove" anything. One of the great problems of human thought is that no matter how one proceeds, one has to pick and choose. And one can pick and choose in ways that are utterly deceptive, and the deception may be extremely difficult, if not impossible, to prove. This is the basic principle of the most insidious types of viciously misleading propaganda. The extent to which most of us, perhaps all of us, are victims of such propaganda is a subject worth far more serious attention than it yet has been given. In some cases, the picking and choosing that is done is easy to locate and identify as grossly misleading, and this is the case with McLuhan.

It is not necessary to look outside of *The Gutenberg Galaxy* and *Understanding Media* to find evidence that McLuhan has not bothered to think through his subject or subjects before holding forth on it or them in public. I invite the reader to contemplate the following assertion concerning the sense of smell in relation to what we have quoted from McLuhan on the sense of touch: "The sense of smell is not only the most subtle and delicate of the human senses, it is, also, the most iconic in that it involves the entire human sensorium more fully than any other sense" (UM 146–47). McLuhan mentions experiments conducted by Wilder Penfield, as briefly as what I have just said, without suggesting what they were and where reported; and we are grateful for this clue, even though we do not have the time to follow it up and find out, as well as we can, whether they really support this statement that they are not clearly said to support, but that we might wrongly guess they are intended to support. Most important, we are left with a question: Are the statements that we have quoted from McLuhan concerning the sense of touch, and this one concerning the sense of smell, contradictory? And if not, how are they related? McLuhan does not tell us.

In most of what he says about the roles of the different senses, McLuhan seems clearly to consider the tactile sense, or the audile-tactile senses, basic. But then he also, as we have already suggested, holds that since the invention of movable type, the visual sense has determined the course of Western civilization:

In fact, of all the great hybrid unions that breed furious release of energy and change, there is none to surpass the meeting of literate and oral cultures. The giving to man of an eye for an ear by phonetic literacy is, socially and politically, probably the most radical explosion that can occur in any social structure. This explosion of the eye, frequently repeated in "backward areas," we call Westernization. With literacy now about to hybridize the cultures of the Chinese, the Indians, and the Africans, we are about to experience such a release of human power and aggressive violence as makes the previous history of phonetic alphabet technology quite tame [UM 49–50].

In this quotation, there is conflict between the audile and the visual senses—not between the visual and the tactile.

Before turning to the testimony of a psychologist against McLuhan's statements quoted above that "scientists . . . concur in praising Berkeley" and that Berkeley supports McLuhan's notions concerning the role of tactility in perception, let me call attention again to the argument McLuhan makes concerning the role of vision in typographic culture. Since the time of Gutenberg, according to McLuhan, vision has been basic. Vision has used the printed word to create literacy, and literacy has displaced the audile-tactile senses from their previously basic role. It has made the sense of vision basic, thus upsetting previously existing sense ratios and, I repeat, homogenizing individuals in society by stripping them of their individual characters, substituting mere jobs for interesting roles and involvement in depth, not only fragmenting society but fragmenting human thought, creating the specialist "who never makes small mistakes while moving toward the grand fallacy" (UM 124). Now, I ask again, what do we mean when we say that something is basic —or, if we prefer, that something is dominant? Do we mean that it plays a determining role—or a role that is determined by something else?

We only raise a dust that we cannot settle, we create unnecessary ambiguities—and there are plenty without our creating any—if we are not careful in our thinking to make these distinctions and to express them as clearly as we can when we speak or write—unless, of course, we are unconcerned about whether we are deceiving ourselves as well as others. McLuhan plays fast and loose when he has the audile-tactile senses basic before typographic culture and vision basic after. Clearly, something else is basic, and McLuhan says nothing that even suggests what that something else might be.

Just above the eye-ear conflict quotation above from McLuhan, he says that: "nothing could be more subversive of the Marxian dialectic than the idea that linguistic media shape social development, as much as do the means of production." McLuhan does not give his reasons for this statement. The reasons seem to me fairly clear. The chief one is simply that if you have a process such as that, say, of life on earth, a process in which there are a number of factors, each necessary to the process, you can attribute the whole process, and any superstructure that arises from it, just as truly to any one factor as to any other—or perhaps I should have said, just as falsely. To argue over what factor is most important in such a process is simply to forget the conditions of the process. I do not intend here to suggest that I think the two processes, the productive processes and the linguistic, are equally necessary to life on earth, for if we think of the earth as the original producer, production is certainly necessary to linguistic media in a sense in which linguistic media are not necessary to it. But in attributing production to the earth, we have to be careful; for the earth probably would not produce anything that would sustain life without the sun; and if we try to explain this relation of the sun to the earth, we get into questions of the greatest difficulty and importance, questions we cannot answer finally and completely by any rational procedures. So the process we have assumed above probably does not exist in the form stated, and the reason, the only reason that McLuhan could give for his statement, is in error.

I pass on now to the testimony that I promised above against the notion that psychologists concur in praising Berkeley for the notion that McLuhan attributes to him.

During the year 1964 when McLuhan's *Understanding Media* was first published, the publishing agency of the university where McLuhan was at the time, the University of Toronto Press, published a book, *Human Senses and Perception*, by G. M. Wyburn, Regius Professor of Anatomy in the University of Glasgow; R. W. Pickford, Professor of Psychology in the University of Glasgow; R. J. Hirst, Professor of Logic in the University of Glasgow. In Part II of the book where Pickford deals with perception of space, size, and distance, we are told that

In man not only is vision the dominant mode of perception, but stereoscopic vision is the predominant way of seeing all external objects. It is surprising what can be achieved with one eye, but it can never compete effectively with stereoscopic binocular vision.[18]

Again,

Man's perception of space is dominated by vision, but the localization of sounds and orientation by the direction of sounds are very important. Here

18. G. M. Wyburn, ed., *Human Senses and Perception* (Toronto: Univ. of Toronto Press, 1964), p. 155.

we have the same general factors as in vision. . . . As in vision, the two outstanding factors in the localization of sounds are connected with the two sense organs being separated in space.[19]

The first U.S.A. edition of *The Gutenberg Galaxy* was published in 1965, the first edition of *Understanding Media* in 1964. The first U.S.A. edition of *The Gutenberg Galaxy*, since it was published in 1965, could have taken notice of the testimony in *Human Senses and Perception*, since the latter was published in 1964. This may not have been possible for the first edition of *Understanding Media*, since it and *Human Senses and Perception* were both published in 1964. The paperback edition of *Understanding Media*, since it was first published in 1965, could have taken notice of this testimony, both in the text and in the Bibliography. No notice of it is taken in either.

Now if I use McLuhan's method, I have to rub in the points I am making here. First, McLuhan talks a great deal about the immediacy and universality of information in the electronic age which we are entering. In this age, "automation forces not only industry and town planners, but government and even education, to come into some relation to social facts." But better-authenticated facts, let us hope, than those that Mc-Luhan gives us. Twice, he tells us, Louis Pasteur was thrown out of the medical profession (UM 202, 329).[20] Pasteur was never in the medical profession. His work was of crucial importance to that profession and caused great controversy in it, and Pasteur was the object of most severe criticism by members of the profession; but, as I have said, he was never in it. "There is no room," McLuhan tells us, "for witless assumptions and subliminal factors" in the electronic age, and "electric speed-up requires complete knowledge of ultimate effects" (UM 355). Knowing and not guessing is becoming of the greatest importance.

But somehow McLuhan, despite the current immediacy and univer-sality of information which he tells us repeatedly is actually here, some-how McLuhan missed knowledge of the book *Human Senses and Per-ception* from which we have quoted above, a book published so nearby that he might almost have smelled and touched it, even if he did not see it, and become aware of it as a publication of the University Press where

19. Ibid., p. 164.
20. I am of course not an expert on the life of Pasteur or on any other of the many subjects I discuss in this book. I depend on experts, and where they fail me, I lose my case. No one of my encyclopedias—Britannica, Americana, Collier's—confirms McLuhan, nor does any of the books on Pasteur that I have been able to consult.

he was and of its importance to his arguments concerning sense perception.

If I use McLuhan's method, I have to go further in the rubbing in. A complete list of the authors that McLuhan mentions, and scolds for missing, or not noticing, or not being aware of pertinent information which, if they had been up to their job, they would not have missed and would have taken fully into account—a complete list of such authors mentioned by McLuhan would not be a short one. Among those he mentions for this reason in *Understanding Media* are Plato (49), Arnold Toynbee (18, 19), Northcote Parkinson (263), Daniel Boorstin (52), Lewis Mumford (147), Oswald Spengler (110, 112), Henri Bergson (244), Theodore White (329), Thomas A. Edison (277), Paul Lazarsfeld (297, 298), Mircea Eliade (155), John Donne (340), David Hume (85), Immanuel Kant (85), Julien Benda (37), Raymond Burr of Perry Mason fame (312), our "cultural historians" (322), our "political scientists" (323), and I do not know how many others that I may have missed.

One final point about McLuhan's reliance on Bishop Berkeley's *New Theory of Vision*, his use of quotations to support his reliance—and his failure to use, from the same source, quotations that show his reliance on Berkeley to be absurd. In the *New Theory* Berkeley clearly holds that there is no visual perception of a third dimension. On this one point, and only on this one, McLuhan and Berkeley are in agreement. McLuhan was in the same bog that Berkeley was in when he, McLuhan, wrote the following passage, trying to follow Berkeley and only getting deeper in the bog, as Berkeley did: "The illusion of the third dimension is discussed at length in E. H. Gombrich's *Art and Illusion*. Far from being a normal mode of human vision, three-dimensional perspective is a conventionally acquired mode of seeing, as much acquired as is the means of recognizing the letters of the alphabet, or of following chronological narrative" (GG 16). First, "the illusion of the third dimension" is a highly ambiguous expression. It can be taken as meaning that a third dimension is seen, but does not exist, that what is seen as a third dimension is not there to be seen and is only an illusion. This is to say that space is two-dimensional. Nobody holds this view, not even Berkeley. It can be taken as saying that while a third dimension may exist, its existence cannot be established by either sight or touch, taken either together or separately. It can be taken as in Berkeley as meaning that vision is strictly two-dimensional, that the "seeing" of a third dimension does not occur for the simple reason that there is no such dimension in vision

—that the conviction of seeing arises from the constant association in time of the seeing and touching of an object that one has to move toward in order to touch. It can be taken as designating perhaps the most difficult problem the artist has when he tries to paint "what he sees." The artist, whoever he is, wherever he is, according to Gombrich—and I see no reason for doubting what he says—grows up in and works in a tradition. According to Gombrich, "no artist can copy what he sees." His book is an extremely interesting and informative variation on this theme. Let Gombrich speak:

It lies in the nature of this problem that it would need a disproportionate number of illustrations merely to show vast numbers of Egyptian servant figures, Chinese bamboo paintings, Byzantine madonnas, Gothic angels, or Baroque putti, in order to prove what an attentive look at museums and art books will confirm—how narrow is the range and how subtle are the variations within which the craftsmen and artists of the past created their masterpieces. *For the real purpose of this book is not to describe but to explain the reasons for the unexpected difficulty which artists encountered who clearly wanted to make their images look like nature* [my italics].[21]

What was the difficulty? Was it that illusion is involved in the sense that there is, as Bishop Berkeley held, no third dimension in visual space and that the illusion of three-dimensional visual space created by the sense of touch in temporal but not spatial association with the visual sense—again as in Berkeley—gave the artist problems almost beyond solution, not only as to what he saw but as to how he could represent truly what he saw? Or was it that even though vision is three-dimensional and perspective therefore genuinely visual, contrary to Berkeley, the artist's problems were still of the greatest difficulty, that to proceed at all he had to adopt some principles that seemed to him to be in accord with what he wanted to do, that his principles would tend to become conventions, and that in the absence of exact knowledge of what he saw and how to represent truly what he saw, his principles would give him a style, a tradition, different from that of others who grew up in different traditions and followed different principles? I believe Gombrich in his *Art and Illusion* is concerned mainly with the second of these two questions.

I come now to the real point. The statement that McLuhan makes that "three-dimensional perspective is a conventionally acquired mode of seeing" while clearly true in the sense that convention enters into the

21. E. H. Gombrich, *Art and Illusion* (New York: Pantheon, 1960), p. xiii.

way artists handle perspective and in this sense compatible with the argument of Gombrich in his *Art and Illusion*, if taken in the sense of Berkeley, that of denying the reality of perspective in vision, is not compatible with Gombrich or with the quotation from *Human Senses and Perception* that I have given above. It would be difficult, if at all possible, to assert the reality of perspective in vision more clearly than in the following quotation from Gombrich: "Now perspective may be a difficult skill, but its basis, as has been stated, rests on a simple and incontrovertible fact of experience, the fact that we cannot look around a corner." [22]

We should be grateful for Marshall McLuhan's two books, *The Gutenberg Galaxy* and *Understanding Media*. They exemplify basic problems in the intellectual world today. They bring together errors of kinds that are widely scattered in much of the writing of our time and, in giving examples, make identification of similar errors a task not so great as to be completely beyond accomplishment. The present chapter would be enough ordinarily to dispose of two books such as McLuhan's. But McLuhanism is far more significant of our time than, say, Bishop Berkeley's tar water, also a universal remedy, was of its time. McLuhanism has been taken to heart by industrial institutions—IBM, General Electric, and Bell Telephone among them—as well as by a host of intellectuals. And while the charms of McLuhanism have now faded, it is, like the Marxism which long ago became old hat, still a power in the land. I proceed with further examination in my next chapter.

22. Ibid., p. 250.

CHAPTER VI

McLuhan Lost and Found

We can, if we choose, think things out before we put them
out

McLUHAN, *Understanding Media*

I shall examine now the cryptic saying "The Medium Is the Message,"
a dictum which McLuhan makes the title of the first chapter of *Understanding Media*, and which he presents as his main thesis. This language
baffled some reviewers, and McLuhan, to help the reader, explains in an
introduction to the paperback edition of 1965, the edition I am using,
that by this saying, "the medium is the message," he means that "any
technology gradually creates a totally new human environment." The
words "any" and "totally" and "new" may cause the critic to wonder,
but if loosely considered, there is nothing in this thesis to boggle over.
Before going further we have to ask how this proposition squares with
the proposition that modes of communication determine cultures. The
answer obviously is that it does not.

Technologies certainly do tend to suggest and, by suggesting, to
stimulate human beings to generate new technologies or add to existing
technologies. The use of a stone with a sharp edge to cut may lead to the
idea that a stone that does not have a sharp edge may be so chipped by
another stone as to give it one; and the use by the hand and arm of such
a stone may lead to the idea that the use of the stone may be more
effective with a handle; and when this process starts it can continue,
increment by increment, until it joins with other processes, started in a
similar way, that also develop little by little until we have modern
cutting implements and machines. McLuhan also tells us that "a new
medium [technology] is never an addition to an old one." [1] In saying
this, McLuhan creates a problem. He leaves us no way of escape from
boggling with him over his definition of a technology. If we take
McLuhan seriously, the statement just quoted forces us to ask, What is

1. *Understanding Media* (UM), p. 174.

a technology? Is the first use of a sharp-edged stone to cut with a technology or the beginning of a technology? I do not like to have to discuss this question, since I cannot imagine any less fruitful way of spending one's time. But really, if McLuhan is to be taken seriously, it is necessary to know what he means when he first says "the medium is the message," then says he means by this that "any technology gradually creates a totally new human environment." I repeat, I do not like to be forced into what may appear to be a quibble over the question whether one or many technologies are involved in the sequence. If, as McLuhan says in the last quotation from him above, "a new medium [technology] is never an addition to an old one," we have a real problem in distinguishing old technologies with their additions from new technologies. I use McLuhan's word "gradual" to designate the sequence or additions from sharp-edged rock to stone axe, to iron axe, to steel axe, with concomitant development of other sharp-edged cutting tools and weapons on to the multitudinous kinds of cutting implements and machines of today. We may say all of this happened "gradually," but we certainly do not mean "gradually" in the sense of changes so minute that human beings cannot distinguish them. There must have been many small but perceptible changes and some large ones. If McLuhan holds that all this proliferation of cutting apparatus constitutes just one technology, I shall not quarrel with his definition; but I shall then want to know how he defines a "new" technology. And if he answers that the development of the hammer or the wheel is the development of a new technology, I shall remind him of implements that combine the cutting edge with the hammer and the cutting edge with the wheel, and these and many other such combinations exist in old implements as well as in highly complicated forms in modern machinery. Furthermore, no metal instruments or machines could exist as these do today without metal-working technologies that have developed "gradually," as McLuhan says, out of primitive technologies. There is no such thing in our time as an absolutely new technology that does not use materials and processes from old technologies and that is not in the strictest possible sense an addition to or subsumption of that which previously existed.

Another of the errors that McLuhan makes is that typographic culture and literacy have brought into being the division of labor, the analysis of jobs, physical or mental, into parts, the arranging of the parts in linear sequences, the handling of the parts one by one in linear sequence; and that these have had vast subliminal effects of kinds hitherto unnoticed, especially in the way of altering sense ratios. As to the division of labor, both Adam Smith and Karl Marx, as well as many others who have thought on this subject, recognized the tremendous increases in productivity that the division of labor made possible; and both discussed what they considered the ill effects of this division on human beings in making them, as they supposed, like machines. Neither considered whether they had been more like animals previously and whether one of the effects of machines could be to take them one stage further toward becoming more fully human. Granted, machines may deaden human perceptions, but for those human beings who have minds, they may sharpen them. They may also have other effects which I shall discuss later.

One has only to have really read, and not merely have glanced over, Adam Smith's description of pin making by hand in the third paragraph of Chapter 1, Book I, of his *Wealth of Nations* to know that the part-by-part, one-thing-after-another process was not introduced by typographic culture and the ensuing literacy, that it had been in all crafts from the earliest times. It is, indeed, not as ancient as walking itself, but it is strictly comparable; and in walking I assume McLuhan does as other people generally do: takes one step after another if he does not ride or fly or hop. If he hops, he does so in the linear sequence to which he attributes vast subliminal effects; and even if he flies or rides, he passes points, one after another, in linear sequence from where he starts to where he goes. There are few things that one can do and not do in sequence. And if the "linear" is insisted on, and the linear is defined as straight, and this threatens to cause us trouble, McLuhan himself gets us out of this difficulty. For there certainly is in all these instances, and far more that we could name, repetition of movement. And we need not boggle over whether the movement is in a straight line since McLuhan tells us, "Any creature in motion is a wheel *in that repetition of motion* [my italics] has a cyclic and circular principle in it." [2]

It is true, of course, reading is a process in which one thing is taken up after another, and the more carefully this is done, the more closely the process is one of taking up parts in sequence. But all this was true before printing when manuscripts were read as well as afterward when printing provided reading materials. Printing did not introduce the part-by-part consideration, the left-to-right reading and the strict linear sequence to which McLuhan attributes vast subliminal effects. Printing has certainly had effects, almost certainly some subliminal effects, but almost equally

2. *The Gutenberg Galaxy* (GG), p. 44.

certainly effects widely different from as well as the same as some attributed by McLuhan to it. The very facts that the alphabet is a very small number of symbols, that it can be easily memorized, that the symbols are meaningless, that the sounds assigned to them were assigned entirely by gradually formed custom, that these sounds vary from time to time and place to place, could have tremendous effects, but in a direction entirely different from that to which McLuhan points. No one who knows anything about the alphabet wastes time considering any alleged present-day meanings of the shapes of the individual characters or the sounds given to them. The fact that combinations of these characters have come by custom to be used as signs for noises, that as noises again the combinations have no intrinsic meanings but only meanings assigned to them by custom—all this removes the necessity for an enormous amount of memorizing, such as is necessary in writing and reading manuscripts in Chinese characters. One of the great consequences of this economy is that time spent in memorizing material of perhaps limited intellectual value is available for thought about meanings and relations among meanings, and—not merely incidentally—about the improvement of man's estate on earth. It is, I grant, highly probable, as McLuhan holds, that a text in Chinese characters tends to force thinking that a text in Roman characters does not require. But thought that is directed by characters that have many and intricate meanings tends to be bound by these meanings, whereas thought is relatively free that is directed by characters—and here "characters" includes words as well as the alphabet—to which one is free to assign whatever meanings he pleases, limited only by such considerations as that if one wishes to communicate one cannot assign totally new meanings to all the characters he uses.

One has never really thought about language if one is unaware of the extreme ambiguities in language entirely aside from the question of the physical forms in which it may be expressed. In pictorial and other closely related forms of writing before the alphabet, these ambiguities were in writing as well as in speech. The main effect of the alphabet and printing was to shift the ambiguities from the physical form of the word as recorded to a form that in itself had no meaning whatever and thus to release time, energy, intelligence for the consideration of meaning with as little reference as possible to the physical form of its expression.

Many other questions might be raised about the proposition that "any technology gradually creates a totally new human environment." Movable type was invented and used to a small extent in China in the eleventh century. Printing from wood blocks dates from an earlier time, but just when is not known. It can be said, of course, and McLuhan says, that movable type could not be used successfully in China because the Chinese language was written in ideographs, and to make type of these and to set such type constituted, at the time, an apparently insuperable obstacle. To say this, however, is simply to admit that there may be cultural obstacles that prevent technologies from being developed beyond certain levels and in more than certain limited ways. And this is simply to say that the generalization "any technology gradually creates a totally new human environment" is false.

While McLuhan leaves himself in this state of self-contradiction, I will go on and say, it is not inconceivable that if the Chinese had wanted to do so, they could have adopted the Roman alphabet, just as the West generally did, and could have gone ahead with the development of printing from movable type. McLuhan comes around to this position in the suggestion that he makes several times that societies can determine, of the technologies available to them, which they will use. He would have saved himself this running to one position, then to another, if he had thought seriously and shaped properly his generalization "any technology gradually creates a totally new human environment" before he made it. There is no room whatever for doubt that the Chinese were perfectly capable of ignoring or removing any obstacles to the use of movable type if enough of them had wanted to do so.

Furthermore, we could have here the answer, as far as an answer is possible, to the question that McLuhan asks: "Is there an instance of any culture that understood the technology that sustained its structure and was prepared to keep it that way?" (UM 93). Such evidence as the Chinese Emperor Chien Lung's rejection of the British proposal of trade made by Lord Macartney's mission in 1793, on the ground that the Chinese had all they wanted, points toward the Chinese as an instance for a long time. But they certainly were not prepared always to keep their culture as it was; and I believe we can be sure no people on earth ever has been. McLuhan's question suggests the possibility of a permanently static condition of a permanently existing culture. There are good reasons for believing that there is no such possibility; and Professor McLuhan's own assertion that "change has become the only constant in our lives" (UM 220) may be cited in support of this belief, but it goes to such an extreme that there is room for doubt whether it says anything at all. Just how anyone can know that change is the only constant is a proposition that needs explaining, and those who make it never explain. It cannot be explained. For if one knows only change, one contradicts one's self if one then adds constancy of change to one's knowledge. And the same is true of constancy. The two terms are really reciprocal in nature. One cannot know change by itself, and one cannot know constancy by itself. And one cannot know either except in the actual events and processes of nature and reason.

Let us move on. I quote below Professor McLuhan's definitions of hot and cold media, and I ask the reader to consider our discussion above in the light of these definitions. *Understanding Media* is a book and is printed in what McLuhan in this passage calls "the phonetic alphabet," and is, in his definition, a hot medium. A hot medium, as the reader will see, is defined by McLuhan as one that does not encourage examination of the terms in which it is expressed, and any filling in to see whether there are any meanings that make sense and, if so, what these are. Why then, have we done the examining, the filling in of assertions in *Understanding Media* that we have done? The reader should consider whether a process somewhat like that in which we have engaged is necessary to understanding, and whether, in the absence of some such process, one is really reading or not rather undergoing a process somewhat like that of hypnosis. McLuhan holds that reading—by which he means superficial reading, merely following the lines of print and accepting what is said without question—tends to have hypnotic effects. On this, I agree with him. The ease of reading printed matter, he argues, and I think rightly, tends with many readers, perhaps most, to encourage reading as rapidly as possible without stopping to think, to ask questions; and the rapid and regular movement of the eye along lines of type from left to right and back again tends to induce hypnosis. The effect of reading manuscripts was, in his view, entirely different. The alphabet used in manuscripts was the same as that used in print, and the arrangement in lines from left to right was the same; but letters were written and lines made by hand, and both had the irregular characteristics of work done by hand. There was in manuscripts little standardization of spelling, much use of abbreviations, which also were not standardized, much running of words together. Manuscripts were usually read aloud, even if there was only one auditor—the reader. Reading of manuscripts was therefore of necessity an activity that required stopping to think. McLuhan makes all these points, and I do not know of any good reasons for disagreeing with him on them—except—and this exception is a large one—that the details of his argument can be used against as well as for his conclusion.

Suppose one has before one a text that one has reason to believe is of very great importance, a text that gives instructions on which, say, the saving of lives depends, and time is limited. The instructions, one knows in advance, are complicated. For some reason or other the text is in a secret code, and the code has to be solved before the instructions can be made available in ordinary language. Obviously, time has to be spent first in solving the code and putting the text in ordinary language. McLuhan is really saying that manuscripts presented for their readers problems closely comparable to those of messages in secret codes, and that struggling with the codes helps to understand the message even after it has been put in ordinary language. One may grant that the intellectual work that has to be done in the solving of secret codes has high value as intellectual discipline, as training of the mind. One may not only grant this, but one may insist that discipline of this kind is necessary to intellectual development. And one may hold that no greater mistake can be made than to assume that ordinary language does not contain problems which, if they are to be understood, require study just as secret codes do. One may hold that this kind of study has in it far greater intellectual value, both as discipline and as acquisition of knowledge and understanding, than any study of secret codes can have, that, in fact, the study of secret codes and learning from them ends where the real problems begin. If this argument is sound, and it certainly has more weight than McLuhan's has, it follows that printed materials constituted a great improvement over manuscripts on precisely those grounds on which McLuhan regards them unfavorably.

Still, as to some of the effects of literacy, I believe we have to grant that McLuhan is not entirely wrong. Much of what is called reading today is not real reading. Unfortunately, we have no two words, one for the "reading" that has effects somewhat like that of hypnosis, the other for the reading that is a demonstrably serious approach to understanding. It would be possible to set up psychological tests that would clearly distinguish these two kinds of "reading." But adequate tests could not be set up by anyone who did not already understand the differences, and there is today very little of this understanding. McLuhan is right, I think, in saying as he does that too many of us have been interested in the cultivation of speed and power whereas what we have needed has been the cultivation of understanding.

Once one understands, or even begins to understand, this problem, one understands that real reading is an absolute necessity to any intellectual life that is not more rather than less a matter of self-deception to those who engage in it. Try as hard as we can, it is highly probable that none of us will ever escape some measure of self-deception. But this is no reason for not trying.

I now give McLuhan's definitions of hot and cold media:

A hot medium is one that extends one single sense in "high definition." High definition is the state of being well filled with data. A photograph is, visually, "high definition." A cartoon is "low definition," simply because very little visual information is provided. . . . hot media do not leave so much to be filled in or completed by the audience. Hot media are, there-fore, low in participation, and cool media are high in participation or com-pletion by the audience [UM 22–23].

The first sentence in this definition suggests that there is hypnotic power in McLuhan's hot media. The possibility that there is such power is worth investigating. But I have, I believe, demonstrated above, in the discussion in which I have engaged, that reading printed matter, which in McLuhan's definition is hot, can, contrary to McLuhan, be *high* rather than *low* in participation, and, most important, that this is nec-essarily so if the reading is real. This is, I repeat, the only form of real reading. The other form is like a form of hypnosis. McLuhan himself grants that reading in depth, that is, reading that is high in participation, can occur, but he has it occurring only with paperbacks:

The paperback reader has discovered that he can enjoy Aristotle or Con-fucius by simply slowing down. The old literate habit of racing ahead on uniform lines of print yielded suddenly to depth reading. Reading in depth is, of course, not proper to the printed word as such. Depth probing of words and language is a normal feature of oral and manuscript cultures, rather than of print [UM 325].

If we are prepared to believe that the binding of a book in paper rather than in cloth-covered, heavily pressed cardboard can make a cool medium out of a hot one, we are, I would say, already in that state, somewhat like hypnosis, that one kind of "reading" induces. It happens that I have read and used the McGraw-Hill paperback edition of 1965 of *Understanding Media* and the University of Toronto Press paperback edition of 1965 of *The Gutenberg Galaxy;* and if I accepted McLuhan I would have to hold that because of their paperbacks, these editions are "cool"—and that this explains my stopping to ask questions and to give or suggest what seem to me reasonable answers to them; and that if I had read and used only the hardback, clothbound editions, I would not have done this. I consider this view so patently absurd that no comment could make its utter absurdity more clear. And therefore I make no comment beyond this on it.

McLuhan's assertion, in the passage just quoted, that "reading in depth is, of course, not proper to the printed word as such," is his conclusion from his discussion of the differences between manuscripts and printed materials. I have already shown that the arguments made to support this conclusion can be made to show that it, also, is absurd.

When a person first sees the cryptic language in which the basic thesis of *Understanding Media* is stated, "the medium is the message," he is bound to wonder, What is meant by that? We have already given Professor McLuhan's answer to this question and found it filled with ambiguity. Professor McLuhan could have written and rewritten, he could have tried as hard as he pleased to make a more careful, a "more highly defined" statement, and he could never have eliminated all ambiguity. I find myself, despite my conviction that perfectly un-ambiguous statement cannot be achieved, rewriting many of Professor McLuhan's sentences in order to make what seems to me sense out of them, and I do not always know at first why they seem to me as they stand not to make sense. I have to examine them to find out.

Here, for instance, are two that, with what appears to me the nonsense left out or repaired, seem to me true and important: "Our education has long ago acquired the fragmentary and piecemeal character of a mechanism. It is now under increasing pressure to acquire the depth and interrelation that are indispensable in the all-at-once world of electric organization" (UM 357). First, I agree our education has acquired a fragmentary and piecemeal character, and I consider this a matter of very great importance. But a mechanism is not of a piecemeal character, except perhaps in its relations to other mechanisms. The very idea and the actual fact of a mechanism is that of an object with parts so related, and only parts so related, that they work together with a minimum of conflict and friction. The universe in Newtonian doctrine is a mecha-nism. There is nothing fragmentary or piecemeal about it. A really well-designed mechanism is in this respect so much like McLuhan's world village in the smoothness of its operation and total absence of conflict and friction as to make one wonder how he can regard the first with extreme distaste and the second with unadulterated admiration. I am not saying there are no crucially important differences between a "world village" and a "mechanism." I am saying that the characters that Mc-Luhan values most in his world village are so much like those that are really present in mechanisms that I find his attitude toward the latter impossible to explain. As to the second sentence, there is no "increasing pressure" that comes from the conscious and openly expressed convictions of human beings today in the direction indicated. So far as public opinion is concerned, the pressure that has been increasing in the last few years has been for specialization, for piecemeal education, for relevance to the most ignorant person's immediate feelings of need—a relevance that will certainly change and become useless in a world that is changing as rapidly as this one is. There is practically no pressure for education which cultivates depth and interrelation in subjects of central importance that will not be out of date and useless within a fairly short time. It is clear, I believe, that Professor McLuhan intends to urge the paramount importance of education in depth and interrelation in subjects that are practically certain to be of continuing importance; and I believe he intends to say there should be increasing pressure from students, public, and educators in this direction; or perhaps that the facts of human experience, even if human beings do not know these facts, are exerting "increasing pressure" toward depth and interrelation. I am in complete sympathy with this intention. I leave out entirely in my rewriting of the two sentences quoted above "the all-at-once world of electric organization." I leave this out because Professor McLuhan seems to mean by these words a world in which, as a consequence of electric transmission speeds and electrical storage and retrieval systems of knowledge, it is possible for everybody to know everything all at once. I do not believe this is possible for anybody, much less for everybody. If we reduce Professor McLuhan's prophecies from the wildest of the utopian to that of a much better world, we still would have the problem of agreement, and avoidance of violent conflicts, over the question what a much better world would be, and especially how to go about getting it. So far as I can see, it is necessary to say at this point that the high and widely varied skills, the specialized knowledge, the general knowledge and wisdom, the willingness to do the very unusual intellectual and moral work necessary to establish and maintain a much better world, despite Professor McLuhan's fervor and ours, simply do not exist, and the prospect that they may exist any time soon is not in sight.

It is in these matters that the intellectual leadership of this time has abdicated from its most important task. McLuhan himself makes an apparently comparable charge when he says:

Nobody in the twentieth century has ever come up with any meaningful definition or discussion of "value." It doesn't work any longer in economics, let alone humanist affairs. It is rather fatuous to insist upon values if you are not prepared to understand how they got there and by what they are now being undermined. The mere moralistic expression of approval or disapproval, preference or detestation, is currently being used in our world as a substitute for observation and a substitute for study. People hope that if they scream loudly enough about "values" then others will mistake them for serious, sensitive souls who have higher and nobler perceptions than ordinary people.[3]

But this charge, while it has some very important truth in it, needs examination to sift the true from the false; and in certain respects it is not compatible with other arguments that McLuhan makes. I point out first the incompatibility. There have been many discussions of value in the twentieth century from two opposed points of view. One of these is the objectivist view that value inheres in objects and actions entirely independently of any notions the observer may have of them. This view is represented in such writings as those of G. E. Moore, Max Scheler, Nicolai Hartmann, W. M. Urban, Eliseo Vivas, and Brand Blanshard. McLuhan himself espouses the objectivist view as I later show him doing when he uses such language as "terrible nihilism." The other of these is the subjectivist view that value does not inhere in objects and actions but is conferred on them entirely by the attitudes and feelings of the observer. This view was most powerfully expressed by David Hume in modern times, and is represented in the twentieth century by a host of writers, among them R. B. Perry, Edward Westermarck, A. J. Ayer, Rudolf Carnap, Bertrand Russell, Philip Noel-Smith, and Charles Stevenson. This classification into objectivists and subjectivists, however, can be misleading in that there are important differences among objectivists and subjectivists, and there have been many writers on value who cannot be clearly classified as either. Value has been a subject of debate for over two thousand years, and is as much so today as ever, probably far more so. It is one of man's perennial problems, and is almost certain to remain one.

Contrary to McLuhan, typographic culture, literacy, has had no homogenizing effects on this debate, no tendency toward "stripping" or "denuding" the individuals who have taken part in this debate of notions peculiar to them. McLuhan argues over and over again that there has been a "stripping" or "denuding" process that makes individuals indistinguishable, that "homogenizes" them. He actually quotes, on the

3. G. E. Stern, ed., *McLuhan: Hot and Cool*, Signet Books (New York: New American Library, 1967), pp. 277–78.

assumption that it supports his argument, the famous passage from John Donne's *Anatomy of the World:*

> 'Tis all in pieces, all coherence gone;
> All just supply, and all Relation:
> Prince, Subject, Father, Son, are things forgot,
> For every man alone thinks he hath got
> To be a Phoenix, *and that then can be*
> *None of that kind, of which he is, but he.*
>   [GG 13]

McLuhan omits the portion I have italicized. Instead of asserting that each individual in society is being made into an atom, indistinguishable from every other individual, this passage asserts the opposite. Instead of the standardization, the equalization that the word "homogenization" suggests—a word that McLuhan uses to designate a process he obviously detests—instead of a fragmenting process that makes the individuals that constitute society indistinguishable, the process actually in operation under typographic culture and literacy has somehow cultivated in each individual characteristics that, at least in his own mind, sharply and clearly distinguish him from every other. While there has been a fragmenting process in society, this process instead of homogenizing as McLuhan holds, has created individuals who consider themselves unique and who in their actions really are so undisciplined, so erratic, so determined each to go his own way, as almost to destroy the possibility of the community, the consensus that is necessary to a peaceful society, not to mention one that is more rather than less just.

The truth in the charge in the quotation above from McLuhan is that which I have suggested when I said above that the intellectual leadership of our time has abdicated from its most important task. It is of the utmost importance that the great debate over the great questions be continued; but it is at the same time necessary that decisions be made and that there be actions on the decisions. If the great debate becomes trivial, a mere threshing of old straw, if it becomes an utterly shallow display of false learning, or, even worse, if it reveals loss of the ability to reason that is the main distinction of man from beast, if it is riddled with non-sequiturs, contradictions, and errors, if it reveals incapacity to learn from the experience of the past and to build on it, the conclusion is no less certain because it is mere tautology that the intellectual activities of man become a source of darkness rather than light. The freedom that is absolutely necessary to the participants in the great debate—if there is to be any debate that is really great—is not a freedom that can stand unlimited abuse. It can be damaged, or even destroyed for a time, by gross misuse just as any other freedom can. The intellectual world is not using its power to criticize and correct abuses of its freedom. The abdication of the intellectuals in this respect has already brought disasters and will bring more until there is a resumption of genuine responsibility for the use of freedom. This abdication has been far worse in the churches and in the universities than elsewhere, for these have been entrusted by society with the cultivation of intellectual leadership. The worst part of this situation is that a type of intellectualism that claims to be rational but is not—a type that denigrates all traditional religion and morality, a type that imagines man is becoming God, has come to be dominant. The natural and inevitable response to the dominance of this type is, as McLuhan suggests, "the cultivation of a backward-looking misanthropy"; but it includes also, as he does not suggest, prophets of false utopias, among them McLuhan himself.

In the absence of the genuine intellectual leadership, which necessarily includes the deepest concern for traditional religious and moral understanding and values, "moral bitterness" becomes, as McLuhan suggests, "a basic technique for endowing the idiot with dignity"; [4] and, he could have added, for others suffering from the same lack of mental competence, moral bitterness along with promises of utopia to followers becomes a great power. Here again I have to point my finger at McLuhan. It is not necessary to read him closely in order to find peepholes that one can look through and see the bitterness in McLuhan, a bitterness that he tries hard but is unable completely to conceal. I confess to sharing this same weakness, and underneath my criticism of McLuhan is a deep sympathy for the purpose, different from that which he anywhere states, that I think he is trying to serve. I cannot, however, put words in McLuhan's mouth and criticize what I think he would say if he had not decided, in my opinion deliberately, to make an intelligence and education tester by means of a superficially attractive argument that was basically false—only to become himself trapped by his argument. The last article in the collection *McLuhan: Hot and Cool*, a transcript of discussion by McLuhan of questions asked him by G. E. Stern, the editor of the volume, is worth close study.

I agree completely with Professor McLuhan that automation makes liberal education mandatory (UM 357), but when I say this, I mean my notion of liberal education, which, I fear, is not at all the same as that of

---

4. Stern, pp. 277–78.

Professor McLuhan. And when McLuhan tells us that "all that we had previously achieved mechanically by great exertion and coordination can now be done electrically without effort" (UM 357), or that "the computer, in short, promises by technology a Pentecostal condition of universal understanding and unity" (UM 80), I am forced to wonder, Does McLuhan really believe what he says?

If we allow ourselves really to think in terms of depth and interrelations, as Professor McLuhan thinks we must do if we are to understand our world—and I agree with him that these are necessary to understanding—we still have to have some knowledge of something other than interrelations in order to have any knowledge of interrelations. Depth, as McLuhan says, also is necessary. The surface certainly does not necessarily show what is beneath. As an instance of interrelations, of breadth that sees facts and principles in their interrelations, I will give a case from personal experience; and I will dwell on it, because it involves far more than at first glance meets the eye. The cryptic language Professor McLuhan uses, "the medium is the message," suggested to me when I first saw it Gertrude Stein's "a rose is a rose is a rose," which she used to puzzle critics and tantalize the public, perhaps also to test their intelligence and education. If one did not know what Gertrude Stein was doing, or did not find out—and as I discovered, finding out, even in a university community, was not easy—one could not establish any relation between "a rose is a rose is a rose" and anything else.

Even Edmund Wilson, the dean of American critics during a large part of this century, in his essay on Gertrude Stein in his collection *Axel's Castle*, gives no clue to what Miss Stein was doing and whether she gave any evidence that even she knew, when she startled the public with the plain truth that "a rose is a rose is a rose." Plato would have understood immediately. He shows this in the *Sophist* when he has the Athenian Stranger say, "And thus we provide a rich feast for tyros, whether young or old; for there is nothing easier than to argue that the one cannot be many, or the many one; and great is their delight in denying that a man is good; for man, they insist, is man and good is good." [5]

One cannot have read much of Hegel and really noticed what he was reading—even if he did not understand it—without getting a clue to the meaning, whether known to Gertrude Stein and intended by her or

5. Plato, *Sophist* 251, in *The Dialogues of Plato*, trans. Jowett (New York: Random House, 1937), II, 259.

not, of "a rose is a rose is a rose." Hegel attributes statements of this kind to the logical law of identity. He not only denies the validity of this law but says, "Utterances after the fashion of this pretended law (A planet is—a planet; Magnetism is—magnetism; Mind is—mind) are, as they deserve to be, reputed silly." [6]

One of the most influential books in the field of ethics published in this century, G. E. Moore's *Principia Ethica,* has as its main thesis the proposition that to say that good is anything other than good is to make ethics into sociology or biology or physics, that is into something other than itself, and further, into something that exists in nature. To do this, in Moore's argument, is to commit the "naturalistic fallacy." Good, says Moore, is good, and only good.

It is not necessary for one to have read Plato or Hegel or Moore to get a clue to the notion that Gertrude Stein was not in this particular case talking utter nonsense, as I think she usually did in her writing. Her roses were the bait she used, just as McLuhan's oracular utterances are the bait he uses. One has only to know a little of the history of atomic theory and its implications for sense perception as discussed by such men as John Locke, Bishop Berkeley, and David Hume to know that the assertion that a quality belongs to a subject as in, say, the propositions "the rose is red," or "the grass is green," is not validated by modern science. In modern science, as should be perfectly clear from our quotations from Einstein, Galileo, Newton and others, as well as from our earlier quotations from Berkeley, a rose is a rose is a rose, and red is red is red, and how the subject and the adjective, the rose and the red get together, and how the rose is seen as red is one of the mysteries that modern science and modern philosophy have not yet explained.

Alfred North Whitehead celebrates this mystery in his *Science and the Modern World* in a passage that has been quoted so often everyone should know of this mystery by now:

... the mind in apprehending also experiences sensations which, properly speaking, are qualities of the mind alone. These sensations are projected by the mind so as to clothe appropriate bodies in external nature. Thus the bodies are perceived as with qualities which in reality do not belong to them, qualities which in fact are purely the offspring of the mind. Thus nature gets credit which should in truth be reserved for ourselves: the rose for its scent: the nightingale for his song: and the sun for his radiance. The poets are entirely mistaken. They should address their lyrics to themselves,

6. G. W. F. Hegel, *The Logic of Hegel,* trans. W. Wallace (Oxford, [1892] 1931), p. 214.

and should turn them into odes of self-congratulation on the excellency of the human mind. Nature is a dull affair, soundless, scentless, colourless; merely the hurrying of material, endlessly, meaninglessly.[7]

I sat in a university audience many years ago and witnessed the mystification of the audience, including myself, by Miss Stein's chant of the rose. I did not learn in any of my many conversations that Miss Stein probably was talking deliberately and knowingly about the ancient problem of predication, the problem of the subject-predicate mode of speech, one of the sources of a seemingly ineradicable ambiguity in language, a problem that Whitehead and others were at that very time advertising to a public, including a public that bore all the symbols of learning, without having any perceptible effects.

Why this failure of perceptible effects?

One should not have to have the actual experience of being in a mob in which everyone is shouting, including one's self, in order to know that under such conditions mere noise is all that is likely to be heard. The voices that shout today on the air, in newspapers and other periodicals, and in books, have made hearing and thinking about what is heard, contemplation, assimilation, and integration of what is heard almost impossible.

I turn now to the question of the all-at-once awareness of everything that Professor McLuhan several times suggests that the computer is bringing. I propose in the following a simple and easy test of the computer in this respect.

In Chapter I above I summarize Edmund Burke's *Vindication of Natural Society*, a work which, if the people of its time had been able to see things as what they are, would have been seen as a hilarious as well as deeply disturbing and highly illuminating satire of the most advanced, the "far out" thought of that time. And if we in our reading of the writings that we have inherited from the past were able to understand these writings, we would be far more aware than we are of the significance of these writings to our time. Marshall McLuhan says in *The Gutenberg Galaxy*, and especially in *Understanding Media*, a great deal about what he seems to imagine to be a universal awareness that the computer has brought or is bringing to human beings. Now I do not believe that the great achievement illustrated by the computer is made any greater by attributing to it powers it does not have, such as the awareness that may characterize human minds. I shall propose here a

7. A. N. Whitehead, *Science and the Modern World* (New York: Macmillan, [1925] 1948), p. 80.

test of the "awareness" of the computer in comparison with that which the human mind may achieve. The test I shall propose is crude, and I am sure others better acquainted with the computer—and better acquainted than I am with the nature of the awareness of the human mind—can propose better tests.

Everyone with any elementary acquaintance with the computer knows that it has a power comparable to that of the human memory, and that this power may be more like the operations of the human mind than those operations of machines that simulate human sight and touch are like the actual sight and touch experiences of human minds. The test I shall propose raises the question whether the computer as now developed can go as far with a certain problem as the human mind can now go.

Here is the test I propose.

I propose that the text of Edmund Burke's *Vindication of Natural Society* be fed into a computer and then the computer be asked to identify in this text and bring out any passages suggested by Marshall McLuhan's proposition, The medium is the message. Here is the passage in Burke's *Vindication* that McLuhan's proposition suggested to me: "the thing, the thing itself is the abuse." [8] It is not what governments do, not the "content" of their actions, but it is the mere fact of their existence and action that is, in Burke's satire, the abuse. Burke says this of governments just as McLuhan says the medium is the message of technologies. The two sayings are exact parallels. The only difference is that McLuhan makes his statement with a straight face, whereas Burke makes his satirically.

I believe that in the present state of the computer, this question cannot be handled; and that no one, not even the most highly skilled and best informed of those working on and with computers, has even the vaguest notion how such information could be derived by the use of a computer.

A comparable problem is that of asking a computer to identify in the *Vindication* text a passage suggested to the mind—the mind that has some depth and a store of more than mere information below the surface of mere awareness—by the passage in Gunnar Myrdal's *An American Dilemma* that expresses the theory of that work:

White prejudice and discrimination keep the Negro low in standards of living, health, education, manners and morals. This, in its turn, gives sup-

8. *Works of Burke,* I, 37.

port to white prejudice. White prejudice and Negro standards thus mutually "cause" each other.[9]

This passage suggests to me the argument, too full to be quoted in its entirety, in Burke's *Vindication*:

The blindness of one part of mankind, cooperating with the frenzy and villainy of the other, has been the real builder of this respectable fabric of political society; and as the blindness of mankind has caused their slavery, in return their state of slavery is made a pretense for keeping them in a state of blindness; for the politician will tell you gravely that their life of servitude disqualifies the greater part of the race of man for a search of truth, and supplies them with no other than mean and insufficient ideas.[10]

But we do not need to look outside the present chapter for test materials. Suppose the texts of Plato, Hegel, G. E. Moore and Alfred North Whitehead fed into a computer. Suppose the computer is then asked to bring out the passages suggested by Gertrude Stein's roses. The computer is not capable of doing anything of this kind in its present stage of development. When it is able to perform such tasks as these, it will be possible to talk of the computer as extending human consciousness, as McLuhan does, without indulging in fantasy and giving impressions that are grossly misleading—so much so as to be socially terribly dangerous if there are no minds around that are able to see and able to identify for the public the grossly misleading character of such talk. The public today is avid for discussion that leads to understanding and reasonable consensus on questions of this kind. The apathy with which the public is so often charged and that to a great extent actually exists could be a consequence of long disgust with public discussion so shallow as to be beneath contempt. The intellectual leadership of the country is not providing discussion that is worth the serious attention of the public.

I take up now the question of the role that McLuhan assigns to morals in relation to technologies. Can we accept this statement of McLuhan's? "Our conventional response to all media, namely it is how they are used that counts, is the numb stance of the technological idiot. For the 'content' of a medium is like the juicy piece of meat carried by the burglar to distract the watchdog of the mind" (UM 18). In this statement, McLuhan says that to be concerned with how, for instance, nuclear fission and fusion are used is to be a "technological idiot." This state-

9. Myrdal, *An American Dilemma* (New York: Harper, 1944), I, 75.
10. *Works of Burke*, I, 48 ff.

ment is, to me, on a par with McLuhan's statement that electric technology is bringing a world of universal Pentecostal understanding and unity in which all we have to do is wish for something, and perhaps push a button or pull a lever, in order to have it.

It is necessary to say again what has been said by others many times in the past to show the nonsense in this statement of McLuhan's. It may be that it would have been better for man to have remained in the condition of the savage, gathering and hunting and fishing to maintain his life; but while this is a question we may contemplate and discuss, it is not one on which a decision is open to us. Decisions that determine the conditions of our lives were made many thousands of years ago. We may be able to reverse or ignore some of these decisions, but how far we can go in doing this is a question not easy to answer. We show little evidence today of being able to ask this question in a way that makes sense, much less to answer it.

The first use of fire, the first use of a stone as a weapon or a tool, the first making of a brush shelter, the first use of a hole, perhaps found in nature, to trap an animal—all these were beginnings of our technologies. We may, of course, speak of them if we please, and as McLuhan does, as extensions of ourselves; but if we begin imagining they are literally so, we simply deceive ourselves. They are no more extensions of ourselves than the world itself is, or than we are of the world. To pile metaphor on metaphor and to reason from metaphors so piled up, without any testing by facts in any except the loosest possible way, is to resort to a type of utterance that has nothing to do with thinking.

There have never been many technologies, if any, primitive or highly developed, that could not be used for vicious as well as for good purposes, as weapons against man as well as means to shorten his physical labor, secure his comfort and his life. Why does McLuhan pick the relatively innocuous photograph for this comment? "If there is, indeed, a terrible nihilism in the photo and a substitution of shadows for substance, then we are surely not the worse for knowing it. The technology of the photo is an extension of our own being and can be withdrawn from circulation like any other technology if we decide that it is virulent" (UM 193). How does McLuhan propose to decide whether anything is virulent? What does virulent mean? In using the term, he has joined those he condemns for using moral ideas, and, so far as his text goes, gives no sign of awareness, that this is what he has done. The expression "terrible nihilism" is an expression of moral condemnation, precisely the kind of expression that, according to McLuhan, only the technological idiot uses. If, says McLuhan in effect, there is something terribly wrong, terribly immoral in the photograph, then we can suppress photography. But, says McLuhan also in effect, for me, McLuhan, to express moral judgments on technologies and propose governing or getting rid of them accordingly is not for me to be a technological idiot. But if you do this, this same thing that I am doing, then you are a technological idiot.

McLuhan condemns without reservation, and he repeats the condemnation over and over, the analytic procedure which has been widely cultivated in the modern world in what is thought to be the rational handling of problems, of breaking a subject down into parts and then dealing with the parts as if one were dealing with the whole subject in all its relations as it exists, and as people have to deal with it, or try to deal with it, in the actual world. McLuhan is certainly right in his condemnation of the procedure that deals with parts as if they were wholes. But McLuhan himself does that which he condemns most severely in others. His whole book, *Understanding Media*, is an exercise in the effort to deal with technologies without considering the obvious moral questions involved in their use. The moral questions are, however, so urgent that, as I have shown in the preceding paragraph, he is unable to ignore them. He is able, however, to create confusion, more and more confusion, in an almost hopelessly difficult subject.

Does analysis have any legitimate part in the consideration of a subject? Of course it has. Technologies can be considered entirely independently of moral problems. But when this is done, moral conclusions cannot be drawn. McLuhan's program calls for him to consider technologies independently of the moral questions involved in their use. But this is not what he does. What he really does is divide moral problems into two kinds in their relations to technologies. One is the kind that is so obvious that we cannot help seeing it, such as that an axe can be used to murder a person as well as to build a house, or nuclear power to destroy or to serve man, and that the first use ought to be discouraged as far as possible and the second encouraged. The other is the kind that is not obvious, that most of us do not and cannot see, and that even if we did see, we might not consider a moral problem. The displacement of the horse by the automobile certainly has given rise to moral problems, but equally certainly was not thought to be one except as it was thought to be a part of human progress, and anything thought to be a part of human progress was thought to be a contribution to morality. Many social scientists today, for instance, are greatly concerned to discover and remove what they think of as the "causes" of criminality and they tend to regard society as the villain because society, according to their theory, allows these "causes" to exist. McLuhan himself subscribes to this theory in one of his moods, but I will not say where, for if the computer can do the job of locating the passage, somebody somewhere should have some incentive to show that the computer can do it. In the effort to do this locating, it would, of course, be to cheat to use the word "society" or to proceed in any way that reduced the locating process to a mechanical-electrical one, for this is not the question at issue. Now let us get back to the supposed villainy of society in allowing the "causes" of criminality to exist. Suppose the "causes" were discovered and removed. Would this be progress? I think it would be; and I would be enthusiastic for this approach, if, after David Hume, I did not regard it as so naive as to be both pitiful and terribly dangerous to both the criminal and society.

Now to tell what the effects of a technology will be before the technology is adopted, to think the technology out before it is tried out as McLuhan suggests, is not an easy thing to do. And whatever notions we may have about causes and who or what is responsible for them, the question of moral effect cannot be avoided, and McLuhan's own statements show this.

McLuhan uses the word "subliminal" to designate an effect to which he gives much attention. According to McLuhan, the alteration of the sense ratio from the dominance of the audile-tactile to the visual by typography or printing was, for the public generally, a subliminal, that is, an unconscious process. He repeats many times in both *The Gutenberg Galaxy* and *Understanding Media* statements asserting the pervasive and dire effects of printing on Western culture, without considering at all the fact that, until the last two centuries or so, the majority, the great majority of the public in the Western world, was illiterate and had no chance whatever to experience any direct subliminal effects from printing. Of course, the illiterate could be affected indirectly and undoubtedly were. There is evidence that printing has had numbing, hypnotic effects in the intellectual world. This book is largely a presentation of such evidence; and this chapter and the preceding chapter can be regarded as evidence of the numbing, hypnotic effect of the type of reading that print induces in McLuhan himself. But we have nothing but McLuhan's repeated assertions to support McLuhan's argument that printing has had numbing, hypnotic effects on the general public. The repeating of assertions is the technique of advertising and publicity, and not of the scholar or the scientist. The general public probably does not, even today, read enough for the numbing, hypnotic effects of rapid reading to be of any importance to it.

A subliminal effect is an effect outside of the area of consciousness. But McLuhan holds that, whether outside or inside the area of consciousness of the artist, this privileged human being, this distinct class with competencies far beyond and above those of ordinary mortals, can protect the public from subliminal effects, and, presumably McLuhan thinks, despite his contempt for moral actions, that this is a good thing to do. McLuhan also holds that

Electromagnetic technology requires utter human docility and quiescence of meditation such as befits an organism that now wears its brain outside its skull and its nerves outside its hide. Man must serve his electric technology with the same servo-mechanistic fidelity with which he served his coracle, his canoe, his typography, and all other extensions of his physical organs. But there is this difference, that previous technologies were partial and fragmentary, and the electric is total and inclusive. *An external consensus or conscience is now as necessary as private consciousness* [UM 57].

I have italicized the last sentence in the quotation to call attention to the word "conscience" that McLuhan smuggles in with this sentence, and I shall use it in connection with the following effort by McLuhan to use Shakespeare to help him build his utopia:

Shakespeare's *As You Like It* provides a good deal to think about. His Forest of Arden is just such a golden world of translated benefits and joblessness as we are now entering via the gate of electric automation.

It is no more than one would expect that Shakespeare should have understood the Forest of Arden as an advance model of the age of automation when all things are translatable into anything else that is desired [UM 58].

What need is there, I now ask, for a conscience in a world in which everybody by mere wishing can get what he wants and in which, presumably, everybody wishes for evil and misery to go away and stay away from everybody, a world from which moral problems have disappeared? What need is there in such a world for artists to protect the public against subliminal or any other effects of technologies, if one can get what one wants by mere wishing, and if one always knows what is good and wishes good for one's self and everyone else?

But somehow the devil is still extant, still around. And the devil, even according to McLuhan's account, is in some technologies, if not all. What can we do about this?

The fact that technologies do interact and spawn new progeny has been a source of wonder over the ages. It need baffle us no longer if we trouble to scrutinize their action. We can if we choose think things out before we put them out. . . . [Technologies] are put out long before they are thought out. In fact, their being put outside us tends to cancel the possibility of their being thought of at all [UM 49].

These quotations call for remarks about books that are not thought out before they are put out, but we pass on. The question of thinking out technologies before they are put out is discussed again toward the end of *Understanding Media:*

The spokesmen of censorious views are typically semiliterate book oriented individuals who have no competence in the grammars of newspaper, or radio, or film, but who look askance at all nonbook media. The simplest question about any psychic aspect even of the book medium, throws these people into a panic of uncertainty. Vehemence of *projection of a single attitude* [my italics] these mistake for moral vigilance. Once these censors become aware that in all cases "the medium is the message" or the basic source of effects, they would turn to suppression of media as such, instead of seeking content control [UM 314].

By "content control" here, McLuhan means (and numerous passages could be cited to show that he intends this and only this as his meaning) the way a technology is used. He is saying here again that if the would-be censors knew what they were doing, they would join him, McLuhan, in the control of technologies or rather their suppression, instead of trying to control their uses. Or is he inviting the incompetents to join him? Is he, after his talk about suppression, backing away from his talk? In any case, he is still holding to his position that the knife, the axe, the wheel, nuclear fission and fusion, and all other such means can be rationally considered only as technologies, that only the "technological idiot" considers how they are used. Here McLuhan engages in that very "projection of a single isolated attitude" which he condemns in "the spokesmen of censorious views," and he is just about as vehement in his projection as it is possible to be. However, despite his vehemence, or perhaps because of the cloudiness that vehemence often generates in those who have it, he never comes to a conclusion on the question he raises about the suppression of technologies. The public is far ahead of him on this. The public in the United States has already made it difficult to establish and maintain some technologies that are used in ways that have adverse effects on the public or any part of it; and the public is currently concerned with exercising more restraint of this kind. The public has also shown deep concern over the helpful and harmful aspects of technologies and has tried to distinguish the two, to curb the harmful without damaging the helpful. One has only to mention the Food and Drug Administration and recently established pollution control agencies to illustrate—inadequately but still it illustrates—this activity.

In parts of his argument, McLuhan clearly tells the reader that the artist can take care of the problem of technologies (UM 65), but beyond a process comparable to that of the laying on of hands, he leaves the reader completely in the dark as to how this is to be done, except to say in effect that if one sees something horrible coming, the mere seeing will overcome the horror. Why, we repeat, if technologies of themselves are leading to the utopia of electric immediacy and universality of understanding and unity, why load artists with any responsibility in connection with them? And if artists choose on their own to bother about technologies because of some peculiar bent and talent that they have, why should anybody bother himself about their bothering?

And of course it has to be asked, if content does not matter, if the content of a book cannot have important effects, if the mere fact of being printed is all that matters, why did McLuhan do the long, hard work that he had to do to write *The Gutenberg Galaxy* and *Understanding Media?* Why could he not put just anything in these books and call them anything and know that, with proper advertising and publicity, they would have the same effect regardless of content? I have, of course, argued in this chapter that McLuhan did not pay as much attention as he should to the content of these books of his—but I have not meant to suggest in my argument that he has not spent an enormous amount of time and labor on them. If his argument is true, he could have saved himself all this.

In his failure to give place, I would say first place, to the question how a technology is most likely to be used and how it is actually used, McLuhan carries far beyond reasonable bounds the truth he states when he says "the medium is the message," or, in other words, that technologies tend to transform societies as well as each other. The truth that he leaves out is by far the most important. This truth is simply, as I have now said many times, that a technology may be used for vicious as well as for good purposes; and I now add that there is a tendency in human beings to abuse technologies. The pollution problem in the United States today is one of the innumerable illustrations of this statement. And the population problem—not just in the United States, but in the world generally—tells us perhaps as clearly as is possible, that even where the effort is made to devote technologies to good purposes, this is not easy to do. An immediate use that appears to be wholly good may in the long run turn out to have created conditions that are not good. McLuhan's urging that thought needs to be comprehensive and accurate is certainly well-founded. But he not only does nothing to help toward the comprehensiveness and accuracy that are needed, he creates confusion that has to be cleared up before the necessary tasks can be attempted.

The effort to control technologies in the interests of human welfare helps to create and maintain the tension between the human tendency toward evil and that toward good. It is only in the making of this effort, and in more than the control of technologies, that human beings become moral beings. To be concerned with how a new or old technology is used is therefore simply one class of the concerns of a moral being.

Thus McLuhan's statement quoted at the beginning of this discussion of McLuhan's notion of the relations of technologies to morals amounts to his saying that to be a moral being is to be a technological idiot; but his implication clearly is that one ought not to be a technological idiot. How he can say or imply an "ought" without having a moral principle that warrants his "ought," I do not know. McLuhan also suggests, but does not say, that technologies ought to be thought out before they are put out. He is obviously avoiding carefully the actual use of the word "ought." But it is there by implication just the same. And since it is there, his obvious meaning is that one ought to be given the best possible chance to be a moral being. So what McLuhan is really saying is that one both ought to be and ought not to be concerned with morals. If it is possible to indulge in greater nonsense than this, I do not know how it can be managed.

McLuhan's argument is further that as a society is transformed by a technology, the transformation becomes visible and "we become what we behold" (UM 19, 45). This, as far as it is simply a repetition of the argument that technologies may have transforming effects on societies, is certainly true. In making this particular argument, McLuhan repeats from Werner Heisenberg's book *The Physicist's Conception of Nature* the story of the Chinese sage Tzu-Gung and the old man. The story is told by Heisenberg with approval of the old man's attitude, and McLuhan joins in this approval. Here is the story:

As Tzu-Gung was traveling through the regions north of the river Han, he saw an old man working in his vegetable garden. He had dug an irrigation ditch. The man would descend into a well, fetch up a vessel of water in his arms and pour it out into the ditch. While his efforts were tremendous the results appeared to be very meager.

Tzu-Gung said, "There is a way whereby you can irrigate a hundred ditches in one day, and whereby you can do much with little effort. Would you not like to hear of it?"

Then the gardener stood up, looked at him and said, "And what would that be?"

Tzu-Gung replied, "You take a wooden lever, weighted at the back and light in front. In this way you can bring up water so quickly that it just gushes out. This is called a draw-well."

Then anger rose up in the old man's face, and he said, "I have heard my teacher say that whoever uses machines does all his work like a machine. He who does his work like a machine grows a heart like a machine, and he who carries the heart of a machine in his breast loses his simplicity. He who has lost his simplicity becomes unsure in the strivings of his soul. Uncertainty in the strivings of the soul is something which does not agree with honest sense. It is not that I do not know of such things; I am ashamed to use them" [UM 63–64].

Now I submit, one may believe in and adopt the old man's way, or he may believe in and adopt the modern scientific way that according to McLuhan is now bringing the utopia of electric immediacy and universality and unity in which to wish is to have; but one cannot believe in and adopt both without creating hopeless confusion. And how anyone can believe in either is a puzzle I will not attempt to solve. Was the old man using, say, something like a five-gallon bucket? Would it have made him feel a lot better to use something like a teaspoon? It is hard for me to escape the conviction that this part of the old man's notion of what should make one ashamed is foolish. And I believe Marshall McLuhan's utopia is equally foolish, except as something by which is to measure human achievement. Strip the alternatives to the use of manpower or the use of the best means that science can provide, and I believe any person who is not bound by some foolish notion will choose the latter. The problem of the best means is not an easy one but it is not beyond better rather worse solutions. McLuhan's comprehensive powers far exceed mine, or at least give the appearance of doing so. He gives the appearance of believing in both the old man's way and the way that leads to his utopia and of adopting both.

I do not see any escape for myself from the view that while technology has given man the opportunity to create grave problems and man has certainly used this opportunity, technology also, more than anything else, has relieved man from a life of unremitting toil, of what amounts to slavery by whatever name it is called. The development of technology appears to have been accompanied by an increase in the "uncertainty in the strivings of the soul," and this, however it came, is one of our great problems today. I believe it came mainly from the dissociation of thought, feeling, and will that occurred in the early work of modern physical science, clearly illustrated by Newton's *Principia*, and since that time widely imitated in social science and the humanities. Aside from the uncertainty in the strivings of the soul and the making of man into a machine, the chief outward effect of the new technologies since the development and wide use of the steam engine has been to substitute power derived from sources such as wood and coal and oil and water for the physical power of human beings.

After all the disagreements with McLuhan that I have expressed, I come to a point of the greatest importance on which, if I understand him, I agree with him. But in agreeing with him on this point, even if I did not say it, I would be implicitly saying that McLuhan does not agree with himself. For the point on which I agree with him is a moral point of the greatest importance. It has to do with the moral effects of technology, and according to McLuhan, again if I understand him, to be greatly concerned with such effects is to be a technological idiot.

It is undoubtedly true that the machine has become one of the major spectacles of our time. The spectacle of the machine, and the human tendency to use anything that saves human labor and that gives men the opportunity to gain power, has led to the transformation of the relatively primitive societies of the Western world into the industrial societies of today. And this spectacle is, at a rapid rate, transforming other societies. This, however, is far from the most important effect of the spectacle of the machine.

I assume that McLuhan picked up from Heisenberg and repeated the quotation that we have repeated above not merely because of the transformation the machine has wrought during the last two hundred years in the outward aspects of the Western world as well as some parts of the East, but rather because of the inward effects this transformation has had—effects that are represented in the old man's concern with "uncertainty in the strivings of the soul." This is the crux of the old man's objection to any improvement in his technology. This can be the only reason that McLuhan quotes the old man. And this is a moral concern. So McLuhan finally joins us in our concern with the moral effects of technologies and we welcome him. Now to the real questions.

Consider for a moment the conditions under which primitive peoples generally live. One of the chief conditions is the rule of custom and habit. This rule could hardly have developed except in a long temporal process in which any strong tendency toward any pattern of conduct became an object of imitation. Since patterns vary so widely among different primitive groups, often having exactly opposite attitudes toward the same conduct and widely different practices on the same subject, either we have to assume that there is no pattern that is really good for all groups and that if lived by would induce peace and justice in and among groups, or we have to assume that even if there is such a pattern, it is either unknown or has no appeal strong enough to secure its adoption. Or we may assume that many, but perhaps not all, human groups have been either unable to discover this pattern, or if able to discover it and actually have discovered it or a part of it, are unwilling or unable to live by it.

Once one becomes conscious of the extreme diversity of conduct among different human groups—of the contrast between, say, the peaceful and relatively just conduct of the Pueblos of New Mexico as described by Ruth Benedict in her *Patterns of Culture* and the horrible conduct of the Aztecs of Mexico in their worship of the god Huitzilopochtli, one cannot sanely reject the idea that some patterns of conduct are better than others and that there may be a pattern which, even if not perfect, is better than any other. The "uncertainty in the strivings of the soul" of which the old man speaks is the uncertainty which arises, produces a tension between the opposite attractions of the old and the new ways, and reflects shattered convictions of better and worse. This tension is essentially a moral tension. And when the animal becoming a human being tries to answer the question this tension raises and succeeds in finding the right answer, he is, as I have said, beginning to become a moral being.

If the intellectual world of this period in human history has not only failed to make any improvements in human knowledge and practice in the field of morals but also has failed catastrophically to understand the great teachers of the past, we cannot rightly attribute this failure to the influence of technologies, unless we assume that man has a flaw in him that deprives him of his freedom in the face of technologies. This is to assume a doctrine of original sin at least as repellent as that of the most predestinarian of the old theologians.

One of the great effects of technologies as they exist today obviously has been, as I have said previously, to release the great majority of human beings, or hold the promise of releasing them, from the necessity of hard physical labor throughout their lives—labor so hard as to be damaging to humanity: "How can he get wisdom that holdeth the plough, and that glorieth in the goad, that driveth oxen, and is occupied in their labors, and whose talk is of bullocks?" [11] There is some evidence that even he can get more of wisdom than some people who spend their lives reading and writing books. Still, I cannot share the enthusiasm that some modern writers express for primitivism. I cannot persuade myself that being infested with, say, hookworm and not knowing it, and resenting, even hating the doctor who wants to cure me, is a good thing. Some primitives, historical and anthropological evidence tells us, may feel resentment on seeing the contrast between their state and the state of the healthy person of civilized society. In this respect, we undoubtedly have many native primitives among us. But many of the real primitives, when they are given the opportunity to rise above primitivism, seize the opportunity and do so. It is hardly possible to overemphasize the part of literacy in this process, first in helping to create the good will and understanding that motivate the civilized man when he tries to help the primitive, and second, in adding to the "magic" which the civilized man commands and the primitive sees him commanding.

McLuhan's *Gutenberg Galaxy* and *Understanding Media* have precisely the distracting effects that McLuhan attributes to concern with the way technologies are used. They take the mind away from the real problems of our time. These two books, insofar as they do not stimulate thought that rejects them on such grounds as I have shown, are "like the juicy piece of meat carried by the burglar to distract the watchdog of the mind" (UM 18). These words of McLuhan's describe perfectly the effect of the two books on minds that do not see their real nature. The quality of most of the attention that the two books have received

11. Ecclesiasticus 38.25.

in the critical world provides little hope for any great intellectual awakening in our time.[12]

McLuhan suggests that the "serious artist" is the one who foresees, in his viscera if not in his consciousness, all possible adverse effects of new technologies and is able to protect the public from them. "To prevent undue wreckage in society, the artist tends now to move from the ivory tower to the control tower of society" (UM 65). For this purpose the work of the artist is "indispensable." This notion might have gained some plausibility if McLuhan had mentioned some "serious artists" on whom there is agreement among other "serious artists" that the ones mentioned are really serious artists, and if he had given some evidence that his "serious artists" foresaw that the steam engine and other new technologies would not only make chattel slavery uneconomic and displace the slave by the machine, but would create a process that involved both wage slavery and the greatest effort the world has ever seen, an effort most seriously made in the United States, to get rid of slavery—but not with any great success, possibly on account

12. R. Rosenthal, *McLuhan: Pro and Con*. This is in my opinion the best collection of essays now available on McLuhan. I have read two others—Stern, *McLuhan: Hot and Cool,* and H. H. Crosby and G. R. Bond, eds., *The McLuhan Explosion* (New York: American Book Co., 1968). *The McLuhan Explosion* is designed to serve the general reader and "students in college Freshman English courses." In my opinion, as the reader of my two chapters on McLuhan will see, the books of McLuhan's that constitute the "explosion" are of negative value, and most college freshmen, even most college instructors, do not have the background necessary to turn this negative into a positive value. *The McLuhan Explosion* includes editorial apparatus such as questions for students to consider. Few of the questions that need to be asked are asked. Many that lead nowhere are asked. A better exhibit, along with McLuhan's two books, of the need for far better general education could hardly be provided. *McLuhan: Hot and Cool* is a much better collection, but not as good as *McLuhan: Pro and Con.* Neither of these two is burdened with an editorial apparatus that is of such low quality as to be worse than useless. None of these three books, nor any of the reviews that I have seen, deal with such basic problems in *The Gutenberg Galaxy* and *Understanding Media* as those dealt with in the three chapters in this book. *The Medium Is the Rear View Mirror: Understanding McLuhan,* by Donald F. Theall, despite its title, is an exceptionally competent examination of McLuhan from a strictly humanistic point of view, developed on a literary basis somewhat comparable to that of McLuhan, but so far as I could see, without his misuse of his sources. In my view, a strictly humanistic point of view, that is, one that excludes theology and religious commitment, while it may be helpful up to a point, is not capable of dealing adequately with McLuhan. For McLuhan is basically a frustrated moralist whose morals stem from a religious commitment. I have suggested this view of McLuhan but have not developed it because doing so would take me too far from the purpose of this book.

of a human propensity to slavery and ignorance concerning the extreme diversity of its forms.

McLuhan's notion that the "serious artist" is the one who can save society from what he imagines to be the wholly baneful subliminal effects of the new technologies could not be taken seriously even if he could show how the "serious artists" could be prevented from showing each other up as not artists, e.g., Whistler vs. Ruskin, William Blake vs. Sir Joshua Reynolds, Leo Tolstoi vs. a long list of the greatest, Jean Jacques Rousseau vs. the arts and sciences generally. These battles among artists are not only amusing, they suggest that it would be difficult, if not impossible, to convince the artists living at any one time who the "serious artists" of that time are. Even McLuhan concurs with the view of Donald McWhinnie, analyst of the radio medium, whom he quotes, that "for most of our lifetime civil war has been raging in the world of art" (UM 48); and McLuhan adds, "Most of this civil war affects us in the depths of our psychic lives . . . since the war is conducted by forces that are extensions and amplifications of our own beings. Indeed, the interplay among media is only another name for this 'civil war' that rages in our society and our psyches." In order to believe that the artist, presented here as a maker of war, is really a maker of peace, as McLuhan also represents him, we have to have better evidence than McLuhan gives us of his part in both roles. Percy Bysshe Shelley tells us in the last sentence of his *Defense of Poetry* that "poets are the unacknowledged legislators of the world." If we believe this, they are already in the control towers of society and have been all along. Are we really to credit our poets with the wars of this century?

One more illustration of the appalling density that one sometimes finds in the work of great artists and critics when one looks. One of the most distressing and at the same time most deeply moving scenes in all literature is that in Shakespeare's *King Lear* when the Duke of Cornwall gouges out one of Gloucester's eyes and, encouraged by his fiendish wife Regan, is about to gouge out the other. A servant, a creature Shakespeare does not bother to give a name—perhaps because he knew very well what he was doing—intervenes and says:

> Hold your hand, my lord:
> I have serv'd you ever since I was a child,
> But better service have I never done you
> Than now to bid you hold.
> [III, vi]

Cornwall, instead of holding his hand, draws his sword on his servant and they fight. The servant wounds Cornwall. Regan seizes Cornwall's sword and runs the servant through from behind. Leo Tolstoi, in his essay on Shakespeare, remarks on these actions:

The Duke of Cornwall tears out one of Gloucester's eyes and stamps on it. Regan says that one eye is still whole and that this healthy eye is laughing at the other eye, and urges the Duke to crush it too. The Duke is about to do so, but *for some reason* [my italics] one of the servants takes Gloucester's part and wounds the Duke. Regan kills the servant.[13]

"*For some reason*," says Tolstoi the critic. Just imagine Tolstoi, one of the world's greatest literary artists looking around for a reason for the servant's action and not finding the reason in Cornwall's action. It is necessary to spell such matters out these days. Tolstoi, in the very act of criticizing Shakespeare for his supposed lack of interest in and understanding of the common people, the nameless, the invisible ones, betrays his own blindness to an action portrayed by Shakespeare, an action as thoroughly admirable as any action could possibly be. One wonders what men like Tolstoi would do if they really were in the control towers of society.

The part of *Understanding Media* that has to do with Tzu-Gung and the old man, except for the problem of "uncertainty in the strivings of the soul," is really just another version of the old argument for primitivism. In one of its last appearances around forty years ago in serious form in the United States, this argument was made by a group known as the Agrarians. The membership was mainly that of a group otherwise known as the Fugitives, most of them poets and critics. The movement was centered in Vanderbilt University in Nashville, Tennessee, and was led by John Crowe Ransom, later of Kenyon College. It was given its best-known expression in a book, *I'll Take My Stand*, by twelve southerners, including John Crowe Ransom, Allan Tate, Donald Davidson, Andrew Nelson Lytle, John Donald Wade, Frank Lawrence Owsley, and Robert Penn Warren. The effect of the Agrarian argument on me was somewhat like that of the effect of the Tar Baby on Brer Rabbit in the story by Joel Chandler Harris. I chose to argue with the Agrarians, but just as Brer Rabbit's paws stuck in the Tar Baby when he hit the Tar Baby, my arguments against the Agrarians ex-

13. L. Tolstoi, "Shakespeare and the Drama," in *Recollections and Essays*, trans. Aylmer Maude, The World's Classics (New York: Oxford, [1937] 1961), p. 323.

posed me to the danger of attaching me to them. McLuhan's arguments are fascinating, and it is easy to get caught by them. But his work is spurious except as evidence of a perennial irrationality and corresponding incapacity for self-examination in human beings, and of the perennail appearance of persons gifted with the mysterious power of getting themselves widely accepted as oracles.

The Southern Agrarians never said so, but their work implicitly committed them to a static society; and their reasons for this commitment, as with McLuhan, had much good in them. Mere speed and power, as they saw, and as I believe McLuhan sees, are not worth seeking. Nor is the reduction of most human relations to a cash nexus necessarily a good thing. McLuhan, as I have suggested previously, is playing with the idea of a static society when he asks: "Is there an instance of any culture that understood the technology that sustained its structure and was prepared to keep it that way?" and when he suggests that the effects of technologies may be thought out and that they may be suppressed if as thought out, they are seen to be "virulent." The static society to which the Southern Agrarians were committed is best suggested perhaps by the view of Thomas Jefferson that the hope of democracy was in the small, independent farmer who lived close to the soil and in whose breast, according to Jefferson, there was a deposit of virtue derived from the soil. This view has genuine appeal to those who have seen the evils, and who have failed to see the good, and the even greater but not unlimited potential for good in industrialism.

The farmer of the Southern Agrarians was modeled on the small farmer of the old South. He was not likely to be a slave owner. At the beginning of the Civil War, three-quarters of the southern white families did not own slaves. In the Southern Agrarian argument, and especially in that part which had to do with "uncertainty in the strivings of the soul," things got just about as complicated as in McLuhan's argument. Somehow the virtue in the breast of the small farmer that he derived from his closeness to the soil also got into the breast of the plantation owner. And the question arose, how did this happen? The Agrarians ignored this question and persons like myself, tainted with skepticism, were left to figure this out for themselves. Since the plantation owner usually rode around horseback to see what was going on, some of us decided that the virtue he derived must flow into him through his horse, though we couldn't answer the question how this could happen. Now McLuhan would not have left a question like this one unanswered. But I think he would have left unconsidered, as most of us did, why we did not see this process working with the Negro, who of all Southerners, was closest to the soil.

The problem of general education is the great problem in the United States and the Western world today. Such problems as "uncertainty in the strivings of the soul," and the use of leisure and of the great power that modern technologies generate cannot be dealt with at all adequately until means of general education that do not now exist are provided. The prospect that the United States will be able to do anything better rather than worse about the world is not good until the United States does something far better about itself.

CHAPTER VII

Babel and Authority

KENT: You have that in your countenance which I would
fain call master. LEAR: What's that? KENT: Authority. . . .
LEAR: Thou hast seen a farmer's dog bark at a beggar? . . .
And the creature run from the cur? There thou might'st
behold the great image of authority; a dog's obeyed in office
King Lear I, iv; IV, vi

The discussion of Marshall McLuhan's two books, *Understanding Media* and *The Gutenberg Galaxy*, in which we have engaged in the preceding two chapters was undertaken, as I have said, to lay a basis for seeing how far Britannica goes in providing answers to the questions we have asked and answered about these books. We are assuming that most people who read either or both will not have at hand the works that are necessary to check McLuhan—say, Berkeley's *New Theory of Vision* and his *Principles of Human Knowledge*, Galileo's *Assayer*, and Newton's *Opticks*. And even if one has them easily at hand, checking takes time, and one does not do this easily if one is not already familiar with them. Such works as these are necessary to the understanding of McLuhan. We are applying our test to Britannica because we know from years of experience with it and other encyclopedias that it is more likely to provide reliable answers to questions such as those that come up in reading McLuhan than any other encyclopedia published in the United States.

We can, of course, not reasonably expect to find in Britannica any help on the question of the misuse of sources such as the several examples we have given in Chapters V and VI. In making this test we have to remember it would be absurd to expect any encyclopedia to answer all the foolish questions that can be asked or correct all the erroneous statements that can be made. If there are any limits on the carelessly considered statements, the gross and misleading exaggerations, the plain errors that human beings can make, as well as the fabrications, no one has ever stated these limits. Writers are of course human beings, and while they may be more careful than others in what they say, they are not always so. It would be beyond all reason to expect Britannica to provide evidence on all the statements that McLuhan makes.

We shall in the following examine Britannica on particular questions that have to do with the subjects Technology, Automation, Rhetoric, Propaganda, Communication, Perception, Perspective, Bishop George Berkeley, Louis Pasteur, and Gertrude Stein.

Let us first look to see what Britannica has to say, if anything, on McLuhan's proposition that "any new technology gradually creates a totally new human environment." Under the word "technology" in Britannica's index there are the following references: see Automation; Engineering; Industrial Revolution, the; Inventions and Discoveries; etc. There is no article "Technology."

We shall begin with Britannica's article "Automation."

There is nothing in the article that bears directly on the quotation above from McLuhan. There is discussion that bears indirectly on it and we shall consider this discussion. The reader may remember the quotations from McLuhan in Chapter V that "the computer, in short, promises by technology a Pentacostal condition of universal understanding and unity," and that "all that we had previously achieved mechanically by great exertion and coordination can now be done electrically without effort." According to McLuhan, the computer, television, and automation will do the job. Here is what Britannica's article "Automation" has to say on this aspect of the subject: "Automation . . . is a way of putting power—usually electrical power—not only at the worker's elbow but also at his mental 'elbow.' It is a multiplier of man's physical and mental ability and in some cases a very large multiplier indeed; it is a unique means of multiplying his range of perception, speed of mental working and powers of co-ordination."

The problem of the use of this power is still the great human problem, just as it was in the days when early man could use a stone either to build a shelter or to bash out the brains of another man. "Automation," the author of Britannica's article tells us, "will not necessarily bring in its wake greater happiness." The author of the article obviously understands that some people can manage so as to clothe and house and feed themselves in ways that leave none of the basic physical needs of life unsatisfied and still be utterly miserable. It has long been known that there is no necessary connection between being rich, well-dressed, well-housed, well-fed, supplied with all the pleasures of life, and being deeply and genuinely happy. And what is true of the individual in this respect has long been known to be true of communities. Britannica's article "Automation" could not be expected to provide us with this ancient knowledge, but the author of the article, knowing the tendency in many quarters to believe that wealth and well-being necessarily go together, shows that he is aware of the ancient knowledge by pointing in the right direction. This is all we could reasonably expect him to do.

Britannica's article "Engineering" is intended only as an introduction to the many long articles on various fields of engineering. The word "technology" does not occur in the article. Since engineering is the application of technologies in practice it would be helpful if this were said. The article "Engineering" is preceded by an article "Engineering (Articles on)" in which around 100 articles on various fields of engineering and related subjects are listed. It would obviously be a waste of space to consider in each of the articles the question of the effects of technology in general. The effects of particular technologies can, of course, be indicated in articles on particular subjects such as, say, the article "Sewage Disposal," where the connection between disease and the proper treatment of sewage is clearly indicated. In recent years it has become obvious that sewage disposal has much wider importance for the environment and information on the subject needs to be added, but the principle that needs to be followed is already illustrated in the article.

The fact that Britannica has broken the subject Engineering down into so many pieces—something which of course Britannica had to do in one way or another, except that in a newly planned encyclopedia the pieces do not have to be scattered throughout many volumes—creates problems to which Britannica has not given adequate attention. For instance, while engineering is dealt with in many articles, there is no article "Sanitary Engineering." There are, however, articles on divisions of Sanitary Engineering, and in its article "Engineering (Articles on)" Britannica lists these articles: "Incinerator"; "Plumbing"; "Pollution, Environmental"; "Sewage Disposal"; "Water Supply and Purification." But suppose one wants a survey of what sanitary engineering has done to get rid of epidemic diseases. This could be dealt with in the separate articles just listed or in the article "Epidemiology," but, except in the most cursory way, it is not adequately done anywhere. And since sanitary engineering has aspects of both an engineering and health-protecting nature, and these are not discussed elsewhere, the question arises whether the omission of these aspects can be justified. The effects of sanitary engineering certainly belong with the treatment of sanitary engineering as well as with the treatment of epidemiology. In epidemiology the effects have medical and health connections. In engineering the effects have technical physical and other aspects that, if the engineering is to be understood, have to be connected with the medical aspects and the purpose of creating and maintaining an environment in which human beings can be healthy.

There is an article "Sanitation, Military" in Britannica which one may find after consulting numerous articles and following numerous cross references; but while the military has made important contributions to sanitation, many contributions of importance have been made by other agencies. One will have to search long to find much more than I have indicated above, and even after long searching, one cannot be sure one has found the more important information on sanitary engineering that is in Britannica. This is, of course, an indexing problem. Britannica handles it very badly. Many readers probably never find information they want that is in the set simply because the indexing is so badly done. The problem of making a really good index for a large encyclopedia has never been given careful study. Indexing is not the simple and easy problem that it is often thought to be. If the current talk about the retrieval of information that may some day be stored in computer banks is ever taken seriously, the discovery may be made that if the makers of encyclopedias cannot solve their indexing problems, neither can the makers of computers.

This is one aspect of the problem that one faces when he wants information from Britannica on the effects of technologies and finds no article "Technology" in which the effects are discussed. The article "Engineering" does not discuss the effects. Particular effects, as I have said, could be discussed in the particular divisions of the subject Engineering; but this, while done to some extent is not done consistently and, even if it were, this would not be enough. The more important particular effects that are known need to be brought together. These would include beneficial as well as harmful environmental effects, including the aesthetic, and other effects that have been discussed for centuries such as those of extreme specialization and division of labor.

In Britannica's article "Engineering Education" it is said that "some specialization is absolutely necessary." But "the trend toward specialization reached a point of diminishing returns. . . . As modern engineering requires an ever more adequate grasp of engineering principles during the undergraduate period, it is inevitable that mastery of specific arts and techniques must, to a greater extent, be left to the engineer's self-education after graduation." The great educational problem of our time, the subject of this book, is the question of the means by which the engineer and others can get this "self-education after graduation." No worse mistake can be made than to assume that the liberal arts as taught generally in colleges and universities today, and as represented in innumerable current books, provide the means for the general education that is needed. The professors of the liberal arts generally—there fortunately are exceptions—have also become specialists, narrow technicians, as have most workers in most fields of what is still called "learning" today. The need for general education is not limited to any one field or group of fields. It exists in all fields and there simply is not time, no matter what the disposition of the educational authorities, to provide all that is needed during the undergraduate or graduate years.

I return now to the subjects listed under Technology in Britannica's index. Britannica's article "the Industrial Revolution," does not attempt to refute any wild propositions such as McLuhan's that "any technology gradually creates a totally new human environment." It does, however, state what all careful writers on the subject have seen to be true and have said in one way or another, that "the process of industrialization so thoroughly transformed society that it may properly be described as a revolution." The article deals with the social as well as the technological aspects of the subject and is excellent in both. One would have to search far and wide to find, and then probably would not find, a better balanced, better informed, more sane, brief treatment of an extremely complex subject. There is nothing in it that could be taken even as suggesting that McLuhan's prophetic utterances may come true.

We take up now Britannica's article "Inventions and Discoveries." Here again there is much that is soundly based on fact and soundly reasoned, but there is one statement to which we feel we should mildly object. It is not remotely comparable to the many wild statements that McLuhan makes, and it is clearly modified in the right direction elsewhere in the article. The statement to which I refer is: "Invention and discovery seem to be universal characteristics of mankind, to be found at all times and all places in human history." But not to equal degrees. And a people that has shown these characteristics to only a very low degree for centuries, perhaps millennia, may at some time begin to show them and then develop them to a high degree. The ancestors of most of the people of northern Europe and of the United States were such people as the ancient Greeks considered barbarians, incapable of becoming civilized. They achieved very little in the way of inventions, until well into the Middle Ages, remotely comparable to the achievements of the Chinese that the author summarizes in the very next paragraph following the statement we have quoted above. If the word "potentials" were in the statement above in the place of "characteristics" there would not only be no grounds for objection to the statement, it would probably be as exact a summary of the facts as they are known and a statement of such wide application and importance that it needs to be generally known and understood. The author uses the word "potentialities" in other places. It has the great advantage of not suggesting something fixed as the word "characteristics" tends to do. This point may seem piddling, but it is not. It has to do with propositions of the kind that are universally denied by the dominant philosophical doctrine of logical positivism and its lineal descendant, philosophical or linguistic analysis. The kind of knowledge that is represented by such statements, and enough of the facts that are needed to validate and illustrate them constitute an essential part of a genuine general education.

The article is excellent in its statement of the relations among technologies:

Had James Watt's invention [of the steam engine] come earlier—and it might have, as witness Giovanni Branca's design for a steam turbine in 1629—the techniques and machines to produce the metal shapes required would not have existed; there may not have been sufficient capital available to manufacture it on a commercial scale; and there probably would have been little demand for it. . . . the need for Watt's invention and the opportunity for its adoption were provided by a series of prior and contemporaneous developments . . .

which the author goes on to describe.

As to social effects, the author reviews the inventions, for which he makes clear the time was ready, necessary to the production of cotton goods and then summarizes briefly, not a word wasted, and with a clarity rarely achieved because of his careful preparation of a background that makes clarity possible, and then goes on to social effects:

the increasing capacity for producing cotton goods in its turn resulted in an increasing demand for raw cotton; there the chief difficulty lay in the large amount of labour required to remove the seeds from short staple cotton, which could be produced in abundance. The problem was solved by Eli Whitney's cotton gin (1793) which more than tripled labour production and provided raw materials for the cotton mills (and, tragically, the economic precondition for resurgence of slavery in the United States).

There is no suggestion in the article of the extreme wildness that is in McLuhan's statement that "any technology gradually creates a totally new human environment." There are no sudden leaps from the effort to talk intelligibly, on the basic of fact, of technologies to talk of utopias as if they were already almost here and certain soon to be completely here, with possibly some extremely unpleasant and destructive intervals before they come into perfect being.

Before passing on from the question whether the subject Technology is adequately treated in the articles to which Britannica referred us under its index entry Technology, it might be worthwhile to ask whether Britannica could give readers any help in understanding the nature of such statements of McLuhan's as that "any technology gradually creates a totally new human environment." We have held that Britannica cannot reasonably be expected in its treatment of technologies to deal with wild statements such as this one. At the same time, we have to admit that in discussions of the technologies that have been used to reduce and in some parts of the world to eliminate, say, yellow fever, notions that are erroneous and that stand in the way of efforts to control have to be discussed if there is to be understanding of the problems that have to be solved before control can be possible. In none of the four books devoted to discussion of McLuhan that have been published so far has this statement of his to which we have given so much attention been seriously considered. This is, in our view, evidence of high significance of the state of mind that is widely prevalent in intellectual circles in the United States today. We cannot help wondering how anybody could read the statement "any technology gradually creates a totally new human environment" and not ask, Does the author understand that this statement is simply ludicrous if the effort is made to take it, in its context, strictly into account? Is the author deliberately using such rhetorical devices as ambiguity, exaggeration, and contradiction in the effort to gain attention? If one began suspecting that the author was deliberately using these techniques—and there is much in both *The Gutenberg Galaxy* and *Understanding Media* that suggests he is doing exactly this —then one might also begin wondering about the state of mind of a reading public, and especially of a critical world, in which these techniques could succeed. There is no room for doubt that McLuhan has met with tremendous success. But we have to ask, Why? Is the art of rhetoric, of persuasive discourse and of persuasion generally, today in such state that it can be practiced without any regard to ethical principles? When we speak of ethical principles, we include logic. For ethics without logic is impossible except by accident; and logic without ethics too often tends to be diabolical. And we include regard for facts. For facts are the only means of tying persuasion to the actual world, for laying a basis for changing for the better, and for keeping persuasion from flying off into fantasy. McLuhan is certainly not unaware of the principles involved here. Why does he misuse his sources, engage in so much nonsense, and contradict himself so often?

One would have to be seriously lacking in the ability to distinguish between the careful, step-by-step factual and logical development of an argument to a conclusion that would stand severe examination on the one hand, and a series of assertions, some factually well-founded, some not, sometimes with logical connections, much of the time without any on the other hand, in order not to wonder about McLuhan's technique. Has he discovered a large gap in the ability of a sufficiently large portion of the intellectual world to recognize and distinguish rational from irrational discourse to make exploitation of the latter worthwhile? In all of Freud's explorations of the irrational, he was usually careful not to make irrational leaps such as those McLuhan makes. One can reasonably argue with Freud's premises, but accept them and his conclusions follow. Freud was a strict rationalist in comparison with McLuhan. What is McLuhan doing? Is he just blundering? The evidence in the two books I have examined says McLuhan is deliberately doing what he does.

The question we have just been discussing clearly involves such problems in rhetoric as ambiguity, exaggeration, the use of shock techniques such as obvious misuse of sources, non-sequiturs, and contradictions. We cannot condemn statements because they are ambiguous. For all language contains some ambiguity, and the effort to remove all ambiguity cannot succeed without removing all the more significant meanings. Are there then no reasonable limits on the use of ambiguity, limits that are necessary if communication is to serve any intelligible purpose? As to exaggeration, we might say it is not only legitimate but necessary if some of us are to be waked from our dogmatic slumber. It is necessary at times if a picture of the good, the beautiful, and the true is to be painted that is powerful enough to exert an irresistible attraction on us.

We have seen the admirable concern that Britannica's authors of the articles "Automation," "Engineering," "the Industrial Revolution," and "Inventions and Discoveries" have shown for the social effects of developments in these fields. The blight of specialization that has lost all relation to its real object, the general welfare, has not been totally and irredeemably destructive in these fields. There is at least a consciousness that there is a general welfare to be sought and served.

We shall now look at Britannica's articles "Rhetoric" and "Propaganda" to see what we find in them in the way of concern for social effects and discussion that distinguishes as clearly as possible between the harmful and the helpful uses of language. We can reasonably expect, say, the teacher of English composition, the professor of American or English or any other literature, and the social scientist to be more concerned with the problem of helpful and harmful social effects than persons in any other discipline except ethics, since the quality of the lives of human beings can reasonably be assumed to be, in their different ways, their particular specialty.

Britannica has an article "Rhetoric." Let us look at it. The word "ambiguity" does not occur in the article. Neither is there any synonym. The word "exaggeration" does not occur in the article, nor do any of its synonyms. There is no discussion of these and other techniques, except the use of ornament and fact, and the little that is said of fact is grossly misleading. The statement is made in the second sentence of the article, and repeated in the last sentence of the first paragraph in a stronger form, that "The study of rhetoric exerted an important formative influence on European culture from ancient times to the 17th century A.D., after which it became less important." There are grounds for believing, contrary to this, not that any less attention has been given since the seventeenth century to the art of persuasion, but that far more has been given to it. The difference is that the attention given has not been that of careful speculative and factual consideration of the subject, built on the best of the grounds laid in the past, but rather of an attention that has been concerned mainly with the cultivation of power, regardless of the purpose for which it is used. The notion that knowledge is power and that the development of power is the great end of human existence has been the hallmark of a large portion of human thought and expression since the time of Francis Bacon. Bacon was clearly concerned about the ethical use of power, but this concern did not occupy the center of his attention, and it has gradually dropped out of sight since his time. Now it is fairly clear that all literature, whatever the purpose of the author, and however great or small his abilities, has persuasive qualities. Modern advertising and publicity and propaganda are deliberately loaded with persuasive qualities. The literature of this century is certainly not devoid of them. The cultivation of the art of persuasion has not only not decreased but has greatly increased since the seventeenth century, and printing has added greatly to the power of this art. This would be no cause for lamentation if it were not for the fact that the cultivation of the art has been to a great extent separated from the question of the worth of the end the persuasion is being made to serve. At the same time, as Michael Polanyi tells us in his excellent book *Personal Knowledge,* "our age overflows with inordinate moral aspirations." [1] We fight wars as never before in human history in order to bring each other into what we, in our particular ways, and without being able to validate our ways, consider the paths of righteousness. The intellectual leadership of the United States is at sea in a storm in a ship it has made unseaworthy, without chart and compass, is in control of the navigation, and is ignorant of the first principles of the art.

One has only to go to the numerous textbooks on English composition or rhetoric, or on advertising and publicity and propaganda, to find almost complete absence of concern with any end to be served by the persuasive powers that the texts are designed to cultivate other than sheer power. Some writings on propaganda tend to treat propaganda as always intentionally misleading, but one has only to consider seriously the writings on propaganda to see that far more is involved. One can easily see the misleading quality of, say, advertising that labels arsenic as sugar and sells it as such, and therefore very little as obvious as this ever occurs. It is not only possible but it is practically certain that some ideas and actions that some think are good but that are really poisonous constitute the most serious problem of propaganda. There certainly are ideas that have powerful natural attractions, but if propagated have socially destructive effects. Our intellectual leadership has divested us of all means of dealing rightly with these ideas. [2]

One does not have to go to the typical teacher of English composition or English or American literature today to find little, if any, ability to reason soundly on such questions as this. Our situation is far worse today than what I have just said suggests. For when one goes to the most influential writings in the field of ethics of our time, one finds the doctrine that there is no such process as sound reasoning on ethical ques-

1. M. Polanyi, *Personal Knowledge* (Chicago: Univ. of Chicago Press, 1958), p. 142.
2. There is an excellent book, *The Ethics of Rhetoric* by Richard M. Weaver (Chicago: Regnery, 1953), that gives the ethical aspect of the use of words the attention that the importance of this aspect warrants. This is the only discussion of which I am aware that attempts this task in our time. We are today as blind as Tolstoi, with Shakespeare's account of the horrible misuse of power by Cornwall and Regan before him (*King Lear* III, vi), utterly unable to see the horror and the thoroughly admirable quality of the effort to stop them. For a stripped-down account of this classic of ethical blindness, see Chapter VI.

tions. One finds the doctrine that ethical propositions are meaningless. Britannica's article "Logical Positivism" summarizes correctly the position of this body of doctrine on ethical questions: "So-called statements about what things are right and good cannot be verified . . . and are therefore without meaning. They are simply expressions of attitudes and ought not to be regarded as conveying knowledge or even opinion. The characteristic value words may serve to move or persuade: they cannot serve to convince us of facts, since they are indefinable in factual terms."

The specialists in the field of ethics have long been divided on the question whether there is any clearly demonstrable better or worse in human affairs, but never as catastrophically so as today. There is no quick and easy remedy for this situation. One cannot suppress that with which one disagrees unless one has the power to do so, and power that is generated for this purpose can be and often has been grossly abused. The consequent evil of suppression by sheer power is often far greater than the evil of the power suppressed. The great object is not that of suppression by the use of sheer power. The great object of education in this connection is that of depriving a body of evil doctrine of its power by understanding its essential evil. This in the end amounts to suppression, but not merely by means of sheer power. One cannot reasonably condemn the use of power to achieve a good end, but if one holds the great office of the teacher, one is under the heaviest obligations first to discover how to distinguish good from evil ends and then to use the power of one's office for the good.

It would seem reasonable that in the course of time agreement could be reached on such questions as whether the way of life of the Aztecs of Mexico in their worship of their god Huitzilopochtli is a way to be cultivated or a way to be condemned—proscribed by understanding, made as far as can be impossible, rather than suppressed by mere power. It is necessary to say "as far as can be" because man, with his volatile nature, can be expected, unless education helps him to get far better habits than any he has yet managed to acquire, to continue to run to this and that quackery as a remedy for his ills. It should not be necessary to mention the great parallels of our time, but the logical positivist should be faced with them and required to show that they are not the logical and emotional consequences of his ideas.

There cannot be any grounds for doubt that the conduct of the Duke of Cornwall and his fiendish wife Regan in gouging out Gloucester's eyes, as set forth in Act III, Scene vi, of Shakespeare's King Lear, was thoroughly evil, and the conduct of the servant in trying to stop this action thoroughly good. There is no instance in Shakespeare of a comparable action by any person in a high position. One could pile up mountains of words on Shakespeare's attitude toward the common man, the invisible man, and the mountain of words, if piled up to support the argument that Shakespeare had no interest in, no sympathy for, no deep understanding of the common man, would look silly if looked at in the light of an understanding not bound by false doctrines, an understanding free to reach a judgment that was true. In the case of Tolstoi in his essay on Shakespeare which we presented in outline in Chapter VI, one can know only that it was an invincible prejudice that blinded him, but just what that prejudice was, beyond the determination willy-nilly to prove Shakespeare was not an artist, would be difficult to establish. In the case of the logical positivist or philosophical analyst, the factors that are responsible for his ethical blindness have been expertly traced by the objective idealist Brand Blanshard in his superb books *The Nature of Thought, Reason and Analysis*, and *Reason and Goodness* to a set of philosophical prejudices, the most seriously delusive of which in our view is that all knowledge is derived from sense experience.

We have recorded in several places and especially in Chapters II and VI our reasons for rejecting all forms of the doctrine that value is subjective. We hold, in opposition to the proponents of the open society, that while a civilized society has to be open to arguments pro and con, some arguments in the course of time should be and have been settled, and one of the duties of the world of learning is to know how and when this was done; and that while the cultivation of understanding requires knowledge of these arguments, it does not require that those who know the arguments be silent when one side is presented to the public or to students in ways that are grossly misleading. We know very well that at times it is dangerous to oppose the mob and that the leadership of the intellectual world can be the most dangerous of all mobs. But, one has to ask, what does the great office of the teacher require on such occasions? If one has not been blinded by false doctrine, one knows the answer to this question.

A civilized society is one that is closed by the personal convictions and the habits of the great majority of its members to the kind of conduct that the Aztecs of Mexico in their worship of their god Huitzilopochtli, that the Duke of Cornwall and his wife Regan in their worship of their god Power, and that too many members of the intellectual world in their worship of their god Success at Any Price illustrate in their words and actions. A civilized society is closed to the kind of conduct that in Plato's *Gorgias* Callicles says is right and good, and that Socrates condemns. Callicles is the exact type of the person being cultivated in education today, or he comes so near being it that we shall let him describe himself. Socrates has just said that "a man should be temperate and master of himself, and ruler of his own pleasures and passions." Callicles calls the temperate fools and then goes on to declare that

they really are fools, for how can a man be happy who is the servant of anything? On the contrary, I plainly assert, that he who would truly live ought to allow his desires to wax to the uttermost, and not to chastise them; but when they have grown to the greatest he should have courage and intelligence to minister to them and to satisfy all his longings. And this I affirm to be natural justice and nobility. To this, however, the many cannot attain; and they blame the strong man because they are ashamed of their own weakness, which they desire to conceal, and hence they say that intemperance is base. As I have remarked already, they enslave the noble natures, and being unable to satisfy their pleasures, they praise temperance and justice out of their own cowardice.[3]

This type of individualism in the course of time becomes socially so oppressive that there is a determined revolt against it, and this revolt turns out too often to be a dour type of puritanism or an oppressive form of collectivism. The failure of all except a very few individualists to distinguish the Calliclean type of individualism from the type which strives for and is necessary to the general welfare, and to condemn the one and support the other, is one of the reasons for the success that vicious forms of collectivism have achieved in the world in recent decades.

Britannica's article "Rhetoric" mentions Plato's *Gorgias* but gives no suggestion of the crucial significance of the *Gorgias* in the history of rhetoric. It is the Hamlet that Britannica's history leaves out. We shall not discover that significance if we examine only what has been defined as rhetoric from time to time by most rhetoricians, with the great exception of Plato and Aristotle. Most of the definitions have been conventional or arbitrary and have failed to take into account the most important question that it is possible to consider about the use of words. This is the aim, the purpose, the end the words are used to serve. This calls for ethical principle to be an integral and governing part of rhe-

3. Plato, *Gorgias* 491–92, in *Dialogues of Plato*, trans. Jowett, I, 551. Robert Elliot Fitch's *Odyssey of the Self-Centered Self* (New York: Harcourt, Brace and World, 1961) is an excellent account of the more obviously vicious form of the Callicleanism of our time and some of its sources.

toric. Britannica's article "Rhetoric," instead of being largely a waste of valuable space, would have been given point if the testimony of Gorgias the rhetorician in the Platonic dialogue *Gorgias* had been quoted on the power of rhetoric:

What is there greater than the word which persuades the judges in the courts, or the senators in the council, or the citizens in the assembly, or at any other public meeting?—if you have the power of uttering this word, you will have the physician your slave, and the trainer your slave, and the money-maker of whom you talk will be found to gather treasures, not for himself, but for you who are able to speak and to persuade the multitude.[4]

Immediately after this speech by Gorgias, Socrates asks him, "Do you know any other effect of rhetoric over and above that of producing persuasion?" and Gorgias answers no. Callicles later enters the discussion and charges Socrates with arguing nonsense—just as the logical positivist does today, though not on the same grounds. Socrates then questions Callicles on whether the cultivation of the power of persuasion without at the same time cultivating the strictest effort to use it only for a genuinely good end is a good thing to do. In the course of this discussion, Socrates makes the classic charge against rhetoric as it was taught in ancient times—and is in the main still taught today. Callicles has just admitted that rhetoric is used for bad purposes, but he says, "There are some who have a real care of the public in what they say," on which Socrates comments:

I am contented with the admission that rhetoric is of two sorts; one, which is mere flattery and disgraceful declamation; the other which is noble and aims at the training and improvement of the souls of the citizens, and strives to say what is best, whether welcome or unwelcome, to the audience; but have you ever known such a rhetoric; or if you have, and can point out any rhetorician who is of this stamp, who is he?[5]

Callicles answers, "I am afraid that I cannot tell you of any such among the orators who are at present living."

Professor Robert A. Dahl, Eugene Meyer Professor of Political Science in Yale University, in his book *A Preface to Democratic Theory* discusses politics as practiced in the United States today. Politics of course involves the relations of the politician with the public, as well as with special groups in the public, and these relations include what is today the equivalent of the ancient art of persuasion. Now if we

4. *Dialogues of Plato*, I, 511.
5. Ibid., I, 564.

define persuasion narrowly, it should be evident, when we consider the following statement by Professor Dahl, that we butcher the subject as it actually is and therefore cannot even begin to understand it. Now before quoting Professor Dahl, I wish to make it clear I am not doing so because of agreement or disagreement with him. I do so because if we define rhetoric as having to do only with persuasive public speech, excluding all questions of ethics and everything that goes beyond public speech, we create hopelessly difficult problems. The exclusion of the cultivation of a genuine ethics in public speech, as well as in all other possible ways, may not necessarily lead to the violation of ethics in practice, but Professor Dahl's testimony is worth contemplating: "In a rough sense, the essence of all competitive politics is bribery of the electorate by the politicians." [6]

Is the electorate in the United States today really following a certain example that the Roman Praetorian Guard set in the year A.D. 193? That example was to put the Roman Empire up for sale to the highest bidder. The example of the Roman Senate was little, if any, better than that of the Praetorian Guard. A wealthy senator, Didius Julianus, actually bid for the Empire in public auction, bought it, and was confirmed in his office by the Senate—only to be tried, condemned, and executed by order of the same Senate when it became clear that the action of the Praetorian Guard in offering the Empire for sale and the purchase of it by a senator from the Guard had so incensed the other branches of the Roman army, and the public as well, that to stand up for the senator was to invite death. The anger of the army and the public unfortunately cannot be taken as proof of high ethical standards. It is just possible that public policy had trained them to expect and to demand their share and that their failure to get theirs was the reason for their anger. The action of the Praetorian Guard and of one senator produced convulsions in the Roman Empire that threatened to break out in more than a constitutional crisis. It threatened to break out in a civil war. Professor Dahl's testimony has, of course, been noticed by some political scientists and perhaps others such as myself. But if it has aroused any deep concern in the public generally, or even been noticed widely, there have been few signs of either. Such is the fruit of the specialization of our time, and of the multitudinous voices that shriek to gain public attention, few or none saying what most needs to be said, all shrieking and

6. Robert A. Dahl, *A Preface to Democratic Theory* (Chicago: Univ. of Chicago Press, [1956] 1962), p. 68.

succeeding only in confusing and deafening the public and debasing the public interest.

There was, once upon a time, a great statement made on this subject by a great statesman. This statement was completely governed by the ethical principles with which both the politician and the public need to be well acquainted in practice as well as in preachment. The statement was made by Edmund Burke. Burke had been sent to Parliament by the City of Bristol. The electors of Bristol expected Burke to vote for what they wanted in return for their votes for him. Burke politely and firmly declined on the grounds that this was not the right way for the elected representative of a group of people to represent them, and, rather than do so, he refused to occupy the office of representative on any such terms. Such is one of the multitudinous forms that the problem of superior orders can take. The evidence that the general public, and especially the supposedly highly educated part of the general public of the United States, has little, if any, understanding of this problem today is overwhelming. This appalling lack of understanding came out clearly immediately after World War II in the actions in which the government of the United States engaged at that time. This lack of understanding was implicit in the failure during World War II to see the desperate need of a balance-of-power policy and in the unconditional-surrender policy. It became explicit in the war-crimes trials and the policy of reeducating the enemy. Even today, full recognition that the same blight that had created the enemy had deeply affected the United States is still to come, despite the widespread public evidence of recent years. The problem of superior orders, important and all-pervasive as it is, is only a part of a larger problem. It is simply a problem in ethics, one that has been coming up from the dawn of man and can reasonably be expected to continue coming up as long as the relations of superior and subordinate continue to exist in society. There is practically no chance, despite propaganda to the contrary, that these relations will ever disappear. They are clearly and necessarily in the nature of things.

Britannica's article "Rhetoric" is written as if these problems did not exist, or if they do, the art of persuasion had nothing to do with them. In discussing the influence of Petrus Ramus, it is said that "Ramism carried the seeds of its own destruction. The dichotomy it established between thought and the words that formulated thought provoked a search for a plain style which would represent facts without adventitious verbal ornament. Rhetoric fell into discredit." We have shown that rhetoric had fallen into extreme discredit with Socrates many centuries before Petrus Ramus. It has doubtless risen and fallen more than once since then. Did rhetoric on the occasion referred to in the quotation above fall into discredit because of "the dichotomy [that Ramism] established between thought and the words that formulated thought" or because of the "*search* [my italics] for a plain style which would represent facts without adventitious ornament" or because the *search* resulted in the finding and use of such a style? Did Ramus establish a dichotomy between words and thought, or did Ramus only become aware of and point out a dichotomy that actually exists? What is ambiguity in language if it is not, in effect, a dichotomy between words and thoughts? Words most certainly are not the thoughts they represent. Any writer who wishes to do so can use modifiers to cut off certain thoughts that words normally represent. And he can, with or without modifiers, use words so as to give them meanings opposite to their normal meanings. As to the advocacy of a plain style and the use of facts rather than adventitious ornamentation, this advocacy occurred long before any effects produced by Ramus and came from the ancient thinker to whom Britannica's article gives the most space—without mentioning this advocacy. Aristotle is perfectly clear: "The right thing in speaking is that we should be satisfied not to annoy our hearers, without trying to delight them: we ought in fairness to fight our case with no help beyond the bare facts: nothing, therefore should matter except the proof of those facts." [7] Ornament may be justified, says Aristotle, on the grounds of defects in the hearers that cannot be otherwise corrected. And as if in comment on the sweeping charge that Socrates has made against all rhetoricians, and perhaps in the hope that if the charge is true, the art of rhetoric can be used—as Plato shows Socrates trying to use it—to persuade the rhetorician to mend his ways, Aristotle says, "if it be objected that one who uses such power [the power to make the worse seem better] of speech unjustly might do great harm, that is a charge which may be made in common against all good things except virtue, and above all against the things that are most useful, as strength, health, wealth, generalship. A man can confer the greatest of benefits by a right use of these, and inflict the greatest of injuries by using them wrongly." [8]

We have not only found nothing illuminating in Britannica's article "Rhetoric" on the harmful and helpful uses of language, we have found

7. Aristotle, *Rhetoric*, trans. W. Rhys Roberts, in *Aristotle's Rhetoric and Poetics*, Modern Library (New York: Random House, 1954), p. 165.
8. Ibid., p. 23.

total failure to take into account the statements on the subject that are probably the best that have ever been made on it.

Let us pass on to Britannica's article "Propaganda." Our purpose still is to find out what light, if any, Britannica throws on the harmful or helpful use of words as this question has been raised for us by McLuhan's use of ambiguity, exaggeration, non-sequiturs, misuse of sources, and contradictions. It would be possible, for instance, for an author deliberately to misuse human sources as a way of showing his contempt for them, as a way of saying human authority is worthless except as a channel for a higher authority: Go to the nature of man and of things and of reason, to the relations between man and man and between man and things, and between man and that which gave him and the universe its being for your authority; your discourse as you have conducted it, thinking it rational, has been thoroughly irrational. Here is what you have been doing: *Understanding Media* is made on your model. Britannica's article "Rhetoric" could reasonably have suggested something of this kind as a possible purpose of an author. This could be McLuhan's real purpose and his reason for the techniques that he has used. But even if this were the real explanation, it should be immediately clear that McLuhan has either grossly overestimated the intelligence of even the best of his audience, or has chosen this way of showing his contempt for them and for the techniques they use. We found no discussion in Britannica's article "Rhetoric" that even suggested possibilities of this kind. We cannot expect to find any in Britannica's article "Propaganda." We now look and exhibit the most important of our findings in the article "Propaganda."

Britannica's article "Propaganda" has a section entitled Tactics in which some propaganda techniques are discussed. There are several paragraphs on how statements have to be fitted to audiences in order to have any chance to produce the desired effect. The word "exaggeration" is not used, but the use of exaggeration is considered in other terms. The article is good in this respect.

The article is particularly interesting, however, on account of the question of the factual accuracy of a statement of great importance in it—the kind of statement to which propagandists resort when there are no means of checking them, as is often the case with statements that McLuhan makes in the two books we have considered. We cannot find any authority other than the carefully and honestly used rational powers of the human mind—powers that can put man in connection with authority far beyond him—to prove that the statement "any technology gradually creates a totally new human environment" is in one sense so highly ambiguous as to be wholly unenlightening and, in another sense, gross exaggeration and, in still another, sheer nonsense. But we could quote many sources that it would be extremely difficult to show are not trustworthy to show that the following statement from Britannica's article "Propaganda," while factually correct except for the italicized portion, could give the uninformed reader a totally false impression: "*Before the seizure of power* [my italics] in Germany, the National Socialist strategy was to prevent a combination of Socialists, Communists and conservatives which would have stalled their advance." It is true that this was the National Socialist strategy. But it was also the Communist strategy. If the Communists had chosen to do so—and the National Socialists before they came to power could not have prevented them—the Communists could have joined the Socialists (Social Democrats) and the conservatives and prevented by legal means the National Socialists under Hitler from coming to power. Only the Communists of the two groups could have had any incentive to stop Hitler. The National Socialists obviously had no incentive to stop themselves. The only opportunity to stop Hitler therefore clearly rested with the Communists. They did not use this opportunity. In this respect the statement above, while factually correct, gives an utterly false impression. Britannica's article "Germany," section The End of the Republic, makes clear that orderly government in Germany was being made impossible by both of the extremist parties, the Nazis and the Communists. These two parties, often in physical conflict with each other, according to Britannica, reduced "parliamentary procedure to a prolonged brawl." And further, on Jan. 30, 1933, according to Britannica's article "Germany," "Adolf Hitler became chancellor of Germany, *legally* [my italics] as he had been determined to do and not by revolution." There was thus no "seizure of power."

The facts, as stated in Britannica's article "Germany," and as reported above, are so well-established that I shall not cite any further evidence for them.

So we have in Britannica's article "Propaganda," the literally false statement that the National Socialists under Hitler seized power, and the grossly misleading factual statement that National Socialist policy was to prevent a coalition that would have stopped them from coming to power. I believe we can be sure these statements were made without any intention on the part of the author to falsify or mislead. Yet we have clear cases of both. The statement that National Socialist policy was to prevent a coalition of the Communists with the Social Democrats and conservatives is a beautiful example of a statement that is literally true but that can have, and is almost certain to have, on an uninformed audience, an utterly false effect. It could be that the writing of an article on propaganda—or a discussion of the subject Prejudice—that escapes being viciously misleading propaganda is not so easy as some of us today clearly think it is.

We are now, let us hope, a little better prepared to find or, if we cannot find, at least to know why we cannot find any discussion that Britannica may have that throws any light on McLuhan's techniques and purpose. And perhaps we have gleaned a little insight into the problem of making statements that someone else cannot show to be false or misleading. The blather that has emanated from the intellectual world in enormous quantities during the last fifty years of this century on the subject of prejudice has been one of the distinguishing marks of this time. Submit yourself genuinely, wholeheartedly, sincerely, to the guidance of the intellectual, the expert, the specialist, tell him you do not want to be prejudiced, you do not want to go through life making one blunder after another on subjects of great importance, ask him for the truth, and he will give it to you without diminishing his bountiful supply. Yet when one looks carefully and seriously at the doctrine that dominates the intellectual world today in one of its moods, one finds this doctrine says that there is no proposition that is self-evidently true; that premises have to be assumed, or established by arbitrary definition, and that the best that can be hoped for is consistency within a system. This is the condition of the mind of the leading intellectuals of today. This mind asserts what this mind denies.

Britannica's article "Propaganda" is not a bad article as discussion of subjects in the field of the social sciences goes these days. In fact, it is worth close study, and such study would be helpful in understanding the problems of propaganda. But there is nothing in the article, beyond what we have said above, that would, without a great deal of pondering, help any reader to understand McLuhan's techniques and from them and other evidences divine his purpose.

The reader may have wondered whether we were digressing and losing touch with the subject Technology when we interrupted our discussion of Britannica's treatment of Technology in order to consider its treatment of Rhetoric and Propaganda. Our purpose has been simply to show that concern only for the generation of power without regard to the use of power necessarily brings disastrous consequences, and that this is true in other fields of knowledge as well as in the field of technology.

We now take up the question whether Britannica needs an article "Technology," and if so, why. Again, we have to engage in what may appear to be a digression in that to show this need we shall have to discuss another article in Britannica. This article shows that the need for it is the same as the need for an article "Technology." The article that we shall use for this purpose is "Civilization and Culture." It is by James Harvey Robinson, formerly professor of history in Columbia University, author of the once famous and widely read but now virtually forgotten book *The Mind in the Making*. A note at the opening of the article informs the reader that the article first appeared in the 1929 edition of Britannica and has been retained since then "because of its interest as a statement of permanent value." If I were to review the article, I would have to question some of the statements in it, but none is so absurd or as factually dubious as many that McLuhan makes. The author makes it clear in his first paragraph that he intends to emphasize the part that man's development of technologies has had in the development of civilization, but he shows throughout the article that the major emphasis has to be given to the development of the human mind—not that the two could ever be dissociated, but rather that there has been interaction, the mind imagining something, making it, finally, perhaps after failures, seeing it work, and being stimulated to imagining other things that might be made and that would serve the purposes of man on earth. In his first paragraph Robinson illustrates the emphasis he intends to give by referring to the dissection of atoms and the manipulation of electrons by men as comparable to the ways in which primitive men might have handled pebbles, and beyond these elementary manipulations by referring to the inventions of man "from the rudest chipped flint to the most delicately adjusted microscope."

In his second paragraph, Robinson anticipates a part of the thesis of this book by speaking of the vast scope of Britannica and the difficulty of writing intelligibly about civilization in a half-dozen or so of Britannica's pages, but still of the necessity of trying to do so, for

there is danger that owing to the overwhelming mass of information given in these volumes, certain important underlying considerations may be lost sight of. There are highly significant questions concerning the nature and course of human development, the obstacles which have lain in the way of advance; the sources of success and frustration which could hardly be brought together in dealing with any of the special aspects of human culture. Accordingly, an attempt will be made under this caption to scan civilization as a single, unique and astonishing achievement of the human species. . . .

Even today with all our recently acquired knowledge, those who strive most valiantly in imagination to get outside of civilization so that they may look upon it dispassionately and appraise it as a whole, are bewildered by its mysteries.

Our new knowledge requires a new view of our subject. We must recast our concept of civilization, "its past progress and its future possibilities." We can now by virtue of the theory buttressed by fact given to us by Darwin in his *Descent of Man*, and by archaeologists and anthropologists, trace man back to a condition that points toward an earlier one that seems clearly to have "merged with that of wild animals, without artificial shelters, clothes or speech; dependent for sustenance on the precarious daily search for food." We must, says Robinson, abandon the notion formerly held that man was originally endowed with a mind. Darwin tells us that "the very essence of an instinct is that it is followed independently of reason." Animals may have, and some seem clearly to have, something resembling the human mind and the human powers of reasoning, but what they have, if mental at all, is clearly no more than rudimentary. "In any case," says Robinson, "the discovery that our ancestors once lived like wild animals raises entirely new and difficult questions as to the nature, origin and interpretation of those powers of his known as *mind and reason, which enabled him to seek out those inventions and come upon beliefs and practices which have produced in the aggregate civilization*" (my italics).

I shall not discuss here the question of the origin of mind and reason further than to say that such words as "development" and "emergence," useful as they are, are mainly labels for our ignorance. To go fully into this subject would take us too far afield. I wish simply to call attention to the priority which Robinson here ascribes to "mind and reason" in the development of civilization and therefore in the technology that Robinson clearly recognizes as one of the determining factors in civilization.

If we reject McLuhan's extreme statement that "any technology gradually creates a totally new human environment," and substitute for it a statement such as "any new technology, or modification of an old technology, with wide possible application, if adopted tends to modify the environment," we have a statement that can be intelligibly defended. This may be because to see it as true, we have to fill it out until it is perhaps indistinguishable from a tautology. In any case, if we accept Robinson, it is the mind that is the active agent in making technologies possible. It, and not they, is the ultimately decisive factor. This is the point that we labored to establish in an early part of Chapter V. This is one of the very important points that Lewis Mumford has made in his highly instructive writings on technology.

There is no discussion in Britannica's article "Civilization and Culture" of anything like McLuhan's statement that "any technology gradually creates a totally new human environment," if this statement is taken strictly. If it is taken loosely, it is obviously old, old hat.

We have to applaud Britannica for having Robinson's article "Civilization and Culture"; but we have to remark that so far as the reader who wants helpful discussion of the relations of technologies to each other and to civilization, Britannica might almost as well not have it. The article should be listed under Technology in Britannica's index and, as we have seen, it is not. The uninformed reader would have little chance ever to find it, and even the best of informed readers would, if he found it, do so only by chance.

Exactly the same reasons that Robinson gives for the article "Civilization and Culture" are valid for an article "Technology." The scope of technology is to some extent the same, to some extent different from that of civilization and culture. The differences in scope are important enough to require separate treatment.

Let us now see whether we can get help from Britannica on McLuhan's thesis that more than any other technologies, those of communication have been decisive in shaping human affairs and human perceptions. Britannica's index tells us there is an article "Communication" and we now consider it.

The article is about two and a half pages long. There is nothing in it that bears on the question whether of all technologies those of communication have been most decisive in shaping human affairs and human sense perceptions. The subject matter chosen for discussion in the article is highly significant in that it helps to reveal the low quality of the discussion in the social sciences today of subjects of wide reach and high importance. If there is anything clear about communication, it is that the study of the feelings, the attitudes, the desires, the convictions of the people of a society at any particular moment, in short, finding out what will please the people most and then flattering them by agreeing with them in order to get the high positions and high rewards that the people have the power to bestow, is one of the major causes of the great social ills, such as wars, that beset the people. Evidence has been assembled, Britannica's article tells us, that carrying a message to an audience and getting the reception that is wanted for it "involves the techniques of adapting the message so closely to the dominating values, motives and aspirations of the audience that the audience is inspired and eagerly welcomes the message."

I shall not quote all the passages in the article that convey substantially this same message. One wonders how the content of this message could be considered an addition to knowledge made by modern social science. There is nothing in the article that suggests that this technique is perhaps not as old as the hills but probably as old as the people who have lived on them and the adjoining valleys and plains. Antony practices it in Shakespeare's play *Julius Caesar* when he follows Brutus and makes a speech that by appealing to the cupidity of his audience reverses completely the attitude of the audience. Shakespeare's Coriolanus prefers death to practicing it. Plato describes the technique in a passage in the *Republic* which is so much better than anything said on the subject by most social scientists today that I quote the passage here:

. . . each of those salaried individuals whom the public call sophists . . . teaches nothing but those beliefs which the multitude express in their assemblies, and this they call wisdom. It is as though a man who is keeper of a huge and powerful beast had got to know its tempers and its desires, how best to approach and how best to handle it, when it has its sulkiest and when its mildest moods and what causes them, on what occasions it is in the habit of uttering its various cries, and what sounds will soothe or provoke it. Now, suppose him, after he had got to know all these things from long experience of the animal, to call this knowledge wisdom, and systematizing it into an art to take to teaching. He has no true knowledge as to which of these beliefs and desires is beautiful or ugly, good or bad, just or unjust. He employs all these terms in accordance with the opinions of the mighty beast, calling things that please it good, things that displease it bad. . . . In heaven's name, do you not think that a man like that would make a strange instructor? [9]

It is possible, given the state of mind that exists today, to deflect attention from what is clearly said in this passage by charging Plato with regarding the public as a great beast. But it is the sophist who does this, and Plato is attacking the sophist. The real meaning of the passage in its application today is that the sophists of our time set themselves

9. Plato, *Republic*, trans. A. D. Lindsay, Everyman's Library (New York: Dutton, [1906] 1940), 492–93, p. 185.

up as teachers of the public and treat the public exactly as if it were a great beast. Or a collection of insects. Britannica tells us that "the communication process has been most profitably studied in such particular biological organisms as bees and termites (See Social Insects)." There is little room for doubt that there is similarity between such mechanical-electrical processes as automation and the communication of insects on the one hand, and that of human beings on the other. If one is to be informed about communication, one has to know its mechanical and near mechanical and insect-like aspects. But the mind of the human being is clearly not entirely mechanical or insect-like in its operations. The human mind can transcend its environment, the physical causes that operate on it, and its own bodily-mental instincts. This process of transcendence is by far the most important process in human communication.

It is possible, as we have already said, to discuss the purely technical side of communication, the nature of words and other symbols, without reference to their meanings, and the development of the various means of transmitting the means from the earliest times until today; and it is possible to speculate, as McLuhan does, on the psychic effects of words aside from their meanings, and the psychic effects of the different modes of communication aside from the particular content of that which is communicated. It is not only possible to divorce consideration of the purpose and possible effects of a technique that is envisaged and not yet actual from the technical understanding and work that has to be done to bring the technique to the state where it can be given purely technical tests in practice, it is necessary to do this if an imagined technique is to be made actual. But at some stage the problem of purpose and effects has to be considered. If the technician is not to be a barbarian, he must himself do this as well as encourage others to do it.

One can use the work one does, technical or other, to open up and look at the world in all its aspects and consider from this point of view, probably better than from one that would have to be imagined, whether what one is doing is, on balance, adding to or subtracting from the good in the world. This is the most important of all questions, and an article on communication in an encyclopedia, where all the more important aspects of a subject ought to be brought together, is worse than worthless if it does not provide help at this point. Britannica's article "Communication" is a total blank at this point.

There is no mention in Britannica's article "Communication" of any of the problems of human sense perception or of possible effects of different modes of communication on the human psyche. We remind ourselves of McLuhan's statements that Bishop Berkeley supports his position on this subject and that psychologists support Berkeley. We are therefore continuing to look for evidence that psychologists support Berkeley and what it is that they support him on. Berkeley clearly held that vision is two dimensional, and he clearly denied unified perception.[10]

Let us consult Britannica's article "Berkeley" and see what we find. We find the statement that Berkeley's *New Theory of Vision* is one of his chief works, "a brilliant piece of pure psychology, on the perception of space, the conclusions of which have been widely accepted." But by whom and on what is not said. The suspicion arises that this the source of McLuhan's statement that we have quoted in Chapter V concerning the attitudes of psychologists toward the doctrines Berkeley promulgates in his *New Theory of Vision.*

Let us see whether Britannica's article "Perception" has anything to say on this subject. First, let us note that Britannica's article "Perception" was written by E. G. Boring, formerly Edgar Pierce Professor of Psychology at Harvard. Except for one short paragraph, and a few scattered sentences, it deals only with the experimental investigation of sense perception as conducted by psychologists and does not review the long history of the speculation on the subject from the time before Plato to Berkeley to the present. This is an inexcusably serious gap in the presentation of the subject. This gap, so far as I have been able to discover, is not filled by discussion elsewhere in Britannica.

Berkeley wrote in the speculative tradition. Experimental psychology as it is known today did not exist in his time. As between the testimony of the philosophical-speculative thinker and writer, and that of the experimental psychologist who knows how to design an experiment so that it will answer correctly the questions he puts to it, no competent philosophers or psychologists today would subscribe to conclusions based on speculation when divergent conclusions based on well-designed experiments were available.

Britannica's article "Perception" provides a definite conclusion on the questions we have raised, despite some ambiguities and the failure

10. *A New Theory of Vision*, Secs. XLIV, XLV, and XLVI. The relevant passages are too long to quote. Some of the statements are not at all clear. Some even appear to contradict others unless all the relevant passages are taken into account. Taken all together, Berkeley's doctrine on the points mentioned is clearly as I have stated it in Chapter V.

to cite sources for the conclusion. The bibliography lists *Human Senses and Perception,* edited by G. M. Wyburn, but the text of the article does not report the experimental evidence on the perception of objects in space that this work contains. This testimony is important in that it supports direct visual perception of three dimensions of objects in space, thus opposing Berkeley's conclusion that vision is two-dimensional. I have quoted the relevant conclusions in Chapter V. We have some reservations on whether the definite conclusion provided in Britannica's article is soundly based. It may be vitiated by the ambiguities in the subject, and the failure to clear up these ambiguities.

Such a statement in Britannica's article as "Stereoscopic vision furnishes one of the best examples of how the characteristics of the stimulating object are reconstituted in perception" illustrates the ambiguity. One of the questions we are asking is whether vision, without any reconstituting by the mind in the completion of the process of perception, is three-dimensional or two-dimensional. The word "stereoscopic" means three-dimensional. The use of the word "stereoscopic" cannot be taken as settling the question whether the work the optical equipment of the eye does is two-dimensional or three-dimensional. The quotation above may be taken as saying that the three dimensions of the stimulating object are *reconstituted in perception* rather than directly perceived without any reconstitution. The next sentence might be taken as answering this question clearly, but we wonder whether we can take it as really meaning that the eye, in its purely optical work, before any reconstitution in perception by the mind, provides three-dimensional objects as they seem clearly to exist in space: "A solid object, viewed with both eyes, produces somewhat disparate images on the two retinas. Since both images are seen in a single perceptual field, one might expect to see this disparity as a double image. Instead, one sees a solid object in three dimensions, with no doubling, in spite of the fact that the two retinal images would not coincide in superposition." The last sentence in this quotation clearly suggests that reconstitution in perception may be what produces the "solid object in three dimensions" and not the optical work of the eye. So far as this statement is concerned, the optical work of the eye could produce only two dimensions and visual perception still be three-dimensional.

Berkeley never doubted that the final product of the process that begins with visually perceiving an object in space was three-dimensional. The question that he raised concerned the part that the optical equipment of the eye plays in this process as distinguished from the part played by other factors. One has to understand the position Berkeley took on this question before one can talk about it intelligibly or test it by experiment. It is not clear that the author of Britannica's article "Perception" had this understanding. No references are made to any psychologists who conducted experiments in which the work the optical equipment of the eye does is shown to be tridimensional. Are we to assume that this view is so well established that no such references are needed—that there is no genuine basis for dissent on the subject? We have quoted from *Human Senses in Perception* in Chapter V. We have no basis on which to judge whether the experimental work summarized in our quotations was so designed as to exclude the ambiguity we have just been discussing. Surely, Britannica's article ought to call attention to this ambiguity and attempt to use language that excludes it. If there is no basis for competing views, what is the explanation of the statement we have quoted from Britannica's article "Berkeley" that Berkeley's *New Theory of Vision* is "a brilliant piece of pure psychology, on the perception of space, the conclusions of which have been widely accepted"?

It is highly probable, I believe, that Berkeley's argument that "the ideas intromitted by each sense are widely different, and distinct from each other; but having been observed constantly to go together, they are spoken of as one and the same thing" has been accepted; but whether this is the case, neither Britannica's articles "Berkeley" or "Perception" tell us. And on the question that Berkeley raises, that of the work done by the optical equipment of the eye as distinguished from other factors, neither article gives any evidence of awareness that for perception to be understood, this question has to be asked and answered in a way that is not filled with ambiguity.

Next we will take up the question raised by McLuhan in speaking of perspective as an illusion. The language he uses, as we have shown toward the end of Chapter V is filled with ambiguity, but in the light of other positions that he takes, such as his acceptance of Berkeley's argument in its ambiguous form that vision is two-dimensional, it is clear that he means vision does not give us objects in perspective. Let us see what Britannica's article "Perspective" has to say on this question.

The question whether vision, with or without the aid of any other sense, or any reconstitution by the mind, is two-dimensional or three-dimensional, is not mentioned in the article. It is said that the representation of perspective in art took various forms and a long time before principles that represented perspective truly were discovered and made available for practice. Since no one holds that space is two-dimensional, it may not be reasonable to expect the question that Berkeley raised, that is, whether the optical work of the eye is only two-dimensional, to be discussed in Britannica's article "Perspective." But it certainly is important enough to be discussed somewhere, and it is not. Furthermore, the ways in which what we now call perspective have been handled in the past suggest the possibility that perspective is merely an agreed-upon conventional mode of seeing. So while we cannot condemn Britannica for not discussing this question seriously, still discussion could have helped clear up a moot point. We are told in the article that "it was not until the first half of the 15th century that the Italian painters made perspective drawing an exact science by the use of the horizon line and the vanishing point." If we accept this statement from Britannica as correct, and the evidence we have given in Chapter V clearly says we should, Berkeley could still be right in holding that perspective is not given by the optical work of the eye; but McLuhan could be in that state of confusion that follows failing to distinguish between the optical work of the eye and the final product of perception. Berkeley certainly held this final product to be three-dimensional. So McLuhan is wrong when he says he agrees with Berkeley.

Now to a test of Britannica—or McLuhan—on fact. McLuhan says twice in *Understanding Media* (pp. 202, 329) that Louis Pasteur was thrown out of the medical profession by indignant colleagues for attacking one of their orthodoxies. I believe it is clear that Pasteur had to be in the medical profession in order to be thrown out. Pasteur is certainly important enough for facts of this kind in his life to be reported in the article on him in Britannica. The article says nothing about his ever having been in the medical profession or having been thrown out. We of course cannot criticize Britannica for not reporting an event that never occurred. Britannica could reasonably take space to discuss this subject only if accounts of this "event" that probably never occurred had reached mythical proportions, as we show in Chapter XI to have been the case in the story of Galileo and the Leaning Tower of Pisa.

Finally, Britannica's article "Computer" gives no support to McLuhan's notion that the computer is an extension of human consciousness. We cannot of course take McLuhan's testimony as evidence that Britannica has overlooked the most important fact about the computer—if this is really a fact. We have proposed in Chapter VI a test that would answer this question if there is anywhere any really serious doubt about it. And incidentally, we have dragged in an explanation of Gertrude Stein's "rose is a rose is a rose" that took us a long time to imagine, and that is so obvious when one once sees it that one wonders how the critical world managed to fail to discover it. We dragged it in because our explanation, right or wrong, would provide a test, along with others that we propose, of McLuhan's notion of the computer as an extension of the human consciousness. When we go to Britannica to find what Gertrude Stein meant by her roses, we find Britannica reports only that she "carried to extremes her weird, repetitious and seemingly nonsensical manipulations of words"—and gives as an example "a rose is a rose is a rose." If the explanation we have given in Chapter VI is correct—and whether true or not, it certainly fits— Britannica, out of an almost inexhaustible supply of examples of nonsensical repetition, picked as an illustration of nonsense the one that makes sense.

The examination of Britannica along the lines we have started could be extended indefinitely. The conclusion that we reach is that Britannica as authority, while better, is not a great deal better than McLuhan. But most important is *not* the question of the qualities of particular articles, important as this is. There are specialists in our time who transcend their specialties and who can put them in the context that is necessary to serve the purpose of a genuine general education. Britannica's great weakness, shared with all of our encyclopedias, is that in its conception and design it reveals no awareness whatever of the crucial importance of general education in our time and how an encyclopedia has to be made if it is to serve this purpose. I shall have more to say on this subject in Chapter XII, especially in connection with Britannica's treatment of the subject logic. I shall use Britannica's treatment of this subject to illustrate certain principles that have to be used if any encyclopedia is to serve the purpose of general education rather than exemplify the habits of the specialist that are making us all worse than barbarians.

We shall examine in our next chapters the best efforts that have yet been made to serve the purpose of general education by means other than the encyclopedia.

CHAPTER VIII

Testimony

The chief wonder of education is that it does not ruin
everybody concerned in it, teachers and taught
The Education of Henry Adams

The most severe and by far the best critic of American higher education during the last thirty years or more has been Robert Maynard
Hutchins, formerly Chancellor of the University of Chicago, now
President of the Center for the Study of Democratic Institutions in
Santa Barbara, California. Mr. Hutchins has been charged with excessive softness toward communism, and I believe this charge is true. But
it was true of the leadership of the United States and probably of a
majority of the people during World War II; and it probably is true
today of a majority of the intellectual leaders of the country. This
charge is not the same as the charge of communism, though the two are
often confused. It may be true for any one of many reasons, among
them that one is opposed to the use of armed force in the settlement of
international disputes, and so much opposed that one prefers acquiescence rather than the use of armed force to resist the growth of communist power. This view most certainly can be honestly held, as can
its opposite. Both can be used stupidly, both can be used for utterly
unscrupulous purposes.

Those who hold that acquiescence is the better course tend to overlook the fact that one may be opposed to the use of armed force in the
settlement of international disputes, but may not be so much opposed
as to prefer acquiescence to the point that one puts one's society into a
position such that it finally has to surrender or fight—and fight when
doing so is only a forlorn hope. They overlook the fact that it is possible to be devoted to peace but at the same time to hold that the worst
enemy of peace and justice and the other principles of a free society
is that excessive devotion to peace, that devotion that chooses peace
at any price.

The charge of being soft on communism poses a grave question, one that is usually dealt with by pooh-pooing and talk about nervous Nellies and obsessions. It is not answered this way. This charge had little force during World War II because it was thought, mistakenly and disastrously thought, that it would be easier to get along with the communists than the Nazis and that a balance-of-power policy was an evil policy and could not be honestly supported by the United States. This view was sedulously propagated before and during World War II and succeeded in controlling United States policy. The necessity of a balance-of-power policy to a free world is still not widely understood in the intellectual world. The facts that anarchism of the extreme type, the type that has become a power in the United States in recent years, always turns into dictatorship, and that the communists have become expert in the use of extreme anarchism to establish their dictatorship, have been in the main invisible to much of the intellectual world because of its softness on communism. Finally, this charge has lost most of its force, though the problem involved in it has become even more serious, as the necessity of trying to get along peacefully with the communist powers of the earth has become clearer and clearer.

Hutchins has made statements as to his beliefs concerning communism and I see no reason for doubting that his statements represent his real beliefs. I shall quote him on this subject below. I have heard on many occasions the charge that Hutchins is antireligious. I do not know of any reasons for believing this charge. I consider myself a religious person, and if his statements represent his beliefs, as far as I know them his beliefs are identical with my own. I consider my religion the unifying principle, the integrating power, the principle and power that give me whatever integrity I have in my life. I believe in the truth of my religion and am concerned that it actually be, not merely in thoughts and words, but in actions as well, what I believe it to be. To manage this calls for a frequent internal dialogue, a frequent process of self-examination, one that at times calls for sackcloth and ashes. (I have to say, I cannot imagine Mr. Hutchins in sackcloth and ashes.)

If religion is the unifying, the integrating influence in human existence, or the dividing, disintegrating influence that in my view it may be according to the nature of one's religion; if religion in some form or other is present in all types of human life, if the word "secular" is an utterly deceptive word, one that has no object, it is necessary in the interests of civilized life to know about religion in its various forms, and particularly to know and be ruled, not merely in words but in actions, by the form that is necessary to civilized life. Hutchins, it seems to me, is helpful on this subject, and I quote passages from him:

By religion I mean belief in and obedience to God. This may not require adherence to a church or creed; but it demands religious faith. . . . We see in St. Augustine's *Confessions* the way in which a man may come to the sort of religious conviction that has meaning" [p. 82].[1]

[Newman and Mill] both feel that moral and religious education is more important than intellectual education. So do I. The question is not whether moral and religious education is important, but what colleges and universities can do about it. No one would favor a nation of highly intelligent and well-trained robbers, murderers, thieves, arsonists, and forgers. And no one would contend that knowledge of the arts and sciences automatically leads to the development of good moral habits [p. 87].

. . . religion is of the greatest moral importance. If the whole world practiced Aristotle's *Ethics*, the whole world would be much better off than it is today. But I doubt if any single man, to say nothing of the whole world, can practice Aristotle's *Ethics* without the support and inspiration of religious faith [p. 91].

Men, simply because they are men, are unlikely to find within themselves the power that can bring the good life and the good state to pass. As Reinhold Niebuhr points out in his Gifford lectures, all anthropocentric ethical doctrines fail at this point: they overlook the fallen nature of man and assume that without grace he can reach a terrestrial end to which almost by definition, no being with such a nature can ever attain [pp. 91–92].

What Hutchins says here seems to me true and important, and along with other statements of his, suggests strongly to me that his religion is in a much healthier state than that of many theologians of our time.

If it is said that Hutchins has not used his religious convictions, as represented by his words, in the selection of his faculty, this is mere repetition of what he himself has said. In refraining from doing this, he has simply followed prevailing custom. None of the leading universities in the United States in its negotiations with a prospective member of its faculty inquires into his religious beliefs. Hutchins says this as clearly as is possible. I quote him:

. . . every day men are appointed to faculties after a most painstaking investigation of their intellectual attainments, but without any inquiry into their moral habits or their religious beliefs. I do it every day myself. We do not ask whether the prospective appointee is afflicted with scientism, skepticism, or secularism. We do not request him to state whether he believes in God or whether or not he thinks morals are indistinguishable from

1. References are to pages in Robert M. Hutchins, *Freedom, Education, and the Fund,* Meridian Books (Cleveland: World, 1956).

the mores and are relative, like the mores, to time and place. We ask what his training has been, what his record was, what his publications are, and what are the prospects of his publishing any more. We ask, in short, whether he has discovered any truth in his specialty, and whether he can be expected to seek for and, perhaps, discover additional truths. . . . everybody would be shocked at the suggestion that it is proper to investigate a man's beliefs, or to ask what, if anything he stands for. [p. 93].

So far as present-day custom is concerned, there is no room for doubt that this statement is true. Our universities are, in the respect indicated, completely dominated by custom. But Hutchins has never been one to let custom govern him, nor has he always avoided doing the shocking thing if he thought it needed to be done.

Hutchins says, and I believe truly: "Without theology or metapyhsics a unified university cannot exist." [2] One might ask, if he really believed this, why he did not violate the custom that has abandoned theology or metaphysics as the source of unifying principles and proceed to find such principles and unify the University of Chicago in accordance with them.

The answer to these questions, in all fairness, is that there are limits to the number and size of the battles in which a man can engage at one time and have any chance to win any of them. I saw Hutchins at work over a period of five years. He was usually engaged in more than one battle. I do not regard prudence as always a virtue, but there are times when it is the virtue of virtues. One can, as I have just said, engage in so many battles at once that one cannot win any. And some battles are far more important than others.

Hutchins expands in his book *Freedom, Education, and the Fund* his argument for instruction in the principles of religion and morality in a university:

The curriculum [of a university] should include the knowledge and understanding of the principles of morality. It should include both natural and sacred theology; for how can a man call himself educated who does not grasp the leading ideas that since the dawn of history have animated mankind? The institution must be committed to taking morality and religion seriously. This commitment involves a third: if the object of higher education is the truth, then, in order to take morality and religion seriously, the institution must believe that there is some truth and some discoverable truth about morality and religion. According to the dogmas of scientism, skepticism, and secularism there is no such truth. If there is truth at all,

2. Hutchins, *The Higher Learning in America* (New Haven, Conn.: Yale Univ. Press, [1936] 1967), p. 99.

it is truth discoverable in the laboratory, by what is called the scientific method. I recently heard a minister of a Protestant church state at a public meeting that no man could tell whether a given act was right or wrong. I replied that he was a moral relativist, thinking that he would be so stung by this reproach that he might reconsider his position. Instead he proudly answered, "Of course I am a moral relativist," as though to say that anybody who is not a moral relativist is an unenlightened, unscientific, medieval reactionary [pp. 96–97].

Again I quote, and again with complete agreement:

Morality and religion cannot be taken seriously unless the possibility of attaining truth by philosophical inquiry and by revelation is admitted. It is necessary to believe that philosophy is something more than words and that it is possible to be rational and religious at the same time [ibid].

I get the impression from Hutchins' writings that he holds religion and morality to be something that a person can have, or not have, as he chooses. I cannot cite any passage to this effect, and my impression may be wrong. I bring the question up because I consider it very important. In my view, religion, like power, is all-pervasive. Merely to be alive, to exist, is to be religious in some way or other, just as merely to exist is to be and to exercise power in some way or other. There is no choice, no possibility of choice as long as one exists as to whether one will or will not be religious, or will or will not be and exercise power. One either worships one's self or one worships the good and the true— abstractions from the transcendent God. And what one imagines to be, and is likely to parade before the world as the worship of the good and the true may be mere worship of self.

I remember as if it were yesterday, the revulsion I felt and the letter I wrote but that I did not send some fifty years ago—on my mother's urgent advice that he would not understand and that my letter would only hurt his feelings—to a preacher who had devoted his sermon to the argument that if one gave one-tenth of his income to the church, one would surely go to heaven. One's real purpose in religion then was not the worship of God. Instead it was to find the cheapest possible price on a mansion in the skies and an irrevocable right to it and infinite delights throughout eternity—in short, it was worship of self.

I cannot take the space to develop the argument in detail, but I say our universities are religious in a demonic way, whereas Hutchins says, if I interpret him correctly, they are irreligious and therefore demonic. The difference seems to me unimportant in this context in comparison with the agreement. But it is, I believe, of crucial im-

portance in other contexts and it is for this reason that I call attention
to it. For instance, Mr. Hutchins seems to me to believe that reason in
men can be developed to the point where it can take the place of the
exercise of power. If to exist is to exercise power just as to exist is to
be in some way religious, this is not possible. The utmost in this case
that reason can do is direct the exercise of power.

I turn now to Hutchins' attitude toward communism. I quote from
him:

I am opposed to Communism because it is a form of tyranny over the mind
of man. It is a system that uses a pseudo-religion to cloak old-fashioned
imperialist expansionism, that sanctions the lie as an instrument of policy,
that is based on the proposition that it is right and proper for a few of the
people to push the rest of the people around, and that denies the essential
elements of the American idea, which are freedom and justice.

This seems to me clear and cogent and true. Hutchins goes on to say:

I do not underestimate the threat of Communism; but I sometimes think
that some people are so neurotically preoccupied with Communism that
they underestimate America. Communism has failed in the United States
[p. 226].

Here I disagree. Communism can come to a country in many different
ways. For instance, at the time I write, the Federal administration is trying to get inflation under control. The cause of inflation is the action
of every interest that has goods or labor to sell to get the highest possible price that it can. Some of the interests involved have been given
power by government policy and are now politically so powerful—
labor unions, for instance—that they can be opposed successfully only
by governmental action. But they are now so powerful that any government that offered really serious opposition to them might be put out of
office by them. The corporations of the country do not control vast
numbers of votes. And government policy is to require them to compete, and this, insofar as this policy is effective, prevents them from
saying to the public: stand and deliver or you can't have our products.
And the profits on which employment depends, depend on them. Labor
has a highly privileged position in comparison with the business and
commercial interests of the country. It can and does hold up the whole
public whenever it pleases. It has virtually dictatorial powers without
any of the responsibility that a dictatorship has, and it has these powers
by gift from the people through their government.

One of the principles in the legal tradition of free societies is that an agreement or contract made under duress is not legally valid. Many of the contracts made with labor in the last quarter century have been made under duress—stand and deliver or go without transportation or communication facilities, or production will be stopped or power shut off; stand and deliver or starve or be buried in garbage. The demands, with the power to make the demands effective, have been so numerous it is impossible even to summarize them here. One actually hears labor leaders today demanding that contracts made under duress be honored. This situation will certainly prove in the long run far more disastrous for labor and for the people of the country generally than is currently imagined, if it is not corrected. It is not at all clear that correction by legislative or administrative or judicial action is possible, unless labor has the wisdom to exercise restraint in the use of its power. The almost unlimited power that organized labor has today will have to be curbed if the country is not to be continually faced with the danger of being driven into some form of totalitarianism by this power.

It would be wrong to give the impression that labor has not had reasons for organizing and seeking power. The problems that labor has made in this respect can be matched by problems that corporations have made. But labor now has by far the greater power, and as I have said, this power was built on governmental action sanctioned by the public. Labor now has virtually unlimited power and it has this power without responsibility for its exercise. If it had responsibility for its exercise of its power, it would be the government instead of now being the power that is almost equal to or even greater than that of the government. The idea of a general strike by labor, if actually carried out, could test the question where power lies. For labor to win this test could be the greatest disaster to labor that has ever occurred in American history. It is true that, at times in American history, corporate power has been almost as great as labor power now is. But fortunately, corporate power has been curbed. Corporations are, like labor unions, creatures of the law. But there are legal and other restraints and possible restraints on corporations that, if needed, prevent them from becoming monopolies that have almost unlimited power.

One of the most difficult problems in the relations of labor and industry today is that industry in recent years has been following practices outside the United States that it followed in the United States until these practices were curbed to some extent by federal laws. One of these practices is the location of industry in low-cost areas where labor that can quickly become highly skilled is available, or purchasing policies that shift industry to such areas. This practice and the purchase of completely manufactured articles and of parts has been extended to foreign countries where savings in cost could be made by doing so. These practices of course shift employment from the United States to other countries. They also make lower prices to the American public possible. And they greatly ease political power problems with the countries where the manufacturing is done and the purchases made. The United States at the time of this writing is in the preliminary phases of the effort to stop the great excess in recent years of imports over exports. This will undoubtedly have some effects, perhaps large effects, on industrial manufacture and purchase of articles and parts abroad. But it can and undoubtedly will create problems of the greatest difficulty with the countries most affected. It is not necessary for cartels to exist in order for governmental intervention in matters of this kind to lead to realignments of international power and international crises. But whoever or whatever is to blame, a situation exists in which the government of the United States has no choice but to intervene.

Now I do not believe that under contemporary conditions free society can exist without organized labor that is reasonably autonomous. But there is also the problem whether free society can continue to exist with organized labor that accepts no limits on its power. This is one of the "contradictions" that, according to communism, exist in free society and doom it to self-destruction. The communist solution is to make labor organizations instruments of government. There is a wide difference between being an instrument of government and being able possibly to dictate to government. If labor pushes to the point of being the government in the United States, whether openly or otherwise, labor will lose its autonomy and become an instrument of government. It already serves to a great extent as an instrument of government in the United States, but it still retains large measures of autonomy. Communist labor has deprived the labor of communist countries of all autonomy. Hitler's National Socialists and Mussolini's Fascists did the same. The problem here is simply that freedom can be used to destroy freedom. As long as this problem is not understood, it is simply fatuous to hold that totalitarianism of one kind or other is no danger in the United States. This is one of the points on which I find it necessary to disagree with Hutchins.

Another point of disagreement with Hutchins is made necessary by his statement in the last quotation that "some people are so neurotically preoccupied with Communism that they underestimate America."

There is certainly some truth in this statement, but this truth cuts in more ways than one. Hutchins himself has done some estimating. When he estimates the universities of America, as he has done, he has estimated the great shaping influence in the country. According to Hutchins, and all the evidence that we have says that he is right, this influence currently is anarchic. At this point he forgets the lessons in his Great Books. The sequel to anarchy has always been some form of dictatorship. Both Plato and Aristotle outline the process in which this occurs. In view of Hutchins' urgent recommendation of their writings as aids to learning, it is difficult to understand why at this point he does not use their aid.

As to neuroticism, Hutchins is certainly right that some people are "neurotically preoccupied with [fear of] Communism"; but he could have said just as truthfully that some are neurotically preoccupied with antagonism to anticommunism. I have had first-hand painful experience with both. I have friends, or rather former friends, who in the early thirties almost joined the Party and who since then have shifted to the opposite extreme. On the Fourth of July weekend in 1965, they informed me that I had to join them in their extremism or they would write me off as a friend. I had know them since college days and had at times not seen them because of their extremisms; but I do not like breaking friendships almost of a lifetime and had, despite extremely unpleasant breaks, renewed friendship when opportunity came along. The neurotic preoccupation with communism in July 1965 was, however, so extreme that I had to let them write me off. I have had the experience recently of being written off by others because they consider me an extremist in my anticommunism as well as in other ways, such as the views I express in this book. Naturally, and perhaps in what might be a merely self-serving way, I might interpret both of these cases as neurotic preoccupation in others rather than in myself. In any case, I cannot help noticing that I am unable to convince the others, nor or they able to convince me. I do not know that any neurotic character is responsible for this failure, though it certainly may be, and, in some cases, it seems to me beyond doubt that neuroticism is responsible. However, I believe this failure is in the main attributable to the failure of our education to help us learn how to use our minds in the governing of what we say and do.

Hutchins appears to be perfectly clear in the following statement that there is one standard that is most important in all reasoning, if the reasoning is not to be self-defeating:

What then are the limitations on the freedom of the faculty of a university? They are the limitations on independent thought. These should be nothing more than the laws of logic and the laws of the country. I would hope that the laws of the country would not seek to control thought. I do not believe that any legislative body can repeal or amend the law of contradiction. *I do not see how it is possible to say that the same thing is both true and not true at the same time in the same respect* [my italics], and I should think it difficult to conduct any communication within the community of scholars unless they all accept the law of contradiction. I should not suggest any other limitations, and if any professor wanted to show, as some of my colleagues do, that the law of contradiction has been repealed by modern scientific advances, I should encourage him to pursue his outrageous course. One might wish that he were more agreeable or more conventional; but he cannot be discharged because he fails to measure up to desirable standards in these respects. As long as his political activities are legal, he may engage in them [p. 157].

The appearance of perfect clarity is, however, completely deceptive. It not only is possible "to *say* that the same thing is both true and not true at the same time in the same respect," Hutchins says it in the words I have italicized in the quotation from him. There is nothing whatever to prevent anyone from contradicting himself. Words are helpless things, and one can use them carefully, or carelessly as Hutchins does here.

Contrary to Hutchins, nobody, not even Mr. Hutchins, is constrained in what he says by the law of contradiction. The only constraint is that if reasoning is to be correct, not erroneous—and it certainly can be filled with error—the law of contradiction must be obeyed. It is often disobeyed. The error that Hutchins makes when he says the laws of logic are among "the limitations on independent thought" is often made. The error could be illustrated with a vast number of examples. I will give only one bit of testimony on the subject, testimony from the very influential British realist, G. E. Moore (1873–1958). Moore became doubtful in his later life about the argument he makes in his essay "The Refutation of Idealism," but he took no risk when in this essay he said: "Many philosophers . . . when they admit a distinction, yet (following the lead of Hegel) boldly assert their right, in a slightly more obscure form of words, also to deny it." This statement of Moore's is just as true with the parenthesis limiting indulgence in contradiction to followers of Hegel dropped out as it is with it in. Moore could have said truly that many philosophers, as well as the rest of us, indulge in the practice of saying something, and then, in other words, of denying what we have said—and the denials do not have to be in a very obscure form. Some of us fortunately have enough intellectual honesty, and knowledge of what it is, to be embarrassed, to feel that we ourselves have made a blot on our intellectual honor when we or someone else catches us in a contradiction.

I shall not comment here on that part of the quotation above from Hutchins in which he says that "the laws of the country" should be, along with "the laws of logic," "limitations on the freedom of the faculty of a university," except to say that if Hutchins abandons "the laws of the country" as quickly and easily as he abandons "the laws of logic" merely because somebody wishes to attack them and thinks he can attack them successfully—if all these laws are for Hutchins limitations that he then finds out are not limitations, then I am forced to wonder how far he has succeeded in communicating with himself on this subject.

I now quote Mr. Hutchins on agreement and the law of contradiction:

Socrates collected opinions, asked questions, clarified terms and ideas, and indicated commitments. That is all he did. All that was required of those who took part with him was that they should try to think and to understand one another. They did not have to agree with Socrates, before or after. They did not have to agree among themselves. If they came to a conviction, they did so of their own free will. The only constraint upon them was the law of contradiction. They could not answer Yes and No to the same question at the same time [pp. 143-44].

Socrates, I believe, never made mere "commitments" without giving reasons for his commitments; he never made commitments without first using logic in the rigorous examination of competing opinions; and he never used his reason except in the quest for an idea of the true or the good by which the quality of all human actions could be judged. He clearly held that some agreement existed, usually implicit, such as that for any discussion to be fruitful, it had to be conducted in a genuine quest for the true and the good. In Socrates we have an example of the unity of thought and will and feeling and of the power of the true and the good to draw them into its service. Socrates was not driven by any physical desires. He was no mere logic chopper. He would have held mere logic chopping, mere skill in reasoning to be diabolical if divorced from service of the true and the good. The portrait that Socrates elicits from Callicles of Callicles—the essence of self-centeredness—in the *Gorgias* is sufficient evidence of this. Socrates clearly held that the reaching of truth as far as possible and agreement on it was the great end of discussion.

If I interpret the last two sentences in the quotation above from Hutchins correctly, they say that the law of contradiction applies itself automatically in human thought and discourse. If this were true, nobody would have to bother about it.

We do not have any dialogue in which Socrates participated in which discussion is now and then interrupted in the effort to introduce irrelevant subjects. Thus there is agreement on the subject to be discussed. Participants in most cases acquiesce and agree with Socrates when he shows them that their arguments are in error because they contain contradictions. Thus there is a large measure of agreement on the law of contradiction. I do not remember any outright denial of it in any of the dialogues. Still, it does not apply itself automatically in thinking and talking. Socrates, or somebody else, has to apply it.

My guess is that in using the word "require" in the quotation above, Hutchins was thinking of pressures on him while Chancellor of the University of Chicago to "require" agreement in his faculty with some one or more propositions. If this is what he is responding to, his response is, in a certain sense, the only one that he could reasonably make. But in another sense, and a crucial one, that of *trying* to get agreement and using his power in relation to appointments to this end, his *not trying* to this extent was simply abdication. At the same time, I recognize that, given the state of mind in the intellectual world today, the trying would have been dangerous to him in that it would have added to the number of battles in which he was engaged.

One cannot get agreement in a free society, and certainly not in a university, by merely in gross fashion *requiring* it. One may get compliance, which may be only external and apparent, by *requiring* in gross fashion, but what is needed is more than any sort of mere compliance, or even willing compliance. One may get compliance by the use, or the threat of the use, of superior physical force; but if one loves genuine peace—and I believe Hutchins does—one acts in the effort to get with others harmonious action that comes from genuine and freely reached agreement that works for a common and good end. This kind of agreement is absolutely necessary to genuine peace, and in failing to insist on it, Hutchins fails to work for genuine peace.

Let us now examine another statement by Hutchins that has to do with the problem of agreement and the purpose of a university: "An educational institution should be a community. A community must have a common aim, and the common aim of the educational community is the truth. It is not necessary that the members of the educational community agree with one another" (p. 99). Is there really no necessity of agreement on anything? What is a common aim if it is not something held in common, something at least implicitly agreed on? And can there be common aim at truth in the absence of agreement in thought and action that this is the aim? The first two sentences in the quotation above, with which I could not disagree and in which I see no flaw, contradict the last sentence. It is, of course, not necessary that university faculties be in agreement on everything. But however this may be, it is impossible that a community should have a common aim without having a common aim, that is, without being in agreement in thought and action that is common. The most important kind of agreement is that of harmonious action that is freely willed—but freely willed harmonious action, as Hutchins clearly recognizes in another place, can be that of thieves and murderers. So, if we want the true and the good, harmonious action must be directed toward them. So, when Hutchins says a community must have a common aim, he implicitly says that agreement at least to this extent is necessary; but then he also says that agreement is not necessary.

Finally, I believe it might be helpful if I present here a collection of comments by Hutchins that, to the extent that they are true—and I believe they are largely true—have important bearings on the prospects for general education in the United States. I have quoted previously a passage from Hutchins in which he speaks of people who are so neurotically preoccupied with what they consider to be the threat of communism that they underestimate America. The estimate of American higher education that Hutchins gives in the following passages is not a high one. It is clearly, according to his own testimony, in one respect a gross underestimate. Now Hutchins' concern here could be called "neurotic." I do not think this would make it so, and I think the loose use of labels of this kind is itself exceedingly unhealthy.

Specialized education in the United States, according to Hutchins, has been a "tremendous success, in material, practical terms." It is general education that for the public generally, including the intellectual world, has been, with the exception of individuals here and there, an abysmal failure. On this, the evidence says overwhelmingly that Hutchins is right.

According to the following quotations from Hutchins, the people of the country do not know what education is, the heads of universities do not know, the faculty members do not know, the boards of trustees do not know.

As to the people:

The people of this country think that education is a perfectly splendid thing and have not the faintest idea of what it is about [p. 44].

As to the faculties:

The tremendous success, in material, practical terms, that specialism instantly achieved in America, led to a greater and greater fragmentation of knowledge, with specialists operating in small parts of each fragment. We have now reached the situation where the work of a man in one part of a fragment is incomprehensible to one in another part of the same fragment, to say nothing of a man in another subject. The unity of the modern American university is therefore geographical, and the topics that can be discussed at the faculty club are the weather and politics [p. 119].

As to administrators:

The academic administrators of America remind one of the French revolutionist who said, "the mob is in the street. I must find out where they are going, for I am their leader." . . . Since the American university has been unable to formulate any idea of its function, its function is to do what any powerful group wants it to undertake. It has no standard by which to judge these requests, because it has no conception of the end. The modern university and the modern department store are therefore almost indistinguishable [p. 179].

As to trustees:

I do not subscribe to the notion that the board should operate the university as the representative of the community. Nor do I subscribe to the notion that the board is a kind of supreme court that should decide educational issues brought before it. This would mean that the board would be determining the educational policy of the institution, something that even the best boards are not qualified to do. . . . a trustee, or a board of trustees, who did not like what the faculty or a faculty member was doing should resign. It should never occur to trustees that faculty members should resign because they do not share the opinions of trustees. The most important right that the trustees have is the right of criticism. I think that two propositions are true: first, a university is a center of independent thought, and second, uncriticized groups inevitably deteriorate. The solution of the problem lies, then, not in regulation or in control, but in criticism. The difficulty is money. Universities always need money. [p. 163].

Further as to trustees, Hutchins argues for self-government by university faculties. But the description that he himself gives, as above, of university faculties hardly shows that they are qualified to govern themselves. And when Hutchins recognizes the right of trustees to criticize, he recognizes their right to bring pressure for resignations. For criticism can certainly generate pressure.

I do not know who can govern university faculties if they are unable to govern themselves. Boards of trustees may be a lot better than the educational influences to which they have been exposed, just as individuals in the public generally may be. Ordinary common sense is hard to destroy completely. But most of us do succumb to the influences around us, just as our evidence shows Hutchins has done, except for his lamentations. Boards of trustees therefore cannot reasonably be expected to be a lot better than the educational and other influences to which they have been exposed. They can hardly be expected to be able to govern except in ways that are gross and as likely to be harmful as to be helpful. But whether harmful or helpful, boards of trustees cannot reasonably be expected to stand in public, and help get money, for education that they consider wasteful or vicious or anything but genuine education. Our real situation is, I believe, that all of us are engaged in a long-time process of trying to educate each other; and I am exceedingly doubtful about any argument that says, even if it is consistent in saying it as Hutchins is not, that this particular group in society has a patent on this process, this group only has knowledge of what it is, and has, with reference to all other groups, the exclusive right to determine the process and to carry it on.

If education is to be genuine, there is no escape from the necessity in all decision-making quarters, which in a free society certainly includes the public, of knowledge of what it is.

In urging so eloquently and so persistently—now for nearly forty years—the necessity of knowledge of general education to the maintenance and further development of free society and the cultivation of this knowledge in the public, Hutchins has performed a service for the people of the United States of the very greatest importance. He has, however, failed to integrate his urging—that is, to free it from contradiction—and has left knowledge of what a genuine education is just about where he found it. As to action, the forces blocking Hutchins' way—if he had one—have been practically all-powerful. But the overcoming of apparently insuperable obstacles is the test of man on earth.

It is impossible to overemphazise the difficulty of the problem of general education. It involves the problem that for centuries has been

embalmed as the paradox of knowledge. One would have to be a super-
man, or have a more than ordinarily genuine revelation to solve this
problem. Even if by some fortunate chance someone should come along
who knows something of what a genuine general education is, would
you be able to recognize the genuineness if you did not already somehow know what it is? But if you already know, why all this bother to
find out?

I have expressed severe criticisms of American education generally
during the last forty years. At the same time, but not for the same
reasons, I have found it necessary in truth to praise American education, and especially American higher education, and to say because I
believe it is true that until recent years it has been the best large influence in the country. It is, as the church was in former times, the
great establishment of its time, and it must somehow be helped to do
better at its great task. The help that is needed is criticism that tries to
find the points of failure and tries to show how they can be rectified.
The points of success are obvious. There never has been an establishment that was superior to this one in its scientific and technical excellence. General education—that is, the cultivation of the knowledge
that is necessary to the proper use of scientific and technical excellence—is where help is most needed. On this Hutchins certainly was
right. Let us turn now to another aspect of the problem of higher education in the United States.

I quote below from an article "Student Politics and the University"
by Nathan Glazer, professor of education and social structure at Harvard, in the July 1969 issue of the *Atlantic*. First, Professor Glazer tells
us what he said when he began to write on the student revolts in
December 1964. He then saw them not as they presented themselves—
as appeals for freedom of speech: he saw them as attacks on this freedom, as attacks that would become more and more serious if they were
allowed to continue. He says he was right in this, and he undoubtedly
was. There were, as usual of course, those who disagreed with him
and those who agreed and, at the time, said very much the same that
he said. "Where were we wrong?" asks Glazer. "Our gravest mistake
was that we did not see what strength and plausibility would soon be
attached to the argument that this country was ruled by a cruel and
selfish oligarchy devoted to the extension of the power and privilege of
the few and denying liberty and even life to the many; and to the
further assertion that the university was an integral part of this sys-

tem." Again, Glazer is right. And he might have gone further and still have been right. There was in the student revolt and other revolts in recent years a use of violence that if it continued and grew would have tended to force the public, either by means of its government or otherwise, to resort to extreme measures in self-protection. One of the lessons of history that is hard to avoid seeing, except by the mentally blind, is that a small, determined, and skilled group can create chaos in a society and arouse an irrepressible countermovement for a dictatorship that will use the severest possible repressive measures. Fortunately, the revolts of recent years have not gone this far. We can be fairly sure that the possibility of the kind just indicated was not seen by those members of the intellectual world who either supported or condoned the revolts or looked on them with indifference—except, of course, for the far-out intellectuals who really wanted a totalitarian dictatorship, assuming that it would do what they wanted done and in a hurry.

The not seeing of which Glazer speaks is one of the grave mistakes that has been made by the leading social scientists in leading American universities since the late thirties. Of course there have been exceptions, but they were ignored by their colleagues, the public, and the government in Washington. This "not seeing" is the mistake that led the United States during World War II to forget the aid that communism gave to Hitler by the pact with him of August 1939, and to assume that only the National Socialism of Germany was a danger to the civilized world. Robert Maynard Hutchins was right when he took the position several decades ago that universities were collections of specialists, that the great tradition of the Western world was not being transmitted by American universities to their students, that in turning out men trained only in specialties, universities were turning barbarians loose on the world and were themselves becoming victims of these same barbarians. Hutchins was, as I have said elsewhere, defeated by these barbarians in his effort to find out what general education is and to establish it at the University of Chicago. I should add that in my opinion the task was far too great, that it could not possibly be accomplished in the time that could be allowed, and that not enough weight was given to the possibility that the teachers needed first to be taught, that there might not be enough already qualified to do very much toward general education. In any case, there is no room for doubt today that the specialists in leading American universities are among the best in the world; but they certainly gave the world in the last five years of the

1960's an appalling exhibition of their inability to govern themselves. And so far as the majority of the people is concerned, education has done no better for them. I quote Hutchins:

Universal education, instead of fulfilling the hopes of its sponsors by liberating the worker and enabling him to get political power and use it wisely, has made him the victim of charlatans in every field of human activity.[3]

The complaint was made to me some years ago by the editor of a university quarterly that book publishing was becoming highly commercialized and he invited me to write an article for him saying why. In the article that I wrote, I said:

I find it impossible to condemn book publishers, or any other publishers for that matter, without first condemning colleges and universities, particularly those that have had the leadership in determining the methods and materials of instruction used throughout the educational system.

I cannot believe that people generally are unable to learn to read books; but the hard fact is that in spite of all the "educating" that is being done most of the products of our educational system do not and cannot read serious books. If "the only perceptible result of the education of the masses" has been "the scribbling of dirty words on public lavatory walls at a level several inches lower than before" the fault must lie in either education or the "masses."

The comics book publisher who, in defending his business, said, "there are more morons than people in the United States and we have to do business with them," may be a horrible example of commercialization, but he at least had the courage to try to face the problem and the honesty to state it as he saw it.

If large numbers of people are incapable of reading books more complicated than comics books, and if these people are not really morons, then it is difficult to arrive at any conclusion except that the educational system as it exists is failing and is failing terribly.

I do not see how publishers can be expected to educate the public when the educational system, with all the support that it receives from the public has failed to create in more than a very small proportion of the public even the least desire for education.[4]

One of the chief developments of the 1960's was the extension of the scribbling of dirty words on public lavatory walls to the shouting and parading on placards of the dirty words in public places, and especially

3. Hutchins, *The University of Utopia* (Chicago: Univ. of Chicago Press, [1953] 1965), p. 9.
4. W. T. Couch, "A Case History in Book Publishing," *American Quarterly*, Winter 1949.

in public places on and near college and university campuses. A large and most important part of the intellectual world seemed bent on providing an arena in which the idiocy of the time could express itself freely and show its contempt for the effort of the human mind to distinguish between and serve the better rather than the worse. This spectacle could cause one to wonder how long it would take for unlimited tolerance to provoke reaction to the other extreme.

I was far from agreeing with all that Hutchins said, and in fact had to criticize him severely on more than one issue in which I was involved with him. But as to the dire need of the country for serious attention to general education, and particularly for some at or near the top to have some of it, I was in complete agreement; and I was painfully aware of being in need of more of it myself. I am now convinced that it cannot be provided in any form that approaches fullness by the colleges and universities of the country—that they can do little more than teach and train in the use of the tools of education, and that the country will be fortunate if they repair the failures they have for a long time been committing in this respect. On the question of student determination of curricula, Hutchins was perfectly clear, and, again, I think right:

> . . . educators cannot permit the students to dictate the course of study unless they are prepared to confess that they are nothing but chaperons, supervising an aimless, trial-and-error process which is valuable chiefly because it keeps young people from doing something worse.[5]

It is, of course, possible for educators to give in temporarily to student demands when they are not able to block the demands and believe that by temporizing they can regain control. But the very fact that demands are made, and have to be acquiesced in, means that the relation between faculty and students is the opposite of what it should be. Still, some of the disgrace that characterized American college and university actions during the last five years of the 1960's will be reduced if the acquiescence that has occurred proves to be temporizing. We can be certain that while the teachers may not know well enough what they are doing and why, the students know far less about these matters —or, if not, the students really ought to be the ones who are doing the teaching. In a sense, and in a most unfortunate but necessary one, it is clear that they are.

5. *Higher Learning in America*, p. 70.

I now quote further from Professor Glazer's article in the *Atlantic* on the student revolts:

I have made some commitments that an orderly democracy is better than government by the expressive and violent outbursts of the most committed; that the university embodies values that transcend the given characteristics of a society or the specific disasters of an administration; that the faults of our society, grave as they are, do not require—indeed, would in no way be advanced by—the destruction of these fragile institutions which have been developed over centuries to transmit and expand knowledge. These are strongly held commitments, so strongly that my first reaction to student disruption—and it is not only an emotional one—is to consider how the disrupters can be isolated and weakened, how their influence which is now enormous among students, can be reduced, how dissension among them can be encouraged, and how they can be finally removed from a community they wish to destroy.

I find it encouraging that a Harvard professor should be willing to make a commitment of this kind in public. This action is wholly admirable, except for one point. I have no doubt Professor Glazer makes allowance in his own mind for the possibility of change in a good direction and I shall not discuss this. The exception I have to make has to do with the statement that "the university embodies values that transcend the given characteristics of a society." It is necessary if universities are ever to do exactly this, that they work seriously at this task and stop congratulating themselves on their being ahead of and superior to the people who support them. A large part of what universities have done in this century has been to turn out technicians who have developed means for destroying all life on earth and who, while incapable of understanding that this is what they were doing while they were doing it, are now incapable of doing much more than lament what they have done. The more, of which they have already done far too dangerously much, is to make bargaining with the communist power in the world almost impossible and to establish a trend toward reducing their country to impotence in the face of this power. The evidence that many physical scientists have given in recent years on the quality of their judgment on political questions is not reassuring. It is no wonder that government subject to the common man is still believed, even by many in the transcendent universities, to be the last best hope of man on earth. I, too, value the universities of America and the world, but not so much for what they are but for what they ought to be and could be if they engaged seriously in that self-examination that is necessary to keep the ego from swelling to self-destructive proportions.

If I understand him correctly, Professor Glazer expresses in the last quotation I have given from him the theory discussed briefly earlier that there are common elements in all educational processes that somehow justify these processes, and that these elements are present in all universities. I assume this is what he means when he says, "the university embodies values that transcend the given characteristics of a society." But then the question arises, Where were these values and what were they in the universities of Germany when these universities gave all their loyalties and used all their resources to support Hitler's National Socialism? And the same question has to be asked about the universities of Russia and their silence during the horrors that Stalin inflicted on the Russian people.

I think Plato came nearer the truth on this subject in a passage of *The Republic* in which the forces that tend to corrupt are being considered. Socrates has already discussed the corrupting power on men generally of inordinate desire for "beauty, riches, strength of body, powerful connections in a city. . . ." Then he asks, "shall we not also say that similarly the most richly endowed natures, if they receive a bad upbringing, become surpassingly evil? Or do you fancy that great crimes and unmixed wickedness come from a feeble nature and not rather from a noble nature ruined by bad education, while a weak nature will never be the author of great good or great evil?" [6]

The members of the faculties of modern universities in industrialized societies of all types possess the technical expertness without which modern industrialized society would die. They and they alone developed the talents without which the two world wars of the twentieth century would not have been possible. They also developed the talents that feed and clothe and house and maintain in a higher state of physical health and comfort more people than ever before in the history of man on earth. Their very accomplishment in the way of enabling more people to live in far greater relative health and comfort than ever before now threatens itself to bring disaster. They are more fully aware of this and of possible correctives than any other part of the population. Without the talents that these men cultivate, the techniques of which they have superb command, modern populations would dwindle in starvation, disease, continual strife, and misery until life on earth became such a horrible burden—not merely for a few, or more than a few, as it has always been—that none would want it; and the operators

6. Plato, *Republic*, trans. Lindsay, Book VI, 491, p. 184.

of euthanasian establishments would be the greatest benefactors of mankind.

The faculties in the universities of the world today are not at the top of the social hierarchy in wealth and power. But they are at the top so far as the power they have in their hands over the future of man on earth is concerned.

The proper use of this power poses a problem of the greatest importance in our time. When we consider that our universities are staffed with the best intelligence that the country has in it, and contemplate the exhibition that this best has given of its incapacity in self-government, we begin, but we only begin, to realize the difficulty of self-government or of good government of any kind and the magnitude of the task that lies ahead. The problem of self-government, of good government of any kind, is in large part, of course, a problem of morals; and if every person, whether he knows it or not, is under the necessity of making decisions about values, about objects of devotion and of worship, and if worship is the essence of religion, then religion is tied to morals in a way such that it cannot be untied.

The present state of our knowledge on this subject—that is, the knowledge that is currently illustrated in the lives of people generally in the United States, and especially in the intellectual world—does not portend good.

It is not necessary, however, to accept this condition as unalterable. There are ways of working for better rather than worse, even when conditions are desperate. Our next chapter will deal with the effort which seems clearly the best yet made to use one of the possible ways, but which failed. Still, even in this failure, something of very great importance was done. A record of the reasoning at the basis of this effort was made and this reasoning can be examined. This examination may help find the right direction. We explore this possibility in the following chapter.

CHAPTER IX

The Great Failure

If you allow the spiritual basis of a civilization to perish, you first change, and finally destroy it.

SIR RICHARD LIVINGSTONE

The great need of our time is for a genuinely educated public that is producing and supporting genuinely educated leadership. The educational system of the United States today produces superb technicians and these technicians have made available to the country physical power beyond the dreams of former generations. A genuinely educated leadership would propose fruitful uses of this power and a genuinely educated public would support such uses. The power of the United States was the determining factor in the physical winning of World War I. Within fifteen years, it was clear that while World War I had been won physically, it had been lost politically and that another World War was going to be the consequence. World War II followed. Again, the physical power of the United States was the determining factor in the physical winning of the war. And again, it is clear that this war has been lost politically. The evidence for this is overwhelming: The crises over Berlin, the cold war, the hot wars in Korea and Vietnam, the intermittent explosions of violence between the Arabs and the Israeli, between the Russians and the Chinese, between the Russians and their satellites, and between the Hindus and the Moslems, not to mention the outbreaks of violence in Africa south of the Sahara and the lesser, but still very serious outbreaks of violence here at home. The United States is so divided politically that in case any really great crisis arose it is not clear the country would not be paralyzed by internal dissension. In fact, the situation relative to the war in Vietnam has been one practically of paralysis. One of the most distressing facts about this situation is that widespread sentiment against violence as a means of making political decisions—a wholly admirable sentiment—contributed perhaps more than anything else to prolonging the violence and to opening the way to the violence that now rages in some parts of the world and that threatens to become even more extensive and destructive.

The basic intention of the United States in both World Wars I and II —the intention to use power to stop the abuse of power—was thoroughly admirable. But it should be known by the leadership of the country and the people by this time that it is not enough merely to have good intentions. The great failure of the United States, I repeat, was the failure of its leadership to understand the nature of the two totalitarian systems, Communism and National Socialism, or more basically, we should say, the nature of man. And the great majority of the people of the country did not understand, either; otherwise they would not have supported this leadership in the policy that built up the power of one of these totalitarian systems.

It should be unnecessary to say anything more—though much more could be said—to show that the United States does not know how to use its power. In saying this, I am not criticizing the present administration, or the preceding one, or any particular administration of this century. I am criticizing, first, the colleges and universities of the country. They have failed in the most important part of their task, perhaps because the education that has been needed is beyond them. I am criticizing also, along with the colleges and universities, the intellectual leadership which, while it may be said to be a product of the colleges and universities of the country, can hardly be considered a mere product, like, say, a stove from a factory that cannot by its own efforts make itself better with the passage of time. It really ought to be possible for some of us to do some learning.

The great need of the United States is for a genuine general education. The most persistent approach to the solution of this problem in the United States was made at the University of Chicago during the second quarter of this century while Robert Maynard Hutchins was chancellor. The work done on general education at Chicago has been described in the book *The Idea and Practice of General Education: An Account of the College of the University of Chicago*, by Members of the College Faculty.[1] The idea of a general education is stated in the first chapter, "The Problem of General Education," by Clarence H. Faust, who was for some years Dean of the College. At the time when this chapter was published in 1950, it was true (and it still is true today),

---

1. *The Idea and Practice of General Education: An Account of the College of the University of Chicago, by* . . . *Members of the College Faculty* (Chicago: Univ. of Chicago Press, 1950).

as Faust says,[2] that no one denies the value of a general education, that to define it as the cultivation of the knowledge and wisdom that every person has to have to be a better rather than a worse citizen is to say something with which in general terms everyone agrees. The disagreement comes over the particular knowledge necessary to this end, and how knowledge and wisdom can be cultivated in ways that have the best chances to be most fruitful. At this point, as Faust says,

... the term "general education" like the terms "liberty" and "equality," has acquired a wide range of meanings, including some irreconcilable ones. ... Almost every college in the country, if presidents, deans, and catalogues are to be believed, provides a general or liberal education for its undergraduates; but it is impossible to discover any substantial, common element in the educational programs of our colleges. The requirement of a course in English composition, one in history, and one in the natural sciences would come closest, perhaps, to meeting this test; but even this agreement proves, upon examination, to be apparent rather than real, for the courses labelled "English," "History," and "Science," in various colleges exhibit such differences in content, method, and purpose—and, indeed, such contradictory differences—as to leave little hope of defining general education by references to what is being done about it.[3]

Daniel Bell of Columbia University, writing in the middle sixties, characterizes the effort "over the past twenty-five years" of the College at the University of Chicago as "the most thoroughgoing experiment in general education of any college in the United States."[4] This judgment almost certainly is correct despite serious flaws in the experiment.

I was at the University of Chicago as director of its press during the period 1945–1950 and had the privilege of seeing some aspects of the College close up. I did not have the time to watch the College constantly, but what I witnessed, I believe, has some significance.

If one is seriously interested in general education, it may be distressing as well as hilarious to contemplate what can come out when one gets a sample of some of what has been done in that name. I had gone to the University of Chicago at the invitation of Chancellor Hutchins largely because of agreement in the main with his ideas on education, and particularly because of the effort he was making to find out what general education is and to establish it in the College of the University.

2. Ibid., p. 4.
3. Ibid., pp. 4–5.
4. Daniel Bell, *The Reforming of General Education* (New York: Columbia Univ. Press, 1966), p. 26.

Here is a sample of what I witnessed in the College. I do not give this as a fair sample, but simply of something that I myself saw and that, along with other things I saw, suggested to me that the College was in some ways not doing what it was set up to do. I quote from an account that I included in an article "Do Intellectuals Have Minds" that was published in the Fall 1947 issue of the *Georgia Review:*

One of the first experiences I had a few weeks after I arrived in Chicago may serve to show why I am concerned with [the question, Do intellectuals have minds?]. I had been strongly attracted to the University of Chicago because I understood that here the unpopular doctrine was espoused that while all truth had not been discovered, some had been, and this had been recorded in books by specially gifted men and that the best beginning in education for young and old was to study these books. I was somewhat puzzled, therefore, when a few weeks after I got here I found that courses in the College, designed for general education, were being changed so frequently and so rapidly that no printing plant could keep up with the changes. The method of providing small quantities most rapidly, mimeographing, was being used for the preparation of materials in many courses—but even that very flexible method was not adequate to meet the demand.

It seemed clear to me, the real difficulty was that the basic problem, whether there was anything worth studying and teaching, had not been faced; and I was strongly tempted to express the heresy that courses ought not to be offered until this problem was solved with some degree of certainty. . . . Later, at a committee meeting, I heard one teacher plead for loose leaf textbooks. All the books in his field, he said, were out of date by the time they were printed. It seemed not to occur to him that any particular combination of loose leaves he used in any course, however changed during the course, would be, on his own reckoning, out of date a few weeks after they were used.[5]

One of the things that you do not do if you are the head of a department in a university is meddle in the affairs of another department. You cultivate not seeing and not saying as far as these are necessary to getting along, and this I had found, before I went to Chicago, to be a long, long distance.

It is clear from the record made by the College of the University of Chicago that it is easy to define a general education in general terms, and it is easy to get agreement on the general terms—even from those who doubt whether any such something as general education that is not a product of specialized education is possible. Everybody, or rather in view of the anarchy and nihilism that are widespread today, I should

5. W. T. Couch, "Do Intellectuals Have Minds?" *Georgia Review*, Fall 1947.

say most people want an educational process that cultivates genuine goodness in individuals, that helps shape the genuinely good citizen, and the educational leadership of the country is particularly and deeply concerned with this problem and in agreement on this objective. But to get agreement on an actual program, and actual work with students, these so far have proved impossible.

Let us examine what former Dean Faust has to say on the question of an actual program in his chapter in the Chicago book, *The Idea and Practice of General Education*. But first let me say to the reader, if he accepts the view that whatever is called education by someone who appears to be an authority, or who is actually accepted as one by few or many, is the genuine thing, he should save his time and drop this book. Dean Faust himself, in the quotation from him given above, clearly exhibits his awareness of the traps in this idea. I accept what Faust says on this point not because he says it, but because what he says is true. Some of what he says otherwise needs serious examination. I proceed with such examination.

The establishment of general education, Faust says,

requires the co-operation of specialists who have undertaken to determine what is basic in a group of related subjects and to work out and correct, in the light of experience, the materials and methods by which students may be led to acquire a grasp of the fundamental principles and methods of thinking needed to form sound judgments in the social sciences, the natural sciences, and the humanities. The attempt to develop courses of this sort has been the major concern of the College of the University of Chicago for the last two decades, and the descriptions which this volume contains reveal the progress which the faculty has made in this direction.[6]

Since the social sciences, the natural sciences, and the humanities can be regarded as including all possible subjects, we cannot criticize this statement on the ground that any subject is excluded. We can certainly agree that we need to know what "is basic in a group of related subjects," and if they are, as is said here, "related," we might find at least one basic something that relates them. The specialist, as Faust proposes, should certainly be able to tell us what this is. This passage was written after some years of effort on the part of specialists to determine "what is basic in a group of related subjects." It would be helpful if Faust had given an example of what they determined. For instance, the notion that the physical universe consists of particles in motion; and, in a wider form, that everything, including thought and emotion, is basically

6. Faust, in *Idea and Practice of General Education,* pp. 16–17.

physical or energy or some neutral something, and that relations of shape and size and motion and number determine the mode of existence of all things—taking the word "things" in the widest possible sense: Is this an example of the something that the specialists in natural science would determine as basic? If not, what would be an example? To mention a fundamental principle and method of thinking "needed to form sound judgments" would have helped bring the discussion from the sky to earth.

In general, there cannot possibly be any disagreement with what Mr. Faust says in this quotation unless one doubts that there is, or can be, any such something as general education and thus doubts that the specialists have discovered any of what it is. Faust says

The importance of general education is not limited . . . to the need for wise citizens. The urgency of the social and political problems with which we are at present confronted permits us easily to forget that society is not an end in itself. We desire a strong, well-organized, smoothly functioning society, not in and for itself, but as a means to the realization of men's potentialities as individuals.[7]

As to the realization of the potentialities of individuals, some young persons possess, and if the doctrine of equality is true in its most important meaning, all possess, the potentials of thieves, murderers, Hitlers and Stalins, as well as other potentials. I am sure Faust would not want these potentials realized any more than I would. The problem posed by the quotation cannot be solved by inserting the word "good" before the word "potentialities," though its insertion would help. Merely to insert the word and go no further is to play with words. The teacher is not really a teacher if he does not take this problem seriously, and if he is unable by precept and practice to help the student discover and serve the good. The subject is today an exceedingly unpopular one, but for that reason all the more important. And it is incredibly difficult.

"Specialized training," Faust says, and certainly correctly, "has been wonderfully successful in this country."[8] But its very success has led to the shaping of education for the production of specialists and a corresponding lack of really serious effort to discover the kind of education necessary to the good and effective individual and citizen. The solution of this problem "by means of a curriculum consisting of

7. Ibid., p. 7.
8. Ibid., p. 5.

vaguely organized courses, handled by vaguely educated teachers, will not do." [9] Faust is here stating and agreeing with an often expressed criticism of courses established to serve the purpose of general education. We have to agree with both the critics and Faust; but, in our observation, the critics of efforts to discover what general education is and to establish it most likely are simply attempting to defend specialization against what they mistakenly imagine are mere attacks on it. Courses can, of course, be vaguely organized and handled by vaguely educated teachers, and it is highly probable that courses established to serve general education do tend to be of this nature. But if general education in a genuine and still-to-be discovered form is necessary to the proper development and handling of specialization, there is not only no conflict between the two, but each is necessary to the proper development and use of the other.

It might be helpful to raise here the question whether specialization is necessarily a narrowing and stultifying influence, or whether one can even begin the cultivation of a general education until after one has made a good beginning toward the command of a specialty. It could be that the two are so closely interrelated that one in any genuine form is not possible without the other. This is not a new question in the history of human thought. It is as old as the great debate over the centuries on the nature of universals. It is possible that specialization has in this century become a narrowing and stultifying influence because specialization during this period has been cultivated under the almost exclusive influence of one side in this debate, the side that in the past was represented by nominalism, and in our time by one of its intellectual offspring, logical positivism. Logical positivism has been the dominant orthodoxy in the United States during this century, but the specialists of our time and many of the would-be general educators, except perhaps for some in philosophy, appear generally not to know this. The effects of this orthodoxy have been pervasive in what is called "education." According to this orthodoxy, there are no necessary connections among the things and events that constitute the universe, there are only conjunctions, associations that constitute regularities that are sufficiently constant to be subjects of study and to establish probabilities as long as the regularities continue; and there is nothing whatever in the nature of things that guarantees the continuance of any regularities.

There is a great body of thought which, except for a few specialists,

9. Ibid., p. 14.

is practically unknown today that directly opposes this dominant orthodoxy. This body of thought says implicitly that no specialty can be understood as well as is possible except in its relations to other specialties and the purpose of serving truth in theory and practice—the purpose for which all specialties exist. In this body of thought, the relations among specialties are not mere surface relations but connections or linkages of a binding nature. If this is true, and so far in the history of human thought no way has been found of determining that it is or is not true—this body of thought is of the utmost importance to the theory and practice of general education as well as the proper development of specialization.

If what we have said in our last two paragraphs is true, if there is today a dominant orthodoxy that has never been proved to be in firm possession of the truth, and if there is a great body of thought directly opposed to this orthodoxy and whose tenets also have never been proved to be true or false, and if this body of thought could become a great competing orthodoxy if the arguments for it were given the attention they deserve, the conclusion is inescapable that our educational theory and practice, while in all its pronouncements condemning indoctrination, has been practicing it in its most insidious form, an almost universally unconscious form, one of which the intellectual world, with rare exceptions has been almost completely unaware.

Furthermore, when the question of indoctrination is given serious consideration, it is likely to be discovered that in some form or other, it cannot be escaped except by abdication of the effort to teach and to learn; and since this effort leads to nihilism, a consequence of indoctrination, there is no escape. It is widely held today in the theory of teaching that opposing views ought to be put before students and they ought to be allowed to make their own decisions on them. But, as we have just seen, this theory while preached is not practiced on a question of the very greatest importance to education. If it were practiced, the orthodoxy that dominates our time would be a conscious orthodoxy, and the great body of thought that is capable of becoming a most serious competing orthodoxy would be brought to light again; and if this were done, it would become possible to discuss the problem of general education and specialization in terms far more intelligible than any that have yet been used. There is little suggestion in Faust's chapter, or elsewhere in the book *The Idea and Practice of General Education*, that a strong theoretical basis for general education is needed—a basis at least as strong as that of the opposition—and when the need is seen for keeping specialization from running wild, one that is far stronger is seen to be needed.

This is the basic weakness of *The Idea and Practice of General Education.* The following discussion will be in the main of instances that illustrate this basic weakness.

It is not possible reasonably to disagree with Faust when he says:

> It is impossible to give every undergraduate all the knowledge that specialists have developed. To give him a part of the specialized knowledge that has been accumulated in one section of the social sciences, of the humanities, or of the physical sciences (the device of the elective system) is not likely to give him the well-balanced understanding of social problems or the ability to appreciate literature and the arts or the understanding of natural phenomena which every educated man ought to possess. Nor, on the other hand, will a piece of economics, a piece of sociology, a piece of political science, and a piece of anthropology, brought together in a single survey course on the social sciences, serve the purpose.[10]

But Faust never states clearly and discusses any approach to a general education that even seems to make such an education possible. One possible approach is by means of the theories that are involved in every field of knowledge. Take, say, the competing theories of economic and technological determinism in social science. It is not necessary to know *all* the facts of social science in order to become acquainted with these theories and to form an opinion on the validity of one or the other, or, if both are held to be valid, on their relations. If knowledge of *all* the facts that bear on a theory were necessary to the understanding of a theory, there would be no chance of ever understanding any theory; and if knowing *all* the facts were necessary to the formation of theories, none would ever have been formed. No one knows, and there is no prospect that any social scientist or anyone else will ever know all the facts of social science. Faust is clearly under no illusions on this score, but if he is aware of the role that theories play in the handling of facts —a role that seems necessary if there is to be intelligible handling of facts—he gives little evidence of this awareness.

It could be that if there is to be any genuine general education, theory is one of the tools that is necessary. While no social scientist could reasonably be expected to state all the facts of social science, it is reasonable to expect him to form an opinion on the question which theories in social science are more important and to be able to state them and discuss their relations in a way that is intelligible. In many cases, there are competing theories. He should certainly have and be able to state his

10. Ibid.

opinion on which are the more important of these. And he should know that theories are not always based on fact. Equality, for instance, is a theory that, unlike evolution, is not based on fact. There is no theory of equality that makes any sense that is based wholly on fact. Its treatment of fact is in many ways very close to that of the more hopeful, the less grim Christian theologies—a subject very much worth exploring. The theory of equality in democracy is a theory that opens possibilities, that recognizes and encourages reasonable aspirations, that emphasizes the potentialities for good and evil in all human beings and tries to cultivate the one and curb the other, that is necessary to mobility from level to level in the social, economic, and political, and other hierarchies. It is necessary to the location, cultivation, and proper use of talent at whatever levels it appears in society.

There are many different sets of relations between theories and facts, among existing facts and facts that may be brought into existence, among theories or ideas that may to a great extent be established as facts —among the ways the world is at any moment and the ways it may be in succeeding moments. And human beings can have effects on these ways—or can they? Freedom and determinism are problems that enter into the two great orthodoxies that ought to be competing and that have been discussed above. They are competing theories, and like the great bodies of thought within which they arise as problems, they too may prove impossible to decide finally and completely one way or another. But it can be said, without fear of successful refutation, that one's understanding of the great problems with which human beings have to deal on this earth remains infantile if one never learns of and understands the arguments that can be made for and against each of these two great competing theories.

It is, of course, not possible for anyone to know that a theory obscurely held today, or not held at all, will not become the most widely held tomorrow. The problem of the style of the moment is a very serious problem in the quest for knowledge, and especially so in social science. Social scientists are human beings and, like other human beings, in the absence of real ballast in their science and in themselves, are likely to be swayed by the styles of thought of the time. If they are to know anything well, they cannot, as they often do, let their minds sway with every wind that blows. And the opposite problem of being bound and practically blinded to new—and old and forgotten—possibilities by their education, education that in one of its aspects however conducted can amount to little more than mere indoctrination—is an equally serious problem. To cultivate knowledge it is necessary to try to learn of that which remains constant in change as well as of change and the patterns that are made by change. A mind stabilized by knowledge of and adherence to principles—theories that have been found to be true— is required to do this. One might reasonably expect in a book on the idea and practice of general education some discussion of the question whether there are any such principles, whether the evidence for them is conclusive, and if so, where it can be found, and the part that such principles and the evidence for them should have, if any, in general education. There is no discussion of this question in the Chicago book.

There are no reasons for believing that there is any better and wider understanding of general education today than there was in 1950 when *The Idea and Practice of General Education* was published. But this, let me say immediately, was not necessarily the fault of the book. A part of the fault lies in the response to it. The critical world simply was not up to the task of turning the effort represented in the book in a fruitful direction.

Daniel Bell, whose book *The Reforming of General Education* was published by the Columbia University Press in 1966, and whose opinion is quoted above that the College at the University of Chicago made "the most thorough-going experiment in general education of any college in the United States," also tells us that when he was writing his book, that is around the years 1964 and 1965, "The College of the University of Chicago is in the throes of readjustment that may lead to the almost complete reversal of general education as practiced there for twenty years." [11] Bell also says: "I am forced to conclude from my inquiry that, for reasons largely different from the ones given by the initial critics of the college, the rationale for general education (however much one sympathizes with its original civilizing intentions) has become enfeebled and the intellectual *structure* (despite the value of individual courses) has lost its coherence." [12] A serious examination of *The Idea and Practice of General Education* suggests that general education in the College of the University of Chicago never achieved any coherent intellectual structure or rationale. But it went much further in this direction than could reasonably be expected, given the pervasive and largely unknown influence of the orthodoxy that dominated that time and that still dominates. Bell is almost certainly right in his judg-

11. Bell, p. 190.
12. Bell, pp. 281–82.

ment that the work in the College was "the most thorough-going experiment in general education," the best in both theory and practice that has yet been made. The need for general education remains, however, as great as ever, if not greater. A new and better approach to the problem of finding out what it is and getting it established must be made.

There is a vast amount of doctrine embedded in the customary ways of thinking, speaking and acting in the life of any people. The child with normal faculties is to a great extent shaped by these ways as he grows up. The great problem of education is not that of withdrawing or nullifying shaping influences—influences that amount to by far the most powerful indoctrination—for that cannot be done even if children are banished into wildernesses to live away from parents and to be brought up perhaps by beasts. Shaping, indoctrination, occurs however children are brought up; and the same is true beyond childhood. Indoctrination is an inescapable shaping influence, but instead of becoming a blinding and stultifying influence, it may be made into a powerful aid to the highest intellectual development by the deliberate asking of questions that bring out the strongest possible arguments for and against doctrines—theories—that are held to be probable or true. Just when this should be done is one of the great unsettled questions of educational theory; but that it must be done at some stage if the inevitable process of indoctrination is not to have life-long blinding effects is hardly open to doubt. Only in this way is there any possibility of helping individuals to get knowledge of a set of doctrines that cannot be easily torn to pieces by a skilled dialectician.

The effort to escape responsibility for determining, as well as can be done, that the influences that shape the rising generations shall be better rather than worse is an effort to abdicate. It is an effort that cannot possibly succeed in the sense of nullifying all shaping influences; but it can succeed in the sense of allowing the savage and barbaric and other influences that in civilized societies become worse than savage and barbaric to do the shaping.

It is difficult to imagine that Faust was unaware of this problem, but whether he was or not, he does not give adequate attention to it. Since it is impossible to discuss education with any degree of seriousness and avoid saying things that bear on this problem, it cannot be said correctly that he ignores this problem completely. We shall now consider a subject that Faust discusses and that has implicit bearings on the problem of indoctrination, that is, of shaping influences.

Faust fails to consider in his article the question whether there are any principles that have been used successfully in the cultivation of science and that are necessary in the distinguishing of correct from incorrect thinking. There is no indication, beyond the bare words, as to what is to be taught to students when he says one of the purposes of the College is to teach students "how to think." We agree completely that "how to think" should be taught as clearly and carefully as is possible; and if the charge is made that this is indoctrination, we accept the charge and we go further and say that it is a most necessary kind of indoctrination. Our reason is simply that if it has taken animals becoming human beings thousands of years to get to the stage where one specially gifted human being could formulate the law of contradiction and give powerful reasons for its acceptance, and if more than two thousand years after the formulation of this law and the reasons for its acceptance, most of the people on earth could not name it or discuss intelligibly its usefulness, or whether it is applicable in all subject matter everywhere and always if reasoning is to be correct, or whether its violation—except in error—can be imagined, or whether there is any other all-pervasive principle that is more certain—it is hardly possible that any group of young people, no matter how brilliant and even if led by a teacher with tremendous evocative powers, will in any kind of discussion or individual thinking generate and state concisely this tremendously important knowledge.

The presentation of one view of the subject logic as authoritative without the strongest possible presentation of the more important competing views, and in a form such that the intelligent and widely informed layman has a chance to understand them is criticized in Chapters XI and XII and no more will be said on this subject here.

All of us, even the greatest of our specialists, tend today, for the reasons set forth in this book, to be laymen outside our specialties. Given the reasons that we have described and that set limitations on all of us that are almost impossible for us to transcend, it could be argued, and rightly, that our criticisms of *The Idea and Practice of General Education* and especially of Faust's chapter are too harsh, that it is unreasonable to expect the teacher to be free from the limitations that, if our argument is true, are universal. Still, it has to be said, it is a large part of the teacher's duty to reach conclusions; and if he is teaching older students, it is his duty to state his conclusions on the subject he is supposed to be teaching and how he reached them, and to help his students tear to pieces his method and his conclusions as far as this can be done. If the tearing process is a wild one, it cannot be tolerated by the genuine teacher further than it is useful to demonstrate its wildness. On the question what is wild, the teacher has to be the judge, and his judgment has to be accepted by the student as authoritative as far as this is necessary for the maintenance of order and the achievement of the greatest measure of success in the teaching. The teacher's authority does not have to be accepted otherwise by the student, and in fact there is no known means of securing acceptance that is genuine if the student chooses not to accept, though fear and force can be used to get the appearance, and under some conditions, the reality of acceptance. There are types of society where the influences are such as to tend strongly to inhibit freedom on the part of the student. The caste society of India and communist societies generally are of this type. A society such as ours that tends almost exclusively to cultivate narrow specialties tends to become of this type. It seems clear that societies can go too far in establishing and maintaining influences that inhibit freedom on the part of the student to raise questions just as they can go too far in the opposite direction.

Indoctrination by the teacher is to be feared only when the teacher does not know his subject well enough to lead his students through it, presenting the competing theories on any principle or fact, or collection of either or both, as strongly as he can, and finally giving his conclusion. His conclusion must be one that he is not only willing but glad to state and defend in public if it is attacked. We shall return to this subject in another context in Chapter X.

One can hardly disagree with Faust's statement:

What is required in general education can best be described by the term "wisdom" rather than by the popular term "straight thinking"; for what students need is not merely guidance in avoiding error, or even smoothness in mental operations, but the competence to establish an adequate relation of the mind to the things which it undertakes to grasp." [13]

But then if the teacher is himself unable to give an example of wisdom in its fullness, leading to the grasp of a conclusion that he can show the student how to defend against the strongest attacks, how can he expect the student, even the brightest, to be able to do this? The answer is simply that the teacher cannot reasonably expect anything approaching this on the part of the student, if he is unable himself to give an example. Teaching that preaches this doctrine and that is completely unable itself

13. Faust, p. 17.

to practice it is gravely lacking, and its wisdom is that of emptiness.

The word "wisdom" certainly can, as any word can, be used as a term of magic, and it is clear that magic, when believed in, may be efficacious. But surely, whatever general education is, it is not in any way constituted by magic. "The curriculum of the College at Chicago," says Faust, "recognizes, on the one hand, that the process of thought for reaching truth about one subject matter differs from the processes of thought required to reach truth in another." [14] Differs completely? The answer to this question most certainly is that there are certain identities in the processes of thought whatever the subject thought about. The logical law of contradiction is one of these. At the same time, it is certainly true, as Faust says, that there are differences in the processes of thought about different types of subjects. There are subjects that cannot be measured or counted, and there are subjects that can. One cannot make sense and use measuring or counting in "the processes of thought" about a subject that cannot be measured or counted. But one can, and one must, if one is to make any sense whatever, use the logical law of contradiction in all "the processes of thought" about all types of subject whatsoever. Only one philosopher of great stature has ever denied this—Hegel. In his great and in some ways extremely baffling body of thought, he holds the law of contradiction to be valid at the lower levels of thought, invalid only at the higher levels. His most cogent follower in important respects in our time, the objective idealist Brand Blanshard, holds the law of contradiction to be valid at all levels of thought. It is not necessary for us to follow this question any further in this discussion since our purpose is only to say that there can hardly be any question in education more important than whether the leading thinkers of all time have accepted any principles as universally valid, what these principles are, and whether the reasons given for their acceptance also can be accepted as valid. These are questions that in our view general education cannot reasonably avoid. Faust does not mention them as subject matter for consideration in general education.

Here is what Faust has to say about the usual type of introductory course:

Recognizing that students do not have time to take introductory courses in all departmental disciplines as a way of securing a general education and convinced, in any case, that introductory courses designed as the first step toward specialization in a departmental area are not the most effective

14. Faust, p. 14.

means of general education, the College has set up an integrated sequence of general courses dealing with the basic problems and methods of major areas of human knowledge.[15]

Even if introductory courses of a pre-professional nature were designed and given that were satisfactory for the purposes of general education, Faust is certainly right when he says the students do not have the time to take all the introductory courses that would be necessary to a general education. And even if far more could be taught and learned in the time that is available, still time, as Faust says, would prohibit this. Furthermore, while Faust does not say so, we can be fairly sure his experience told him that in order to develop pre-professional introductory courses that would help toward general education as well as toward professional purposes, the specialists who now teach and who write the textbooks would have to transcend the limitations that have been drilled into them and that constitute the greatest obstacle to the discovery and practice of what is needed for a genuine general education. We have already said and will repeat here and below, the great obstacle is a narrow and blinding type of indoctrination that is largely unconscious and therefore far more insidious and difficult to correct than any conscious kind.

In the integrated sequence that was set up in the College, says Faust, three fields "are distinguished . . . the humanities, the social sciences, and the natural sciences. The general courses provided in these areas have placed increasing dependence upon the reading and discussion of original writings of scientists and of masterpieces of literature rather than upon textbook summaries and lectures." [16] In order to follow this procedure, while Faust doesn't say so, it is clear beyond question that selections have to be made. If the selections are of excerpts, then the method is that to which Faust has objected—that of presenting the student with mere pieces or parts of works. If the selections are not of excerpts but of complete works, then the amount of reading is far beyond that which is possible. The only possible solution of this problem in the terms that Faust himself has specified might seem to be in textbooks that were specially written to serve the purpose of general education. But if selections and summaries are not allowed, textbooks cannot be written. The making of selections is not limited to the selecting of excerpts from existing works. Every writer makes selections of some

15. Faust, p. 21.
16. Ibid.

kind when he writes; and if teaching is to be teaching, summaries must somehow be provided; and wherever thinking that is worthy of the name occurs, they always are. Whatever approach to this problem is made, the result is necessarily a survey. No course of instruction, however it is conducted, whatever the materials used or not used, can escape being a survey in the sense of being necessarily made up of selections and summaries. The whole question here is that of the quality, relevance, and adequacy of the selections and summaries.

Finally as to the subject matter that serves the purpose of general education, Faust says in a long statement that summarizes his argument:

It has seemed clear that a mere array of facts, however impressive, would not serve the purpose. For one thing, the sheer mass of knowledge accumulated by science is too great; but even if this were not the case, and even if a wise selection from the vast accumulation of facts could be made, science refuses to stay fixed, and much of the science of today will be obsolete tomorrow. Even those facts, moreover, which maintain their scientific status cannot be truly grasped and really understood as mere items retained in memory. They come to be intelligible, come to be truly known and significant, only through understanding the methods by which they have been established. For all these reasons, but perhaps especially for the last, the College curriculum in the natural sciences has increasingly provided for the study of the nature, methods, and role of science rather than for the presentation of the present state of knowledge in such subjects as physics, chemistry, geology, zoology, botany, etc. For this purpose it has increasingly turned from the textbooks on science to the writings in which scientists themselves report their discoveries and announce and defend their theories, and it has turned from the memorization of textbook facts to the analysis in class discussion of the ways in which scientists have formulated their problems, the nature of the principles they have used, the methods of argument and proof they have employed. It is not expected that such study will produce original scientists but, rather, that it will bring students to an understanding of the nature, processes, possibilities, and limitations of science and will prepare them to distinguish between scientific sense and mere quackery. Experience has meanwhile shown that students retain a larger number of facts from courses pursuing this method than from the traditional textbook and lecture courses.[17]

If we take the word "facts" to mean details such as those that Charles Darwin presents in massive array in *The Origin of Species* to support the theory of evolution, and if we make a highly selective array of such details or facts as those that Darwin reports, an array sufficient to illustrate the theory, we have done probably the best we can for a positive

17. Faust, pp. 21–22.

presentation of the theory of evolution in general education. Faust is
certainly right when he holds that it is not possible in a course designed
for general education to present all the facts recorded on the subject in
scientific literature. He could have gone further and said truly that this
is not possible even in professional courses. Furthermore it is extremely
doubtful whether any scientist, even one who has taken the study of
evolution as his life's work, knows all the recorded facts. Even for the
specialist, time and ability to memorize fix limits.

Now if what we have said thus far is true, some theories, such as
that of evolution, are supported by facts, others, such as that of equality,
are not; and still others, as we shall see, involve apparent facts; and getting beyond the appearance, the apparent facts, to the reality, the real
facts, so far in the course of human thought, has constituted a problem
beyond solution. Here again, the problem that is involved cannot be
understood as far as is humanly possible except in terms of theory—in
this case, the understanding of competing theories, such as, say, the
theory of the solar system of Copernicus and Newton on the one hand
and that of Einstein on the other. Theory and its various relations to
fact, or apparent fact, would seem clearly to be a large part of the great
subject matter of general education. There is very little in the Chicago
book, either in Faust's introductory chapter or in other chapters, that
points in this direction.

When Faust says "science refuses to stay fixed and much of the science of today will be obsolete tomorrow," he makes a statement that is
true but one that raises the question whether knowledge that changes
in the sense of being real today but not real tomorrow is really knowledge. Science would not be possible if there were nothing permanent,
or of a high degree of permanence, in change. It is practically certain
that there are rational factors in science which are permanent, are always
present and decisive in the determination of facts, and constitute the
relations among facts. These relations, as well as events in time and space,
may be referred to as facts. It is not possible to take the space here to
discuss the extreme ambiguities in the word "fact," even in the ways it
is ordinarily used; and the specialists in the various disciplines add many
ambiguities to these ways. A general education would throw some of
the light that is sorely needed, in the intellectual world as well as elsewhere, on this extremely confused and confusing subject.

When Faust says that facts "come to be intelligible, come to be truly
known and significant, only through understanding the methods by
which they have been established," he makes us wonder just what he

meant when he said, as we have quoted him above, that "science refuses to stay fixed and much of the science of today will be obsolete tomorrow." In one of the two statements just quoted, he clearly says that some facts have been established by science and in the other he makes a statement which, taken along with the first, amounts to saying that while there are some facts that are established, fixed for all time perhaps, the science that has established them—including presumably its methods —"refuses to stay fixed and much of the science of today will be obsolete tomorrow."

In this discussion Faust is obviously pointing toward the problem of permanence and change and, we have to say it, illustrating the confusion in most modern discussion of this problem. It is not at all likely that even the best general education would any time soon, if ever, lead to the solution of this problem. But it could, at least, lead to the recognition that it exists.

We cannot discuss in this chapter, without running to inordinate length, all the questions that would need to be discussed in order to understand as well as possible the long quotation above from Faust's chapter. We have already indicated points at which questions of a most difficult nature arise in connection with his statements concerning the role that method plays in science, and particularly in the "establishment" and understanding of facts. We come now to the question whether facts "come to be intelligible, . . . to be truly known and significant *only* [my italics] through understanding the methods by which they have been established."

When we know how to establish or change a fact, we may imagine that we have come to understand it; and it is beyond doubt that we have gained some understanding of at least that class of facts over which we have this power. But when one man kills another, he certainly changes the fact that the other was living to the fact that he is dead; yet it is obviously false to say that to know the method of the killing provides understanding of the living or the dying, or of life or death. One of the great illusions of our time is that man has real knowledge of that which he can make and that he can *make* many things. Man's making is always limited to that of merely changing, in accord with principles or laws that he did not make, things in nature that he did not make. And while there are many things that he can change, there probably are far more that he cannot change. We need only remember the heavenly bodies millions of light years distant to have examples of the latter. The methods that man may use in "establishing" fact, or, where he is able to make changes, the methods he uses to change facts certainly are aids to the understanding of facts, but they are far from sufficient. The facts that Darwin collected and that he reports in his *Origin of Species* would be utterly unintelligible if he had not tried to show that they are tied together by indissoluble links and in doing so illuminated his facts by a great theory.

Now to understand the problem that we are discussing, it is necessary to know that the theory of knowledge that dominates our time, logical positivism, holds that all knowledge of all kinds, without any exception of any kind whatever, is derived from sense experience. It has been argued, and with great cogency, that sense experience that establishes even one fact necessarily arouses and goes beyond sense experience to rational factors that are then found to be involved in all experience. If there is anything certain about human knowledge, it is held in one of the great bodies of doctrine of our time, it is that such knowledge necessarily involves experience that goes beyond sense experience. This that goes beyond is the work of the mind with the rational factors that the mind, when it is doing its proper work, sees in the constitution of facts. It is these rational factors or indissoluble linkages in such facts as those that Darwin reported that provide whatever truth there is in his theory.

It has been held by reputable scientists that the theory of evolution is so well-established that it should be no longer referred to as a theory but as a fact. It would be as infantile to argue against this notion as to argue for it. For the real question is whether rational factors are always involved in facts. If the mind can see a rational factor in one fact; and, if this factor exists as a link among many, the mind may see it among many also. Sense experience by itself in this theory, cannot establish even one fact or discover the rational factor in even one fact, much less can it do so in many. The potentiality that is in an acorn to become an oak has never been an object of sense experience and by its nature cannot be.

Myth is still the only means that man has of trying to understand the basic facts of existence and non-existence. It is, on the most difficult questions, the only means available. It is impossible to draw and establish a clear line between myth and theory; but the term "theory," while often applied to propositions that are extremely difficult and highly debatable, generally does not attempt to be as comprehensive as myth. In his theory of evolution, for instance, Darwin does not attempt to explain the origin of life; and no explanation has ever been given that does not contain mythical elements. We have only to remember the particles that in modern physics constitute the physical universe—and perhaps everything in the universe including human thoughts—and that no particle, not even one, has ever been an object of sense experience; and that this fact has been the occasion of a lively debate because if their existence as more than mere conveniences, necessary for purposes of calculation—a purely logical factor that cannot be found in sense experience—has to be recognized as existing in nature and reflected in the mind when the mind makes inferences, then the case for the ruling orthodoxy of our time is seriously weakened if not destroyed. The ruling orthodoxy denies the existence of any rational factor in nature. The relation of the debate over the existence of the particles that in modern physical science are used to study the nature of the universe to the great orthodoxy of our time and to the problems of myth and theory in learning is not even suggested in Faust's chapter or in any other chapters in the Chicago book.

We have made in this discussion statements that may appear to be dogmatic, and in form they certainly are. But not in spirit. They are made in dogmatic form because this is necessary to clarity. And clarity is necessary if there is to be any chance to get the ruling orthodoxy to relax its rule sufficiently to give its potentially most powerful opposition more than a hit-and-run hearing. If the purpose of this book were merely to displace one orthodoxy by another, it would, in our present state of knowledge, not be worth any attention. For no orthodoxy can be understood and held in a way that is not filled with confusion unless it is held with the best possible understanding of its active and potential competitors. The means for cultivating this understanding do not exist in our society today. Our great purpose is to show the need and then propose a means adequate to serve it.

We have suggested above that there are rational factors in science that are permanent insofar as there is any science and that these are always present and decisive in the determination of facts and that they in reality constitute the relations among facts. Science is largely the discovery of these relations, of the networks of facts that exist from time to time in space, and of the relations among these networks.

An event in the early stages of modern physical science illustrates the paramount importance of the rational factors in the development of science. When the Copernican theory was accepted, it was not accepted because anyone had ever seen or had any actual experience other than imaginative of the earth rotating on its axis or moving around the sun. So far as any supposed motion around the sun is concerned, to see or have any other sense experience of this motion from the earth is not possible. If sense experience is the decisive factor in the cultivation of science, as is held in logical positivist doctrine, this doctrine receives a mortal blow when it is understood that verification of this motion by sense experience is not possible. The patch that is made on the doctrine by verification in principle is a thoroughly rational patch, for if the motion actually occurs—and relativity theory raises some doubt about this—and if one could get to any point in outer space where one could see the motion, one would undoubtedly see it.

Galileo understood as well perhaps as anyone ever has the decisive role of reason in the development of science and remarks on it in a way that is completely unambiguous through Salviati, who impersonates him in his *Dialogue on the Great World Systems*. One of the persons in the dialogue, Sagredus, has just expressed wonder that so few persons hold the Pythagorean opinion that the earth and not the sun moves. Galileo, speaking through Salviati, replies:

But my wondering, Sagredus, is very different from yours. You wonder that so few are followers of the Pythagorean opinion; and I am how there could be any yet left till now that do embrace and follow it. Nor can I sufficiently admire the eminence of those men's intelligence who have received and held it to be true, and with the sprightliness of their judgments offered such violence to their own senses that they have been able to prefer that which their reason dictated to them to what sensible appearances represented most manifestly on the contrary. That the reasons against the diurnal vertiginous revolution of the earth, by you already examined, do carry great probability with them, we have already seen; as, also, that the Ptolemaics and Aristotelians with all their sectators did receive them for true is indeed a very great argument of their efficacy; but those experiences which overtly contradict the annual motion have yet so much more of an appearance of convincingness that (I say it again) I cannot find any bounds for my admiration how reason was able in Aristarchus and Copernicus to commit such a rape upon their senses as, in despite thereof, to make herself mistress of their belief.[18]

Despite the flamboyance of Galileo's rhetoric, the message in this passage will come through clearly to any careful reader, at least as far as it involves the question immediately at issue.

Faust specifies as a part of the Chicago College program the study and analysis of the original works of scientists, on the assumption, I suppose, that they do what they say they do and that they know and state

18. Galileo Galilei, *Dialogue on the Great World Systems*, trans. Salusbury, ed. G. de Santillana (Chicago: Univ. of Chicago Press, [1953] 1957), p. 341.

the assumptions, the principles, the theories involved in their work.

Albert Einstein tells us in his Herbert Spencer Lecture, "On the Method of Theoretical Physics," delivered at Oxford, June 10, 1933, that

If you want to find out anything from the theoretical physicists about the methods they use, I advise you to stick closely to one principle: don't listen to their words, fix your attention on their deeds.[19]

In his *Autobiography*, written when he was between sixty-seven and seventy-three, Charles Darwin says of his preparation for writing *The Origin of Species:*

I worked on true Baconian principles, and without any theory collected facts on a wholesale scale, more especially with respect to domesticated productions, by pointed enquiries, by conversation with skillfull breeders and gardeners, and by extensive reading.[20]

It is evident that the first part of this statement, "I worked on true Baconian principles, and without any theory collected facts on a wholesale scale," is made somewhat dubious by the part that follows. Darwin did *not* collect miscellaneous facts. Those he wanted and collected by the means he mentions had to do "more especially with respect to domesticated productions" and had all of the character further defined by the words "skillful breeders and gardeners." Darwin's notion of what he was after may have been, probably was in its earliest stages, vague; but there is little room for doubt that he had a notion and that he worked on it until it became clearer and clearer in his mind. Gertrude Himmelfarb in her highly readable book *Darwin and the Darwinian Revolution* tells us that the time when Darwin shifted from his "original impression that species being immutable, had originated in special acts of creation" to "the possibility that species were not immutable and had gradually changed and evolved in the course of time" [21] can be dated with a high degree of certainty. Miss Himmelfarb gives reasons for thinking the shift occurred in the spring or early summer of 1837 and not on board H.M.S. *Beagle* as Darwin says in the first paragraph of the Introduction to *The Origin of Species*. When the scientist leaves only one record on one subject, and says only one something on that subject, one still has

19. Einstein, *Ideas and Opinions* (New York: Crown Publisher, [1954] 1963), p. 270.

20. Charles Darwin, *Autobiography*, ed. Nora Barlow (New York: Harcourt, Brace, 1959), p. 119.

21. Gertrude Himmelfarb, *Darwin and the Darwinian Revolution* (London: Chatto and Windus, 1959), p. 123.

the question whether he understood and did what he said. But when two or more records exist, and what is said in the records about the same subject do not jibe, one has some problems that cannot easily be solved by merely studying records.

The following statements made by Darwin and quoted by Miss Himmelfarb do not jibe with the statement quoted from Darwin's *Autobiography.*

How odd it is that anyone should not see that all observation must be for or against some view if it is to be of any service. . . .

No one could be a good observer unless he was an active theorizer.[22]

After the publication of the *Origin,* in justifying the work, says Miss Himmelfarb, Darwin "defended the procedure of 'inventing a theory and seeing how many classes of facts the theory would explain.' " [23]

Two items by Darwin are given in the lists of readings in the book *The Idea and Practice of General Education* for students in the College to study and analyze to find out about Darwin's method. One is Darwin's *Origin of Species,* the other is "Provisional Hypothesis of Pangenesis," in *Variation of Animals and Plants Under Domestication.* The facts about Darwin's method, brought to light by Miss Himmelfarb, are from miscellaneous sources. They are not in *The Origin of Species,* and they are not in the selection from the *Variation* cited above.

Whatever else may be said of Darwin's method, and wherever we have to go to find out about it, we have in the last quotation above an interesting and perhaps significant anticipation of Einstein's view that theories are free inventions of the [disciplined] intellect. I quote from Einstein's paper "On the Method of Theoretical Physics":

The structure of the theoretical system of physics is the work of reason; the empirical contents and their mutual relations must find their representation in the conclusions of the theory. In the possibility of such a representation lie the sole value and justification of the whole system, and especially of the concepts and fundamental principles which underlie it. Apart from that, these latter are free inventions of the human intellect, which cannot be justified either by the nature of the intellect or in any other fashion *a priori.*[24]

There is much that students need to know on the subject of fact and theory of which Faust does not give even a hint in his article. And

22. Ibid., p. 130.
23. Ibid.
24. Einstein, *Ideas and Opinions,* p. 270

neither do any other articles in the book. One of the more interesting and influential discussions of the relations of fact and theory during the last half century is Appendix 2, "A Methodological Note on Facts and Valuations in Social Science," in Volume 2, pp. 1035–70 of the 1944 edition of Gunnar Myrdal's *An American Dilemma*. The lists of readings in *The Idea and Practice of General Education* in the section on the social sciences includes selected passages of Myrdal's *An American Dilemma*. Myrdal's Methodological Note is not among them. Moreover, Myrdal nowhere states the one most important fact about his method. This is simply that he adopts for social science the current model provided by mathematical physics. Myrdal's model, as Myrdal clearly says, does not provide for any self-evident truths. Equality thus has for Myrdal a basis totally different from that which it had for Thomas Jefferson and the committee that directed Jefferson in his drafting of the Declaration of Independence. Myrdal does not, however, discuss this departure from the theory on which the Declaration is based. If the reader, or the Chicago student, does not know something of the history of the doctrine of self-evident truth, the connection of this doctrine with both the idea of equality as self-evident truth in the Declaration of Independence, and the idea of self-evidently true axioms in Euclidean geometry, and, finally, the effect of the development of non-Euclidean geometries in weakening and possibly destroying the doctrine of self-evident truth, he lacks an essential element in the understanding of Myrdal's method. In Myrdal's method, equality has no roots in the nature of things; it is not an idea necessary to opening the way to individual and social improvement; it is a mere convention, something agreed upon that may continue to be agreed upon as long as sentiment for it lasts, and abandoned if the sentiment for it disappears—and abandoned without necessarily devastating effects on individuals and society. This subject is one of the great meeting-places of various disciplines. Subjects such as this are at the center of human knowledge. They constitute the subject matter of general education. They are practically unknown today.

Faust greatly underestimates the importance of memory, and so do most of those who talk about the growth of knowledge. If we wish to say that books and other printed materials, micro cards, computer storage-and-retrieval systems *know* the materials recorded in them, there is nothing to stop us. When a computer storage-and-retrieval system, or something else, is constructed that recognizes that Gunnar Myrdal's use of the expression "self-evident" is totally different from that of Thomas Jefferson, and when the computer storage-and-retrieval system then, on being asked, tells the interested person where he can find informed and illuminating discussion of these two meanings and their tremendous implications for the quality of life possible for societies and individuals, there will be a real basis for talking about the growth of knowledge. The truth is that the knowledge that is most important to human beings is being lost while immense masses of detail are being recorded and stored. No one has yet discovered any way to locate this detail except by means that require the use of human memory. And human memory is not being properly developed and stored today. Gertrude Stein's rose is a rose is a rose would long ago have been recognized as what it is if the human memory were being properly developed and stored. A change such as that which Gunnar Myrdal has imported from mathematics and physical science into social science in the meaning of the expression "self-evident" is not a trivial matter. The great importance of changes of this kind goes unnoticed today.

One cannot even begin to talk about anything without having in his memory words for the things he wishes to talk about. And there are ideas or theories, such as that of self-evident truths, that have wide connections which, if not understood and *in the memory*, open one to gross deception and to the practice, without intention, of deception on others. One cannot begin to talk about history without having a wide variety of names—of persons, places, events, epochs, and developments that can hardly be called events such as, say, the beginnings of agriculture (the Neolithic Revolution) or the Industrial Revolution. A word such as "evolution" approaches the meaningless—even if the whole process is by scientists given the apparently Gibraltar-like hardness of a fact—to anyone who does not know any facts that illustrate and help to constitute the process, and is ignorant that the reality of the process depends entirely on an inference from external appearances to internal realities of a totally different nature from any experience available to the senses. In the chapter dealing with the course in the History of Western Civilization in which the effort to see how the integration of the natural sciences, the social sciences, and the humanities in history is possible, it is said: "It has been found useful to prepare date lists for the students and to require memorization of about a hundred key dates." [25] It would have been helpful if Faust had recognized in his chapter the necessity of memory work to learning—and far more than is suggested in the quota-

25. *Idea and Practice of General Education*, p. 230.

tion above from another chapter. Whatever theory of learning one accepts, the careful and bountiful storing of the memory is essential if the work of the mind is to be fruitful.

I turn now to a statement in one of the articles in *The Idea and Practice of General Education* that I believe should have been developed in more detail both in the article in which the statement is made and in all the other articles in the book.

In the article on the social sciences the author says that the staff of the College is committed to a free society:

The positive relation to action is implicit in the aim to develop rational habits of deliberation about public policy. We as teachers would not organize a program aiming at this result if we did not expect that some day the student will himself exercise this habit in the making of real decisions in a free society. In reality, then, *we have committed ourselves to the building and maintenance of a free society. Without this assumption, the ends of the program would make little sense* [My italics]. Further, we are committed to the use of those methods of free and impartial discussion which are essential not only for the continuance of a free society but for the very existence of the scientific spirit as well.[26]

This is so well said that I can think of very few criticisms that I would care to make. I would use the word "reasonably" to modify "free society" and I would somewhere say why. The reason I would give is, as I have said in previous chapters, that freedom can be used to destroy freedom. To fail to understand this is to fail to understand one of the necessities of what we call free society. Another of the necessities is stated in the phrase "free and impartial discussion" in the quotation. Here again the words "free" and "impartial" are needed, but they can be misleading. If by "free" is meant doing or saying what one pleases in discussion without strict regard to what the exploration of the subject requires, then to be "free" is to be destructive; if by "impartial" is meant lack of concern for the truth of the subject, that is indifference, then, as Immanuel Kant truly said, the principle we have adopted is "the mother, in all sciences, of chaos and night." The true scientist and scholar is deeply concerned, despite the conventionalism of our time, to get as near as he can to the truth of his subject. He is also concerned not to let his concern get in the way of his effort, as it easily can. "The partisan," Socrates tells us in the *Phaedo,* his last talk with his friends just before his execution,

26. Ibid., p. 134.

Now the partisan, when he is engaged in a dispute, cares nothing about the rights of the question, but is anxious only to convince his hearers of his own assertions. And the difference between him and me at the present moment is merely this—that whereas he seeks to convince his hearers that what he says is true, I am seeking rather to convince myself; to convince my hearers is a secondary matter with me. . . . I would ask you to be thinking of the truth and not of Socrates: agree with me, if I seem to you to be speaking the truth; or if not, withstand me might and main, that I may not deceive you as well as myself in my enthusiasm, and like the bee, leave my sting in you before I die.[27]

In order for "free and impartial discussion" to escape mere wrangling, or me-tooism, or any of the other numerous varieties of fruitless discussion, all participants have to obey, whether as a matter of habit or otherwise, the principles that are necessary to this end. And to do this the principles must be known, at least in the sense of being habitually observed. A genuine general education would try to cultivate in students, and I believe we can be sure the Chicago College staff did try to cultivate in its students, knowledge of and habitual obedience of these principles; but it would not leave their discovery to the students. The teachers should know these principles, should be able to state them and demonstrate their necessity to "free and impartial discussion."

The Chicago College program would have been a far better program if teaching had started with principles, not of yesterday or today, but principles which have been well-established throughout the history of Western civilization and for which validating discussion exists, such as, say, Aristotle's discussion of the law of contradiction in Book Gamma of his *Metaphysics;* or the particle theory in Lucretius' *Nature of Things,* even though the theory as in Lucretius is in important ways entirely different from modern theory; or the theory of political and social power as stated by Thucydides in his discussion of the Melian Conference in his *History of the Peloponnessian War*. Too many of the readings in the Chicago list have not been tested by time.

It is unreasonable to expect college students, no matter how carefully selected or how brilliant, to derive from texts principles that are not explicit in them. The statement of a principle or theory in a way that is clear and relatively unambiguous and defensible is not an easy task. Very few principles or theories in the social sciences have ever been so stated, and even fewer in the humanities. If the experts have not been able to do very much in this direction, it is entirely unreasonable to expect students to do much.

27. *Dialogues of Plato*, trans. Jowett, I, 475.

I have expressed severe criticism of the effort under Chancellor Hutchins and Dean Faust to find out what general education is and to establish it in the College of the University of Chicago. In my criticisms, I have been applying, as far as I think it valid, a principle of great importance stated by Hutchins. I quote from him: "I do not think that I exaggerate when I say that in a democratic society controversy is an end in itself. A university that is not controversial is not a university. A civilization in which there is not a continuous controversy about important issues, speculative and practical, is on the way to totalitarianism and death." [28] I do not go so far with Hutchins as to agree that in a university or outside a university, "controversy is an end in itself." On the contrary, the idea of controversy merely for the sake of controversy is abhorrent to me. And even when real issues are involved, the rights of the issues are likely to be forgotten in the desire to win by any means, fair or foul; and sheer meanness tends to creep in. I have found controversies often to be so distressing that I have always tried every possible means of avoiding them. I could give numerous instances when I have seen persons in positions of power do ill-advised, even outrageous things, and I, to avoid controversy, have been silent, deeply distressed, and ashamed of myself. But when the rights of the question are strictly regarded, and the egos involved suppressed, controversy is as necessary to the life of a university as Hutchins says it is.

Most of the pressures of American society are toward making persons more concerned with personal advancement, regardless of what they have to do to get the advancement, than with anything else. The other extreme, excessive devotion to notions of the general welfare that are compatible only with blessed innocence, that have not been subjected to informed criticism, may be equally or more destructive. It is good for young people to be seriously interested in getting ahead in the world—really necessary that they should be determined to do so; but only in ways that are compatible with the general welfare. To manage this is not easy, and Adam Smith was not the first or the last to understand this fact. Adam Smith knew, as we should today, that declarations of devotion to the general welfare may be mere masks for the promotion of special interests, and these special interests may be academic as well as other. It remains true, however, that there is never any promotion of the general welfare that does not promote individuals and groups, some more than others. The problem of serving the general welfare in ways

28. *University of Utopia*, p. 91.

that cannot be made to appear to be the service of special interests is not as easy as is often assumed today, and especially in intellectual circles.

The processes that have shaped the Adolf Eichmanns of the world are terribly in need of attention in the United States as well as elsewhere. The healthy community life that is necessary to a healthy national life cannot be achieved by a nation of Adolf Eichmanns.[29] But neither can it be achieved by a nation of Callicleans, or anarchists, or nihilists, or others without good principles embodied in good customs and habits.

The effort in the College at the University of Chicago under Chancellor Hutchins and Dean Faust, with all its shortcomings, was one of the really great efforts of this century to perform a service absolutely necessary to the maintenance and further development of free society. Ways must be found to continue this effort and make it succeed. The Western heritage from which the American heritage is derived is far too precious to let it disappear from the face of the earth.

29. Adolf Eichmann is perhaps as clear an example as can be found of the type of person who takes and carries out superior orders without concerning himself about the quality of the orders. His only concern seems clearly to have been personal advancement and he appears to have been willing to do almost anything to get it—if the doing did not at the moment endanger him. Modern society, in the United States as well as elsewhere, in all of its institutions, spawns persons of this type. And worse, it spawns the type that goes wildly moral over the moral problem when it discovers the existence of this problem. Such books as Hannah Arendt's *Eichmann in Jerusalem* warrant serious study. The problem of superior orders is far more extensive and difficult than Miss Arendt suggests in this book. The viciousness that Eichmann expressed in the part he took in Hitler's National Socialist program of exterminating the Jews can be expressed in multitudinous ways.

CHAPTER X

Distilled Experience

The dialectical method finds . . . the soul embedded in what is really a swamp of barbarism.

PLATO, *Republic*

The most important effort that has been made in the United States to solve the problem of general education for the public outside of colleges and universities, as well as inside, was made by Robert Maynard Hutchins. This effort assumed, as to some extent the University of Chicago College program did, that the great books of the Western world provide the materials from which a general education can be derived and that there is a consensus that identifies these books. This effort took two forms: one, the organization of groups throughout the country for the purpose of reading and discussing the great books of the Western world; the other, the production of a set of these books with suitable aids for study. For several years there were many groups over the country reading and discussing the great books. Interest seemed genuine and growing for a time. But this did not last. The groups did not generate enough interest to become self-perpetuating and greatly to multiply, and gradually this part of the effort weakened, perhaps because there was no well-endowed national organization that provided continual stimulus and skilled supervision.

I have not read and I would consider it a waste of my time to read some of the books in the set *The Great Books of the Western World*. Many of those that I have read, however, I have read many times, and I read them long before Hutchins and his associate, Mortimer Adler, made their selections. Most of my selections are in the Hutchins and Adler set, and only one that I have felt worth close study, Hume's *Treatise of Human Nature*, is omitted. If the opinions of persons who have tried to determine whether there are any books that, because of their qualities, are really great were asked, I believe there would be rough agreement on the Hutchins and Adler selections.

I regret the limitation of the set to the great books of the Western world. Why not the great books of the whole world? The answer could be that if the title of the set were, say, *The Great Books of the World*, and if there were then in the set only a relatively very small number of volumes of Oriental origin, the charge of bias, of cultural chauvinism would almost certainly have been made and could have seriously embarrassed the project when the set was published. To limit the set to the great books of the Western world and use this as a title would avoid openly raising this issue. But then the question necessarily arises, if anyone bothers to think seriously about the matter, that if the great books, and only the great books in the set, really contain the materials necessary to a general education, the presentation of the great books of the western world as containing these materials is an implicit claim that they are really the great books of the whole world. The claim cannot be avoided regardless of the set title. But it can be clouded and I think probably it was best to avoid the controversy that could have arisen if the claim had been made explicit.

Still I feel it necessary to take my courage in my hands and say I agree with Thomas Babington Macaulay's statement on this subject. I quote:

I have no knowledge of either Sanscrit or Arabic.—But I have done what I could to form a correct estimate of their value. I have read translations of the most celebrated Arabic and Sanscrit works. I have conversed both here [in India] and at home with men distinguished by their proficiency in the Eastern tongues. I am quite ready to take the Oriental learning at the valuation of the Orientalists themselves. I have never found one among them who could deny that a single shelf of a good European library was worth the whole native literature of India and Arabia. The intrinsic superiority of the Western literature is, indeed, fully admitted by those members of the Committee who support the Oriental plan of education.[1]

In judging this statement it should be remembered that the dilution of the printed materials on library shelves in the West had not yet been accomplished when Macaulay made this once celebrated statement. A more exact statement of what I believe is true on this subject today is that, except for the Bible, there are not more than a half-dozen Oriental books of earlier times comparable in their contribution to human knowledge with any of the 443 works that make up the 54 compact volumes of the Hutchins and Adler collection published by Britannica under the

---

1. Macaulay, *Selected Speeches*, The World's Classics (New York: Oxford, 1935), p. 349.

title *The Great Books of the Western World*. To regard a statement of this kind as cultural chauvinism is not to know what cultural chauvinism is. Cultural chauvinism is the abandonment of standards in the interests of local loyalties. In trying to avoid cultural chauvinism—which one should certainly try to avoid—one can easily slip into an inverted form, one that tries to escape self-centeredness and fatuous assertions of quality by giving up on the problem of quality and resorting to judgments that are merely representative, that assume the equal excellence of the productions of all peoples, and in doing so, give up on the real questions toward which all genuine education is directed: the question of excellence and truth in human existence.

The question of quality, not who made the books and where, and certainly not the color of the cloth in which they are bound, should determine judgments of excellence. If we do not have standards by which to make such judgments, and if these standards do not completely exclude irrelevant matters such as color or geographical point of origin, we have not learned anything that is very much worth knowing. The great books are the great heritage of the whole world. They constitute the most important part of the kind of property that cannot be held by anyone, or any group, to the exclusion of others. The values they contain cannot be transmitted by legal, physical possession. The Western world has made the contents of the great books easily available to people generally so far as physical access is concerned. But still a person willing to work and with a mind is necessary to gain more than physical access.

It is entirely possible and highly probable that the people of the Orient will take possession of this great heritage. It is fortunately that kind of property that the more of it that is taken and really possessed, the more there is to be taken and possessed. And in this respect, a respect that is sometimes dealt with as if true only of the world's knowledge, it is possible there has been serious error. Karl Marx made much of the capitalist practice of taking what he called surplus value from labor. He did not notice that in those parts of the world where there was little of what he called capitalism and little taking of surplus value from labor, there was also the most intense poverty.

Important as the great books are, to study them is not enough. Most people, including most specialists with Ph.D. degrees, cannot read many of them; and those that they can read, such as Darwin's *Origin of Species*, will pose for them questions—if they think while reading—that are not answered in the works themselves, nor are they answered in the two-volume collection of excellent essays, *The Great Ideas*, edited by Mortimer Adler and William Gorman, and part of the set of Britannica's *Great Books of the Western World*. This is simply to say that no one set of books can do everything that is necessary to the cultivation of a genuine general education. This set is by far the best of its kind and should be in every home where there are people, young or old, who are able to read and who are willing to work to get first-hand knowledge of the intellectual effort that has been most important in shaping the Western world and that is now, mainly in its Hegelian-Marxian version, shaping the Eastern world. It is a great improvement in crucial ways over the effort that was made to establish general education in the College of the University of Chicago. Of greatest importance, the execution of the work is actually guided by the purpose that the editors say it is designed to serve; this purpose is to give the public access to the great books of the Western world with editorial apparatus that is genuinely useful to the reader. Instead of leaving to the reader, as the Chicago College program left to the student and teacher, the whole task of analyzing the works and discovering the great ideas in them, this task was performed by a well-trained staff under highly skilled direction, which had a purpose and knew how to serve it. The analysis that was made of the works locates and proves beyond question the permanence of certain ideas in the midst of controversies about them for a period of over two thousand years. This does not mean, of course, that one has only to read the works, the list of great ideas, and the essays about them to gain understanding. It is still necessary to discuss, even if the discussion is conducted only in one's own mind, whether there are any permanences in change, and what these are, because the permanences can be understood only if they are continuously distinguished from the protean characters with which they are always associated. The Hutchins and Adler set provides aids to the reader that cannot, of course, be compared with the aid that Arabic numerals have provided in the making of calculations, or the Phoenician (Roman) alphabet in communication; but it does suggest that it is still possible to invent great aids to learning.

In the largest and most general sense, the most important information we can have about the great books is that they are, with reference to subjects of great scope, efforts by great minds to establish orthodoxies on the subjects with which they deal. Now a great orthodoxy can have widely different effects on the human mind, depending on the quality of the mind and the other stimuli it receives. It can bind or it can free and support the mind in its work. It is not sufficiently well understood that no intellectual work beyond the most primitive response to impulse is possible if it is not conducted in the context of an orthodoxy, either within the orthodoxy as a further development of it, or outside it and as an effort to replace it with another orthodoxy.

Some intellectual tools have in practice throughout human history been proved necessary and common to all intellectual work that has had any chance to stand long enough to become an orthodoxy. The first task of education has always been to teach, to instruct, to indoctrinate as carefully and as firmly as possible the young in the necessity of knowledge of and skill in the use of these tools and actually to teach and train in their skilled use. The same is true concerning knowledge of the great orthodoxies. The great task of the educator at the highest levels is to cultivate in the learner the correct and firm grasp of these orthodoxies and the tools that have made them possible. The cultivation of this correct and firm grasp is a necessary part of the preparation for the task of criticism and of improving on existing orthodoxies. At every stage in this process, the teacher fails to do his duty if he does not help the learner understand why some orthodoxies are better than others. And all good teachers do this and this is indoctrination. If the teacher is genuinely a teacher, nothing else that he can do is so important as this. It is this that makes his profession, his office one of the greatest in which human beings can engage.

The problem of indoctrination is not an easy problem. Indoctrination can be conducted in ways that, if successful, block the way to learning. But it can be conducted so as to open up the way to learning and make learning by far the most attractive activity that the human mind can cultivate, and the most helpful to man, both as an individual and as a member of society. Indoctrination is almost certain to remain indefinitely, if not always, the chief problem of free society. There is no prospect whatever of any final and complete solution of this problem. It did not exist before the establishment of the relatively free societies of the modern world. Or perhaps I should say, if it was a problem, very few if any people knew that it was a problem. Indoctrination for most people almost always and everywhere until recent times has been routine accepted without question. And it probably still is for most people even today. Deliberate indoctrination is being constantly practiced in free societies in multitudinous forms, many of the forms competing for time and interest and acceptance. The freedom in free societies also allows constant competition in the formation and reformation of orthodoxies even to the extent of the development of new and the destruction of old and the enlistment of partisans. Totalitarian societies do not allow activities of this kind. In them the effort is made by the state to maintain only one orthodoxy and to outlaw all others. Indoctrination in this one orthodoxy, as long as there is great outside opposition, may provide tremendous stimulus, but if this one orthodoxy wins over the outside opposition, this stimulus is lost, and the power of binding the mind that has so long been cultivated, in the absence of the outside stimulus, is likely to produce its deadening effect.

The background that acquaintance with the subject matter of *The Great Books of the Western World* provides is necessary to the best handling of the problem of indoctrination in the interests of free and good society. But *The Great Books of the Western World* are not focused on the problems of the contemporary world. There is no pretension in or about them that they are so focused; and it is no criticism of them to say that they do not serve a purpose they were not designed to serve. The great books of the past cannot be accepted as providing complete and final models for guidance in the future; but they make clear beyond doubt the kind of work that is now most needed and they provide some, if not all, of the basic principles needed for this work.

The purpose and work to serve it that I shall now discuss is of the greatest importance, and no institution now in existence is serving it.

We have seen, or should have seen, in Chapter IX, a contradiction in the work of the College at the University of Chicago. First, a dean of the College says that the purpose of the College is not to teach "what to think" but "how to think." Second, a member of the College staff, the author of the article on social science, says the staff is committed to "the building and maintenance of a free society." The question arises whether this "building and maintenance" requires certain thinking and doing, and whether this in turn requires teaching "what to think." But to start at the right place, it seems necessary to remark that there may be a necessary connection between what is taught about "how to think" and "what to think." Or, to say the same thing in another way, if there is no "what to think" that is necessary and trustworthy on "how to think," it is impossible that there should be, or could be, any real teaching of "how to think."

It may be that the best method of teaching "how to think" is to face the student with the problem and make him work it out for himself. It could be held, just as reasonably, that the student should not even be allowed to read books that he or his teacher might think would be helpful, that he should be deprived of all such aids. If the teacher is forbidden to help, that is, to indoctrinate or teach what is necessary on "how to think," it seems clear other aids should not be allowed. The notion that the student can make himself into an intellectual giant by his own un-aided efforts can be made very attractive, but when we look at it seri-ously it makes no sense whatever. To follow this procedure is really to say, whether we know it or not, that there should not be any teachers, any schools, any colleges and universities, or any books and libraries to which the student can go for help. To hold that the teacher should not guide and instruct and indoctrinate as far as he can is really to say that neither the teacher nor any other aids to the student are needed, that he should do everything for and by himself.

Now if there is no body of knowledge that the teacher should com-mand and that enables the teacher to help the student learn what it is necessary to think on the question how to think—if the thinking is to be done correctly—then the educational process is a hopeless enterprise. We know, as well as we know anything, that there is knowledge of what to think on how to think and, if we are not in a seriously befuddled state, we know it is the teacher's duty to teach what to think on how to think. Until the student has received and understood the body of knowledge that the teacher, if he does his duty, conveys to him on this subject, he can reasonably be expected and required mainly to accept this knowl-edge. The teacher cannot reasonably be expected to explain and justify to students matters which the best minds of all time have been unable to explain and justify. The student cannot be expected to understand at first everything that he needs to be taught. Some never understand. They receive knowledge only as, say, a swamp receives water. Some understand early and sometimes so well that they are able to see grave flaws in the teacher's understanding, and some of these may choose to torture the teacher with questions that he should be but is not able to answer. There is no cure for these conditions except better teachers and better students; and when both teachers and students are perfect, there will be genuine cause for celebration.

However we consider the educational process, there is no escape from the duty of the teacher to drill into his students what to think on how to think. And this drilling is indoctrination. Whatever we may say on the subject, if there is any real teaching of what to think on how to think, indoctrination is inescapable. In one form or another, it always occurs. This does not necessarily mean that the student's mind, if he has a mind, will be bound by the indoctrination. But there is always this danger, and while it can be reduced by good teaching—by teaching that always warns against imagining that one is becoming or has become god, by teaching that warns of human fallibility without paralyzing human enterprise—still even the best of teaching can be defeated by the materials it has to work on. The student's mind, if he has a mind, can be damaged by worse rather than better orthodoxies. It happens all the time. The only corrective is the effort to get the student to accept and understand the better rather than the worse, and there is no infallible method of making this effort successfully. But still the effort has to be made if the great office of the teacher is not to serve a purpose the opposite of that it is intended to serve. The chances are that the student with a mind will use fruitfully the help of the really good teacher. The student who appears to be mindless is as likely to revolt against sense as against nonsense. He poses a problem for which no really satisfactory solutions have yet been found. The student who has a mind will certainly revolt at times against nonsense, but not in a way that renders all teaching a hopeless effort. The student owes the deepest respect to the great office of the teacher, and even if he cannot respect the person occupying the office, he will, if he has a mind, not make a shambles of the educational process in order to show his disrespect. Of course, when teachers themselves do not respect the office of the teacher and disgrace it by bad teaching, or allow students to rampage freely and to do things that damage, perhaps irreparably, teachers who have not curried student favor, there is little that can be done until better teachers are found.

No real teacher, I repeat, leaves his students without the best help that he can give them on questions within his scope, such as what to think on how to think. If the teacher can play the midwife with the students, as Socrates did with the slave boy in the *Meno,* and by skillfully directed questions evoke the right answers, this is certainly one excellent mode of teaching, perhaps the best there can be; for in this process the student indoctrinates himself in a way that, if developed, enables him to correct false indoctrination. If one takes the position that there are no right questions to ask, and no right answers to such questions, then one is lost indeed. If the teacher takes this position, he is no teacher. To occupy the office, to be called a teacher and really to be no teacher of anything other than chaos is so popular today that there are many who plume themselves on being this kind of teacher.

Now there is hardly any room for disagreement on the proposition that to be committed to a free society is to be committed to everything that is necessary to a free society, and to find out what these necessities are. I assume that no one knows *all* that is necessary and that *all* probably cannot be found out, but that some such things, beyond what is already known, can be. And when these necessities are found out—and this finding out is no easy task—one knows, as well as a human being can know, not only what to think but what to do. To deny this is simply to hold that there are no valid ways of thinking, that "how to think" is a phrase empty of meaning. All science is testimony that this view is false.

Now I do not deny—on the contrary, I hold—that there are extreme difficulties in the way of doing what this argument plainly says should be done. But whatever I think on this question, and whatever the truth may be, this is the problem posed for us in one way by the great books of the past. This problem is to improve on their orthodoxies. Another of the problems it poses for us may be illustrated by considering the doctrines stated by qualified members of the College of the University of Chicago on the program of the College during the years while the effort under Chancellor Hutchins was being made to cultivate general education. According to its own testimony, the College both had and did not have the purpose of "the building and maintenance of a free society." I now proceed to show this.

For any purpose to be served, whether the purpose of going to the moon and getting back to earth, or the purpose of "the building and maintenance of a free society," there are necessities that have to be discovered, and the means to meet these necessities when and where they arise have to be provided.

There is no such thing as "the building and maintenance of a free society" any more than there is or can be a "going to the moon and returning to earth" as a consequence of the mere repetition of the words. The repetition does not have magical powers. To go to the moon and return calls for the working out, step by step, of everything necessary to the going and returning. To say in detail what this calls for in knowledge would be to give an account of all the valid conclusions bearing on the problem of going and returning, or, to say the same thing in another way, on what to think and what to do. Now to teach knowing how to think on this subject in the best form in which it is known is indistinguishable from knowing what to think and necessary to knowing what to do. Shall we say this knowing should not be taught as carefully, as clearly, as precisely as possible, because to do this would be to indoctrinate?

In denying the necessity of indoctrination, the College denied the connection between teaching how to think and teaching what to think. But if there is no necessary connection between how to think on the one hand, and what to think and what to do on the other, it is impossible that any teaching by the College of how to think could be of any help to students in determining what to think and what to do to serve the purpose of "the building and maintenance of a free society." In one breath the College declared this purpose, in another it declared a different and, by its own showing, an incompatible purpose.

The orthodoxy on the question we have just been discussing is in a state of almost hopeless confusion. I shall risk adding to the confusion by elaborating on the argument I have made.

Imagine for a moment the catastrophes that would ensue, no matter how many billions were spent on the effort, if what to think in the most exact, the most rigorous possible way as to what was necessary to do the job of going to the moon and returning was not first worked out for every foreseeable contingency.

It can be said, of course, that "going to the moon and returning" is an entirely different matter from "the building and maintenance of a free society." I would agree. Going to the moon and returning is in many ways entirely different, and incredibly less difficult. Yet raw students, so we are told, were taught "how to think" in the Chicago College program on the assumption that once they knew "how to think," they would be able—still relatively raw students, knowing presumably little more than what the College taught them about "how to think"—without any further help to work out "what to think" on the question of "the building and maintenance of a free society." No one in his right mind would expect raw students, after having been taught this "how to think" to work out even the basic principles, not to speak of the innumerable details, involved in going to the moon and returning. And while going to the moon and returning is probably the most difficult single achievement by man since he has been on earth, it is almost certainly easy in comparison with "the building and maintenance of a free society."

While most of the problems involved in going to the moon and returning are different from those of "the building and maintenance of a free society," so different as to make it impossible to formulate comparisons that are not in some ways, totally misleading, still the logic involved in both is the same.

It is extremely rare to find writings in the humanities and social sciences today that are so clear, so compelling in their cogency that one cannot reasonably deny their truth. One hardly ever finds today a piece of writing as illuminating as the following from Samuel Clarke's *Dis-*

course Upon Natural Religion. In this quotation, a logically conclusive
answer to all the current varieties of subjectivism in morals is given:

... if there be no such thing as Good and Evil in the Nature of Things,
antecedent to all Laws, then neither can any one Law be better than another, nor any one thing whatever, be more justly established, and inforced
by Laws, then the contrary; nor can any reason be given, why any Laws
should ever be made at all: But all Laws equally, will be either arbitrary
and tyrannical, or frivolous and needless, because the contrary might with
equal Reason have been established, if before the making of the Laws, all
things had been alike indifferent in their own Nature. There is no possible
way to avoid this Absurdity, but by saying, that out of things in their
own Nature absolutely indifferent, those are chosen by wise Governours
to be made obligatory by Law, the practice of which they judge will tend
to the publick benefit of the Community. But this is an express Contradiction in the very Terms. For if the practice of certain things tends to the
publick benefit of the World, and the contrary would tend to the publick
disadvantage, then those things are not in their own nature indifferent, but
were good and reasonable to be practiced before any Law was made, and
can only for that very reason be wisely inforced by the Authority of Laws.
Only here it is to be observed, that by the publick Benefit must not be
understood the interest of any one particular Nation, to the plain injury
or prejudice of the rest of Mankind, any more than the interest of one City
or Family, in opposition to their Neighbours of the same Country: But
those things only are truly good in their own Nature, which either tend to
the universal benefit and welfare of all Men, or at least are not destructive
of it. The true State therefore of this Case, is plainly this. Some things are
in their own nature Good and Reasonable and Fit to be done, such as keeping Faith, and performing Compacts, and the like; And these receive not
their obligatory power, from any Law or Authority, but are only declared,
confirmed and inforced by penalties, upon such as would not perhaps be
governed by right Reason only. Other things are in their own nature absolutely Evil, such as breaking Faith, refusing to perform equitable Compacts, cruelly destroying those who have neither directly nor indirectly
given any occasion for any such treatment, and the like; And these cannot
by any Law or Authority whatsoever, be made fit and reasonable, or ex-
cusable to be practiced.[2]

Such arguments as this of Clarke's are usually held today to be dis-
qualified on either of at least two grounds, and sometimes more. Clarke's
argument is, of course, a rational ethical argument. It does not deny the
role of feeling in ethics but holds rather that reason has to be used to
establish order among feelings, that feelings have to be kept under

2. Samuel Clarke, *Discourse Upon Natural Religion*, in *British Moralists*, ed.
L. A. Selby-Bigge (Oxford, 1897), II, 8–9.

control by reason, otherwise they can become socially destructive. Logical positivism holds that ethical propositions depend entirely on feelings and that when one asserts such a proposition one is merely expressing one's feelings while imagining that one is saying that something is really characterized by some quality such as being good or bad. Thus logical positivism says the quality of evil did not inhere in the action of Cornwall when he gouged out Gloucester's eyes, that what Cornwall's servant thought he saw as evil was merely a feeling in himself which he projected on the action. Thus any proposition that says this action was evil is meaningless. All ethical propositions, according to logical positivism, are of this nature. The playwright Harold Pinter presents the same problem from a different point of view, one that, whatever Pinter's intention, reveals the influence of the theory that everything in the universe, including human thoughts and feelings, consists only of particles in motion, in his play *The Homecoming*. All of the characters in the play are extreme sensualists, committed to the sexual exploitation of themselves and others, except one. This one is a professor in an American college on a visit to England with his wife. He sees his wife plan with his father and brothers to become a prostitute and is entirely unconcerned. At a certain point in the play there is what the participants imagine to be philosophical discussion of the nature of a table, discussion that points toward the obviously false reductionist notion that has penetrated to some extent the popular mind that everything in the universe is only particles in motion. The professor's wife states the notion when she says:

"Look at me. I . . . move my leg. That's all it is. But I wear . . . underwear . . . which moves with me . . . it . . . captures your attention. Perhaps you misinterpret. The action is simple. It's a leg . . . moving. My lips move. Why don't you restrict . . . your observations to that? Perhaps the fact that they move is more significant . . . than the words which come through them. You must bear that . . . possibility . . . in mind" [ellipses the author's].[3]

And of course the same view may be taken when an atom bomb is dropped on a great city and hundreds of thousands of human bodies are torn to pieces, or put into such condition that having been torn to pieces would have been merciful. Now what shall we say of a doctrine that regards the ultimate constituents of the universe, whatever these may

3. Harold Pinter, *The Homecoming* (New York: Grove Press, 1966), pp. 52–53. By permission of Glove Press, Inc., and Methuen & Co., Ltd. Copyright © 1965 and 1966 by H. Pinter, Ltd.

be, as of the same moral value—in this case of no moral value—whether they are in the form of healthy, or dismembered, or suffering human bodies? All, in the particle theory that we are now considering, are only particles in motion. We not only grant, we insist on, the existence of extreme difficulties in the way of fair and honest judgments on military actions; but what are we to say of a doctrine that holds that the discussion of the morality of such actions is meaningless?

Those of us who concentrate our fire on the military have a target nearer home that cries for our attention. This target is ourselves. We are the victims of a widespread and tremendously powerful notion of which we are often completely unaware. This notion is the most powerful factor in the implicit dominant orthodoxy of our time. Such is the depth and width and height of the learned ignorance that has us in wandering mazes lost.

This is, of course, the homecoming, in a perverted form of a doctrine that in this perverted form has reached the status of an orthodoxy. It could really be true that ideas, orthodoxies, that get into circulation may have consequences. We can be sure David Hume did not intend anything of this kind when he said that "reason is, and ought only to be the slave of the passions, and can never pretend to any other office than to serve and obey them." Hume has been almost certainly the most powerful influence in the shaping of logical positivism.

Another criticism of Clarke's argument is that it tends to transform ethics into political and social and legal philosophy. It would be hard to find and hold any view more obtuse than this. It is like the specialization that is cultivated as if the subject with which it has to do existed in a tightly closed compartment with no relations with anything else. If ethics can be transformed into political and social and legal philosophy, they also can be transformed into ethics. And insofar as they involve ethical problems, what more could be desired for them and it?

There certainly are great dangers in indoctrination, in teaching "what to think." But there are far greater dangers in imagining that there is in existence no implicit dominant orthodoxy while in fact there is such a doctrine, and one that says in essence that there are no ethical truths that can be known and taught and that teachers must not take sides on questions of this kind. Most teachers today are unaware that there is in existence an implicit dominant orthodoxy.

The good teacher today, in the generally accepted doctrine of the teacher, is one who presents "both sides" or perhaps all the more important sides of a question, and never becomes an advocate of any one side. The doctrine of the teacher is thus that he, like Buridan's ass, stand paralyzed between two sides, or among many, unable to make up his mind, or if he is able to make it up, unable to make it up rightly, thus proving his intellectual incompetence or ignorance. The reasons for the doctrine all derive from the notion of specialization, the notion that one can be competent only in the subject on which one specializes. As long as specialization of the extreme kind continues, with little or no general education, the effort obviously has to be made to maintain the doctrine, even though maintaining it consistently is impossible.

It would be grossly misleading to give the impression that there is any easy solution of this problem. It almost certainly is beyond any completely acceptable final solution. But at the same time it is simply fatuous to assume, as is currently done, that current notions about racial relations, especially about integration in schools, colleges, and universities, are the only notions necessary to free society that have been discovered and that warrant the backing of law and law-enforcing agencies, and that it is the duty of the teacher who in his regular work has to do with this subject to indoctrinate on it and on no other.

We are told indoctrination is against American principles. Thomas Jefferson was certainly a good American. Let us see what he had to say on this subject. We owe, so Bernard Crick tells us, to Jefferson's

discussion with James Madison, Joseph Cabell and other Visitors of the University of Virginia about what texts to prescribe, a remarkably illuminating statement of what were considered by the gentlemen of Virginia in 1825 to be the "principles of government" and a proper way to teach and to insist upon them.[4]

This is the resolution on this subject that, under Jefferson's leadership, the Visitors finally approved:

Whereas it is the duty of this Board to the Government under which it lives and especially to that of which this University is the immediate creation, to pay especial attention to the principles of government which shall be inculcated therein, and to provide that none shall be inculcated which are incompatible with those on which the Constitutions of this State and of the United States are genuinely based, in the common opinion; and for this purpose it may be necessary to point out specially where these principles are to be found legitimately developed: Resolved, that it is the opinion of this Board that as to the general principles of liberty and the rights of man, in nature and in society, the doctrines of Locke in his *Essay concern-*

4. Crick, *The American Science of Politics* (Berkeley: Univ. of California Press, 1960), pp. 14 f.

ing the true original extent and end of Civil Government, and of Sidney in his *Discourse on Government* may be considered as those generally approved by our fellow citizens of this, and the United States, and that on the distinctive principles of the government of our State and of those of the United States, the best guides are to be found in (1) the *Declaration of Independence,* as the fundamental act of union of these states, (2) the book known by the title of *The Federalist,* being an authority to which appeal is habitually made by all, and rarely declined or denied by any as evidence of the general opinion of those who framed, and of those who accepted the Constitution of the United States, on questions as to its genuine meaning, (3) the *Resolutions of the General Assembly of Virginia* in 1799 on the subject of the alien and sedition laws, which appear to accord with the predominant sense of the people of the United States, (4) the valedictory address of President Washington, as conveying lessons of peculiar value; and that in the branch of the School of Law, which is to treat on the subject of Civil Polity, these shall be used as the text and documents of the school.

Crick makes the following obviously correct comment:

This attempt at Republican prescription was obviously an extremely fit choice of books for American higher citizenship and was a splendid evocation of what Jefferson had called "the American mind"; but it was none the less flagrant prescription and indoctrination.

John Adams, Crick tells us,

had good cause to protest that in the Visitors' Resolution Jefferson "carried his patriotism rather too far . . . he was guilty of narrowing political science to a party platform."

And Crick tells us in a note:

Even Madison had remonstrated with Jefferson that the inclusion of the Virginia Resolutions might brand the University as purely partisan; only at his suggestion did Jefferson then include Washington's Farewell Address as a kind of venerable makeweight.

The same Thomas Jefferson who along with his Board of Visitors to his University advocated "flagrant prescription and indoctrination" of Republican as opposed to Federalist principles also said in a letter to Benjamin Rush that he had "sworn upon the altar of God, eternal hostility against every form of tyranny over the mind of man" and had on other occasions suggested the need for a revolution every twenty years or so. Such contradictions as these could be reconciled only in the blood of the martyrs that Jefferson said watered the tree of liberty.

I suggest that American history properly understood may illustrate a dialectical process in which principles of the utmost importance to the quality of human life on earth have been given free expression, that some of the more important of these principles have been faced by others equally important and in direct opposition to them, and that this free and public conflict among principles of the greatest importance has brought some improvement in the quality of American thought and life. But I also suggest that this process is not an inevitable one, that it does not inevitably bring improvement, that it can meet obstacles that impair its quality and make advance to a higher level of discussion impossible. In other words, some human thought, necessary to the quality of the process can ossify and can make mistakes so gross as to render discussion a source of darkness rather than light. But however this may be, there seems no room for doubt that commitment to the cultivation of the highest possible quality of thought in this process is basic to an American orthodoxy which needs sorely to be stated and understood.

I suggest further that in the absence of a consciously held orthodoxy and of an established system of indoctrination in an orthodoxy in some institutions of the highest intellectual integrity, public discussion tends to become chaotic and meaningless, and even if powerfully persuasive, mere sound and fury, settling nothing. The indoctrination proposed here would be provided only to those who wanted it.

The habit of the world of learning today is to connive at indoctrination when the indoctrination is of a dogma that is currently popular. Jefferson's *Resolution*, which we have just looked at, clearly shows that he too could fall into this pattern. Yet the question that his *Resolution* poses is one that cannot safely be shrugged off.

Let us give an illustration of current indoctrination in dogma, a dogma of which we have spoken several times. Here is one of the most influential books of the last fifty years or so of this century in the field of philosophy, *Language, Truth and Logic*, by A. J. Ayer, formerly Wykeham Professor of Logic in the University of Oxford, more recently Grote Professor of the Philosophy of Mind and Logic in the University of London. Chapter VIII of *Language, Truth and Logic* is entitled "Solutions of Outstanding Philosophical Disputes." Here is one of Professor Ayer's solutions:

. . . the questions with which philosophy is concerned are purely logical questions; and although people do in fact dispute about logical questions, such disputes are always unwarranted. . . . Accordingly, we who are interested in the condition of philosophy can no longer acquiesce in the existence of party divisions among philosophers.[5]

5. Ayer, *Language, Truth and Logic*, 2d ed. (New York: Dover, [1936] n.d.), p. 133.

And, says Professor Ayer in effect, this is not to be taken as any intention to suppress differences of opinion or to exclude from the profession of philosophy those who express differences: "it must be understood from the outset that we are not concerned to vindicate any one set of philosophers at the expense of any other." [6] We just won't "acquiesce in the existence of party divisions among philosophers," says Professor Ayer, but just how this can be done without vindicating one set at the expense of another, Professor Ayer does not say.

And, according to Ayer, debates about the rightness and wrongness of ethical judgments are just as nonsensical—and therefore perhaps beyond the bounds of tolerance—as debates about logical questions:

. . . ethical judgments . . . have no objective validity whatsoever. . . . If a sentence makes no statement at all [as is the case with ethical sentences], there is obviously no sense in asking whether what it says is true or false. And we have seen that sentences which simply express moral judgments do not say anything. They are pure expressions of feeling and as such do not come under the category of truth and falsehood.[7]

The chief sources of Ayer's doctrine are David Hume's *Treatise of Human Nature* and his two *Enquiries.* Hume labored manfully to get his ethical theory out of the bog into which he put it when, instead of basing ethics on all of the faculties of the mind—reason, feeling, will, imagination, memory—he based his theory on feeling. But one cannot really read any of Hume's discussion of feeling and not see that he is continually using in this discussion all of the faculties of his mind, including his reasoning powers, as well as he can. Hume several times recognizes more or less vaguely, as Socrates or Plato did some two thousand years before him, that in order to base ethics soundly on feeling, the same feeling has to be aroused in all human beings everywhere and at all times, and to the same degree, by every situation, every relation, every action that involves an ethical question. Hume knew very well, as Socrates and Plato did and as every informed person for more than two thousand years has known, that such universality in feeling does not exist. All of Hume's efforts to get his theory out of the bog into which he put it when he adopted feeling as its foundation failed. Logical positivism is wrongly interpreted if it is regarded as a complacent acceptance of this failure. Logical positivism is a belligerent assertion of this failure and of determination to maintain it.

6. Ibid., p. 134.
7. Ibid., p. 108.

Logical positivism is the most powerful factor in the implicit dominant orthodoxy of our time.

So our ruling orthodoxy says the servant in Shakespeare's *King Lear* who gave his life to stop his master the Duke of Cornwall from following the advice of his fiendish wife Regan that, after gouging out one of Gloucester's eyes, he not leave the other, really had no good and sufficient reason—no reason necessary to decent life on earth—for his action. Ayer does not even look around, as Tolstoi did in his essay on Shakespeare,[8] for a reason. He does not see that mere habituation, as in the doctrine of Hume and logical positivism could not possibly have been the cause of the servant's feeling and action. Ayer, in his own estimation, did not have to look around. He has already looked, found nothing, and made further looking unnecessary. He has settled matters of this kind. In his doctrine there are no moral or immoral actions, and one only wastes time if one looks around for any moral significance if one has already looked around and found these words without meaning. There are, according to Ayer, no reasons of a necessary nature, only vagrant feelings, why the servant should have tried to stop the cruelty of Cornwall and Regan, no reasons why in the name of decent life on earth, Cornwall and Regan should not have gouged out Gloucester's eyes. They felt at the moment like gouging, so why not gouge? To say of such actions as those of Cornwall and Regan, as Ayer implicitly does, that they are "pure expressions of feelings," is about as clear a way of characterizing feeling that enslaves reason as is possible. In our view, and clearly also in Shakespeare's, either reason or feeling, divorced from or enslaved by the other and not guided by a genuine notion of good, escapes only by accident being diabolical. But the logical positivist of our time has rendered his judgment: out with ethical judgments; they are meaningless. And this sentence on ethical judgments and debates about ethical judgments, just as with debates over logical questions, does not "vindicate any one set of philosophers at the expense of any other." Of course, it does not *vindicate*. But if it gets power back of it, even if the power is only that of a determined but small minority, it can achieve practical rulership. For another part of the implicit dominant orthodoxy of our time is: Don't rock the boat. Logical positivism has gained great power. It tends to exclude from departments of philosophy in universities persons otherwise qualified merely because they disagree with the implicit dominant orthodoxy. Fortunately, Britannica's article "Logical

8. See Chapter VI above, toward the end.

Positivism," from which I have quoted previously, is clear on the doctrine of logical positivism, so I do not have to cite the many writings that could be cited to validate this point. Now to the question whether they have succeeded in grasping power.

There is testimony from thoroughly trustworthy and well-qualified observers that there has been a grasping of power and, in fact, that this was happening decades before Professor Ayer, convinced opponent of any and every form of ought, argued that this is what *ought* (of course without the word "ought") to happen in philosophy. Let the logical positivists and philosophical and linguistic analysts be the philosophers in all institutions of higher learning and then, obviously, as Professor Ayer says in the quotation from him above, there would be, at least on the question of the objectivity of moral judgments and perhaps even in logic, no parties and no party disputes in philosophy.

According to Brand Blanshard, Professor Emeritus of philosophy in Yale University, author of *The Nature of Thought, Reason and Analysis*, and *Reason and Goodness*, and generally regarded by his peers as the world's leading exponent of objective idealism:

At the turn of the century rationalism was in a complacent ascendancy in Britain, Germany, and America, though it was being sharply challenged in France. The form it commonly took was absolute idealism. . . . Of course the idealists were familiar with Hume's arguments. . . . Granting that we could not now answer [the questions] why roses are red or the sky is blue [or] why one billiard ball rolls away when another strikes it, [we were convinced] there must be some reason for the colour of rose and sky; and if billiard balls, rivers and planets follow an invariable course, we cannot suppose this to happen by chance or miracle. . . .

. . . Bosanquet in his Gifford Lectures of 1911 argued that the test of truth appointed by logic, namely coherence within a system, provided also an objective standard of taste. And it was the thesis of Watson, Royce, and the Cairds, of Ward and Haldane and Sorley, in an impressive shelf-full of further Gifford Lectures, that religion itself could become adequate to its object only as this object was conceived, and continually reconceived, by an advancing reason.

To mention these philosophers is to evoke an era that seems already more remote than that of Hume, though they are all within easy memory of persons still living. There are very few philosophic chairs in Britain or America now occupied by persons of their outlook; their philosophy is gone like Prospero's pageant, leaving hardly a wrack behind. Their main conclusions are either rejected or set down as merely meaningless.[9]

9. Blanshard, *Reason and Analysis* (Chicago: Open Court, 1962), pp. 28 f.

It is necessary now to remind the reader of our use of Ruth Benedict's *Patterns of Culture*, Galileo's *Two Great World Systems,* and Velikovsky's *Worlds in Collision* to illustrate further what may be an ineradicable tendency of the human mind to form orthodoxies when it engages in the effort to think seriously. This clearly applies to scientific thought, as well as thought in other fields; and it applies despite, or we might as well say, because of the prevailing orthodoxy in physical science that says all facts and all theories are hypothetical. This doctrine was the accepted orthodoxy in physical science long before the controversy over Velikovsky's *Worlds in Collision.* This controversy suggests, among other things, how easy it is for the scientist, as well as the rest of us, to say something and then in his actions contradict what he has said.

The orthodoxy in anthropology during this century has been that of cultural relativity. It is now being questioned as one may see in the article "Cultural Relativism" in the new *International Encyclopedia of the Social Sciences.* Cultural relativism, as we saw in Chapter II, says there is no better and worse in the customs and habits of different peoples and, in this, is in complete accord with logical positivism. Miss Benedict, as we saw in Chapter II, immediately after describing in language that definitely conveyed notions of better and worse three different patterns of culture, threw out the judgments she expressed in the language of her descriptions and, as we quoted the Editor of *Psychology Today* also in Chapter II, "refused to argue for one style pattern of life over another. . . . *Among the professionals of anthropology, anything but neutral categories might have been attacked as 'unscientific'—the sin of sins*" (my italics).

I have said enough, I believe to suggest that orthodoxies, established ways of thinking and doing things, exist in all fields of knowledge; and that teaching always, and necessarily, involves the effort to indoctrinate the student in an orthodoxy. It is necessary to harp on this because the fact has gone virtually unobserved and it is a fact of crucial importance in the educational process. It is a fact that many of us would prefer not to have to recognize in its great importance because recognition would bring home to us, and especially to members of the world of learning, a responsibility this world has been evading.

It would make no sense whatever to begin teaching children to read by discussing with them the merits of the Roman alphabet, in comparison with pictorial modes of writing and other possible modes, and giving the children their choice as to which they should learn. The society of the children long ago made certain choices. The children have to learn to use what has already been chosen before they have any chance whatever to improve on this. Sooner or later, if the children are to learn to read, they must learn the Roman alphabet, and the sooner they memorize the letters in the conventional order and learn to use them to recognize words, the sooner they will be able to begin learning from printed materials; and as they gain skill, the use of the alphabet and the recognition of words will become an unconscious process. The mind in its operations establishes an economy in which after a time thought about the alphabet and the recognition of words is no longer necessary. The thought that was directed toward using the alphabet properly, and gaining skill with it, can now be directed entirely toward the subjects with which the alphabet enables one to deal. Unfortunately, one may then never concern one's self with the question how the alphabet came into existence, how it came to be more and more widely adopted, and whether something better is not possible. But while a thoroughly engrained habit, such as the use of the alphabet becomes, may constitute an obstacle to the consideration of its value and to finding something better, a person who does not know the alphabet and who is not thoroughly familiar with its uses can hardly be relied on to make valid judgments about it in comparison with other means that might be used; and, certainly, if one does not know thoroughly any system, he is not likely to invent a system better than any that already exist.

No invention of any complexity, such as that of movable type and printing from movable type, has ever been made except by persons familiar with some of the earlier and simpler processes that enter into the more complex process of printing from movable type. Inventions always are of specific things or processes, and in the industrialized societies of today with their advanced stage of invention, inventions always involve antecedent parts and processes. It is inconceivable that anyone without knowledge, say, of such a process as that of making pins by hand by one person could divide the process among a number of persons in order to improve the product and increase production. It is no less inconceivable that the invention of a machine to make pins without knowledge of the process of making by hand, and particularly of how this process could be divided and actually was divided when pins were still being made by hand, would be possible.

The manipulation of material things and the making of them into forms in which they are wanted is incomparably easier than the manipulation of ideas and the making of them into forms that serve human good and that are wanted and accepted and put into practice.[10] If this were not so, utopian communities would long ago have become numerous on the earth. It is not at all clear that any great advances have been made in this respect since Moses brought the ten commandments down from Mount Sinai. The self of the human being, the self-centered self, is still the chief object of human worship; and many of the prophets of our time have not yet arrived at the point at which Moses had arrived when he brought warnings against this worship. Some animals in the human form are still a long distance from realizing any of their better and more important potentialities.

It would have been possible at any time in human history to establish utopias, if people generally had been willing and able to concern themselves seriously with the conditions necessary to their establishment and maintenance—and if they had been willing to act in accord with these conditions.

It happens that I do not believe utopias on earth are possible. However, I consider it absurd to be against them—except as the belief in their possibility; the belief that "the establishment" stands in their way and has to be destroyed if they are to be brought into existence is a belief in the use of violence, even civil war, even world war. Shabby and utterly deceptive orthodoxies about utopias are among the chief causes of war in the world today. But while I doubt the possibility of establishing and maintaining any utopia, I see no room whatever for doubt that societies can be made better or worse; but I also believe that to make them better is not as easy as falling off a log. Making them better is not something that one knows how to work for merely because one has been born since World War II and engages in marches and carrying banners against war, and for freedom and justice and peace, and perhaps for an income for which one does not have to work, so that one can live pleasantly, enjoy fighting the establishment that feeds, clothes, and houses one and that creates the conditions that enable one to live as one wants to live, doing one's thing and nothing else, living on the fat of the land and having all the fun one can stand with sex and perhaps drugs. This is the world that Marshall McLuhan tells us is coming when he says in the quotation I gave from him in Chapter VI, and which I now repeat: "We have now only to name and program a process or a product in

10. Plato's form of the good, which has puzzled many minds for many centuries, could be that pattern or configuration of factors in a culture that induces in a society the best life that is possible for human beings.

order for it to be accomplished. Is it not rather like the case of Al Capp's Schmoos? One had only to look at a Schmoo and think longingly of pork chops or caviar, and the Schmoo ecstatically transformed itself into the object of desire!" (UM 352). Al Capp, as I have said previously, created his Schmoo as satire. McLuhan is using him seriously. And this would be merely amusing if it were not so pathetic. This is an orthodoxy which, if it were not in a vague way so widely believed, so very influential, would not be worth attack. Satire is the only possible method of effective attack, but that is not possible for me in this book.

I shall make a few additional remarks now about indoctrination and an orthodoxy that has been worth attack.

It could have been argued above in the discussion of the child and the Roman alphabet that the child should not be taught the Roman alphabet, that teaching him this system fixes this system in his mind, binds him to it, and stops him from the effort to discover and propagate a better system. There is no end to the absurd arguments that can be made. Actually, the indoctrination in an orthodoxy gives the mind something to work on or with; and even when society inflicts penalties on minds that work and give public expression to their working, an orthodoxy may be an invitation to attack by an active mind. It must be granted that some orthodoxies have not had this effect. The reason for this may be either in minds or in orthodoxies. We simply do not know. But this does not mean that we are completely in the dark on this subject.

The history of Christian orthodoxy, a body of doctrine that has often been represented as an orthodoxy with hopelessly stultifying effects on human minds into which it has been drilled, can be written only in terms of attack on doctrines and counterattack with doctrines, of heresies as well as orthodoxies. It should be well-known today that there is no one generally accepted body of doctrine common to all those who consider themselves Christians, and that the extreme variety of Christian doctrines was created despite the efforts of centuries to establish and maintain by indoctrination one and only one body of doctrine. How do we explain this diversity despite indoctrination?

The orthodoxy about minds that is generally accepted today says that there are no basic differences among minds in what we might call their pure state, that is, before they have become accustomed to or indoctrinated in some particular culture or some particular elements or system or configuration of elements in a culture such as normally constitutes an orthodoxy in religion. If we accept the current orthodoxy about minds, we are forced to look to such orthodoxies as those in Christian doctrine for elements that arouse curiosity, stimulate the asking of questions, and lead to diversity in doctrine. Christian doctrine or doctrines, on this assumption, must have a high concentration of this element; and contrary to the notion that it has stultifying effects must have more effect of the opposite kind than any body of doctrine the world has so far had. It would, I believe, be a mistake to assume, as is often done in the intellectual world, that Christian doctrine is spent, finished. It is still the yeast in the Western mind, even if the Church in our time has ceased to be the great generator and bearer of it.

The orthodoxy that exists in physics and mathematics is a massive, monolithic structure in comparison with the "orthodoxy" in Christianity. There are, of course, attacks from time to time within physics on the orthodoxy. Professor E. A. Milne of Wadham College, Oxford, for instance, indulges in the heresy of advocating gravitation without relativity.[11] But Isaac Newton ruled physics from 1687 until the advent of Albert Einstein. Einstein now rules physics. One cannot do anything in the realm of thought without having an orthodoxy. It provides a system within which one can work or against which one can work. One may have a mind of incomparable potentials, but without an orthodoxy, one would be like an eagle trying to fly in a vacuum.

It is time for the intellectual leadership in free society to begin thinking seriously about the necessities to the continuance of this type of society. Such thinking, if at all properly conducted, would lead to the establishment of an explicit orthodoxy. Then there would be something worth indoctrinating in the young beyond such elements of learning as the Roman alphabet, the Arabic numeral system, and that people, regardless of race or color, should be treated like human beings. Then there would be something for students in the colleges and universities of the United States to revolt against in ways that might make some sense. An orthodoxy, or if we insist on the plural, *orthodoxies*, much clearer and better ones, are needed for the public also. The revolts of today could be seen perhaps more truly as revolts against meaninglessness than anything else.

The question of an orthodoxy for free society is one of the problems with which a program for general education should deal. There are persons scattered in colleges and universities in America and elsewhere

11. See E. A. Milne, "Gravitation Without General Relativity," in *Albert Einstein: Philosopher-Scientist*, ed. P. Schilpp (New York: Tudor, [1949] 1957), pp. 411 ff.

who are qualified to deal with this problem. Their active participation in a program of the kind contemplated here would be an absolute necessity.

The reading and re-reading and serious study of the great books is necessary to understanding the present-day world. But the immature mind cannot engage in this process most fruitfully unless far more and better help is provided than is now available. The help that is most needed is commentary on the great problems of the present-day world in the light of the great discussions of these problems as they have appeared in their different guises in the past.

One of the difficulties in working out a program for general education is that to conceive of education at all it is necessary to conceive of it as directed toward some purpose. One purpose of education, as we have seen, is the training of specialists. Free society, as well as other types of society, has to have them. Another purpose of education is the development of the good person, the good citizen. Free society becomes impossible without a majority of persons of this kind. All education involves the cultivation of skills that are necessary to further education. No one boggles over whether the cultivation of these skills is necessary, whether this is a form of indoctrination which the student has to accept whether he likes it or not. All education involves the transmission of information, including information concerning methods of acquiring information, and methods of handling it as illustrated by theories. All education is of necessity to a great extent an authoritative procedure in which the student has no alternative but to receive what is given to him and master it if he can. The mastering necessarily includes a vast amount of memorizing, unless information is ordered in theoretical form, and even then the theories and facts that illustrate them have to be remembered. The mastery of information, that is, the remembering and understanding of it, consists precisely in the ability to give information theoretical form and to test by fact, or imagined fact, the validity of competing theories.

Understanding that is genuine cannot be conveyed from one person to another. Each person has to do, of necessity, his own understanding. But there are ways of cultivating understanding where the necessary mental equipment exists. Among these are the examination of competing theories, the testing of theories by each other and by facts and by consistency, the revelation of dubious and unconsciously held assumptions by the asking of properly directed questions, the posing of dilemmas—all questions that have to do with the problems of knowledge and belief.

But no matter how skillful the teacher, the student has to do the understanding; and information given to him will remain mere information—if it is not forgotten—until a light dawns that is not on the surface of the information. This light is the theory that makes possible economy in learning. To understand the role of theory is a basic necessity in learning today.

Of course the information given to students can be of the wrong kinds and in the wrong proportions. Some kinds of information are certainly more important than other kinds. But mere information even though right and important is not enough. Information has meaning only in a context, and in human thinking this context is a theory. To learn how to determine more carefully the right kinds and the right proportions and the right theory is the great task that remains to be undertaken if general education for free society is ever to have any chance to be more than empty words with no object in existence. I turn now to an effort to state at least some of what is necessary to serve this purpose.

CHAPTER XI

General Education

... happiness can only come to a state when its lineaments
are traced by an artist working after the divine pattern
                                        PLATO, *Republic*

I have in the foregoing pages presented evidence more than sufficient
to show that it is extremely improbable that any college or university
will be able, any time soon, in any courses it might establish, to do a
great deal more for general education than it has been doing. The three
leading encyclopedias in the United States for adults—Americana, Britannica, and Collier's—are such that a person already has to have a
large part of what constitutes a general education in order to use them
for this purpose, and even then they are almost useless. This same problem exists for the person who has easy access to large libraries and perhaps a large collection of books of his own. The reader today, even the
doctor of philosophy in any of the more important disciplines, unless
he has been extremely fortunate in stumbling on books worth reading,
or has had extraordinarily wise guidance from extremely rare teachers,
is helpless in the wilderness of printed matter. If a person is a specialist
in some field, as more and more people are today, he may find it impossible to keep up completely with the new literature in his field, not
to speak of related fields; and he may be unable to find the time to read
the older seminal works that are usually of a much more general nature.
Such a person, as well as others, simply does not have the time to do
the roving that is necessary to find printed material that is of a genuinely broadening and really instructive nature.
  How do we know what is worth reading or of a genuinely broadening and instructive nature? We of course mean by these expressions
whatever would contribute to a general education. What do we mean
by a general education? We mean knowledge of the more important
theories that have to do with permanence and change and knowledge
of enough facts to illustrate the theories. But most important, we mean
knowledge of that pattern of culture, of living, that form of the good

which the animal becoming human has been seeking now for some thousands of years.

The word "general" is unfortunate. But there is no other that is any better. One objection that may be made is that every situation, every problem that people face, is specific. Every thought, every action about any situation or problem, is specific, so it may be said. There is, it may be held, literally no such thing as a general situation or a general problem or a general thought or a general action. An argument that appears to be conclusive can be made to this effect, and, in fact, has been generally accepted since the time of George Berkeley by most of the people who think seriously about such matters. This condition of general acceptance suggests that there may be holes in the argument, and, despite Berkeley, while it is true as he argued that there is no such thing as a triangle that does not have a particular shape or other particular characteristics, there is such a thing as having the character of being a triangle that is common to all triangles; and there are many other characters that are common to all triangles, one of which is that of being bounded by three straight lines. But we cannot take the space to develop this argument here. We have to be content here with the appeal made by D'Alembert in his "Preliminary Discourse" in the first volume of the great French Encyclopedia: "Let us not imitate those philosophers of whom Montaigne speaks, who, when asked about the principles of men's actions, were still trying to find out whether there are men."

The word "general" most certainly can be seen as having meaning of crucial importance in the expression "general education." One of these meanings, while including that suggested by the word "training" goes far beyond it and in one of its senses is opposite to it. This opposite meaning is the ability to look over a situation that contains a problem and not be limited by training to seeing it in the routine way that training establishes. There is no intention here of disparaging training. Training for particular tasks is necessary. But there is always among people who bother to think about what they are doing, and who realize that improvement is possible, a tension between established ways and ideas of better ways, and between those who begin practicing the new ways and those who continue the old.

The kinds of tasks to be done change. General education is necessary if people are to see that specific training has to change as tasks change. To make training as wide and as versatile as possible is clearly best, but with every increase in versatility, there seems to be a loss in specific ability. To restate the problem: the men who get their subsistence by gathering and hunting and fishing will be left behind by the men who first imagine settling down and using a stick to stir soil, and who then settle down and use the stick and make things grow that formerly they gathered; and these will in turn be left behind by those who imagine how animals can be made to help with something better than a stick and who are able to put what they have imagined into practice.

The ant, the bee, all insects exemplify perfectly the meaning of training, even though they are not trained. They rarely, so far as we know, transcend their specific instinctive practices, which correspond to the practices drilled into human beings by specific training.

General education includes training for specific tasks. It would be worse than worthless if it did not. It also cultivates the imagination, but not just any kind of imagination. It cultivates the imagination in ways that enable the human being to transcend any particular training and discipline himself for new training for new tasks and better ways of accomplishing the old tasks.

It is not possible to talk intelligibly about general education without also talking about specific problems, specific situations, specific processes. But we cannot talk about any of these without talking about far more than the subjects that are specifically mentioned. For instance, in the preceding paragraphs we have, without mentioning them, talked about processes that involve subsistence, survival, competition, learning, evolution, and many other subjects, including that of a world in which things can happen and men can make things happen. General education has to do with the understanding of this world and of the necessities and possibilities in it.

It is highly probable that, say, ten thousand years ago there was little knowledge of what are today called the basic skills or tools of education. Today the basic tools—language, rhetoric, logic, mathematics—are necessary to life above the primitive. There are no known substitutes that are generally practicable for the institutions—the elementary schools, the high schools, the colleges and universities—that give training in the use of these tools. Individual initiative has done the job for some individuals. But it is possible that some of the potentially best do not have the drive necessary for this and have to be both pulled and driven, at least for a time. In any case, the condition of each today is so thoroughly tied up with that of all, the interest of each and all is so far one interest that the greatest possible educational effort at all levels and in all ways is necessary.

The tools of education are most certainly subject to improvement, as is also training in the use of them. General education by cultivating the imagination opens the mind not only to the possibility of better use of these tools but to their improvement. In order to make improvements, however, it is necessary to be thoroughly familiar with the tools that already exist and to have the highest degrees of skill in their use. General education as conceived here could be limited to the few, those who have gained the best possible contemporary command of their specialties. This, in our view, would be a mistake of the greatest magnitude. The search for talent in the public generally, at every level, and the provision of means for the cultivation of this talent are among the commitments of free society, and are also necessities for the maintenance and further development of free society.

There are some tools of learning that in our view already exist in a high degree of perfection. I do not mean to say they cannot be improved. I do mean to say that until their use in their present form by the general public, as well as by specialists, is greatly improved there is little chance for improvement of them as tools. It is highly probable that the human imagination would never have worked on the problem of imagining something better than the digging stick unless it had first learned how to use the digging stick more productively than the previously existing ways of gaining a subsistence.

Of all the tools of learning by far the most important are the laws of thought in logic, and of these the most important is the law of contradiction; but this is true, not in the sense that logic can take the place of language or of rhetoric or of mathematics, but rather that the laws of logic must be used in language and rhetoric and mathematics and all other thinking and doing if the reasoning that is always basic in these is to be more rather than less truthful.

A genuine general education would pick out all the great principles that seem to be universally valid, or valid within a large field such as, say, human relations, and would illustrate them sufficiently to make their importance understood, even if it could not be demonstrated finally and completely that they really are valid everywhere and always. The universal validity of the law of contradiction has been sometimes denied, but it is hard to see how this denial can be maintained and still have any correct reasoning. John Locke wavered in his treatment of the law of contradiction, regarding it at times as necessary to valid reasoning, at other times as having no positive and necessary role in the advancement of knowledge. Locke was writing at a time when the practice of engaging in long chains of deductions from general principles was beginning to be questioned, both because the general principles were suspect and because the law of contradiction somehow had come to be regarded as a principle that could be used without reference to fact to establish a basis for knowledge. Locke was justified in criticizing this practice, but he went much too far. The science that came from Newton and that Locke was following as well as he could would have been impossible without the rigorous use of the law of contradiction, both by Newton in his reasoning and by those of his predecessors whom he followed in his *Principia*. For instance, Galileo's theory of tides was based on Galileo's theory of inertial motion. Galileo held inertial motion to be the exclusive cause of the tides, except of course that local shapes might give them special effects. In his *Principia*, Newton held gravity to be the exclusive cause of the tides, with the same exception as to local shapes giving special effects. Galileo's theory and Newton's were thus incompatible. Both might be false, but both could not be true.

One of the most significant experiences I have ever had was in connection with efforts I made while I was editor in chief of *Collier's Encyclopedia* to get a biography of Galileo that told and exploded the myths that had clustered about him. These myths were contradicted by the facts in important details and, as we shall see, one statement by Galileo himself, which we shall quote below, contradicts one of the myths. The contradictions were unknown to our scientific advisers and they accepted the myths as true. Their first response to our efforts toward correction was that we were allowing an author prejudiced against Galileo to persuade us to allow him to make a vicious attack on Galileo. I now tell one of the myths and how its mythical character was exposed, and who did the job.

Lane Cooper, professor of English Language and Literature in Cornell University—note the fact that Cooper was not a scientist or an historian of science—had published in 1935 through Cornell University Press a book, *Aristotle, Galileo, and the Tower of Pisa*. I happened to get the book and read it shortly after it was published. It seemed to me then, and it seems to me now, a book of great significance. Its significance lies in its revelation of the common—the *general*—addiction of human beings, scientists and scholars, as well as the rest of us, to the making of myths about great subjects, and the resistance we give to efforts to expose our myths. We can adorn them almost as we please; but expose them? No, not if the guardians of the sacred deposit can have their way; and in one way or another, all of us are guardians. I now quote extensively from the opening chapter of Lane Cooper's book. These passages are classic in their clarity and significance:

It is still a common belief in America that Galileo, having ascended the leaning tower at Pisa, by a single dramatic experiment refuted an assertion of Aristotle that had not been challenged since the days of ancient Greece, nor then. Thus in a text-book of "science" for our intermediate grades, the children at school, it is said, find a picture in which a little dark Italian man observes from the height of a slightly oblique tower two balls of different size that are airily poised, as it were, on their way to the ground; together the unequal objects are supposed to be falling, together they must land below. I have at length got hold of some such picture; the Library of Congress found it for me on page 28 of a book by Francis J. Rowbotham called Story-Lives of Great Scientists, which first appeared in England and then in America about fifteen years ago. In this illustration, on the left, the apse of the cathedral is partly in view. Above, on the right, Galileo leans from the summit of the tower; two spheres, one far bulkier than a man, the other small, are beginning their descent; and at a safe distance a crowd of spectators below spreads out from the cathedral. The unique experiment is supposed to have been performed about the year 1590, and to mark a turning-point in the history of science. I wish to call in question the correctness of this picture, and shall ask the reader to suspend judgment concerning the story it is supposed to represent until he has some grasp on the substance of the following pages.

  And first, whatever Galileo did, or failed to do, at Pisa, in all his extant writings he never once mentions the leaning tower, and never talks of experimenting from it. Next, let us remember this: half a century and more before we have conjoint mention of him and the leaning tower, Simon Stevin of Bruges, according to his own assertion, had let fall two balls of lead, one ten times the weight of the other, "from a point about 30 feet high" to a plank below, and "they landed so evenly that there seemed to be only one thump." In a book dated 1605, Stevin says that he had done this "long ago" with his friend John Gretius; the two men were bent upon demonstrating by "experience" a mistake of Aristotle in the *Physics* and *De Caelo*.

  Then why mention the speed of "falling" bodies in our title? Because Aristotle in his writings on physics never once uses the Greek word for "fall" in relation to speed.

Lane Cooper's book, as I have said above, was published in 1935. Twenty years later, all three of the encyclopedias—Americana, Britannica, Collier's—as well as all other encyclopedias that I was able at the time to check, were repeating the story of Galileo dropping the balls from the Leaning Tower of Pisa as if there was no room for doubt about it. And not only encyclopedias were repeating it.

Now it would, of course, be a mistake to take Lane Cooper's book as the law and the gospel. Cooper himself is perfectly clear on this point. But so far as I have been able to discover, no one has improved on or corrected his account in any substantial way. All of the repetitions of the Leaning Tower story that bother to locate the event in time locate it about the year 1590. I now quote another passage from Lane Cooper which includes a quotation from Galileo's *De Motu* which shows from Galileo himself what he thought about falling bodies around the year 1590:

Galileo himself is not incapable of straining a story to make it lively; and all of us are capable of mistaking illusion for reality in what we hear and see. The reader may even ask himself a question about the credibility of the following passage. It is the only one I know of in which Galileo seems to say clearly that he dropped objects of different weights from a tower. I beg the reader to attend with care to what is said, for I merely translate a passage, from the treatise *De Motu* (of about 1590), that would be contemporary with the alleged experiments which Favare accepts on the word of Viviani; Galileo takes issue with Borri his predecessor, on the reason why wood, as Galileo still thinks, in the beginning of its fall moves more quickly than lead. The following is from Galileo's *De Motu:*
"If the large amount of air in wood made it go quicker, then as long as it is in the air the wood will move ever more quickly. But experience or 'experiment' shows the contrary; for, it is true, in the beginning of its motion the wood is carried more rapidly than the lead; but a little later the motion of the lead is so accelerated that it leaves the wood behind; and if they are let go from a high tower, precedes it by a long space; and I have often made test of this. So must we aim to draw the sounder reason from the sounder suppositions.
"Oh how readily are true demonstrations drawn from true principles." [1]

It would be impossible to imagine a more direct contradiction of the legendary story which, Lane Cooper tells us, "first appeared in Viviani's life of Galileo. This earliest biography must have been written more than twelve years after his death, and well over sixty years after the assumed date (1590) of the episode at Pisa." [2] Lane Cooper was not the first to suspect that the legend was merely a legend. Cooper gives full credit to the German Emil Wohlwill for first examining the legend seriously in his work *Galilei und sein Kampf für die Copernicanische Lehre*, which was published in 1909. I go into this detail to show how long it takes for word of the exposure of a myth to get around—or

1. Lane Cooper, *Aristotle, Galileo, and the Tower of Pisa* (Ithaca, N.Y.: Cornell Univ. Press, 1935), pp. 54–55.
2. Ibid., p. 17.

perhaps I should say, how difficult, if at all possible, it is to expose one, once it gets a good start. Lane Cooper quotes from a half dozen or so popular books, available in libraries in 1935, that repeated the story, with embroideries. I am sure he could have quoted many more if he had felt it worthwhile. As I have said above, Britannica, Americana, and Collier's were repeating it in their 1950 editions. Cooper notes: "The article on Galileo by Agnes Clerke in the last edition of the Encyclopedia Britannica still retains the story as a fact." [3] Britannica had been retaining it, and reprinting Agnes Clerke's article from its great ninth edition, for over fifty years.

I took a day in the New York Public Library some years ago and located the repetition of the story in more than a half-dozen popular books published since 1935, when Lane Cooper's book was issued. The repetition is not limited to popular works by authors who might be expected to be none too careful with their facts. Among the scholars, scientists, and philosophers of the highest repute who have repeated it, as I have said in Chapter III, are John Dewey, Alfred North Whitehead, C. I. Lewis, W. D. Ross, C. A. Coulson, Louis Trenchard More, and Albert Einstein.

The junior encyclopedia *World Book* in its 1963 edition refers to the story as "an often-disputed story." I have not made a special study of the subject, but as far as my reading goes, the facts are exactly the other way around. Lane Cooper's book was practically ignored for decades after it was published. There has been no "dispute" in the English language except for Lane Cooper's book. This book caused a flurry when it was published, but it was promptly forgotten and the facts recorded in it ignored—buried in the mass of print a few months after the book was published. There was no "dispute" beyond this until the late 1950's, and there was none then that was worth any attention. Contrary to *World Book*'s account, there could not be any dispute by anybody who paid any attention to and was guided by the clearly authenticated facts. Of course, someone may have discovered and published discordant "facts." But if so, these too have been lost in the mass of print.

I would regard a special study to find out whether there was a "dispute" as unimportant, very nearly of the drivelish kind, unless it was focused on some much larger problem, such as, say, the question whether the scientist is free from the myth-making propensity that seems to

3. Ibid., p. 21 n.

prevail generally among human beings, or the question how far even the most intelligent persons today can find their way to relevant facts in the current wilderness of printed matter. The computer storage-and-retrieval systems offer hope of making relevant facts available, provided one knows the right questions to ask. We can be certain the scholars, scientists, and philosophers mentioned in the second paragraph above, all of great distinction, did not know that there was any question to be asked about the story they accepted. It will be some time, I think, before any solution is found of this problem, either of a mechanical-electrical or any other kind.

If all the literature in all languages relating to the Galileo Tower of Pisa story were stored in computers it would be possible by asking the right questions in the right way in the right language to find out whether *World Book*'s reference to the story as "an often-disputed story" is more true than the opposite. In any case, I think we can be fairly sure the author of the *World Book* article had no adequate grounds for this statement. *World Book* is an extraordinarily good encyclopedia for the young, by far the best for the young that is in existence, but the author of the article on Galileo in the 1963 edition shows little acquaintance with his subject. Moreover, *World Book*'s notion of a dispute may be a consequence of the reporting of the facts as recorded by Lane Cooper in Americana, Britannica, and Collier's, in editions later than those of the 1950's; by Harvey Einbinder in an article in the Winter 1960 issue of the *Columbia University Forum* and in his book *The Myth of the Britannica;* by Arthur Koestler in his highly readable and excellent book *The Sleepwalkers,* and by at least two recent historians of science, A. C. Crombie and Herbert Butterfield that the often repeated story may now become "often-disputed." But any such disputing will be done only by those, as I have suggested above, who do not concern themselves with the facts of the case, that is, who prefer myth-making to guidance by fact. For it is fairly clear from Galileo's own words, quoted from Lane Cooper above, that short of the introduction of words not by Galileo into his *De Motu,* or something else also highly improbable such as error about the date 1590, that there is no room for dispute. The myth seems clearly to have been a fabrication, but, I believe we can be sure, not an intentional one. The myth tells the truth about what modern theory says would happen if two bodies— say a feather and a piece of lead—fell in a vacuum. Now I do not know that scientists have yet been able to establish a vacuum. But if we secure as near a vacuum as is possible and let a feather and a piece of lead fall in it, they appear to reach bottom at the same time. This is what modern science says happens in a vacuum, and this appears to be true. Now the myth-making faculty appears to come into play and have Galileo do something which in all probability he did not do. Here is the way it seems to work. Galileo was a great scientist. Great scientists discover what actually happens, what is true. Galileo certainly worked on the problem of falling bodies. He himself said so. Therefore Galileo conducted the Leaning Tower experiment and demonstrated this truth. To doubt this is to doubt the greatness of one of the world's greatest scientists.

But whatever the real explanation, this, in a confused form, is what was met when editorial advisers in the field of the physical sciences were asked about an article on Galileo for Collier's Encyclopedia that explored the Tower of Pisa myth and the question what the real argument was between Galileo and the Inquisition over Galileo's book on the great world systems. The article was finally printed, but before it was printed, the discussion over whether it should be printed revealed the attitude I have just summarized.

There is no evidence whatever that the author of the first great statement concerning contradiction—made by Aristotle in Book Gamma of his *Metaphysics*—held the view that reasoning, without any reference at any point to fact could be reliable. Yet the persons who tended to disparage fact generally thought of themselves as Aristotelians, and were charged by their critics with using contradiction in this spurious way because the critics also thought this practice was derived from Aristotle. Both were wrong. I have quoted Aristotle previously on this question and will repeat the quotation here. According to Aristotle, if our theory of a subject is wrong "the facts have not yet been sufficiently grasped; if they ever are, then credit must be given rather to observation than to theories, and to theories only if what they affirm agrees with the observed facts." [4]

This statement of Aristotle's is not, I believe, an adequate statement of the relations of fact and theory, since it seems to be true that in some fields of thought and action, for human beings to think something is so, that is, to have a certain theory of something, and to act accordingly, may actually make it so. The relations of theory and fact have never been adequately explored. The subject is of basic importance,

4. See the entry "Aristotle" in the index for passages quoted from Aristotle on fact and their location in his works.

and to cultivate knowledge of it would be to cultivate a part of the knowledge that is necessary to a general education.

The Aristotelian law of contradiction illustrates so perfectly the type of knowledge that is universally valid, or which approaches universal validity, and it is given so little and such inadequate attention except in textbooks on logic that I shall give three more illustrations of its importance. All of these illustrations have to do with logic as it is involved in other subjects. Logic as a separate discipline has to be cultivated if the subject is to be as well-known as is possible; but it cannot even be illustrated in ways that are not misleading except in connection with other subjects. Labor has to be divided here as well as elsewhere; but division that does not at some time lead back to integration destroys rather than develops knowledge.

The customs and habits of a people may determine such notions as that a condition in a person beginning with a fever, leading in a couple of days to a skin eruption which then passes through the stages of papule, vesicle, and pustule, then dries up, and if the patient does not die, leaves more or less permanent scars, was caused by an enemy who employed a medicine man to use his magic to produce the condition. The belief that the condition was determined by any rites, spells, conjurations used by a medicine man is among the beliefs the modern world has for some centuries held to be superstition.

A medical man, trained in a present-day Western medical school (and the school would not have to be a good one) would certainly not attribute the condition to an enemy working through a magician. The medical man today is trained to diagnose by a rational process in which, whether consciously or unconsciously, he uses such propositions as some of the conditions of this particular case are common to a wide variety of diseases, others are common only to a less wide variety, and some, perhaps only one, are common to only one disease. Some conditions may be so clear that they can with relative safety be diagnosed by external symptoms. And some physicians, even when external conditions leave other physicians entirely in the dark, are able to diagnose from external conditions with high accuracy. This aspect of medical practice is thus certainly not a rigorous science, but it is also and certainly not the practice of magic. There may appear to be psychic effects, and these are in a sense mysterious, but there is no mumbo jumbo about them.

I have stated only in the roughest sense what seems to me to be the process involved in diagnosing the type of case involved. This process,

I believe can be stated in logical terms, though in some fifty years of reading, including biographies of leading medical men, in books and in encyclopedias, I remember seeing it suggested in only one book. I do not intend to suggest that any physicians actually go consciously through a logical process in diagnosing a case or that almost immediate intuitive recognition does not occur. I do intend to say that diagnosis today is far more reliable than it was, say, two or three thousand or even one hundred years ago, and that this greatly improved reliability is a consequence largely of three factors that are interdependent: (i) improvement in methods of examination or observation of patients, that is, of determining the conditions of the illness; (ii) the gradual elimination by logical processes of magic as a cause; and (iii) the gradual connection, again by logical processes, of specific causes with specific diseases. I do not know what is possible in the way of accurate description of this process as it existed in earlier periods, and how far it would be possible to go in showing improvements in the process with the passage of time. I suggest that the role of logic in the history of medicine is sufficiently important to be given specific attention. By this I mean something like the following. The description given of a disease above is intended as, and is the best this layman can give, of a case of smallpox. Contact with the body or with the clothes or other objects that a person who has the disease in a contagious stage is generally accepted, I believe, as a necessary condition for the spread of the virus that causes the disease. If it could be established that the disease occurred without contact, then some carrier of the virus other than human bodies with the disease or things that had touched such bodies would have to be sought if there was to be any good chance to control the spread of the disease. Whether it is ever said so or not, in the reasoning that is done on these questions, there comes a moment when the evidence requires a decision on the two propositions: contact, in the sense indicated, is a necessary condition to the spread of smallpox; or contact is not a necessary condition to the spread of smallpox. This can be restated in the form of the law of excluded middle in the one proposition: either contact in the sense indicated is necessary or it is not. Contact may of course be necessary but not sufficient, meaning of course that one or more cooperating causes as well as contact are always present. The patient examination of this problem along strictly logical lines is necessary to its solution; and this work may be done successfully even though the one who is doing it has never had a course in logic or opened a book on the subject. The logical law of identity also plays its part in that the symptoms accurately observed point unambiguously toward smallpox. The presence of the virus along with the symptoms and all the conditions that are working in the body, some beyond observation, are identical with the disease.

It may seem a waste of time and labor to show logical principles at work in every human activity that claims to be scientific, but if there is any desire and any need to know, and not merely to guess or suppose, that there are any principles of universal validity, this is necessary.

Let us now consider a simple case of observation, one that, contrary to dominant notions, involves far more than mere observation made by the senses. The role of logic in this observation is decisive. Take a pencil and put it in a tall glass of water. If the pencil is then moved around in various positions it will appear differently. There are positions of the pencil and points of view such that the pencil appears to be broken. But the observer can take his finger and run it along the pencil and discover whether the pencil is to his sense of touch broken or not. One thing he knows as certain before his observation—and the adequacy of his observation and his reasoning about his observation are utterly dependent on this something—is that the pencil cannot both be broken and not be broken as he looks at it at any particular time. He can look as long and as hard and as carefully as he pleases and he will never discover this principle by any mere sense observations.

It could be argued that in the case above we have assumed that touch is reliable but sight is not. It is sometimes held that touch is the basic sense and that the validity of other senses can be tested by touch. The sense of touch cannot, however, be used in astronomical observations, and it was in astronomical observations that modern science got its start. The sense of touch has had relatively little application in comparison with the sense of sight. There are in touch contradictory appearances just as there are in sight, but they are of relatively little importance. This is not to say that touch is of no importance. On the contrary, the problem of touch in the sense of two or more objects in contact, as the cause of action has been for centuries the chief competitor in physics of the idea of force at a distance as the cause of action.

In the case of the pencil, doubt about the validity of the sense impressions gained by sight is first created by the widely different appearances according to the position of the pencil and the position or point of view of the observer. There are, as I have said above, positions such that there appears to be a practically complete break in the pencil. If one then withdraws the pencil from the water, the pencil appears to be straight and unbroken. The law of contradiction does not say that the water does not have the effect of breaking the pencil and withdrawing it does not have the effect of putting it back together and making it straight again. It is possible, however, to make what might be regarded as a preliminary check on whether water can have this effect. In doing this it is the sense of touch that is used, or can be used, to suggest that the different appearances to sight are illusory. The study of the refraction of light in different media is necessary to provide further and apparently irrefutable evidence that touch in this case tells the truth whereas sight gives appearances that do not represent the object as it really is. In all work of this kind, the law of contradiction is absolutely necessary to the distinguishing of appearance from reality. If it is not used consciously, and in the great majority of cases it is highly probable that it is not, it is an unconscious assumption. Moreover, as to distinguishing appearance from reality, there are no means of ever doing this completely. If there were, there would be no problem of knowledge left for philosophers to wrangle over.

Galileo was perfectly aware of the primacy of reason over observation—at least in the case of the Copernican theory. I have quoted in a previous chapter his praise of Copernicus for using his reason to prove that the motion that every person observes of the sun rising in the east, passing across the sky and setting in the west is an appearance and not the reality.[5] In Einstein's relativity theory, it is held, as has been said previously, that in dealing with the problem of motion one may choose his point of rest at will. It is not clear that Einstein intended to suggest, as is sometimes held, that there is no real difference between appearance and reality, that point of view determines appearance and whatever appears is equally real. It is hardly possible that this was his intention, and, so far as I have been able to discover, he never said that it was. But he also, so far as I have been able to discover, never said that it was not. In any case, to accept any doctrines of Einstein's as beyond criticism would be utterly repugnant to specific statements of his on the subject of acceptance of authority, and no one except makers of idols or false gods—or perhaps slaves by nature—accepts without question any human authority.

The Aristotelian law of contradiction is universally used in reasoning

5. Norwood R. Hanson in his extremely interesting *Patterns of Discovery* (London: Cambridge Univ. Press, [1958] 1961), p. 182, n. 6, says that Galileo sees the horizon drop. But Galileo's own testimony does not confirm this view. See the quotation from Galileo in Chapter IX above.

processes that are valid. It would be possible to show that this is true in all fields of knowledge, but I shall discuss only one more field here. Take the field of law, even what is called positive law, usually defined as the command of the ruling power, and we find that if the law is applied uniformly, if special privilege is not allowed, the law of contradiction is an absolute necessity to the proper application of the law. Consider the case of a person X charged with murder. If there are only two witnesses and one says that X committed the murder and the other one says that X did not, we can be certain that one or the other is wrong. Every court in the civilized world acts on this basis, and the basis is so universally assumed to be beyond question that it is never attacked in court trials. On the contrary, when there is contradictory testimony such as that I have just given, the effort of both prosecution and defense is to bolster the testimony of its witnesses and to destroy that of the opposition. If a witness contradicts himself he discredits his testimony to the extent that the contradiction affects it. Even if the contradiction is on what appears only to be a side issue, it weakens the credibility of the one who commits it; and it may be held by the court as a sufficient cause for the charge of perjury.

In summary, the knowledge that today is called science, as well as all procedures such as court trials that can sustain with good reasons claims to be seeking truth, use logical principles on crucial questions. These principles have, however, become so habitual in scientific work and other procedures such as that of courts that they are practically forgotten. The logical principles are really embedded in the procedures, and when the student specializes in a field, he learns the procedures and entirely too often is unaware of the logic in them. This is one of the reasons that specialists in one field often find it difficult to understand procedures in another. I have known scientists who are scrupulously careful to get and pay due regard to facts in their own field, but who do not hesitate to form opinions and to express them, even on matters of great importance, in other fields without bothering to get the facts and without even trying to give them due regard. The importance of fact is all-pervasive just as logical principles are.

This importance is difficult to discuss without the utterance of nonsense. Suppose, for instance, that it is said that Caesar crossed the Rubicon is a fact and that he did this will always remain a fact. No one who says this means that Caesar is still repeating this event and will forever continue to be crossing the Rubicon. What is meant is that *if* an event is ever established, finally and definitely, as having occurred at some time in the past, it is in this sense fixed and never can change. To assert this is merely to assert a tautology, and to doubt it is to engage in the nonsense of doubting a tautology. Such assertions have nothing whatever to do with the question of change and certainly do not amount to denials of change. One cannot find one's way through the jungle of discussion of questions of this kind without the help of logic.

It is sometimes said that human beings are not governed by logic, that they are governed by emotion, and that we might just as well forget about logic. This would be to forget about science too, and about other kinds of knowledge that cannot be regarded as scientific, and it would be to forget about beliefs, for some beliefs are basic to science. Logic does not exist for itself. It exists to establish order in beliefs and emotions—it exists to keep them from being self-defeating; and it exists as a necessary element in the pursuit of knowledge and the just handling of human affairs. It is even involved in mercy, when mercy is not self-defeating.

Since the principles of logic are to a great extent embodied in customary procedures and habits, it might be thought that they can safely be forgotten—and they can, as long as the customary procedures and habits are not self-defeating and are followed. But when there are customary procedures and habits that are self-defeating and good procedures and habits are breaking down, carefully cultivated thinking processes that are adequately informed become absolutely necessary to correction.

It is highly probable that the breaking down of customary procedures and habits has more serious effects on human beings than it has on animals. It is well-known that mental illness can be produced in animals by contrary stimuli or breaking down or blocking habits that have been learned and that have led to a reward, or by the removal of the reward. For an animal such as a rat to learn a maze may be to some extent like the learning of new sets of habits by persons, though we like to think that persons are endowed with reason. But to be endowed with reason means ability to learn even when contrary actions that in the absence of learning tend to produce neuroses are involved.

A person may be reasonable without knowing anything whatever about the laws of logic in the sense that he can state them; but when he is reasonable, he is so most likely only because of the quality of the logic that is in his customary procedures and habits. The quality of the logic in the configurations or patterns of value embodied in cultures is to a great extent that which makes one culture better than another.

There is little room for doubt that different groups of the animal becoming human are at different stages in passing from the merely associative, conjunctive, or extensional logic of the animal to an entirely different type of logic. This better type of logic—instead of resting entirely on the response of the animal to the stimuli that occur in association with other animals and with things in a way that involves only his drives for food, sexual satisfaction, and rest—is a type that begins to arouse and involve rational faculties and bring them into action.

The logic that appears to be that of the animal—we have to use the word "appears" here, for we are engaged in speculation for which there is no conclusive evidence—has been set forth in great detail during this century by Alfred North Whitehead and Bertrand Russell in their *Principia Mathematica* and Ludwig Wittgenstein in his *Tractatus Logico-Philosophicus*, and by a host of followers in numerous other books. But if the possibility has been considered that this logic is the logic of the animal, and not, in more than a most primitive way, the logic toward which the human being has been striving for over two thousand years, one may search far and wide without finding out who has so considered it and where. This logic that may be merely an elaboration of the logic of the animal is being widely taught in colleges and universities today as an advance on the logic that stems from Aristotle. The logic that stems from Aristotle has proved necessary to every advance that has been made in human knowledge. As an elaboration of the logic of the animal, the associative logic seems clearly to be a tremendous intellectual achievement. It could reasonably be used as a landmark in the history of human reasoning powers from which to measure advance. But if the associative logic is really the logic of the animal, there cannot be any worse mistake than to teach it as the logic which ought today to be learned and practiced—that is, unless the service of good requires the abandonment of the human quest and the return by the human being to the animal state.

It has to be admitted that the logic of the animal is still, even today, in large measure the only logic that is available to human beings. Any careful analysis of the means available for dealing with any of the great human problems will show this. Consider, for instance, the means that are currently available in the effort to establish truth in trials in court. Such trials generally contain elements such as the Aristotelian law of contradiction, elements that depend wholly on thought—elements that cannot be derived from mere association or conjunction. But trials in court also still contain many elements of a merely associative or conjunctive nature. And until human reason is perfected, a prospect that is exceedingly remote, it will be impossible to get rid of all of these merely animal elements.

The discussion of the elements that human thought has so far brought into logic is even today often of a totally misleading nature. The misleading character of this discussion can be to some extent corrected if criticism is not only allowed but actively cultivated. Let us illustrate. Here is an elementary textbook by P. F. Strawson, Fellow of University College, Oxford. In trying to explain the law of contradiction in the first pages of his first chapter, Strawson says: "Suppose a man sets out to walk to a certain place; but when he gets halfway there turns around and comes back again." [6] Then Strawson says that "from the point of view of a change of position, it is as if he had never set out." And this is certainly true. But what does physical action have to do with the law of contradiction? The answer clearly is that it has to do with physical action only in that one cannot both engage in any particular physical action and not engage in it at the same time. One cannot take a walk and not take a walk at the same time. Awareness of this principle, and use of it, is purely mental and necessarily so. For one cannot even try to violate this principle in any physical action. Such action is not only not possible, it cannot be imagined. It can, however, be violated in words, and easily. It often is.

The use of physical action to illustrate the law of contradiction is totally misleading unless it is used to distinguish between physical action and mental action. If one holds a doctrine, an orthodoxy, that says this distinction is false, one will, of course, if one knows one's own doctrine and is consistent, not make this distinction. Strawson does not use his instance of physical action to distinguish it from mental action. It is hardly possible that Strawson does not know that his procedure involves an assumption that may be false. The uninformed and unskilled reader is entitled to know about assumptions of this kind and why they are made. As an introduction to logic, Strawson's discussion at this point is grossly misleading. And it is important because it is characteristic of a large portion of the writing of our time.

It should not be surprising that in the type of logic that Strawson writes about—the associative type—the character of mental action should not be clearly distinguished from physical action. So far as we know, the animal does not make this distinction. There is no place in

6. Strawson, *Introduction to Logical Theory* (London: Methuen, 1963), p. 2.

the associative logic of the animal for more than the most primitive thought—thought of the kind that is necessary to habituation, but that does not go beyond it. The particular type of logic that governs the animal is normally utterly primitive and impeccable. The animal never engages in self-contradiction. When the human being begins to burden himself with thinking and trying to solve at least some of his problems by thinking, he finds it necessary to seek better means than the mechanisms of association and stimulus and response.

Now the ideas we have presented in this discussion did not originate with us. We have merely brought together ideas that we have found elsewhere, widely scattered, and utterly unavailable for study until they are collected, fitted together, and the effort made to show that there is at least enough plausibility in them to warrant serious attention to them. Furthermore, it just could be that there is some connection between the great human disasters of this century and the persistent and widespread efforts that have been made in this century to cultivate in the human beings of this century the mind of the ape.

Human beings are the only creatures that can contradict themselves; and they have to be far advanced beyond their primitive condition to be able to do so.

I repeat, for an animal such as a rat to learn a maze may be in some ways like the learning of new sets of habits by persons. Our experimenters have taught us that neuroses can be produced in rats by cultivating habits in them, by fixing these habits in repetition and then by breaking the habit pattern. We are supposed to learn from this that the same may happen with human beings; and there are good reasons for believing that the human being is still to a great extent like the animal in this respect.

Why do we harp on problems of this kind? Simply because human beings have been searching ever since human minds have become conscious for statements about man and the universe that can be relied on, that can be reasonably accepted as true. Such statements can then be used as premises in further thought about man and the universe. The search for such statements has been to a great extent given up in our time. The kind of truth that is generally sought in our time is that of systems built of elements that are defined arbitrarily and that make no claim to have any connection with the nature of man or the universe. This seems to us one of the most important breaks that could possibly occur in the habit that human beings have cultivated for over two thousand years of studying man and nature in the effort to find truths about them. Whether this break has been accompanied by a pervasive neurosis in contemporary intellectual leadership, we shall not attempt to say; but if what has been learned about the causes of neuroses in rats is valid with reference to human beings, there is a question here of no little importance, one that obviously warrants most serious attention. And the public is entitled to know all that it is possible to know about it. As we have now said many times, the public today has no way of knowing about numerous questions as important as this one.

We hear much these days about the analysis of language and about how philosophers in the past have created problems by misusing and misunderstanding language; and there are good grounds for believing that there has been some of this. But as to clearing up these misunderstandings, let us take an elementary instance. Who is telling us today that when we speak of such matters as, say, extreme disorders in society, we contradict ourselves? The word "society," like the word "community," is a name for the constancy of conduct that we in turn call "custom" or "habit." And it is possible that the relations of these words to each other and to what they designate is not arbitrary but instead so deeply rooted in reality, even though these relations were formed largely by the associative logic of the animal, that alteration that is more than superficial, and that has a good chance not to produce widespread neuroses, is one of the most difficult of all human tasks. The appeal to reason in this task, when the only type of reason that is available is that of the associative kind that created the problem that is to be solved, would be ludicrous if it were not so productive of the disorders it is intended to cure. Furthermore, it is impossible to make a greater mistake than to assume that the rule of any type of mere reason can be a substitute for the rule of custom and habit in society. The real problem is that of discovering what is reasonable and embodying it in custom and habit; and this is difficult enough.

The search for premises that are true and the development of a logic that is powerful enough to secure agreement without false rhetorical embellishments is the greatest of human quests. It should be clear that agreement is of only a superficial nature if it is not reached in a contest in which the strongest possible arguments against that which is agreed on are given due consideration. No method of doing this has yet been found except that provided by the working out of the implications of competing sets of premises; and even with the best logic that human beings have yet been able to develop, the working out of such implications so that all men, or even a majority, understand the process and accept its conclusions has so far in human history proved practically impossible. The associative logic of the animal has been developed into a system that has tremendous appeal because, like the great animal principle of association, if one accepts the system, one can work it mechanically and without more thought than is required to push the buttons or pull the levers that set a well-constructed machine to work. The logic that stems from Aristotle cannot be reduced to a system that can be worked mechanically; and this in a world that looks to the machine as the great instrument of human salvation is no small defect.

It is not only the animal element in the human being that derails the Aristotelian logic. It is, as John Locke argued, with less cogency than the point deserves, the practical impossibility of conducting in words long chains of argument without making mistakes so serious as to render the argument absurd. Still, when custom and habit break down, the effort to restore sanity has to be made, and, in most general terms, only five means have been discovered in human experience that serve this purpose. One is physical force. (In our view the associative logic enthrones physical force). Another is correct information about the actual situation. Another is logic—but just what logic in its genuine form is, if our argument has any large measure of truth in it, human beings still have much to discover. Another is the will to use these in the best forms in which they are known. And this leaves us with the problem with which we started: if any of us knows the best forms, we still have to learn how to persuade others. We are thus reduced to saying what we believe, and without any rhetorical flourishes or other spurious effort to persuade, in the hope that what we say will of itself persuade.

For instance, in our view the notion that law, unsupported by custom and habit, can establish and maintain a decent order in society is a notion that can be entertained only by persons utterly ignorant of the crucial role of custom and habit. But I do not mean to say custom and habit are so important that, whatever they are, they should be sanctified. I mean to say they are so important that they must be kept sane and healthy; that the tensions between them and the forces working for change must not be allowed to become so great as to destroy the whole structure; that the only means, the necessary means to sanity, is better reasoning than the associative logic of the animal, or any mechanical devices based on this logic. And of course, law, and force based on law, are both necessary as long as the animal becoming human is still mainly mere animal. There are interrelations here that are not superficial, not of a merely surface nature. The relations between good customs and habits, a logic better than the associative logic of the animal, and law and physical force cannot be given arbitrary definitions that, when put into a machine, can answer the great question what is necessary to getting and keeping a good society. Human aspirations, even if often hopelessly wild, are incomparably better guides to human good than any directions that can be derived from machines, whatever the logic involved in the mechanical process. And this is not to say that machines do not have an important place in human life.

I have now gone further than perhaps was necessary in criticism of the associative logic of our time and in trying to show the crucial role of the logic that stems from Aristotle, and particularly of the law of contradiction. I assume that I have said enough above to suggest that this is the central principle in all reasoning that goes beyond the level of that of the animal, that its conscious use has become more and more necessary to the maintenance and development of civilized life, and that not to know this law, and not to have any skill in its use, and not to be able to recognize violations of it, is simply to be unable, except by accident, to play any constructive part in modern society. I have suggested also that there are many subjects such as the relations of fact and theory that have universal importance and that need to be better understood; and the same is true of particular facts and theories. All these constitute part of a general education.

General education does not have any marks by which it can be infallibly recognized. And no man's judgment about it is or can be infallible. But if it is at all possible it must consist of knowledge of the permanent in the changing. The effort to discover this knowledge is the kind of effort that led to the development of modern science, the greatest achievement of men on earth that is to this time generally accepted, one which is today receiving wider and wider acceptance by all peoples on earth. Modern physical science provides men with knowledge of the laws, the permanences in change in the physical world. If it provided men with knowledge of themselves, especially with knowledge of how to control themselves, of how to use the knowledge that physical science provides in living together healthily, peacefully, justly, and creatively, and most important, with the indomitable will to discover and actually to live in these ways, then there would be no need for general education, or rather, the continued development of modern physical science would in time fill this need. It may be that something of this kind is in prospect, not because of anything special in physical science, but because of something that may be, but that has not yet clearly shown itself, in the men who cultivate it.

Now if there are no principles that are known to be true or any great facts that, whether we understand them or not, always have compulsive power in them, if there is nothing of the nature of, say, a hierarchy of knowledge, that is, the possibility of ranking subjects in accord with their importance, or, to say the same thing in another way, if all facts, all principles, all theories, are of equal importance, then there is no subject matter that warrants the widest possible attention and that in a genuine sense can be said to constitute a general education.

The position taken in this book is that there is a hierarchy of knowledge. To say this, however, is to say nothing unless we know what we mean when we say it and can give good reasons for what we say. No one has ever succeeded in doing this in a consistent and complete way that would stand the test of time. We are not able to do it; but we are able to state enough principles of universal validity and to identify enough permanences in change to be sure that work in this direction has a good chance to be fruitful. The law of contradiction and death and taxes are not the only certainties in this world. Many more have been discovered and many more remain to be discovered.

The statement is often made today that this is a time of great increase of knowledge, that knowledge is doubling or quadrupling every so often. It is not said where this knowledge is that is increasing. It most certainly is not in any one person's mind. It is not in any collective mind, for, so far as we know, there is no such mind. If it is the marks on paper or the electric impulses stored in a computer, that are available to anyone who knows how to get at this material and has access to it, then, I suggest, another and very great difficulty has been added to the problems of peace and justice among men. Now instead of having merely the problems of knowledge and action that have vexed the best minds of the earth for over two thousand years, we have these problems plus the problem of knowing how to control the man who controls the computer that we, the public, are allowing to control the power that is generated by the new knowledge. The computer does not provide its manager with knowledge of the ends that it ought to be made to serve. The computer is a mechanical-electrical machine made to serve strictly mathematical calculating and literal memory purposes. The mere existence of a machine that serves these purposes as superbly as the computer does can have, but does not necessarily have, the effect of drawing attention to it and of creating the illusion, as modern science generally has done, that it can do things it cannot do. There are good reasons for believing, as the old man says in our quotation of him from McLuhan and Heisenberg toward the end of Chapter VI, that "He who does his work like a machine, grows a heart like a machine, and he who carries the heart of a machine in his breast loses his simplicity. He who has lost his simplicity becomes unsure in the strivings of his soul. Uncertainty in the strivings of the soul is something which does not agree with honest sense." But the old man did not say all that needs to be said on this subject. For the man who controls the computer may have eliminated all the strivings of his soul to operate in ways other than the mechanical-electrical mathematical calculating and literal memory ways and thus have established his certainty, but he will have done this only by eliminating his humanity.

The control of power has always been a problem, one at which human beings have so far achieved some but not nearly enough success. There has never been a time when, as I have said and will repeat, if human beings had been able to control themselves and act decently toward each other, life on earth could not have been in large measure idyllic, despite the horrors that nature imposes. The new knowledge has brought power sufficient to destroy all life on earth. It has not brought knowledge of how to control this power. On the contrary, it seems highly probable that as knowledge of the generation of power has increased, knowledge of how to control it in the interests of human good has decreased.

The problem that is being created by the so-called additions to knowledge that are being made today go far beyond, are far greater than the need this increase creates for the doubling every twenty years or so of the size of libraries or, as an alternative, the creation of compact storage-and-retrieval systems. This problem raises in crucial form the need for judgment in human beings that is able to distinguish between drivel, trivia, and facts and principles or theories of more or less importance. If it is not possible to rank facts and theories in a hierarchy of importance, then what is called knowledge tends to become illusion or, at best, learned ignorance. I shall now illustrate with what I consider drivel or trivia and later with the subject that I consider of the highest importance. I have already given many illustrations of what I consider of high but not of the highest importance, such as the law of contradiction in logic, which is important only as means but, in this respect, necessary and universally valid.

Some years ago I read a number of Bertrand Russell's books, among them potboilers as well as more serious works. Russell's *History of Western Philosophy*, one of the potboilers, is highly readable, as a potboiler ought to be, and, I think better than most works of the potboiling class. In his account of Pythagoras, Russell tells about a rule Pythagoras made for his followers concerning beans:

Pythagoras is one of the most interesting and puzzling men in history. Not only are the traditions concerning him an almost inextricable mixture of truth and falsehood, but even in their barest and least disputable form they present us a very curious psychology. He may be described, briefly, as a combination of Einstein and Mrs. Eddy. He founded a religion, of which the main tenets were the transmigration of souls and the sinfulness of eating beans. His religion was embodied in a religious order, which, here and there, acquired control of the State and established a rule of the saints. But the unregenerate hankered after beans, and sooner or later rebelled.
  Some of the rules of the Pythagorean order were:
  1. To abstain from beans.
  2. Not to pick up what has fallen.
  3. Not to touch a white cock.
  4. Not to break bread.
  5. Not to step over a crossbar.
  6. Not to stir the fire with iron. . . .[7]

Russell gives twelve "rules" of which I give above only the first six. He has a footnote in which he quotes the following passage from Shakespeare's *Twelfth Night* on the theory of Pythagoras concerning the transmigration of souls:

CLOWN: What is the opinion of Pythagoras concerning wildfowl?
MALVOLIO: That the soul of our grandam might haply inhabit a bird.
CLOWN: What thinkest thou of his opinion?
MALVOLIO: I think nobly of the soul, and in no way approve his opinion.
CLOWN: Fare thee well; remain thou still in darkness: thou shalt hold the opinion of Pythagoras ere I will allow of thy wits.

Now if all the literature of the Western world were stored in a computer, just imagine all the statements on the Pythagorean theory of the soul that might be dredged up. I will not say that such dredging would be useless, because it might prove to be and I think would be extremely useful, a most efficient timesaver, but only for some mind that had some judgment as to how to use it.
  We are illustrating here the problem of drivel in higher education.

7. Russell, *A History of Western Philosophy* (New York: Simon and Schuster, 1945), pp. 31 f.

University departments tend to adopt for study anything that there is pressure to adopt. They have no standards for determining the importance of subjects, or if they have, they do not use them or tell anybody what they are. The consequence is numerous courses on drivel, and Ph.D.'s turned loose on the world qualified only to teach drivel and with a concomitant almost complete paralysis of critical judgment, one of the great purposes that higher education ought to serve. Our illustration here is extreme and I have deliberately made it so in order to show how far down in the hierarchy toward utter drivel it is possible to go. I doubt whether much work in higher education ever goes this far down, but I also doubt, as I have said, whether much thought is given to where any subject belongs in the hierarchy of subjects.

If such a computer as we have imagined had been available to Bertrand Russell and he had chosen to ask it to produce all passages that include the two words "beans" and "Pythagoras" in English and other languages, the computer, if properly instructed, would have located for him a plausible explanation by Plutarch of Pythagoras' antipathy to beans: " 'Abstain from beans'; means that a man should keep out of politics, for beans were used in earlier times for voting upon the removal of magistrates from office." [8] One can imagine a clever writer with a wide store of information of this kind making merry with Russell and perhaps achieving a best seller. But such stuff remains drivel, trivia, unless it serves some purpose that far transcends the details we have just recorded concerning Russell, Pythagoras, and beans.

I will go further with Russell and beans, despite the triviality of the subject.

Russell is among the writers of our time who have made much of David Hume. Hume provides a clue to the meaning of the word as it might have been used by Pythagoras, but he does not mention Pythagoras in connection with his use. Now I have no idea how much stuff our computer would dredge up if it were instructed to dredge for all uses of the word "beans." The passages dredged up might be so numerous that going through them would be a hopeless task. This is just one of the numerous problems that the use of the computer poses and for which no solution has yet been found. So we just do not know whether the computer could have been helpful in locating the clue provided by Hume. Anyway, I cannot pass on without this jibe at Rus-

---

8. Plutarch, *Moralia*, trans. F. C. Babbitt, Loeb Classical Library (Cambridge, Mass.: Harvard Univ. Press, [1927] 1960), I, 61.

sell. If he had read closely the book that Hume considered one of his two most important, *An Enquiry Concerning Human Understanding*, Russell would not have missed a passage in which Hume tells of an imaginary conversation with a friend in which his friend says: "I shall suppose myself Epicurus for a moment, and make you stand for the Athenian people, and shall deliver you such a harangue as will fill all the urn with white beans, and leave not a black one to gratify the malice of my adversaries." [9] The clue to the meaning of the word "beans" as used by Pythagoras is in this passage; but the whole matter insofar as it has to do merely with a lapse of Russell's is of no importance whatever. If there are many lapses of this kind, they can create a suspicion of carelessness and can suggest checking for lapses in dealing with more important matters. But otherwise, this is drivel. Such information is of importance only when it is brought to bear on a larger question such as why anyone should or should not engage in politics, and this again with a still larger and still more important question such as why a person should live his life in one way rather than another. And these become as fully meaningful as human beings can make them only when related to the largest questions that can be imagined, such as, why is there something rather than nothing? Is it really possible that a universe could just happen to exist? How did this something that we call a "universe" come to be? Does it have any purpose, and if so, what is this purpose? If I have a part in this purpose, what is my part, or, as McLuhan says, my "role." We very carefully avoid talk these days about one's having a place or role in the world and staying in it and doing one's duty in it; but if the universe and one's presence in it are not chance happenings and thus utterly meaningless, one cannot escape thinking in terms of one's station and its duties unless one wishes deliberately to make his life meaningless or worse.

And so it is that if the treatment of any such subject as what Pythagoras meant when he said "abstain from beans" is not to be sheer drivel, it must be dealt with in a context that includes the largest of subjects and all subjects in between. When no such context exists, it has to be created in order for discussion to escape being sheer drivel.

I now proceed to discussion of the question which, of all that can be asked, is the question of greatest importance.

The largest questions in what is often thought to be a purely secular

9. David Hume, *An Enquiry Concerning Human Understanding* (Oxford: Clarendon Press, 1902), p. 134.

sense are those that have to do with the physical origin of the universe and particularly whether a power beyond and greater than the universe had anything to do with this origin. In dealing with this question, the problem of bias or prejudice arises in its most difficult form. Anyone dealing with this subject has to make some assumption relative to the questions whether the universe was made and whether it exists to serve a purpose. In the most general sense, there are only two possibilities, one that it has a purpose, the other that it does not have a purpose. It may be said that this question can be ignored. To ignore it, one might say, is like seeing a great structure made by human beings and asking, What is that? And then after getting the answer, that is a machine made to enable men to travel to the moon and back to earth, beginning to quibble over the question whether such a machine could have been made without this purpose. One might say further that there is no real seeing of such a structure unless it is seen in terms of its purpose.

There has for a long time been a tendency in scientific work to consider efficient causation as the only type of causation. When the distinguished psychologist E. C. Tolman put the title *Purposive Behavior in Animals and Men* on a book of his, he also said in his Preface:

I wish now, once and for all, to put myself on record as feeling a distaste for most of the terms and neologisms I have introduced. I especially dislike the terms *purpose* and *cognition* and the title *Purposive Behavior.* I have, I believe, a strong anti-theological and anti-introspectionist bias; and yet here my words and my title seem to be lending support to some sort of an ultimately mentalistic interpretation of animal and human behavior. Actually, I have used these terms *purpose* and *cognition,* and the various derivatives and synonyms I have coined in a purely neutral and objective sense.[10]

This has been a governing attitude in scientific work for around three centuries. There are reasons for it. These reasons have been exhaustively and exhaustingly set forth in the writings of men who have watched scientific work most closely and commented on it most cogently— such men as John Locke, David Hume, and Immanuel Kant. The word "objective," as meaning "unbiased, without prejudice," has long been accepted as truly characterizing scientific work directed toward the discovery of truth. But when the idea of truth is abandoned, this idea of method in the pursuit of truth loses this meaning. At the present time, objectivity in the sense of fairness to a subject, or lack of bias, has

10. Tolman, *Purposive Behavior in Animals and Men* (Berkeley: Univ. of California Press, [1949] 1951), pp. xi–xii.

meaning only in the sense of excluding any purpose except the purpose of establishing a closed system all elements of which are known. The word "system" here means absence of contradiction of one statement by another within a set of statements. A considerable portion of scientific work today is devoted to the construction of closed systems, all elements of which are known in the sense that they have been defined or accepted as indefinable by their maker. To ask the purpose of such a system is held to be indulgence in nonsense. But then such systems do have makers, and there is no possibility of utterly and completely downing "once for all" the question Why? What do their makers make them for? Play? Intellectual exercise? For the glory of God— and if so, what is that? The late C. I. Lewis, formerly Edgar Pierce Professor of Philosophy in Harvard University, makes the following comment on this question:

. . . the fact that purposive behavior is a physical happening, argues nothing as to the adequacy of exclusively physical categories for description of it, since the feature which is in point is one which it does not share with physical doings in general. No anathema pronounced by any psychologist against such words as "purpose" will exorcise this initiative as a distinctive and observable character of certain modes of conscious doing. . . . if use of the term "behavior" serves to fudge the distinction in question, then once again we have again a double-meaning which obscures a fact; though now the fallacy is opposite in its direction to that which primitive man commits. . . ."[11]

I think this is true and well said. However, I have no difficulty understanding Tolman's antitheological bias, though I do not share it. On the contrary, as I have already suggested, theology is to me the greatest of all subjects, and it is not possible really to understand anything without understanding it in terms of theology. But there are theologies and theologies, some of them so wild as to tend to discredit all theology. There are reasons for the wildness. Base a theology on facts, and accept the theory of evolution, as one then has to do, and one cannot escape the view of nature as red in tooth and claw, and all the past as a scene of torture in which one form of life preys on another. If one gives the facts their due weight and concludes from them, the only possible conclusion from the facts so far visible is that the pleasures of life exist as powerful lures to cause living beings to multiply themselves so that there will be more and more preying by living things on one an-

11. C. I. Lewis, *An Analysis of Knowledge and Valuation* (Chicago: Open Court, [1946] 1950), p. 6.

other, more and more torture. It is not possible, if one thinks in terms merely of facts and searches for a purpose compatible with the facts, to escape the view that the world that man inhabits was created for the purpose of torture. Bertrand Russell was being entirely reasonable when he suggests this conclusion at the beginning of his theological essay, *A Free Man's Worship*. Russell is not the only one who has come to a view as thoroughly pessimistic as this one. Arthur Schopenhauer was thoroughly pessimistic. Eduard von Hartmann in his *Philosophy of the Unconscious* holds that the process of learning leads to the view that non-existence is better than existence:

We have seen that in the existing world everything is arranged in the wisest and best manner, and that it may be looked upon as the best of all possible worlds, but that nevertheless it is thoroughly wretched, and worse than none at all.[12]

Hartmann's conclusion is that only cosmic suicide can end the misery of existence:

What would it avail, e.g., if all mankind should die out gradually by sexual continence? The world as such would still continue to exist, and would find itself substantially in the same position as immediately before the origin of the first man; nay, the Unconscious would even be compelled to employ the next opportunity *to fashion a new man or a similar type* [H.'s italics], and the whole misery would begin over again.[13]

The first edition of Hartmann's *Philosophy of the Unconscious* was published in the year 1869, a little over one hundred years before the time at which I now write. One can imagine how, if he were living today, he would adapt his views to fit present scientific knowledge. He could hold that nuclear energy might be used to destroy the world in its present form, and it is clear that he could hold, compatibly with modern science and with the last quotation from him above—and with ancient views other than the Hebrew doctrine of a beginning and an end—that escape from repetition is not possible.

There are more than a few people in the world today, and there seem always to have been more than a few, who have met with what they and the world consider success, and many of these few are satisfied with the world and themselves. William James makes an illuminating and disturbing comment that is relevant to this satisfaction:

12. v. Hartmann, *Philosophy of the Unconscious* (London: Routledge and Kegan Paul, [1931] 1950), III, 125.
13. Ibid., p. 129.

. . . if the hypothesis were offered us of a world in which Messrs. Fourier's and Bellamy's and Morris's utopias should all be outdone, and millions kept permanently happy on the one simple condition that a certain lost soul on the far-off edge of things should lead a life of lonely torture, what except a specific and independent sort of emotion can it be which would make us immediately feel, even though an impulse arose within us to clutch at the happiness so offered, how hideous a thing would be its enjoyment when deliberately accepted as the fruit of such a bargain? [14]

Can we say truly that there has ever been a time when there have not been such tortured souls, or that there is any prospect that there ever will be such a time? Do we implicitly make a bargain—whatever we may think or say—when we continue to exist, knowing as we must, if we are not intellectually and morally blind, of this condition that seems to go along with our existence? And even if the problem of "the certain lost soul on the far-off edge of things" could be solved, what of the suffering of the past? What kind of creature are we if we can even begin to be satisfied with the idea of a better world based on the suffering of the past? "Until the nineteenth century," John Kenneth Galbraith, professor of economics at Harvard and voice crying in the wilderness for more of the new economics, tells us, and all our evidence says truly, "grinding poverty had at all times and in nearly all places been the fate of all but a minority of mankind." [15] According to this voice in this modern wilderness, the new economics will save from grinding poverty the nation that is in a position to accept it and that actually does so. It is not my intention here to disparage the saving power of the new economics or any other economic system, but merely to suggest that the new economics can be stated, as far as it goes, in terms of theology. It ignores the great question of concern about the past. We, living today, are soon going to be a part of the past. If saving the past is of no importance, of what importance then is saving this present that is soon going to be past? Is exclusive emphasis on the future just a new form of the doctrine of election, and an especially shallow one? The human condition is such, I suggest, that human beings are never able to escape the necessity of both the effort to find piecemeal solutions of their problems, and the effort to find comprehensive solutions. Theology is an effort to find a comprehensive solution; and so far as I have been able to discover, human beings have always engaged

14. William James, *Essays in Pragmatism*, ed. A. Castell (New York: Hafner, 1949), p. 68.
15. J. K. Galbraith, *American Capitalism: The Concept of Countervailing Power* (Boston: Houghton Mifflin, [1952] 1956), p. 24.

in it and, I believe, always will. It is, by definition, but not merely by definition, in reality the most inclusive, the greatest of all subjects.

Endless, meaningless, repetitive existence, some of it self-satisfied, some sunk in physical self-enjoyment, most of it tortured—this is just one of the great problems of theology. How do you get rid of meaningless repetition? Well, if it really exists, you cannot. Do you know whether it exists or not? You do not. Does it matter what you believe, or whether you suspend belief? If beliefs are programs of action, as John Dewey held (and on this Dewey was, at least in part, certainly right), your beliefs may make the difference between one kind of world and another. If you are bothered about the world you live in and at the same time are not careful about your beliefs, you are most likely yourself, along with others like you, producing the world that bothers you. You are, in short, a moral idiot.

What does it make sense to believe about endless, meaningless, repetitive existence, some it self-satisfied, some sunk in physical self-enjoyment, most of it tortured? A little skepticism could be helpful at this point. One can ask where did the idea of endless, meaningless, repetitive existence come from? The answer is simply that it was derived from analogy with limited human experience extended endlessly by the imagination. Is there any warrant for the belief in this endless extension other than the argument from analogy and belief in the validity of what is imagined? There is not. If the argument from analogy can be used, and if the imagination can be used to develop notions that make some sense rather than none, is it really good to refrain from this effort? Theology is essentially the effort to make more rather than less sense out of existence. I confess to a bias in favor of more rather than less sense. I am therefore in favor of this effort in theology. At the same time, it seems clear that not all efforts in theology have been equally successful. But however this may be, if the facts are as I have stated them, and if the reasoning I have done about them is correct, theology is the most important of all subjects. It is the discipline that is necessary to the prevention and cure of slums of the mind and heart. It is not understood today that slums of the mind and heart can exist under any external circumstances, under conditions of poverty as well as wealth, that such slums are not subject to physical correction except as pain and suffering may, but do not necessarily, provoke thought and a movement of the spirit toward the recovery of health. Whatever else is known of the mind and heart, the spirit and soul of man, their existence or non-existence, or their coming into being and their going out, their operations, real or imaginary, there is certainly nothing here that is merely physical or mechanical.

The boldest and most radical of all theories of man and the universe is that which denies the ultimate validity of what are normally regarded as the facts of human experience that say that human existence is ultimately meaningless or worse. But this denial can lead to other problems of the greatest difficulty. For instance, we have said above that one cannot know in any final and complete way that any of the testimony concerning misery in human experience other than one's own is true. The doubt that we have expressed can, however, lead to solipsism; and solipsism makes so little sense that it has to be rejected. It is not possible in this book to show that the line of thought that begins with the doubt we have expressed leads to solipsism. This has been done in other writings. But the reader who wants to know of these has no practicable way of finding out about them, and most are far beyond the ordinary reader's grasp. On this subject, good summaries of the reasoning that has been done in the past and that readers of good intelligence can with some work understand simply are not available. This is true of numerous other subjects of great importance.

The task of discovering what general education is, of establishing it in a more rather than a less genuine form, and of providing means by which the public can have access to it would undoubtedly be a very difficult one. But it is a task that must be attempted. It can be worked at with blinkers on or with blinkers removed as far as that is possible. This book is written in the hope and belief that the blinkers can be to some extent removed, that the eye of the mind can be made more rather than less open.

CHAPTER XII

Necessary Institutions and Functions

Civilization is only possible if, by renouncing the nihilism of formal principles and nihilism without principles, the world recovers the road to a creative synthesis

ALBERT CAMUS, *The Rebel*

The purpose of this book is to suggest a new approach to the problem of general education for free society, first, by the establishment of an institute for general education for free society; and second, after a period of preparation, for the institute to work out the basis for the writing and editing of an encyclopedia that it would design to serve the purpose of general education. The encyclopedia would be published by a commercial organization, preferably one already in existence. The institute would be financed by whatever means it could secure during its first several years. After the publication of the encyclopedia, it would be financed in substantial part by royalties from the encyclopedia. It should, however, find other sources of support since one of its important services would be the organization of public forums on topics of contemporary interest involving principles of perennial importance.

In making this suggestion, it is assumed that general education cannot be cultivated in the absence of institutions that are established to serve this purpose, that the institutions that are needed can be largely self-supporting and can be brought into existence by the institute that is here proposed. There is no room for doubt whatever that a genuinely good encyclopedia that really served the purpose of general education could be sold in large quantities and could be more than self-supporting. The real problem is to design such an encyclopedia and then to make it.

The institute probably should not be part of a university, but should have informal relations with one or more. It should be located in a university community. It should have a small governing board consisting of public-spirited citizens, university faculty members, and university students. The informal connections of the institute with one or more universities should be such that it would be used by them to organize or help organize public forums on university campuses and on educational television. Educational television now consists of a little bit of this and a little bit of that, without any program of any kind whatever that is of service to a genuine general education. The need for programs that go to the roots of current subjects is extreme.

The superficiality of our lives has cut us off from the great sources of human inspiration. To restore connections with these great sources is necessary if free society is to survive. This calls for transcendence of our present condition, something that is utterly impossible if the doctrine that dominates our time is true. Let us look again, most briefly and hard, at our condition. Our condition is such that we can dig up and exhibit and discuss and repeat our examinations and discussions of the roots of our problems without even minimal understanding of them. The human mind only too often is like a talking or recording machine that has no understanding of what it says and hears, no ability to examine a statement or an experience and recognize the meaning of it. We have given many instances in preceding chapters of this lack of understanding in what are generally regarded as among the highest quarters in the intellectual world. We have no prescription for the correction of this condition except the patient, continued, and concentrated effort to discover and use the help that is necessary to remove the blocks and to go beyond and cultivate the means that are necessary to better understanding.

It is clearly the case today that not all the dangers to free society come from persons and groups committed to its destruction. The greatest dangers almost certainly come not from its declared enemies but from its own ignorance and blundering toward its own destruction. If there is anything clear about free society today, it is that if there is in free society much knowledge of that which is necessary to its health, this knowledge is unavailable to the public. Despite all the talk about the right of the public to be informed, to know, to have the means of cultivating understanding, this opportunity for more than a very few simply does not exist.

The low level of understanding that in this book is exhibited in quarters among the highest in free society is a dangerously unhealthy condition. There are in American life today two powerful forces working to transform free society. These are right-wing and left-wing forces. Both are really working, in the main unknowingly, for dictatorships, and dictatorship is going to come if the widespread and deep sentiment in the public for the restoration of sanity in public and private life is not given effective expression. The great purpose of the institute would be to organize, educate, and help guide this sentiment. This will not be easy to do. The spectacle that leading American colleges and universities have provided during recent years is convincing evidence that this is a tremendously important task and as difficult as it is important.

The encyclopedia that is envisaged here might be in its outward as well as its inward aspects different from the currently available major adult encyclopedias—Americana, Britannica, Collier's. The chief inward defects of these three as they now stand are these:

1. None was designed to serve the purpose of general education for free society. None shows any awareness that general education for free society is the great educational problem of the United States.

2. All three contain large amounts of material that can be of interest and importance to only a very few persons in a hundred thousand or even a million. Each is entirely too much a helter-skelter collection of material. Information of a highly specialized nature needs to be available, but it could reasonably be available in libraries or in new types of storage-and-retrieval systems. No distinction is now made in any of the three major adult encyclopedias between material on obscure and highly specialized subjects and that necessary to a general education.

3. While no thought was given in the editing and writing of articles to making them serve the purpose of general education in a free society, some articles are so written as to demonstrate that this can be done. For instance, Britannica's articles (1967 edition) "Adam Smith" and "Caste" are excellent for this purpose. Collier's (1967 edition) "Galileo" is superb. It could be improved most by quoting and discussing Galileo's speculation on the particle theory. The article should not be cut to make this addition. More space should be allowed. Collier's article "Equality" goes a long way in the right direction, but could be improved. The excellence of the articles "Adam Smith" and "Galileo" consists in their accurate presentation of their subjects and incidental demolition of myths that have falsified them. A myth may be the best, in fact, the only way of representing some subjects. To use myth rightly is work of the highest art; but it can also be used for viciously misleading propaganda purposes, to obscure and prevent the understanding of problems as well as to illuminate them. Britannica's article "Caste" is a model of the way in which the pros and cons of a subject can be made highly instructive. A close reading of this article will give the reader a better understanding of problems that are common to all societies. This is what is required

for general educational purposes. One of the tasks of the institute would be to direct the writing of model articles on different types of subjects to be used as guides to further writing.

4. Many of the articles in these encyclopedias are written by specialists in such manner that only specialists can read them. I shall take some space to discuss this problem because it is so very important. The 1967 edition of Britannica has two long articles on Logic, one under the caption "Logic," the other under the caption "Logic, History of." In the article "Logic" extensive use is made of the characters of symbolic logic. The layman who wants to know about the present-day status of logic is not likely to have the time to learn the symbols and gain the skill with them necessary to read the article with understanding. There is no need whatever for laymen generally to know the symbols of symbolic logic and to have any skill in their use. To give a section of the article to symbolic logic would be appropriate, but a short section would be sufficient for the layman. This section should give the arguments against as well as those for symbolic logic. Since the symbolic logic that is presented is the association logic of Hume, the giving of the arguments for and against it are of prime importance. The article in the 1967 edition does not do this. The knowledge that the layman needs most to have of logic as the experts conceive of the subject today has to do with the present-day status of the laws of thought, the pros and cons on this subject, and an explanation of Hegelian, Marxian, and present-day communist use of contradiction. No one of the three encyclopedias gives any information on the question, of great importance since Hegel and especially during this century, how contradiction in traditional Aristotelian logic becomes contrary movement in communist logic. No one of the three encyclopedias discusses the present-day status of the laws of thought and the pros and cons on them.

Now consider. There is an article "Cosmogony" in Britannica, and in this article it is said:

For almost three decades after its formulation, the theory of the expanding (or dispersing) universe suffered from an annoying *contradiction* [my italics]: the age of the universe, as observed rate of expansion (the mutual recession velocity of galaxies), was considerably shorter than the age of the Earth as estimated by reliable geological methods and the age of stars of the Milky Way as given by more recent astrophysical studies. The discrepancy was not removed until 1952. . . .

It would be possible to multiply many, many times, and to fill many volumes with illustrations of the use of the Aristotelian law of contradiction in scientific work from the earliest times to the present. More than one encyclopedia of many volumes could be filled with such illustrations if illustrations were extended beyond the field of science. The mother who is questioning her child about a story the child has told and is trying to get the child to tell the truth is aware of the importance of contradiction even if she has never heard of the law and its absolute indispensability to all knowledge. To assume that the general public knows the points at which the law of contradiction has been decisive in the development of human knowledge is to make a false assumption. The role of this law at decisive points in crucial cases needs to be made clear.

Britannica's article "Logic, History of" devotes a paragraph to the law of contradiction, but this paragraph does not even suggest the crucial role of the law both in the history of human thought and in all work today that is directed toward the discovery of the truth about anything. In the section on Modern Logic, it is said that "in many of his works Leibniz seems to overestimate the importance of one or both of the laws of contradiction and identity."

It seems clear that this is true. The law of contradiction says nothing whatever about the facts of the universe except that this or that cannot both be and not be a fact in the same way at the same time. The influence of Leibniz was largely responsible for the pseudo-metaphysics that flew into the empyrean and deduced from supposedly self-evident premises supposedly profound truths. This was the practice that John Locke attacked more than any other in his *Essay;* but, as T. H. Green showed in his long and important, and currently neglected, Introduction to his and Grose's edition of Hume, Locke, in his attack on metaphysics untested by fact, enmeshed himself in absurdities as grotesque as those of the followers of Leibniz. The attack made by Immanuel Kant on metaphysics was by far a more judicious one than that of Locke.

Britannica has a reference at the end of its article "Logic, History of." This reference leads to an article "Thought, Laws of." Here is the first sentence in the article: "Traditionally, special importance has been attached to three of the simplest laws of logic, the *law of identity*, the *law of contradiction*, and the *law of excluded middle* (or *tertium non datur*). These were called "laws of thought," a name which may conveniently be retained even by those who do not accept the implications which the name suggests."

So, if one finds it convenient to call arsenic sugar, perhaps label and sell it as such, there is no good reason why one should not do so. I confess to a strong bias against this principle, or lack of principle. There is no discussion in the article of the pros and cons of the subject, no suggestion of the problem that would arise in connection with any subject, such as "Cosmogony," if contradictions in the subject came to light and were not treated seriously.

All of the three articles—"Logic," "Logic, History of," and "Thought, Laws of"—except for a section in "Logic, History of," were written by the same author.

Now here is what the distinguished logician Ernest Nagel of Columbia University and coauthor of a leading text on logic has to say about the logical principles that Britannica disposes of in cavalier fashion—without even hinting that other views directly opposed to those presented by Britannica, such as the following, are widely held by distinguished logicians: "As principles of being, logical principles are universally applicable. As principles of inference, they must be accepted by all, on pain of stulifying all thought." [1] The author of this statement adds, as in fairness to his readers he should: "We must mention in passing that this view of the nature of logic is not accepted by all thinkers."

5. The fair presentation of a subject in an encyclopedia requires that if there are contradictory or divergent views on it among those considered experts that the arguments for the opposing views be presented as strongly as their best exponents are able to present them. Britannica does not present the arguments for and against the view that the laws or principles of logic are necessary to correct thinking, nor does it present the arguments for and against the special brand of logic that it presents. In its article "Logic," it merely presents symbolic logic in the authoritarian manner that implicitly says: this is it and there is no other, and who are you to ask for reasons? This is the way the deadly dullness of our encyclopedias is made.

Americana and Collier's give "Logic" incomparably better treatment than Britannica for the layman. But neither allows enough space for the treatment that is needed to be given. The author of the article in Americana is Professor Ernest Nagel of Columbia University from whose text I have quoted above. In the article he recognizes that the principles of Aristotelian logic are sometimes denied, as they have been from the earliest times; but again, he comes to the conclusion that they "are relevant whenever men engage in reflective and responsible thought."

Professor Irving Copi of the University of Michigan is the author of the article "Logic" in Collier's. The traditional laws of logic are not

1. Morris R. Cohen and Ernest Nagel, *An Introduction to Logic and Scientific Method* (New York: Harcourt, Brace, 1934), p. 186.

discussed in the article, but their existence is implicitly recognized in the discussion of other logical principles and processes. Professor Copi is the author of a widely used text, *Introduction to Logic,* in which he says that "objections have been made to the principles of identity, contradiction, and excluded middle from time to time, but for the most part the objections seem to be based upon misunderstandings." [2] Professor Copi then discusses the misunderstandings in a way that is lucid. He also discusses in the opening chapter of his book the phrase "the laws of thought" and notes that the definition of logic as "the science of the laws of thought, is not accurate." [3] Professor Copi then makes it clear that psychologists may also be concerned with thoughts and even with the question whether there are any "laws of thought"—but, by the phrase "laws of thought" the psychologist is likely to mean psychological rather than logical laws of thought. The two are often totally different.

It would be a complete misinterpretation of what I have said on this subject to conclude that I am objecting here to attacks on the logical laws of thought. On the contrary, I cannot imagine any greater aid to light on this subject than the most powerful possible attack along with the most powerful possible support. The best arguments against any position on any subject must be known before it can be known that there is an adequate or more than adequate defense. The misunderstanding of this principle is the major factor in creating the weakness of free society in the face of communism today. None of our encyclopedias applies this principle as it should be applied. Our encyclopedias reflect the failures in our universities.

6. It would be unfair to take Britannica's treatment of logic as typical of Britannica. Britannica has many excellent articles. Britannica has, however, a large number of articles on subjects of highly specialized interest, that are written, as are its articles on logic, in such manner that they are useless to the layman. And all of us are laymen so far as fields in which we are not expert are concerned. The expert in a field does not need an encyclopedia article on his subject. He has access to the important literature on his subject. An encyclopedia article on his subject can be no more for him than evidence that somebody else also has more or less command of his subject. Articles in encyclopedias supposed to be designed for the general public written by the expert to exhibit his

2. Irving M. Copi, *Introduction to Logic,* 2d ed. (New York: Macmillan, 1961), p. 271.
3. Ibid., p. 4.

command of the subject to other experts on the same subject are mistakes of a kind that ought not to be indulged.

7. The problem of articles on highly specialized subjects was entirely different around two hundred years ago when Britannica began its distinguished career. At that time there were relatively few, if any, highly specialized subjects such as there are today. The language that was available then to discuss the frontiers of knowledge was such that the moderately well-educated layman could understand it. The technical vocabularies that exist today simply did not exist then. The technical virtuosity of the performance that the author of the article "Logic" in Britannica gives in its 1967 edition was not possible until years after 1900. It is highly desirable, necessary if they are to do their real jobs, that the major adult encyclopedias of the country keep up with the frontiers of knowledge; but for them to do so in ways that make this part of their work practically useless to the layman is certainly neither necessary nor desirable. Americana and Collier's as well as Britannica offend in this respect, but not nearly as much or as seriously. Despite the criticism of Britannica I have just expressed, it is in my opinion the best of the three, Collier's is next best, and Americana last. Each of the three has some articles better than corresponding articles in either of the others. Britannica is much the larger of the three sets, it has more articles that are of first-class quality, but, as I have said, it also has more that, like the article "Logic," are useless to the general public.

8. It might be asked why I have not included the Columbia Encyclopedia in my discussion. The reason is that the Columbia is designed to provide quick access to facts. It is what in encyclopedia editorial work is called a spot information encyclopedia. It merely presents information with very little effort to cultivate understanding. Columbia is as good as an encyclopedia can be in which facts and theories are dealt with as if theory never determines what is thought to be fact as well as the other way around. This way of always dealing with "fact" and "theory" is, at crucial points, to cultivate ignorance rather than genuine knowledge.

I have never seen a discussion of the logical law of contradiction remotely comparable in its fairness, cogency, and convincing power to that of Aristotle in Book Gamma of his Metaphysics. I have never seen this statement quoted in full in a textbook on logic or metaphysics, or in an encyclopedia article on logic or metaphysics. If there is any way of presenting the law that contributes more to understanding of it than Aristotle's way, this way should certainly be used; but I doubt whether there is any. In any case, the giving of reasons why something is thus and so, and where there is doubt on a subject, the giving of reasons pro and con for this or that view is necessary to the cultivation of understanding. Columbia does very little of this. As we have seen, Britannica in its three articles, "Logic," "Logic, History of," and "Thought, Laws of," does none of this. On the contrary, the author proceeds as if he were a second Moses, had been on Sinai and received the law on the subject of Logic, and is simply pronouncing it in his article.

The pros and cons of subjects are absolute necessities to the cultivation of understanding. Britannica, Collier's, and Americana do very little of this, but they do enough to distinguish them clearly from all other American encyclopedias.

9. None of the three encyclopedias has given any really serious attention to the problem of aids that are necessary if readers are to make full use of their encyclopedias. For instance, none of the three encyclopedias has a complete classified list of its articles, with repetition of titles in different classes where this is proper. Such a list could be tremendously helpful to the reader. It could be used in connection with reading for the purpose of general education as well as for other purposes. Suppose, for instance, a person remembers that there is a Greek myth that has to do with the effort of men to fly, but has forgotten the names of the figures in the myth. A list of articles dealing with figures in Greek myths would make possible the recalling to memory of the names and the location of the information that was wanted.

Suppose a person gets interested in the subject of earthquakes and wishes to find out about geological faults. The article "Earthquake" might give the names, locations, and important data on the more important ones. None of our three encyclopedias has such information in its article "Earthquake." Americana has an article "Fault," but it does not give this information. The article seems unnecessary since the subject has to be covered in the article "Earthquake" if the latter is to be understood. Neither Britannica nor Collier's has an article "Fault." The reader who wishes to know the names, locations, and major information on the more important geological faults of the earth cannot get this information from any of our three encyclopedias. I am not suggesting that this is a defect. On the contrary, it may be a sign that the importance of different subjects has been compared, and some relatively objective way of making decisions on this question has been worked out, and the less important excluded. I doubt whether this is the case. Much material of very little importance is in all three of our encyclopedias. I do not know of any objective way of making decisions on the question of comparative importance. The question is important and the only something that I know of that can be used to make decisions on it is that something that is called judgment, and judgment, so far as I can see, that is worth anything is formed only by wide and hard experience in judging.

All three encyclopedias have the index entry "Fault." None has the name of any particular fault under this entry. This does not mean, however, that there are no separate articles in any of the sets on particular faults. Collier's, for instance, has an article "Balcones Escarpment," on a fault in south-central Texas; but the article is not listed under Fault in Collier's index. The names of particular articles are sometimes listed, sometimes not listed under class names in the index in the three encyclopedias. There should be some system for locating articles on related subjects, and whatever system is adopted should be carried out consistently. There is, as we have seen, woeful lack of consistency now. A separate classified list would enable the reader who does not know the names of the more important faults to find out quickly whether there are separate articles in the set on particular faults. In the absence of such a list, when the reader does not know the names, his only way to find out is to look through his set from one end to the other. There are many problems of this kind that our encyclopedias completely ignore.

10. The information in the article "Fault" in Americana, as I have said above, could have been given only in the article "Earthquake," and the article "Earthquake" could have been a section of the Physical Geology division of the article "Geology." This is the problem of breaking a subject up into parts or keeping parts together, or more generally, that of different kinds of arrangements, such as short vs. long articles, systematic vs. alphabetical arrangement, and compromises such as the systematic-alphabetical arrangement.

Take, for instance, the subject Physics. It can be broken up into parts such as Electricity, Heat, Light, Mechanics, Nuclear Physics, with a general article "Physics" that attempts to show the relations of the parts, and each of these can be put in the encyclopedia in its alphabetical place. This is the alphabetical arrangement. It lends itself equally well to either short or long articles. An alternative to the alphabetical arrangement with the articles that constitute the subject Physics scattered in their alphabetic places, would be to bring all these articles together under the caption Physics and then arrange them according to their complexity, starting with the simplest subject matter and proceeding to the more complex. I do not know that this could be done in a way that would make sense. If it could, it would be worth considering. But many factors would have to be taken into account—for instance, the simplest subject matter from the point of view of physics, the particles or energy or whatever that constitute the universe, is from the point of view of understanding probably the most difficult.

If arrangement from the simplest to the most complex is not feasible, alphabetic arrangement under Physics might be better for general-education purposes than scattering in alphabetical positions throughout the set. Or, even better, a table of contents showing subdivisions of long articles on large subjects such as Physics could be given, as Britannica often does, at the beginning of an article.

An encyclopedia designed for the purpose of general education, would I believe, serve this purpose better if it presented the parts of knowledge together that are by nature more closely joined together. Physics, Mathematics, Chemistry, Botany, Zoology, Anthropology, etc., seem to me clearly to be such parts and have the advantage of being generally known. It would be a mistake, however, to come to any conclusions on this question until the different possible modes of organization had been considered with specialists in the different fields. There are some subjects that do not fit any classification; there are others that overlap divisions. It would be possible only after a complete list of contents was made to see whether all contents could be made to fit in a convenient way in a systematic or systematic-alphabetical arrangement.

It is also necessary to take into account the question of plans for marketing. A set organized by sections of a few volumes to each section can, without changes in the sections, be marketed both as sections and as a set, whereas a set organized alphabetically can be marketed only as a complete set.

11. The question how far the encyclopedia should be made editorially to serve only the purpose of general education is as much a marketing as it is an editorial question. The set that probably would have the best chance in marketing is one that in the provision of information would be as ample as but more carefully selective than its chief competitors, and that in addition corrected the deficiencies in Americana, Britannica, and Collier's.

12. It is highly probable that short articles on such subjects as Architectural Terms, Plants, Animals, Trees, Birds, now scattered widely in their alphabetical places, would be more useful if collected and either appended to articles on the large subjects to which they are most closely

related, or where there are no such articles, put in alphabetical order under such captions as Architectural Terms, Trees, Birds. There are many short biographical articles on persons of some importance in the history of their countries. These might well be collected and located after the article on the country. The same might be done with small towns and cities of no great historical importance—or these might be relegated to an Atlas and Gazetteer. Some of this collecting suggested here is already done on some subjects by some encyclopedias. Collier's (1967 edition) provides a good model in the section Film Personalities that constitutes the last part of the article "Motion Pictures." Both Collier's and Americana have sections on Architectural Terms following their articles "Architecture." They could just as suitably have sections Legal Terms following their articles "Law." The junior encyclopedia World Book has for years been running its brief articles on personalities important in the States of the United States just after the State articles. These modifications of the alphabetical arrangement are great helps to the reader in that they bring related subjects together. It is highly probable that careful study would discover additional possible substantial improvements.

13. There are some subjects of very great importance that are given little or no attention in our encyclopedias. Among these is Hierarchy, in the sense that societies always are in some ways and to some extent hierarchical in structure. Another is Objectivity, in the sense of fairness in the treatment of a subject. Objectivity as it has to do with scientific subjects can be dealt with in an article on scientific method. But the problem of objectivity as fairness to a subject extends beyond what are normally considered scientific questions.

For instance, it is held by most philosophers today that none of the traditional "proofs" of the existence of God are really proofs. But, in view of the belief in many quarters that there is no God, or that God is dead, the question arises, can there be any proof of non-existence? This question is sometimes discussed in purely definitional terms, such as, if one can define God in such terms as to show the necessity of his existence, why then cannot one just as fairly try to show by definition that his existence is impossible?

Substantially the same approach was made for a long time to the discussion of motion. A thing cannot move where it is, because if it did, it would not be where it is. It cannot move where it is not, because it is not where it is not. Therefore, it was concluded, motion does not exist. But we look around us and see it. Motion certainly exists. It probably is one of the great all-pervasive facts of the universe. Instead of there being a problem whether motion is possible, the real problem is whether anything else is possible in connection with the physical things of the universe. It is, I believe, not recognized by many scientists what a tremendous revolution in human thought occured when Galileo developed his idea of inertial motion—and especially what a long history of hard thinking, from the time of Parmenides and Zeno on, went into the development of this idea.

The idea of motion is simple and easy in comparison with the idea of God. Our major adult encyclopedias do not throw much light on the problem of objectivity in the sense of fairness to the subject in the discussion of ethical, aesthetic, and theological questions. Somewhere the arguments of the logical positivists and others who assert atheism should be faced with the question: You insist on sense experience as the source and test of all knowledge. How did you get your "knowledge" that the word "God" does not refer to anything? The answer today does not make sense if it is given in terms of the pre-Copernican universe, or of God as existing only in time and space, or as an object that can be found, as one can find a cup or chair. No theologian of any repute today thinks of God as an object in the same sense as he thinks of any object in time and space. To argue about this in literal terms, to cite passages in the Bible and treat them literally is to indulge in the type of thinking that has been scorned as stupid and ignorant fundamentalism, and it is precisely this, whether it is that of the critic who imagines he is enlightened or that of the stupid and ignorant fundamentalist. The stupidity and ignorance in both cases are exactly the same stupidity and ignorance.

The most illuminating discussion of which I know of objectivity in the sense of fairness to subjects is Michael Polanyi's *Personal Knowledge*. Discussion of the quality of Polanyi's is not now in any of our encyclopedias.

Again, none of our encyclopedias has anything to say (or if they do I have not been able to find it) on the relations of fact and theory. They have very little on fact and value and fact and reason.

All give estimates of the number of Jews exterminated by Hitler's National Socialists. None give estimates of the numbers starved to death, worked to death in labor camps, and otherwise exterminated under Stalin, and before and after Stalin. The information that is necessary to the formation of clear and definite judgments on the qualities of communist governments in comparison with those of free societies is not given in any.

The subject Sacrifice is handled by all of our encyclopedias as if it were a subject that has to do only with primitive societies. This century has seen probably more human sacrifice than in all preceding human history.

Slavery is a very large and very important subject. Our encyclopedia articles on the subject are good as encyclopedia articles go, Britannica's much more extensive and much better than either Americana's or Collier's, but none measures up to the importance of the subject. Americana, for instance, tells us that "the slave trade . . . existed among primitive African tribes at a very remote period," but drops the subject after saying this, and there is no bibliographical reference to any information on it. Americana also tells us that "in the mid-20th century slavery still exists in many parts of the world," but does not say where, or how the reader can find out where and what the conditions of slavery are in those places. Both Britannica and Collier's corroborate this statement in Americana, and Britannica gives some definite information as to places, but little as to conditions. Collier's speaks of "brutality and inhumanities inflicted by the Arabs on their slave victims as late as the twentieth century," but does not say what these are or where the reader can find out. Britannica contradicts Collier's on this point. Britannica characterizes slavery under the Arabs as mild.

Britannica has an excellent bibliography, arranged so as to give important help to the reader. Americana has no bibliography. Collier's bibliographical references are to books that bear only on United States subjects, and none of them have to do mainly with slavery.

There are many subjects such as these that are in sore need of more serious attention than they are anywhere now given. Picking out subjects that provide the best opportunity for comprehensive and illuminating discussion is not an easy matter. Sustained study by a specially qualified staff over a period of time, and this time cannot be estimated at this stage, with the advice of scholars and scientists, is necessary if list making and other work of a preparatory nature is to be well done.

14. Britannica's bibliographies are by far the best among our three encyclopedias, but there is room for improvement on Britannica's bibliographies. The seminal works on a subject can often appropriately be mentioned and characterized in an article. Brief characterizations of works in bibliographies could be more than sufficiently helpful to war-

rant the space this would require. People in the world of learning have no idea how difficult, how practically impossible it is for the layman to locate really good discussion of difficult subjects. Bibliographies should always, on subjects on which there are important competing theories or important differences, list and characterize the books that present them. No encyclopedia yearbook now lists and characterizes new books in connection with its articles. The usefulness of yearbooks would be greatly increased if this were done with care.

15. While I was editor in chief of *Collier's Encyclopedia*, I received many letters from purchasers of the set, most of them criticizing deficiencies of one kind or another. One that I received was from a purchaser who said he had bought his set because the salesman had said he could find out from it almost anything he wanted to know. The purchaser went on to say that a couple of years previously he had bought a lot, he now planned to build a house on it, the lot had many trees, he wanted to identify them, he tried to use his encyclopedia for this purpose; but after spending hours in the effort, he found he just couldn't identify his trees by using his encyclopedia. Perhaps, he said, he had overlooked something, and I could tell him how to use his set for this purpose.

Well, I couldn't. When the set was planned, this problem, and a lot of others comparable to it, had been overlooked. So I had to write a nice evasive letter, thanking the writer, and carefully avoiding telling him that we just had not done our job properly.

The articles on particular trees were scattered in the set from A to Z as required by the alphabet. All the articles were illustrated, but the illustrations that were used gave little or no help on the problem of identification. One could scan every page in all the volumes of the set, locate every article on every particular tree, and even though there were articles on every tree to be identified, still be unable to identify his trees.

The solution of this problem was easy if anyone, learning that it existed, then bothered to think about it and get the necessary information. As to information, first, trees have characteristic shapes, both overall and as to branching. The characteristic shapes of broadleaved trees can be seen most clearly in drawings or photographs if the drawings or photographs show the tree without its foliage. If the tree is shown with foliage, the branching cannot be clearly seen. Second, the shapes and sizes of leaves offer probably the easiest means of identification. A leaf can be taken from a tree, carried home and compared with an illustration. Flowers and seeds are also useful in identification, but they are available during only a short period in a year, whereas leaves are available for a long period. Third, the bark of a particular tree has its particular characteristics, but one cannot easily take a piece of bark from a tree to compare it with a picture and a description in a volume of an encyclopedia. Of course, one may rely on his memory, but an actual sample is better.

As to arrangement, it was obvious that an article under the caption "Tree" that included illustrations of the nature described above of the various trees would solve the problem. An article of this kind was put in the set.

I do not know why short articles such as those on trees need to be scattered alphabetically throughout an encyclopedia. They could all be collected under the caption "Trees" and their interest and usefulness greatly enchanced. Such an article would be as long as a thin book, and, if properly prepared, could be sold separately as a book. Much of the material in encyclopedias is susceptible to treatment of this kind—if there has been proper preparation. Such treatment would do better service to education and would certainly be more profitable to the publisher—but again, I repeat, because it is crucial, only if there has been proper preparation. Deficiencies in preparation, in planning in advance, cannot be corrected except by starting again and planning properly.

16. One of the questions that has to be considered in designing an encyclopedia for the purpose of general education is that of the allocation of space to types of subject matter. It could be argued, for instance, that if control of the power generated by science and technology is the world's and the country's most serious problem, emphasis should be placed on the subjects having to do with this control, or even that an encyclopedia dealing exclusively with control is the one most needed and therefore the one that should be prepared. I have no doubt that control is the most important problem. I doubt whether a set could be so designed that a few volumes devoted exclusively to this problem could be sold separately as well as a part of the set. But as to publishing a set that has to do only with control, I believe that basic scientific theory in the sciences generally has to be understood in order to understand the problem of control. The humanities, properly handled, also have their contribution, and it is, I believe, a necessary one. At the same time, the whole set can be planned so that parts will make units that can be sold separately.

17. One of the features of Diderot's *Encyclopédie* that is not as well-

known as it deserves to be is the articles and engravings showing the state of the industrial arts and crafts of the time. It is possible today to make as great a contribution in this field as Diderot made in his time— and perhaps a greater one.

There is today a widespread feeling of antagonism to modern industry. Modern industry is held responsible for the hideousness of vast areas and for the pollution of air and water that has become so serious all over the country. One has only to have watched, and to know from actual seeing, the effects of the disorderly habits that large numbers of people have in the disposal of their debris to know that modern industry alone is not responsible for the filth that threatens to engulf us. The bad habits of modern industry can be corrected far more easily than the bad habits of large parts of the American public. Most important is the utterly simple, elementary, and inescapable fact that modern industry, and only modern industry, has relieved human beings from long hours of hard physical labor, that modern industry is one of the large factors in the best hope that human beings have of better life on earth. Among the great needs here is, of course, careful and readable representation of the science and art in the various industries; but also needed is special attention to cases where industrial plants have been made beautiful, where they are attractions rather than hideous spots on the landscape, where they do not pollute the water and the air; and where the problem of location has been handled so that workers do not lose as much or more in travel time than they have gained in shorter working hours. I do not mean to say that the foul blots, the wasteful arrangements should not be represented. On the contrary, I say that here again there is opportunity for genuinely fruitful pro and con treatment of a great subject.

18. The great French *Encyclopédie* of Diderot gained the tremendous influence that it had during the eighteenth century mainly through its attacks on the orthodoxies of its time. The attacks were made by various means, one being that of an article that presented the orthodox views on a subject, and to have a cross reference to an article that attacked the orthodox views. It is still necessary in encyclopedias to use cross references to lead readers to closely related discussion and to avoid needless repetition; but it is unnecessary today to present pro and con discussion of the same subject under different captions because of any problem of censorship. The pro and con discussion can be in different parts of the same article. The more important competing ortho-

doxies in the world today, as well as those of the past, are sorely in need of serious pro and con discussion.

19. The problem of making an adequate index to an encyclopedia is not easy. It is possible for an encyclopedia index to be far better than Britannica's—as, say, Collier's is—and still not be as helpful as an encyclopedia index might be. There has never been a careful, comprehensive study of the problem of indexing an encyclopedia such as Britannica with the purpose of finding out how to make an index that would be most useful to the general public. A careful and comprehensive study of this problem and of other aids, such as complete classified lists of articles, with equally careful attention to the problem of retrieval from computer banks, is sorely needed. I have suggested in the text important points at which definitive tests might be made of the retrieval of information from computer banks. This is, of course, not the only problem in connection with the idea of using the computer as a substitute for the encyclopedia—in fact, it is not the most important problem—but it is one that needs to be understood.

We are now near the end we had in view when we set out to write this book. This end now exists as an idea in one of its earliest stages. This idea is the need for a new type of encyclopedia, one that would serve the purpose of general education for both the intellectual world and the general public. The general education which is contemplated here would be designed to provide the opportunity for every individual in the public who is able to read and capable of learning to gain a better understanding of the great as well as the small issues in life; and particularly to understand, better than is now possible, the relations between the well-being of a society and the understanding and actions of its members. The information that the most comprehensive encyclopedias are supposed to provide would be made available, but in contexts that serve the purpose of understanding far better than is now done.

The question might be asked, since we have many definite ideas on how the proposed encyclopedia should be made, why bother with an institute that might take a long time to study the need that we say exists and how to meet it? Why do we not go ahead and outline the encyclopedia that we think is needed, submit our outline to a possible publisher and take our chances? The answer to this question is that no one person today knows enough to do this job as it should be done. The very asking of this question reveals the ignorance that turned the marvelously good intentions of Jean Anouilh's Antigone II into viciously destructive forces. The difficulty of doing this job well is of the order of that of going to the moon and returning safely. The knowledge of how to do this was not possessed by any one person. It was not generated in a day, or in a few years. It was generated by the thought and experimental work of many persons over many centuries. This knowledge was put to work only in the cooperative effort of highly qualified persons completely dedicated to the task. The financial resources that would be required for the institute that would study the problem of general education and plan the encyclopedia would be far less than were required for the moon project, but still the expenditures required would be large. The results, if the project were reasonably successful, would be far greater than any that can be imagined as coming from the moon project.

CHAPTER XIII

The Human Potential

> What is a man
> If his chief good and market of his time
> Be but to sleep and feed? a beast, no more.
> Sure, he that made us with such large discourse,
> Looking before and after, gave us not
> That capability and god-like reason
> To fust in us unused.
>
> *Hamlet*, IV, iv

This book bears the title *The Human Potential* despite the fact that we do not know in any final and complete way what this potential is. Let us now explore this question.

The most puzzling obstacle to understanding the great problems of human beings on this earth and what to do about them is the opinion in high places as well as low of already knowing. On some matters, to be sure—such as whether fire burns, or whether human beings have to act whether they know how they should or not—it seems clear that the claim to knowledge is beyond reasonable dispute. We have ignored these matters and have directed our attention to those over which dispute has been more important in human history and on which knowledge better than yet achieved seems necessary if the potential of the animal becoming human is to be given a better rather than a worse chance for further development in a good direction. We make no claim to know in any final way what is good, but we do claim that there are evidences in human history that, if handled with care, can be trusted.

In Chapter I we illustrated the *problem of already knowing* in three periods prior to our time—in ancient times in the case of Creon in the play *Antigone* by Sophocles; in the eighteenth century in the case of the gross misunderstanding of Burke's *Vindication of Natural Society* by the intellectual leadership of the day; in our own time in the case of Antigone II in the play by Jean Anouilh. We show how this problem affected two of the leaders in the French Revolution; and we could have done the same for cases of leaders in the United States in our century. We can be sure that neither Woodrow Wilson nor Franklin D. Roosevelt, two of our greatest leaders, intended some of the more important results of their leadership. The United States today is torn with dissension over its leadership and this dissension again illustrates the problem. Not all of those on the antagonistic sides can really know. Much of this dissension arises from a background that is as ignorant of the realities of this life—realities that in various forms appear to be perennial—as was Jean Anouilh's Antigone II. We refrain from discussion of this great human problem in the specific forms in which it has existed in recent years for the simple reason that memories are short, righteous feelings and convictions strictly comparable to those of Jean Anouilh's Antigone II pervade and overflow our time, and the background necessary for intelligible discussion and the cultivation of understanding rather than anger and more dissension, even to the point of violence, does not exist. One of the purposes of this book is to show the need on this particular subject, as well as many others, for the knowledge that has been developed in over two thousand years of highly pertinent discussion, knowledge that can be made available generally by the specialists of our time, if they are given the opportunity.

One of the two most difficult problems in the discussion of wars is that of determining where rightness lies—if there is any rightness to lie anywhere. The dominant doctrine among the experts on ethics in the English-speaking world of our time, as we have shown in previous chapters, is that there is no such something as rightness. At the same time, large parts of our world are hurling charges of violations of right against other parts. Most of us cannot accept the idea that there is not and cannot be any rightness or wrongness in conduct but do not know enough to appeal to the great tradition that says there is. This tradition is today in eclipse. There are those who have provided light on this problem, but their light today is as under a bushel, unavailable to the general public. The parts of the intellectual world that are being heard from most frequently today give no signs of having had the benefit of this light.

The other of the two most difficult problems in the discussion of wars is that of capturing imaginatively in their fullness and urgency the motives and feelings of the participants, of both leaders and followers on all sides. Why do the leaders lead and the followers follow? The answer to this question can be summarized in the words rewards and punishments. These can range from service freely given to an ideal which may involve the sacrifice of one's life, to service for less worthy motives, such as the desire for glory, great distinction, excitement, the fear of punishment by government or society, the chance to escape from boredom or a nagging wife, in ancient times the sharing in captured booty, in modern times the securing of a pension and other benefits of a veteran in a war. The ideal that one thinks one is serving may be that of an ignoramus, but still as thoroughly admirable as that to which Antigone II was devoted, and it may ignorantly and innocently be put into the service of viciousness and acquire destructive powers as in her case. The sacrifice that Antigone II makes of her life is apparently useless, utter waste—as she recognizes when, near the end of her life, she says she doesn't know why she is dying.

We have seen close up, in the two plays in which Antigone is the central character, samples of the kinds of causes that are always present in wars; and in the case of Creon II, the virtual impotence of the best type of rule against the sheer viciousness and superstition that are able at times to command ignorance—even though the ignorance is imbued with the most admirable feelings and intentions. The two plays, especially Jean Anouilh's *Antigone*, reveal perhaps as clearly as is possible the motives and feelings of the participants. They make clear that the motives and feelings of people that are necessary to decent human life are, if wrongly directed, among the great whys of wars. How do we tell right from wrong direction? Anouilh's *Antigone* is an almost impossible achievement in many ways, but especially in that it provides examples of the real problems involved in doing this. If it were really seen and understood today, the quality of the judgment implicit in much current discussion of wars, past and present, would undergo a great transformation. The means for creating the background necessary to the cultivation of this understanding, which in turn is necessary to the cultivation of the best in the human potential, do not exist today.

In Chapter II, while we recognize the great contribution to understanding implicit in Ruth Benedict's *Patterns of Culture*, we criticize the book because this contribution is not only left implicit but is contradicted by the conclusion. This conclusion, as we have said, supports the orthodoxy that was dominant in anthropology when Miss Benedict wrote *Patterns of Culture*. This orthodoxy, as we have seen, is the doctrine of cultural or ethical relativity. It says that no culture is better than any other. If this is true, there can hardly be any human potential worth discussing.

If we were to discuss all the evidence and speculation that bears on the human potential, we would discuss all myths, all theology, all philosophy, all anthropology, all history, all literature, all science and art, for all these bear on the nature and destiny of man and the universe. The subject "the human potential" is encyclopedic in scope, and this is the reason we have chosen it for our title.

The work of the anthropologist in the study of preliterate peoples has to be considered in the study of the human potential. The doctrine of cultural relativity obviously bears on the problem of the human potential. For if there is no better and worse among cultures, nothing can be learned by any kind of study of them, or of anything else, that is worth knowing about the human potential. However, if the testimony of human beings in their lives in the various cultures that have existed on earth is given decisive weight, the notion that there is no better and worse has to be rejected. There is no room for doubt that as the consciousness of the individual human being has developed, the quest for better rather than worse and the effort to establish the better has also developed.

If we try seriously to understand why anthropologists generally have adopted the doctrine of cultural relativity, which we have discussed and criticized in Chapter II, we have a difficult but not an impossible task on our hands. The first task of the anthropologist in the study of a culture is to discover and describe the actualities of the culture, and these include the customs, the attitudes and feelings, the beliefs and motives of the people. If he knows what he is doing, he knows that his work involves, and necessarily, value judgments of his own; but he knows to some extent what these are and discounts them as far as he can. He knows, for instance, that the facts and other topics of a culture do not select themselves for him, that he has to do the selecting, and that he can select and treat his facts and other subject matter in such manner as to misrepresent completely the culture he is trying to describe. To say this is not to say that facts and topics and attitudes with which he is totally unfamiliar may not thrust themselves upon him and so impress him that he recognizes their importance and treats them accordingly. He certainly selects when he does this. Selection is inescapable. For there is no way of knowing whether facts and topics of great importance may not thrust themselves upon him, but which he does not recognize and therefore does not select.

In his effort to be objective, that is to describe truly, the anthropologist will use language that as far as possible excludes his own value judgments and conveys only the value judgments of the people of the culture he is describing. But there is no neutral language available to him and no possibility of any. He does the best he can in this situation. Thus a ritual in which a person is killed will not be spoken of as involving a murder, and possibly not even as a killing. It most likely will be spoken of as a sacrifice thought to be necessary to some social purpose held in common. Such purposes are always designed to serve what is thought by the people to be better for them rather than worse. And some things are valued so highly that life itself will be risked, if necessary sacrificed, for them. The valuations of preliterate peoples tend to establish ethnocentrism in each culture—the notion that of all possible ways of doing things, its ways are the best. Thus far anthropologists seem to be in general agreement, and we see no good reasons for disagreeing. The anthropologist cannot, of course, accept ethnocentrism. But the notion that all cultures are equally good is also absurd, and he has accepted it in his doctrine of cultural relativity.

We now go beyond the anthropologist, or perhaps to work that should have been a part of his, but has not been. Somebody, somewhere, some time has to consider the question of the quality of the various social purposes that various peoples have had and the means they use to maintain them; otherwise the work of the anthropologist and historian at its most important point is largely wasted.

One of the great differences between preliterate and civilized societies is that in the latter the equal excellence of the cultures of all peoples may to some extent be seriously questioned. We say "to some extent" because civilized societies do not always encourage such questioning and sometimes penalize it heavily, and, in our view, sometimes for good reasons. There is no self-deception greater than that widespread in civilized societies today that they have freed themselves from the condition that has prevailed generally in preliterate societies, i.e., that if the values of the society are threatened, life may have to be sacrificed to maintain them, that the values are necessary to the quality of life thought to be worth living.

If there is to be any chance for the human potential to be developed beyond its present level, this condition as it exists today must somehow be changed. It is highly probable that complete freedom from it is not possible, that if the good in the human potential is to continue to be developed, there must continue to be individuals able to imagine unachieved but possible good, and willing to sacrifice their lives if necessary in order to give others the chance to achieve it. But there must be a reduction in the price that has to be paid, if this price is as high as world wars; otherwise the outlook for man on earth is worse than bleak.

It seems clear today that if reason continues to be the slave of the passions, as it has been during this century, the human potential will not only not be further developed but life, if it continues very long to exist at all, will become nasty, brutish, and short for the unfortunates still living in the world. The time has come to work on the problem of making the passions work with reason toward the further development of the potential for good in human beings.

Our purpose in our discussion so far has been to bring out as clearly and as briefly as possible the basic causes of violence within and among societies. These must be curbed, but not destroyed, if the human potential is to have any chance for further development. The basic causes of our wars have clearly been the needs and desires of human beings ungoverned by principles that make harmony within and among societies possible. The discovery of such principles has been one of the great objects of reason, but reason itself has been and still is a subject over which dispute rages. All doctrines are in agreement that the establishment and maintenance of harmony within and among societies is the great object to be achieved. But this agreement, or apparent agreement, itself is a problem of the greatest difficulty. For the differences over the kind of harmony that is necessary to a tolerable peace, and what kinds are possible, if any, are so wide, so much opposed to each other as to be themselves the cause of strife—even to the point of more world wars —that the harmony is intended to make impossible. We shall now continue our discussion with summary statements of certain facts of history, despite the fact that the body of doctrine of our time that is shaping the world holds that we cannot learn anything from these facts and should ignore them.

No society beyond the most primitive has ever been discovered in which complete harmony has existed. The so-called progress of civilization during most of the history of the animal becoming human seems to have been progress in the creation of disharmonies within and among societies. The most primitive, perhaps because of their distance in time, seem to have been internally the most harmonious. And even in the most primitive, our evidence says that at times brother deliberately kills, murders, brother. It just could be that the story of Cain and Abel represents a possibility that at times becomes an actuality that still exists everywhere among the animals which, we may still hope, are somehow becoming human beings. It may be also that the effort to find means of offsetting the actualization of this possibility has been widespread, and that it has been this factor, expressing itself in manifold ways, that has led to the formal development of the governments that existed previously in the form of custom and habit. When we begin realizing this, we begin realizing that the animal becoming human has from ancient times been at least vaguely aware that harmony among peoples and governments offers the only possibility of escaping the devastation of wars. But how achieve this harmony? By force? By persuasion that does not include force or the threat of force? By an ideal that of itself, if widely propagated and understood, would create unity? There has been a perennial search for such an ideal. There have been many claims that such an ideal has been envisioned and that it can be brought to earth and made real. But no ideal that has consistently condemned the use of physical force and refused to use it, or to accept any benefits derived from its use, has ever gained more than temporary power—power that has soon been shown to have been more illusory than real.

It is claimed in Communist doctrine that the time will come when people will accept and act in accord with this body of doctrine, a time when the lawlessness of individuals and factions will disappear, the state will wither away, and the rule of reason will bring harmony among individuals and groups, including nations; and the need for the use of physical force to secure harmony will completely disappear. The fact is, however, that there has never been any system of government or state that has used more physical force against its own people than have those governments that claim to be developing Communism. And so-called wars of liberation rather than peaceful persuasion have become their method of spreading their theory and practice.

The forces that are working today for more civil wars and for another world war unless free society surrenders cannot be stopped by mere verbal expressions of feelings, no matter how vociferous these are. The notion, widely held in the United States today, that the world judges adversely the agents of violence, as it often does temporarily, is belied by the fact that the remembrance of the use of violence in the effort to persuade is today highly selective, that reference is made only to cases that one chooses to prove one's point, never to those that disprove it—that cases equally or more significant which work against one's point are simply ignored. The interest that the intellectual leadership and the public generally has in death caused by the violence of governments is clearly indicated by the fact that there is no source easily available to the intellectual leadership or to the general public that gives an account of the numbers of persons who have died on account of the deliberate actions of the governments of Russia and China from the inception of the Communist revolutions until the present.

It might be said, as it often is today, that interest in this subject could best begin at home. And we agree. The question arises why has this interest not been cultivated, why is reliable information on it practically unavailable, quickly and easily, in the United States today? The government of the United States does not interfere with the provision of this kind of information (or any other kind) in articles, books, and encyclopedias. If information on the American treatment of the American Indian is not quickly and easily available to anyone who wants it, one can only point to American editors and publishers, and particularly to American encyclopedias and the American public, and ask why. The answer obviously is lack of serious interest. The subject as brought up today only confuses issues. Some of us bring it up for this purpose, and many of us in our ignorance of the great issues of our time follow this lead and add to the confusion. If we were really interested, we would demand reliable information and discussion of this information that made some sense.

Many Americans today believe that the United Nations, despite the exhibit it has given since its founding, can make reasonable decisions, and that if the more powerful nations of the world turned all their armed forces over to the United Nations and then consistently backed all the decisions of the United Nations, and if the United Nations then consistently used this power, or the threat of it, to stop international strife, and if the strife within nations could somehow be kept from becoming international and destroying the United Nations or making it impotent so far as the prevention of war is concerned—international war would be stopped. And it undoubtedly would. But the ifs in this set of beliefs, wholly admirable when taken as starting points for studying the questions on which they depend, have the effects of powerful narcotics when they are taken as settling the questions they raise. The whole set of ifs taken this way, as they usually are, is strictly comparable to the notion that if wishes were Cadillacs, beggars would ride and no longer be beggars. They would be able then, along with everybody else, to parade their egos, and, along with Herbert Marcuse, of whom we shall speak below, to bewail the misery their good fortune had brought them and prescribe an infallible cure not only for their own good fortune, but that of multitudes of others as well.

Why has the ideal—a wholly admirable ideal—of a United Nations proved unworkable in the prevention of war in our time? The obvious answer is that the commitments of the more powerful governments of the earth stand in the way. It may be that these governments, or some of them, do not have the support of the great majority of the people. But while this is a question on which one may speculate and express opinions in speech and in writing in a relatively free society such as that of the United States, one cannot do this in Russia and China. The most reliable knowledge that human beings can get on questions of this kind can be got only at the risk of life in these countries.

The necessity of fear and force in some degree to government and the equally great necessity of widespread moral convictions that are well-informed, well disposed, active, and to high degree right if force and fear are to be rightly used and kept at a minimum, have all been demonstrated in informed writings of the greatest cogency; and yet these necessities are little known in the intellectual world of our time. This world currently provides the ludicrous and distressing spectacle of widespread conviction that there is no genuine right and wrong, no notion of good or of better and worse that is valid, while at the same time pointing at this and that individual and group and making the charge of vicious and destructive prejudice and action. This is as if a doctor said to a patient,"There is no possible cure for your condition," and then, in his next sentence, said "There is a cure." One would without hesitation drop any doctor, lawyer, accountant, or other professional person one had been using who one discovered habitually engaged in actions in accord with such nonsense.

It can be said with a high degree of certainty that the quality of the understanding of problems of this kind that prevails among a people determines the degrees of the fear and force that their government finds it necessary to exercise over them in order to maintain itself and do its work. There are many necessities of this kind that are little understood in large segments of the intellectual world today. But it has to be said in fairness and truth, as we have shown in some detail in this book, that our intellectual leadership has little opportunity to know. It is in this respect better off than our public generally, but not enough to make any great difference. Our intellectual leadership is lost in a wilderness of ignorant opinion that it has helped to create. To find a way out of this wilderness is no easy task.

In one of the *Federalist* papers (No. 10) the instruction that is in human history for anyone able to get it is demonstrated when the wisdom of more than twenty centuries is focused on the problem of breaking and controlling the violence of the factions which, after the American Revolution, threatened to destroy the newly won freedom. Two great necessities in the government of a reasonably free people are demonstrated: first, the necessity of an overall government that has the duty and the power to intervene and break the power of factions that threaten the general welfare; second, the necessity in the interests of the general welfare of keeping this government from becoming either so powerful as to become a tyranny or so weak as to be impotent. The whole purpose of the *Federalist* papers was to help cultivate among the people of the time enough understanding to gain their support for this vital service to their own welfare. Fortunately, enough people of the time were able to understand the arguments put before them; and they established the government which, perhaps as well as the public allows, is guided by principles that make possible the serious and sustained effort to discover and serve the general welfare.

It is beginning to be thought and said in the United States today that there are peoples in the world that have not yet reached the level necessary to understand the problems involved in establishing and maintaining the type of government necessary to a reasonably free society. One wonders immediately how this notion can be distinguished from that of Hitler on the subject of superiority and inferiority among peoples; and one wonders about its relation to the American doctrine of equality. Is it a denial? So far no one has openly advocated extermination. This would be too crude. Extermination can be managed without open advocacy. Now if equality is not a fact, and none of its great exponents has ever held that it is, what then is it? John Stuart Mill could be cited in support of the doctrine of levels among peoples, and on this point his best critic, James Fitzjames Stephen, would have agreed with him. Even Abraham Lincoln and Thomas Jefferson could be cited to the same effect. Shall we study these men with a view to understanding and accepting them as authorities? We urge the importance of study of men such as these, but not for the purpose of accepting them as authorities. Any study that is sufficiently wide will discover that a well-informed and reasonable notion of equality is necessary to the general welfare of human beings on earth and that it involves the potential in the animal becoming human to cultivate and realize reasonable aspirations. Whether one agrees or disagrees with the approach the United States has made to this problem as it exists among other peoples of the world, one can hardly accept the view that this is a problem of no concern to the people of the United States.

The problem of the general welfare has become incomparably more complicated and difficult in our time than it was when the United States was founded. It should not be necessary today to argue that the degree of interdependence among the nations of the world is such that the United States cannot safely retreat into isolation. Nor can it run the world. It seems clear the United States cannot perform the functions that a United Nations ought to perform and that the effort to do so can lead only to destructive dissension at home and defeat abroad. But does this mean that so far as the most important participation in world affairs is concerned, the American idea is dead, that it offers no hope to human beings elsewhere in the world, regardless of the level at which they are living? If the American idea, so far as other people in the world are concerned, is dead, can it still be alive at home? This is no appeal for more effort to run the world exclusively by physical force, or for more effort to implant ideas where they are not wanted. It is an appeal for thought on a question of the greatest importance to the quality of American life and to the possibility that this quality is indissolubly linked up with the quality of life of peoples elsewhere in the world.

The understanding and the vital service that are necessary to the general welfare are receiving, except in superficial and hit-or-miss ways, too much cultivation in the United States today only in ways that create the Antigone II's of our time.

The words "the general welfare," we can be sure, despite certain very influential judicial opinion, were not written into the preamble to the Constitution of the United States as mere façade, mere decoration. On the contrary, they state the great purpose of that document. But like many of the words in the Constitution, or any other writing or speaking, they do not bear their meanings on their face. The great problem of understanding them exists today just as it did when the Constitution was first presented to the representatives of the people in the states for their ratification.

The reverence with which the people of the United States generally and rightly regard the Constitution can mislead them into treating the words "the general welfare" as terms of magic that do not have to be understood in order to be effective. These words, correctly understood, serve to open the way to the further cultivation of the potential for good that is in human beings. The cultivation of this potential has been in process for many thousands of years. During most of this time the animal becoming human almost certainly has not been aware of any effort on his part to improve his condition. What it was that started and particularly what has continued this development beyond a growing consciousness of unrealized potential, we do not know, nor do we know how far this development may go. The word "potential" in our title *The Human Potential* is our name for this "what." This "what," unlike the potential in the acorn which in our ignorance we know somehow becomes an oak, is in large measure a mystery to us, but not wholly so.

The notion of potentiality is not new. It is important in Aristotelian, Hegelian, Darwinian, Marxian, Marcusan, and many other bodies of doctrine. In Aristotle it is limited by the doctrine of fixed species. In Hegel's earlier writings, a doctrine of perhaps unlimited human and natural potentiality is dominant. Not only man but nature is malleable, and within the limits only of reason—and those limits are not easy to discover because of certain extreme ambiguities in Hegel's notions concerning the nature of things. The things of the universe are objects of reason and are created by reason. The potential that is in things to become other than what they are, that is, to change, Hegel takes as authorizing him to hold and take seriously the view, which he states in many ways, many times, that a thing is what it is not. Hegel presents his views generally as authorized by Aristotle, but Aristotle clearly says in Book Kappa of his Metaphysics (§ 9, 1065b) that to be and to be potentially are not the same. Contradiction, in Hegel's sense, is the moving principle of the world. In Aristotle's sense, contradiction is that it is impossible for the same thing at the same time to belong and not to belong to the same thing and in the same respect (Book Gamma, § 3, 1005b). We cannot take the space to present further evidence that the view, widely accepted, that Hegel subsumes and carries further Aristotelian doctrine is extremely dubious. If Hegel himself misrepresents his sources, it would seem that we cannot, except at the risk of gross and absurd errors, accept his logic without serious question, and it is his logic on which Hegel stands or falls. But, to go on with his doctrine —the doctrine that as modified by Marx and his successors (who have certainly modified Marx) has been transforming the world in this century—at every stage in human development, nature and human nature are understood in terms of reason that also is developing in human consciousness. The reasonable at every stage corresponds with the world and it corresponds because it creates the world. Human potentiality is limited only by the perfection of reason. But as we shall see, there is a problem here that Hegel does not solve. In the development of the human potential, according to Hegel, man achieves freedom. This freedom in Hegel's later work is, however, freedom under law, and not the absence of external constraint that has often been held and is still often held to be the only genuine freedom. It is necessary at this point to distinguish between that in this subject on which it is possible to agree with Hegel and that on which one has to disagree. As to disagreement, there most certainly is, contrary to Hegel, some freedom that exists as a consequence of absence of constraint. This freedom exists most importantly in the realm of thought—less so and rightly less so in the realm of public expression, as is recognized in such laws as those of libel. And despite John Stuart Mill's argument for no limits on freedom of speech except in the case of an immediately present danger, there is a real problem, an especially serious problem of free public expression on the part of those who occupy positions that tend to give authority to their expressions. Exclusive attention to the side of this subject that Mill takes in his great essay *On Liberty* and complete ignoring of the side that James Fitzjames Stephen takes in his powerfully reasoned attack on Mill's essay in his book *Liberty, Equality, Fraternity* is not the way to cultivate understanding of this profoundly difficult and crucially important question. We have given in a previous chapter instances that illustrate this problem.

It is on the nature of freedom that Herbert Marcuse, widely known and of international influence for his *Reason and Revolution, Eros and Civilization, One Dimensional Man, Soviet Communism, Negations,* and other works, completely abandons his great preceptor Hegel, espouses freedom as total absence of constraint—a doctrine completely opposed to that of Hegel and attainable only in never-never land, where in our view Hegel's logic may really work. In this revolt against Hegel, Marcuse illustrates the ease with which Hegelian doctrine can be turned against Hegelian doctrine. In the Hegelian doctrine that every thing and every idea contains and turns into its opposite, there is nothing to keep freedom as external constraint in the form of law from becoming the complete absence of any form of external constraint—and, as Marcuse would have it, the absence of internal constraint as well.

The total absence of external and drilled-in internal constraint is not and never has been a tenable notion of freedom. In this respect, Hegel is right and Marcuse wrong. Human beings have always lived under conditions, both external and internal, that have strictly limited them, except for rare individuals who have not been hedged by some of the limitations that have kept others within their bounds. Only the rare individual has been able at times to transcend (overcome) some of the limits that have hedged others. How he is able to do this is utterly mysterious even though mountains of words can be piled up in the effort to locate and explain the how. The word "genius" and all its equivalents are mere labels for we know not what, in this respect just like John Locke's substance. So far as the limits on human beings are concerned, many seem to change without the exercise of any human initiative; others seem to require human initiative; but no changes of any kind have ever led to the absence of limits, and, according to one portion of Hegel's doctrine, anything of this kind would be utterly impossible. Things, ideas, in this doctrine exist by virtue of their limits.

It is not necessary in the effort to escape the doctrine of historicism attributed to Hegel that says human beings always and everywhere are the products exclusively of the conditions under which they were born and live to fly off to Marcuse's never-never land of totally un-limited freedom, a freedom that according to Hegel cannot be other than nothing. If one is a Hegelian, one has to assume that historicism contains and becomes its opposite. One is then authorized to join in singing that we shall overcome.

But, if we accept Hegel, we accept the notion that there is only one route of escape from one set of limits, and this route leads inescapably into another set. For, as we have said, things—and Hegel uses the word "things" in the widest possible sense to include persons, ideas, objects that we normally think of as physical, everything in the universe— things, according to Hegel following Plato, exist only by virtue of their limits. Hegel would thus have to hold that if one escaped into freedom unlimited—Marcuse's freedom—one would be escaping from existence. It would not help, so far as Marcuse's doctrine is concerned, if one then held, in accordance with Hegel's doctrine, that this "non-existence" was indeterminate being, indistinguishable from being, and this being indistinguishable from nothing, that these passed freely into each other, pure being into pure nothing, and that out of this nothing something came; and that this whole process could occur immediately, since logic exists outside of time. But if this process started with a per-son, could the something that Hegel would have resurrected out of nothing be a person and the person the process started with? Hardly, short of miracle. And could this person exist if his condition were that of freedom unlimited? In Hegel's doctrine, we repeat, neither persons nor freedom nor anything else can exist without limits. Marcuse aban-dons Hegel's logic at this point. Marcuse does not consider this basic problem in Hegel. He just uses Hegel's logic as far as it suits his pur-poses, and then abandons it. And perhaps for good reasons. Pehaps be-cause Hegel's "logic" is not logic at all except in the sense of being able to make what appears to be a good case for anything out of nothing at all. In this sense, his "logic" has proved to be one of the most powerful instruments ever devised by the human mind and made available for human use. We have suggested previously that the treatment of this subject in our encyclopedias is most seriously defective. Our discussion— that of a novice—is intended only to bring out, on the one hand, the questions about this "logic" on which the novice is most in need of light; and, on the other hand (whether Hegel's "logic" is really logic or not), to urge the importance of cultivating understanding of the nature of this instrument because of its great power. It clearly poses some of the problems of primitive magic in that if one believes in its efficacy, it tends to work, and to work in a strictly sober sense what can be regarded only as miracles. There is no room for doubt that there are scholars of great learning and of the highest intelligence capable of discussing this question pro and con, with competent editorial help, in a way that would be highly illuminating and within the compass of encyclopedia articles of reasonable length. No such discussion is available today, and the encyclopedia is the only practicable means of making such discussion on this and other subjects of comparable importance generally available.

If there is any subject on which the general public is sorely in need of more light, it is that of Freedom. Britannica does not have an article under the title "Freedom." There is no index entry of the word "Freedom" that refers to an article on the subject but under a different title. There is an article under the title "Liberty." The article is about one-quarter of a page in length. This is a fair indication of the quality of the judgment embodied in Britannica—the best of our major encyclopedias —in the allocation of space to subjects. This allocation cannot be corrected by patchwork. To correct it in any basic way, the set would have to be redesigned, rewritten, remade.

The need, in the interests of the human potential, for discussion that shows the interrelations of ideas and facts is crucial in our time. In Chapter I a fatal weakness in empirical doctrine is briefly shown. But this does not necessarily entail the conclusion that the facts of the universe are unimportant, or that reasoning that makes any sense can be conducted without reference to them. It suggests the need for distinguishing between a wild and a sober metaphysics, a wild and a sober dialectic. I use the words "wild" and "sober" instead of the words "unreasonable" and "reasonable" because of the division in the world today over what it means to be reasonable—but still, I cannot avoid the fact that by the word "sober" I really mean reason in the sense in which

I understand the term. I believe I have made this sense as clear as possible.

It happens that the problems involved in the nature of facts and ideas and theories—or rather some of the more important of these problems—can be brought out about as clearly as perhaps is possible in the discussion of Hegelian doctrine. The reason for this is that Hegelian doctrine raises crucial questions about fact, questions that need to be raised if facts are to be understood, whereas empirical doctrine generally does not raise such questions. If the discussion of fact is conducted only in, say, an article by an empiricist who asks none of the crucial questions concerning empiricism, the effect of the article—when it does not bring revulsion and criticism by the reader—is really to cultivate ignorance rather than knowledge. The reader who understands this and who finds the articles he consults often of this nature will soon become convinced that his encyclopedia is useless except perhaps for such matters as the more or less correct statement of dead orthodoxies and the checking of names and dates.

Let us now look at the questions Hegelian doctrine raises about the nature of facts. Hegel's early notions concerning the potentiality in man and nature were, after Hegel, greatly strengthened by Darwin's theory of evolution. This occurred despite the fact that in his philosophy of nature, Hegel characterized the idea of evolution as inept. Darwin rested his theory on facts and regarded his facts as realities. Hegel emphasized the notion, basic in Plato and his followers, that facts, in the sense of occurrences, happenings, events, are mere appearances. This immediately raises the question, is an appearance any less real than a so-called reality? Plato's answer was yes. The word "appearance" and the very idea that it represents can be taken as suggesting a low degree of reality or a defect.

But can there be degrees of reality and if so, how? Let us see whether we can get any light on this question by considering the meaning or meanings of the word "fact." It is sometimes said that once a fact, always a fact. But this cannot mean that Caesar having once crossed the Rubicon is still crossing. Can it mean that the snows of yesteryear still exist in some imaginary land? If not, where are these facts that are always facts? We usually have no doubt whatever that it makes sense to say that $2 + 2 = 4$ is a fact, but this is obviously not a fact in the same sense that if Caesar really once crossed the Rubicon, it is a fact that he once did so. But still, if $2 + 2 = 4$ is really true, it is certainly also a fact. It should be immediately evident that the notion of a fact as an occurrence, a happening, an event, is totally different from the notion of a mathematical fact as involved in the proposition that $2 + 2 = 4$. Now whether $2 + 2 = 4$ is a truth in the nature of things or a mere convention, it can be held and a mass of data can be cited in support of this holding—and none can be cited against it—that no society anywhere at any stage has been discovered that has not had its customs and habits. These, however derived, amount to conventions. So it might be held we have always and everywhere among human beings in societies the fact of conventions. So it might be said further that the necessity of conventions to societies is in the nature of things, unless evidence can be brought to the contrary—and there is no such evidence. This is among the facts that Herbert Marcuse would use "the power of negative thinking" to negate. He uses the sanction of Hegel's proposition that "Thinking is, indeed, essentially the negation of that which is immediately before us," to authorize his "power of negative thinking." [1]

Dubious as these notions of Hegel's and Marcuse's are, there is certainly some truth in them if logic has to be designed to follow nature in order to be valid. For nature, whether created by reason (logic) or not, certainly "negates" those facts that are of the type we have called, and that traditionally have been called, "appearances." It certainly brings them into being, apparently from nothing, and takes them out of being and puts them back from where it took them, that is, apparently into nothing. Thus nothing is at least in part something and is the great receptacle or custodian of Caesar's crossing of the Rubicon and of the snows of yesteryear and of all that which has appeared on earth and disappeared, including all the persons. Now this nothing, we may say, is obviously something, but it is utterly beyond any human sense-experience, and therefore our empiricists ignore it when they do not deny its existence. It is, except for the language that is used to designate it, indistinguishable from the receptacles that Christian doctrine provides for some of that which for a time exists, then disappears.

It is possible to raise serious doubts about the validity of Hegelian doctrine as we have done, but it has to be said for Hegel that, whether rightly or wrongly, he did not shirk the task of dealing with questions of the greatest interest and importance to human beings—questions that have to be considered if the arguments, the conflicts, the wars over how the human potential can be given its best development are not to sink

1. See for both quotations the first paragraph of the Preface to the second edition of Marcuse's *Reason and Revolution*. (Boston: Beacon Press [1941], 1960.)

to the level of mere sound and fury, signifying nothing but the incapacity of man to rise higher than nihilism.

Hegel obviously held also that there are propositions that are universally valid. His logic in his view consisted of such propositions. It is possible to doubt the validity of Hegel's logic, as we do, but we join Hegel in believing that there are propositions that are universally valid, such as that $2 + 2 = 4$—and many more, such as that conventions of some kind, good, bad, or indifferent, exist always and everywhere in societies, and that the quality of the life of the people of a society depends on the quality of its conventions, its pattern of values or form of the good, and these in turn depend on the quality of the thought and action of the people. In these crucially important aspects of his doctrine, Hegel in our view is right and profoundly important to the development of the best in the human potential.

Our encyclopedias today, while made and used mainly as compendia of fact, provide no help whatever to the reader who becomes aware of the extremely different uses of the word "fact," and perhaps of the profound importance of these differences in his effort to understand himself and his world. There is no article in any of our encyclopedias on the subject Fact, there is no index entry of the word "Fact," there is no way for the reader to locate the meager discussion in various articles that bears on this subject—this subject of basic importance in the logical positivism that is the implicit dominant orthodoxy in the English-speaking world of our time.

Finally, on this subject, let us say that the facts which seem to be written off as realities of low degree or no degree at all, by the word "appearances" used to designate them, are among the realities of the highest degree with which human beings have to live their daily lives. At this point, Hegel and modern science (implicitly) and John Dewey and his followers are in agreement. But beyond this point, cleavage comes. In the doctrine of modern science and of John Dewey, facts of the type of appearances are consequences of deeper realities of which human beings can by understanding gain some measure of control. In the doctrine of Hegel, the deeper—or higher—realities are at every level created by the reason that exists at that level; reason develops, and contradiction is the principle that moves reason and makes it develop; and as it develops, it re-creates or develops further the deeper realities. In short, the deeper realities are creatures of reason or mind, and reason exists in two aspects, one as subject, the other as object.

John Dewey, the most original and the most influential of American thinkers, and easily the equal of any in modern times, started his great career as a Hegelian and then revolted against him. The main thrust of Dewey's revolt was against Hegel's monism, his reduction of the universe to mind. Dewey went so far in his revolt as virtually to deny the role of mind in his own monistic doctrine of nature. At the same time he exemplified in much of his work a high degree of excellence in the use of mind. However, his doctrine is not free from serious problems, though perhaps less so than Hegel's. No doctrine yet stated in the history of human thought has been sufficiently clear and free from unsolved problems as to gain and hold general acceptance.

If we are to gain the best possible understanding of such great exemplars of the use of mind as Dewey and Hegel, if we are to be able ever to do more than chirp the words of their followers, if we are ever to be able to gain the best possible understanding of ourselves and our world, it is necessary that we have far better help than is now in existence and that this help be generally available. The Antigone II's of our time are not wholly to blame for their condition. The kind of help that is most needed is exemplified to some extent by articles we have mentioned in one of our earlier chapters—one on Adam Smith in the 1967 edition of Britannica, and one on Galileo and one on Equality in the 1967 edition of Collier's. The provision of help of this kind on all the great subjects is necessary if the best in the human potential is to be given further development.

The worst of all mistakes in a democracy is to assume that the common man—and all of us today are such common persons—is not interested in trying to understand the conditions that determine the quality of his life; or that generally he is not capable of achieving this understanding, and then, on such grounds as these, or on account of sheer lack of thoughtful concern with the real problems of a free and self-governing society, to fail to do the best that can be done in the provision of the means necessary to give democracy a chance to work and to demonstrate its potentialities for excellence. This is to betray the last best hope of man on earth.

If evolutionary theory is true, there was a time when there was no life on earth. Evolutionary theory as held today is that the universe also has evolved and did so for aeons before the appearance of life. If we take the trouble to think, the question arises whether the stuff, whatever it is, of which the universe consists ever had a beginning, or whether it has existed always. There have been many theories and myths, much speculation on the relations between the myths and the theories, but even if we knew enough, which we do not, we could not take the space to give even the briefest review of these here. Let us consider in the briefest possible way only the origin of life and mind. As we have suggested above, modern cosmic theories generally hold that there was a time when there was no life or mind on earth as these are known today, even in their most primitive forms. Life is held to have been, possibly still to be, potential in what we today call matter—without knowing any too clearly just what we mean by any of the words, "life" or "matter" or "potential." These words are, we might say, like the word "mind," symbols of our ignorance as well as of some knowledge and pointers toward the possibility of more. Life, as we have said, is held in modern cosmic theory to have developed from what we speak of as inanimate matter. And the same is held to be true of mind insofar as it is held to exist at all.

Now there is at least one important difference between modern theory and ancient myth which we need to mention, and this is that ancient myth tended to be accepted by its adherents in a way that said nothing further could be discovered by study, that even if this account is not the whole story, it is as good a representation as can be achieved by human beings, that no matter how far one goes in the study of origins or continuities, one will never get any final answers any better than those embodied in our myth. Ancient myths thus tended to be final pronouncements and to close the subjects with which they dealt to further investigation and speculation. The question we now wish to raise is whether there are comparable forces, perhaps inescapable, that are at work in modern thought and even in modern science. In considering this question, we need to remember that the associative logic of David Hume which has been the most important influence in the shaping of the logical positivism of our time has also been a powerful influence in modern science. There is a problem here that is important to the further development of modern science and thought about modern science, and to thought or metaphysics of the kind in which Hegel engaged—perhaps even to all human thought.

In the effort to cultivate the human understanding and the human potential, such almost certainly true and fairly well established doctrines as that which says that the customs and habits into which persons are born and which are drilled into them and which they drill into themselves have powerful shaping influences cannot be safely forgotten. No matter how absurd they are, they are extremely difficult to overcome. The most important of the influences of custom and habit is the conviction of rightness they usually create. The customs and habits of a people, again no matter how absurd, always seem intelligible to them (until somehow they begin breaking down), so much so that the raising of questions concerning them is taken as a sign of something badly wrong in the questioner.

There is no more serious illusion than the one widespread in the intellectual world today that a society dominated by one set of customs and habits can easily pass, without struggle, conflict, perhaps civil war, from the established set to another. The possibilities here obviously involve the nature of the established set of customs and habits and the quality of the influences that are working for change. In the absence of a great idea, an ideal that can be brought to earth and put into practice, one that cultivates the minds and hearts of the people, one that has far more powers of attraction than mere material prosperity, important as this is, the prospects are not good. The ideal of exclusive material prosperity has tended always in the past to degenerate into the ideal of sensuality—the ideal, if we may call it such, that Herbert Marcuse, Norman O. Brown and many others in our time advocate in one way or other. As this "ideal" tends to be established—and it is far along in the United States today—the material prosperity tends to disappear. And then come all the disorders, the horrors of anarchy and desperation and despair among the people. The desperation generates determination and action that eventuates in reaction and the establishment of a regime that is virtually despotic.

The study of human history, including the study of preliterate peoples, can be illuminating; but if the historian or anthropologist is really a nihilist—and it is easy to be one without knowing that one is— he is likely to stand in the way of the light that is most needed.

Now the customs and habits that govern the work of scholars and scientists are, from any view that takes the study of the universe and man seriously, also customs and habits and just as much subjects for study and the exposure of absurdities and worse as are the customs and habits of primitive peoples. It is a mistake, and an appalling one at this time in human history, to assume that the familiarity that creates the conviction of rightness and intelligibility among primitive peoples ceases to operate among civilized peoples. David Hume, the source of the thought that has been most effective in shaping the intellectual life of the English-speaking world of our time, knew very well the power that association and repetition have in the fixing of ideas; in his *Treatise* and *Enquiries*, as is well-known to his students, he reduces intelligibility to association and the familiarity that comes from association. And this, if we take the trouble to think, leads us to certain considerations.

If one spends many years studying any one great subject that involves an orthodoxy—and practically every subject of any importance does—and one is never exposed and never exposes himself to serious criticism of the orthodoxy in which his subject is embedded, never seeks such criticisms out and becomes thoroughly familiar with them, he may never discover that the learning he thinks he has done has not been learning at all, that he has allowed himself to be a victim of the ease with which familiarity creates notions that will not stand serious examination. Our encyclopedias in their almost total failure to raise questions where questions most need to be raised reflect the level of awareness of this basic problem in American education.

As we have said above, evolutionary theory as it exists today poses a problem of the utmost difficulty in science and human thought. John Dewey, by far the best and the most persistent and consistent exponent of empirical naturalism in our time, states this problem in a way completely in accord with his native New England toughmindedness when he says in his *Experience and Nature* (1929 ed., p. 23): "That professed non-supernaturalists so readily endow the organism with powers that have no basis in natural events is a fact so peculiar that it would be inexplicable were it not for the inertia of the traditional schools [of thought]." Dewey's empirical naturalism is in our view untenable in certain of its basic assumptions, as we have held in our brief remarks on empiricism in Chapter I. But despite his professed empiricism, Dewey is a metaphysician in the great tradition in such works as *Experience and Nature*. Furthermore, no one in the history of human thought has made a better case for naive realism, the philosophy of the common man, and the philosophy of the philosopher when he is not philosophizing, than John Dewey. This great contribution of Dewey's is not mentioned in Britannica's article on him. The words "naive realism," by far the best-known name for the philosophy of the common man who, whether he knows it or not, certainly has a philosophy, are not used in the article and they are not in Britannica's index. There is an article "Common Sense, Philosophy of," in which the common sense philosophy of the Scottish critics of Hume is very briefly, too briefly, stated, and in which a few lines are given to the British realist G. E. Moore. John Dewey's empirical naturalism is so great an improvement over that of the Scottish critics of Hume that it might seem inappropriate to mention him in the same article. But so is G. E.

Moore a great improvement. Dewey's naive realism, or empirical naturalism, is a highly sophisticated body of thought that begins with common sense or naive realism. To fail to mention him and briefly to characterize his thought in an article on Common Sense Philosophy is simply, along with the failure at least to index the words "naive realism" and refer to the article "Common Sense, Philosophy of," to fail to perform one of the tasks that an encyclopedia must perform if it is to do its job.

Two paragraphs in the article on Dewey are devoted to his view that the experimental methods of science provide "the most promising approach to all problems, social and ethical as well as scientific." This doctrine has been widely criticized on the grounds that modern science throws no light whatever on the great question what ends the power it has put at the disposal of man should be made to serve. The modern scientist as a person may disagree completely with the dictum of David Hume that " 'Tis not contrary to reason to prefer the destruction of the whole world to the scratching of my finger," [2] or that of G. E. Moore that "no sufficient reason has ever yet been found for considering one action more right or wrong than another," [3] but his science, so far as has yet been shown, provides no basis whatever for any system of morals. Modern science, whatever its major concern has been, has in its application led only to the generation of power. The needs of human beings, and the desires that grow as needs are met if there is no ethical control over them, have determined the use of this power. The wars of this century, or the conditions that made them inescapable, the chief of which has been the absence of easily demonstrated ethical principles and control of inordinate desires by such principles, are sufficient evidence to establish the truth on this question.

It is irresponsible in the highest degree for encyclopedias to be so made that readers cannot get from them information that is more than merely tantalizing on subjects of this kind. The question whether Dewey or anyone else has ever found a basis in modern science for ethics is of the greatest importance. Readers are entitled to some clues as to how this has been done, if it has been done, and who has done it and when and where, if it has been done in a way that is worth mentioning. If it has not been done, readers are entitled to this information.

One of the greatest problems in ethics is whether the human potential contains the possibility of human perfection, and as some would have

2. *Treatise of Human Nature*, ed. L. A. Selby-Bigge Oxford: at the Clarendon Press [1888] 1949, p. 416. (Bk. II, Pt. III, Sec. iii)
3. *Principia Ethica* (Cambridge: at the University Press [1903] 1956), p. 152.

it, even that of man's becoming God. Even though Herbert Marcuse uses Hegel mainly to grind his own axe in his book *Reason and Revolution*, his discussion throws important light on the doctrine of potentiality as derived from Hegel, clarified in one crucial respect by Feuerbach, and made by Marx into the instrument that during this century has been gaining greatly in power and rapidly transforming the world. Feuerbach's clarification consisted in showing, more clearly than Hegel did, that Hegelian doctrine correctly interpreted leads to the view that man is becoming God. Feuerbach gave his enthusiastic support to this view without considering the possibility that this notion might prove wholly deceptive and disastrous flattery. This development calls for comment.

There is a tendency in human beings, so human history clearly says, on achieving great power and on being flattered as the powerful always are, to begin acting as if they are gods. When two such human beings on earth get in each other's way, strife usually follows. Divide the world between two such gods and their followers and let them have their shares of the nuclear power that exists today, and the consequences, unless these gods have become angelic, almost certainly will not remain purely imaginary. Those moves in human thought which led to the banishment in thought, and even in imagination, of gods from the earth, were moves toward peace—moves that need sorely to be understood today, and not only in the Communist countries. Feuerbach's clarification of Hegelian doctrine in this vital respect was not only not disputed by Marx but implicitly strengthened by him. And many who are not consciously followers of Hegel or Marx adhere to this notion that man is becoming God—or if they do not consciously adhere to it, they act this way as far as they can. Their own desires are their God.

It would be difficult to overemphasize the significance of this doctrine, now the religion of our time, that man is becoming God. This doctrine is a fully developed version of the doctrine that man is becoming perfect—a doctrine that implicitly recognizes the possibility of oneness in many. For perfection, in the ordinary rather than the Hegelian or Marcusan or other senses of the term, can hardly be other than a character that modifies in the same way other characters as these exist in different individuals. It can only be a pervasive kind of oneness, with no internal opposition, that is exactly the same in all the individuals who are perfect. If this oneness exists among human beings, we may search for it as we please, but we do not find it. We find instead frequent and obvious incompatibilities that at times grow into wars. Only governments that have the power to break and control factions so far in human history have been able to prevent wars even among their own people—and even governments, well-designed and well-conducted governments have not always been able to do this. There is no evidence whatever to the effect that man on earth has any chance to achieve a state of perfection. The great insight that one of the greatest obstacles to a decent peace among human beings on earth is the notion that some persons have become perfect, or are achieving perfection, was achieved in the arguments over Christian doctrine. To be perfect would be to be above the law, even the best devised law. This is antinomianism. Hegel agrees with Christian doctrine in condemning antinomianism. Marcuse preaches it.

If the insight in the rejection of antinomianism by Christian doctrine were understood today, the notion that man is becoming perfect, or a god on earth, would be treated with the understanding derision that it deserves.

Britannica has an article "Antinomianism" but it is written as if the problem of antinomianism were peculiar to Christianity and had no everyday practical importance in the lives of ordinary human beings, as well as in the thought of some contemporary philosophers such as Marcuse. The treatment of this subject by Britannica is exactly on a par with that of its treatment of sacrifice. The reader may remember our criticism of our encyclopedias for treating sacrifice as if it posed problems that come up only among preliterate peoples. This academic separation of subjects from the realities of this world serves only to cultivate a knowledge so narrow as to have the effect only of the deepest ignorance. The human potential cannot be given any good development, except in revolt, in an atmosphere such as this.

Human beings have always been under the necessity of developing standards, and the quality of their lives has always been largely determined by the standards they have developed and practiced. Just as all the basic arguments concerning the origin of life and mind can be reduced to two types, one that assumes creation out of nothing—a supernatural, utterly miraculous process—the other that the potentiality of life and mind exists in apparently inanimate matter, that is, in original nature, whatever that is; so the basic arguments concerning the origin of notions of standards may be reduced to two types, one which assumes a supernatural process, and another which assumes a natural process. It is obviously impossible to prove either. Both rest on notions that may be held either as assumptions or beliefs. The chief value of assumptions is that they can be loosely held, easily made, easily given up, and that while held may be used for sheer speculative purposes in order to develop systems of thought and compare them with each other. But if the comparison of systems is to be fruitful in the sense of helping to determine better and worse, standards of judgment that have been found to be more rather than less trustworthy have to be used. If any such standards exist in the intellectual world of our time, our encyclopedias do not tell us what they are. Nor can one discover easily from them that our time is one of notions presented as standards competing for acceptance throughout the world.

It is mainly in the comparison of different systems of knowledge and the assumptions or beliefs on which these systems rest that human reason is in dire need of exercise in our time. It is not our idea that the new type of encyclopedia we are proposing be wholly devoted to discussion of this kind. Such an encyclopedia would not be as useful as possible to the general public today. Nor would it be as useful as possible to the intellectual world. The encyclopedia we propose would be even more encyclopedic than any that is available today in that it would present the more important pros and cons on the great subjects; and all the subjects necessary to make the work as far as possible encyclopedic would be dealt with in contexts that meet the great as well as the small educational needs of our time.

We see some of the unfolding of the human potential in what we assume to be the truth of the theory of evolution and in the records that the animal becoming human has created and left to us of his activities in the past. It is impossible for most of us to read and study these records. This has been done by persons specially qualified for this task. It is possible for the essence of what they have learned to be made available to the public in a way that cultivates thought and understanding. This type of activity is one of the great commitments implicit in the founding of the United States. This commitment has been greatly served by educational institutions that have been established before and since that time; but the establishment of institutions, no matter how well-conceived when first established, does not guarantee that new needs will not develop that call for new institutions.

The problem of serving the general welfare is, of course, a problem first of knowing at least to some extent of what this welfare consists and the necessities to its service. It is generally agreed today that the general welfare depends on the maintenance of standards that there are at least some good reasons to believe are valid. We really do not want to feed our children food that harms them. The need for more rather than less trustworthy standards is not limited to food. It extends into all aspects of human life.

One of the standards of American life today is that no one shall be allowed to starve. This standard may be raised to that of seeing that everyone somehow is provided with the necessities of physical well-being. A large portion of the American public gives evidence today of wanting this standard established and maintained, at least for Americans and, as far as is possible, for others. But since the charitable disposition toward which our public is strongly inclined can be subjected to gross abuse and can, if abused, lead not only to the further impoverishment of the poor but to widespread revulsion against the charitable disposition, we try all the expedients we can to prevent this abuse. For this purpose, as well as many others, we create and maintain institutions designed to cultivate the minds of the individuals that constitute the public. And since the word "mind" has tended to designate and the very notion of mind has tended to become that of a more or less perfect mechanism, one that like a machine has nothing to do with feeling and valuing and willing but that can somehow remember and calculate and engage in thinking—but not as well as a thinking machine—we still tend, or some of us do, to think and speak of human beings as having souls and spirits as well as minds and bodies—or, as is often said, "the whole person." Many of us take seriously the problem of providing what we consider the best possible cultivation of the human potential.

We have, as a consequence, a wide variety of a multitude of institutions. The question necessarily arises, however, whether we have enough of different kinds to meet the different types of needs that exist in our public. There are problems here that can prove fateful in American life that are not getting any really serious attention. For instance, there has been no institution so necessary to the quality of American life as the American university. But the American college has also been necessary. So has the technical institute. So has the vocational-training agency. So has training on the job given by innumerable commercial and industrial establishments. So have elementary and secondary educational institutions, private as well as public. In the creation and maintenance of institutions it is not impossible to make grave mistakes as well as to fail to do things that the general welfare requires.

In the state of North Carolina where I write these lines the University at Chapel Hill which was a few years ago the only institution that bore the name "The University of North Carolina" is now The University of North Carolina at Chapel Hill. There are fifteen other institutions that by state action in recent years have been given the name "university."

Why fifteen publicly supported universities in the State of North Carolina in addition to that at Chapel Hill? The answer to this question, we believe, is that with all their shortcomings, American universities generally have obviously contributed so much to raising the external standards of American life that it is difficult to imagine that more and more of the same will not have the same effect. No community in North Carolina can fail to see the apparent effects on the state and especially on the Chapel Hill, Durham, and Raleigh area of the three great higher educational institutions in this part of the state. It is hardly possible for any resident of the state to be unaware of the apparently permanent prosperity that is being experienced—if not always enjoyed—by many of the residents of this area. Who does not want prosperity?

We do not care to argue the question whether this has been the chief reason for giving the name "university" to fifteen additional institutions. No one today would expect the mere name to create the reality. To expect this would be to expect magical effects. The intention must have been in time to create the reality. Whatever the reasons, North Carolina now has, in name at least, sixteen universities supported by the state. Will all strive to be universities in actuality as well as in name? If not, will North Carolina have provided a really big problem for Mr. Ralph Nader? If they strive and succeed, will they duplicate each other? If so, when all become Ph.D.–producing institutions, how many will they produce? And what will these Ph.D.'s be capable of doing? Who will need, who will employ them?

It is possible, we think highly probable, that North Carolina has developed the need for fifteen additional state-supported educational institutions. But is it possible that fifteen additional universities in reality as well as in name will be needed at any time in the foreseeable future?

One of the great problems in Germany in the twenties and early thirties was the extreme over-production of Ph.D.'s. It is not generally understood today that the Ph.D. tends to be as highly specialized in his employment, if not in his mind, as the garbage collector, and so far as the everyday activities that make human life possible—as distinguished from improving future activities—much less necessary. The labor unions of our time, if they had never done anything else, have performed a tremendously important service in making our Ph.D.'s, our intellectual leadership and the top levels of our society at least dimly aware that they and the top levels may be thrown to the bottom if they do not pay serious attention to the basic needs that have to be met in order to have a decent society. One of these needs is attention to the problem of numbers needed in the near future in one kind of work as compared with another.

The technologies which have been used successfully to create American wealth, but which have also tended to ravage and pollute and exhaust the natural resources of land, water, and air, offer the only hope that human beings have of cleaning up the pollution and cultivating the natural resources. The technologies as they now exist fall far short of this task. This is one of the fields in which far more institutional effort is needed, and probably more institutions and more support to existing institutions.

Many young people today are not interested in higher education of the type that is currently being widely cultivated. It is often held in educational theory and practice that to give special attention to the needs of these young people and to find ways to meet these needs would be to create differences in education that in turn tend to create fixed classes in society. This theory ignores at least two great facts in American life. One is that there is at present a fairly large class of unemployed simply because the members of the class do not know how to do and are, because of their lack of trained skill, incapable of doing anything well. This class is becoming larger and more important with every day that passes. It cannot be made to disappear by being simply ignored, or, if not ignored, merely talked about. The other great fact is that where native ability exists, it is possible to cultivate this ability later when it is not possible to cultivate it earlier. The problem of institutions designed to meet this need has not been given nearly as much attention as the proper development of the human potential requires.

One of the features of institutional behavior that has been much discussed but that so far as American education and higher education are concerned has to a great extent baffled intelligent action is the tendency of institutions that have enjoyed apparently great success to ossify or develop absurd aberrations, to forget that they were brought into existence to meet certain needs of society, that changes in needs require changes in institutions. It is necessary that needs be classified as to type; and if the health of society is to be cultivated as well as is possible, provision has to be made to meet as well as is possible each type of need. One of the most distressing aspects of American higher education is the extreme difficulty of getting discussion of this subject that is helpful to the people outside of educational institutions who have the power and are under the necessity of making decisions.

We can be fairly sure that if the faculties of American universities do not give this problem far more serious attention than they have yet given it, others who have the zeal but not the qualifications necessary to do this job will undertake it; and the combination of reasonable conservatism and well-tempered radicalism, of holding to the best of the past and at the same time experimenting, exploring, discovering, that has to some extent characterized our universities, will most likely be gravely damaged if not destroyed. The universities of America today are tending toward failures widely different from but still in important ways comparable to those of the regimes that existed in France in 1789 and in Russia and Austria-Hungary in 1917.

There is a functional relation between universities and the societies in which they exist that neither the societies nor the universities can safely ignore. Once the great institutions of society begin making caricatures of their functions, or even give the public the impression that in crucial ways they are failing, they and their society are in grave danger.

The present-day university has had no alternative but to cultivate specialization; but the exclusive cultivation of specialization can go so far as to be the cultivation of ignorance. We have shown that the modern university and college cannot do much more than they have been doing in the way of general education and that a new type of institution is necessary if this purpose is to be served as well as is possible.

It is hardly open to doubt that, with a few great exceptions, modern man is not using anywhere nearly as well as he might the means that have been developed in the past for the better cultivation of the human potential. This means is the great inheritance of modern man. This inheritance has the peculiar character that it cannot be automatically conveyed or possessed. Unlike wealth in land and other limited resources in high demand, any number of individuals may take all they can of this inheritance, but no matter how much they take, they cannot diminish the supply. The more they take and take seriously, the greater the chances of improvement in the quality of the supply. The human potential, when given genuine cultivation, improves and stabilizes that on which it grows.

The time has come in human history when the cultivation of the human potential in ways that serve both the best interests of the individual and the general welfare is necessary if the level of human life is to be raised rather than lowered. There is no possibility that the present level will cease to move; and it can go down as well as up. If this book helps to make clear the institutions and the work necessary to cultivate the human potential for better service to the general welfare, it will have served its purpose.

Index

tion, understanding, 261 ff., 284–304; Socrates on arguments, 25, 275–76; Hutchins on, 277; Mill vs. Stephen, 369; Galileo vs. Newton on the tides, 46; Diderot's *Encyclopedia,* 354; dialectics in U.S. history, 293–94; smallpox: truth about vs. primitive magic, 315–7; Buridan's ass and beyond, 24, 291–92

Aristotle, myth that he was a mere theorizer, 43; motions of the heavenly spheres, 44; on the logical law of contradiction, 55, 314; man a social animal, 70; desire to know, 79; observation, facts, theories, 110–113; metaphysics, 110–12; potentiality, 117, 368; origin of names (words), 137–38; *Rhetoric,* 213; on rhetoric, 137–38, 209, 213; *Ethics,* 229; fixed species, 368

Aristotle, Galileo, and the Tower of Pisa (Lane Cooper), 43, 309 ff.

Artist, art in the ideal society, 15; McLuhan's notion of role of, 184, 193; maker of war or of peace, 193; Shelley and the wars of this century, 193; Tolstoi, 193–94, 208, 296

Assumptions, role of in present-day thought, 22, 49–50, 216–17; time and space in Newton and Einstein, 110–11; in theory of evolution, 140; prejudice, 215–17

Atom, theory of the early Greeks, 146; Copernicus, Galileo, Newton, 146–48; theory in present-day physics, 268–69

Authority, has to be accepted in learning if beginning is to be made, 21–22, 303; of physical nature, 21–22; some inescapable, 49–50; of the expert, 253; of the teacher, 21–22, 261–62; acceptance without question, 318, 341–46, 366; in encyclopedias, 66, 341–46; in logic, 261, 341–46; in facts, *see* Facts; in currently accepted theory, *see* Theory, orthodoxy. *See also* Communism; Democracy; Free Society; National Socialism

Automation, 73, 132–33; liberal education mandatory, 175; work, mental, moral, physical, 175

Automobile, moral problems, 182

Awareness, of human minds and omniscience and computers, 141–42, 179 ff.

Ayer, A. J., and contradictions, 22; on physics and perception, 149; *The Problem of Knowledge,* 149; *Language, Truth and Logic,* 149; subjectivity of value, 173, 295; censorship, 294–96

Aztecs, Huitzilopochtli, and cultural relativity, 58, 190, 208, 360–61

Bacon, Francis, and knowledge is power, 205

Baconian principles and scientific method, 271

Balance of power, 122–23, 212, 228

Beans, Pythagoras and Bertrand Russell on, 329 ff.

Belief and moral idiocy, 336

Bell, Daniel, *The Reforming of General Education,* 250, 259

Benedict, Ruth, *Patterns of Culture* and Ph.D. requirements in anthropology, 34; cultural relativity, 35, 58, 190, 208, 360–61; facts contradict conclusion, 40–42; "lost manuscript," 41–43, 51 ff., 59; orthodoxy, 42, 298; *see also* Knowledge; Orthodoxy

Berkeley, Bishop George, and course of Western thought, 151; on mode of existence of secondary qualities, 145, 151; *Principles of Human Knowledge* and *A New Theory of Vision,* 151–56, 197; Johnson's refutation, 151; doctrine of mind, 152–53; on number, 154; visual perception two-dimensional, 155; tar water, 162; Britannica on, 222; on general words, 306; *Visual Language, Vindicated and Explained,* 155

Bibliographies, 85, 351–52

Blanshard, Brand, *The Nature of Thought, Reason and Analysis, Reason and Goodness,* 208, 297; on logical positivism and university philosophy faculties, 297; on symbolic logic, 65; on contradiction, 263

versities of Germany and Russia under national socialism and communism, 247; more difficult to get along with than the communists?, 228